Critical Essays on
F. Scott Fitzgerald's
Tender Is the Night

Critical Essays on
F. Scott Fitzgerald's
Tender Is the Night

Milton R. Stern

G. K. Hall & Co. • Boston, Massachusetts

Library of Congress Cataloging-in-Publication Data
  Main entry under title:

Critical essays on F. Scott Fitzgerald's Tender is the
  night.

  (Critical essays on American literature)

  Includes index.
  1. Fitzgerald, F. Scott (Francis Scott), 1896–1940.
Tender is the night — Addresses, essays, lectures.
I. Stern, Milton R.
PS3511.I9T454   1986   813'.52   85-17601
ISBN 0-8161-8444-5

This publication is printed on permanent/durable acid-free paper
MANUFACTURED IN THE UNITED STATES OF AMERICA

CRITICAL ESSAYS ON AMERICAN LITERATURE

This series seeks to anthologize the most important criticism on a wide variety of topics and writers in American literature. Our readers will find in various volumes not only a generous selection of reprinted articles and reviews but original essays, bibliographies, manuscript sections, and other materials brought to public attention for the first time. This volume contains thirty-four essays and reviews on F. Scott Fitzgerald's most complex novel, *Tender Is the Night*. There are reprinted selections by many of the leading commentators on American letters, including Matthew J. Bruccoli, Gilbert Seldes, Philip Rahv, Malcolm Cowley, Arthur Mizener, Edwin Fussell, James F. Light, and Alan Trachtenberg. In addition to an extensive introduction by Milton R. Stern, which surveys the history of scholarly comment on this work, there are original essays by James W. Tuttleton and Milton R. Stern, and a bibliography compiled especially for this volume by Joseph Wenke. We are confident that this volume will make a permanent and significant contribution to American literary study.

JAMES NAGEL, GENERAL EDITOR

Northeastern University

To
Robert Vrecenak and Isabelle DiCenzo,
Interlibrary Loan Department of the
Babbidge Library of the University
of Connecticut,
this volume is gratefully dedicated.
Always available, they make everything
available.

CONTENTS

INTRODUCTION

The manuscript of *Tender Is the Night* went to Scribner's in October 1933. It was published in April 1934. The delays occasioned by revisions presaged the course of its reputation. The book had to wait many years for its completion; in germ or in draft Fitzgerald worked on it off and on for seven years. It had to wait seventeen years for its revised publication, and despite some strong commentaries in its behalf, it had to wait approximately a quarter of a century for general recognition of its value.

Every student of Fitzgerald's work is familiar with Hemingway's remark that in retrospect *Tender Is the Night* gets better and better. The observation is a paradigm and encapsulation of critical attention. When Alexander Cowie published his historical survey of the American novel eight years after Fitzgerald's death, he spared only a one sentence reference to F. Scott Fitzgerald—a comment on *This Side of Paradise*.[1] And even in that, Fitzgerald had to share equal billing with Percy Marks, a very minor writer whose works, especially *The Plastic Age*, belong to the five-and-ten of mind and materials that Fitzgerald shopped in for *This Side of Paradise*. In 1963, when Arthur Mizener—who early championed *Tender Is the Night* as Fitzgerald's most brilliant novel[2]—published *F. Scott Fitzgerald: A Collection of Critical Essays*,[3] he assembled nineteen articles. Four were devoted to *The Great Gatsby*, two to *This Side of Paradise*, and twelve to general evaluations. Even Mizener allowed only one entry for *Tender Is the Night*—a 1934 review.[4] And as late as 1973, in Kenneth E. Eble's collection, *F. Scott Fitzgerald: A Collection of Criticism*,[5] there are three essays on *The Great Gatsby*, five on special topics, and one apiece for *This Side of Paradise*, *The Beautiful and Damned*, *The Last Tycoon* fragment—and *Tender Is the Night*. Partly this neglect of *Tender Is the Night*—and this is especially true for Mizener's collection—resulted from the fact that through the nineteen-fifties some of the best observations about the book existed in general considerations of Fitzgerald rather than in criticism that concentrated upon the novel itself (of which there was relatively little). In fact, in 1969, when the first collection of essays on *Tender Is the Night* appeared,[6] one fifth of the inclusions were general essays rather than concentrations upon the novel. Attention to the

1

book was spurred by the two appearances of the revised version (1951 and 1953), but it took almost two decades after Fitzgerald's death for critics to realize how much "better and better" *Tender Is the Night* became.

In almost every way Fitzgerald's richest book was his unluckiest. While he was writing it, his life fell from the golden excitement of early success to leaden despair and disrepute. As the world came apart in the postwar horrors that led to World War II, his personal world crumbled into Zelda's sickness, his own alcoholic and suicidal woe, and his debts. Before, during, and after the composition of the 1934 version of *Tender Is the Night*, Fitzgerald felt the significant and strangling tie between his life and his world, both full of present miseries and wrenching memories of the good, gay, gone times.

The very heart of *Tender Is the Night* is a composite of nostalgia, remorse, lost hopes, broken dreams, disintegration, and the emergence of a hateful, harsh new world from the death of old ideals and idealisms. It was inevitable that early reviewers and Fitzgerald's friends and acquaintances should have seen the novel as disguised autobiography, a judgment reinforced by Fitzgerald's use of "composite" characters.[7] Even as late as the 1950s, some commentators continued to see the novel rather narrowly as fictional autobiography, "a documentary of the novelist's own collapse."[8] Only a few reviewers saw the unlucky novel in its true dimensions, dimensions that either overwhelmed or escaped many readers when the book appeared. Those dimensions are enormous, for Fitzgerald made his novel—his "testament of faith"[9] in his greatest abilities—something much wider than a fictitious documentary of his own experiences as an individual. The book's materials are, as Gatsby would have said, "only personal": the merger of people Fitzgerald knew with refractions of those personalities in parts of his own self; his own deterioration; Zelda's psychosis; his own times and places. But the theme of the book is history itself, the Spenglerian process of the collapse of a civilization into barbarism.[10] The central subject of *Tender Is the Night* is the moral history of the western world just before and after World War One, and most especially it is the continuing history of the American Dream.

The term "the American Dream" has degenerated almost into meaninglessness through overgeneral popular usage and through the sloppy, overabundant, witless rhetoric of politics and advertising. When there is a clearly discernible meaning, the phrase generally has come to indicate upward social and economic mobility: having a lot, being secure, belonging—some money and some power. But for Fitzgerald, the idea of America was the opposite of secure belonging. It was total risk and plunge. It was "a willingness of the heart," as he phrased it, a response to a dream of unrestricted being, a dream of freedom that allowed the exercise of the most transcendent imagination and the realization of its goals. That imagination was nothing less than absolute belief in fulfillment of the endless possibilities of the self. It was a dream of existence not subject to time, limitation, or mortality. It was a dream of triumph over history, of a condition in which human beings finally are liberated from a fallen state and all the consequent corruptions of the past — a dream of ultimate freedom indeed. This belief is exhilarating almost beyond expression, and of all writers F. Scott Fitzgerald best expressed the excitement of Romantic American hope, when all the world seemed to be in its golden morning with every fantastic realization of heroic desire and youthful expectation just ahead. The greatest dimensions of humanity, of self, and of society were attainable and almost palpable, as they had been for the Puritan's City on a Hill, for the Deist's Jeffersonian dream, for achievable Emersonian divinity, and as they had been for Woodrow Wilson's Fourteen Points. The enlargement of spirit that goes into such expectation is at one with a naiveté of vision; idealism is at one with neglect of history; incredible effort, discipline, hope, belief, and accomplishment become one with ultimate and destructive disillusion. Of all this national magnificence and these internal flaws Dick Diver is the central representative. Amid the murderous madness of World War One, he studies for the future. He will give himself entirely to curing the corruptions of the past, and just as America was to "make the world safe for democracy" through "the war to end wars," so Dick was to be the greatest psychologist who ever lived, and once and for all would cure the world of its sickness.

Dick's boundless hope and dedication were those of his nation's dream. And as his cure of Nicole took form in circumstances bitterly different from his dream-vision, so too America's dream-liberation from history shattered against its own realities — history's obdurate and endless restatements of mortal limitation, hypocrisy, selfishness, corruption, and lies — even for America — in a fallen world. No less than that is the subject of *Tender Is the Night*. But much less than that is what early readers recognized.

II

At first, most readers did not see that Dr. Diver's marriage and career — his "case" — was a summation of the book's materials, a vehicle for the theme of history. Consequently, most of the reviews in the nineteen-thirties placed *Tender Is the Night* in one of three categories, few reviewers acknowledging more than one category: (1) a study of abnormal psychology, one more in a spate of "psychopathic" fictions growing out of the fashionable triumph of "Freudianism"; (2) a study of domestic intranquillity, a "marriage novel" scrutinizing the breakdown of a relationship; and (3) yet one more Fitzgerald tale of glamorous, decadent Jazz Age playboys and girls, and, worse yet, in the outworn mode of expatriation. Whatever the critics' classifications of theme, their objections tended to reiterate two observations: (1) there was no convincing — or at least clear — reason for

Dick's disintegration, and (2) the shift in point of view and the chronology after the Rosemary beginning was confusing.

Categories of classification seem now to offer the interest of antiquarian curiosities, for the novel has far outgrown the limitations placed upon it by most of the early reviewers. The limitations themselves did not dictate or grow from critical approval or rejection. For instance, Mary Colum ("The Psychopathic Novel," included here), in her obtuse review saw nothing beyond the psychological materials, didn't like those, and pronounced the book at once a minor work and a major failure. On the other hand, Michael March ("Page After Page," also included here) read the book as the breakdown of a marriage, and, in his cliché-ridden and error-riddled appreciation, hailed the novel as a masterpiece.

The question of rich expatriate jazzbabies as subject matter for readers burdened by the Great Depression, however, requires a bit more attention. Some of the Depression era reviews were intensely political (Philip Rahv's *Daily Worker* essay, "You Can't Duck Hurricane Under a Beach Umbrella," included here, is a strong example) and took Fitzgerald to task for being stubbornly retrogressive in ignoring contemporary economics and the rise of fascism. Although not all the reviews picked up this note, several did, and that fact became an explanation for later critics in accounting for the commercial and, to some extent, critical failure of the novel. The reviews that followed Malcolm Cowley's 1951 edition of *Tender Is the Night*, and then again after the 1953 *Three Novels of F. Scott Fitzgerald*, created the impression that leftist political reviews like Philip Rahv's accounted for the failure of the novel and for Fitzgerald's desire to revise it. Malcolm Cowley's introduction to the revised version (included here) influentially strengthened that impression.

In the 1960s, Bruccoli's *The Composition of "Tender Is the Night"*[11] attempted a corrective for this assumption. This corrective had been anticipated by Charles Poore in 1951[12] and was consolidated by Bruccoli in "*Tender Is the Night* — Reception and Reputation":

> "But it is not demonstrable that Fitzgerald was the victim of a hostile, New Deal oriented press. In all fairness, the assassination of *Tender Is the Night* cannot be added to the catalogue of Democrats' iniquities . . . . A glance at the ten best-selling novels of 1934 provides nothing to suggest that the readers of the Depression rejected Fitzgerald because they preferred socially significant novels about slums: *Anthony Adverse; Lamb in His Bosom; So Red the Rose; Good-Bye, Mr. Chips; Within This Present; Work of Art; Private Worlds; Mary Peters; Oil for the Lamps of China;* and *Seven Gothic Tales.* This is a typical mixture, and there is not one proletarian novel in the lot. Indeed, *Within This Present* is a nostalgic look back at the twenties . . . the three top sellers of the year were historical novels. . . . People who lament the failure of *Tender Is the Night* generally ignore the fact that Fitzgerald had not had a best seller since *This Side of Paradise*, and even it was not one of the

top ten in 1920. Fitzgerald was a popular figure, but he was never really a popular novelist in his lifetime.[13]

The history of the novel's reception, then, may be seen as an assumption (in the 1950s) that political reviews and social attitudes of the 1930s, continuing into the sparse attention Fitzgerald received in the 1940s, accounted for the novel's failure; that this assumption was corrected in the 1960s and 1970s, and that the political and economic atmosphere of the 1930s had little or nothing to do, after all, with the book's reception.[14]

However, the corrective itself requires a slight correction. For one thing, Fitzgerald did not think of *Tender Is the Night* as popular fiction subject to the standards of dime-store best-sellerdom. He was entirely wrapped up in it as the great work that would be his bid for removal from the list of popular romancers and for placement among the serious artists. For another, the more intellectual journals, like *Harper's*, the *Atlantic*, and the *Saturday Review of Literature* among wide circulation magazines and like the *Modern Monthly* among smaller periodicals,[15] did not pay the kind of attention to popular best-seller fare that they did to books they took seriously. To a large extent, Fitzgerald *was* identified among serious readers with Jazz Age parties and expatriates, and serious readers and serious journals were without question seriously involved with serious matters of world politics and the Depression. The reviews that tended to classify *Tender Is the Night* into categories of subject matter — and most of them did — did not encourage consideration of the novel by serious readers. C. Hartley Grattan's review (included here) was one of the few appreciative notices that cut across easy categories and hinted at the dimensions of the novel. It is not insignificant that Fitzgerald wrote to the Marxist, George Goetz, who used the pseudonym V. F. Calverton for his own books and his editorship of the *Modern Monthly*, that "Grattan's review in the *Modern Monthly* . . . pleased me more than any I got."[16] Moreover, Fitzgerald, like most of his literary contemporaries, was at least mildly sympathetic to politically conscious, left-leaning positions in the 1930s, both while writing *Tender Is the Night* and then when reading reviews of it. In sum, although Bruccoli's corrective is necessary, there remains more justification than Bruccoli allows for Cowley's assumption about the effect and general context and ambience of the reviews of the 1930s in relation to Fitzgerald and the retail reception of *Tender Is the Night*. The nature of the best-sellers in 1934 does not account for the special nature of *Tender Is the Night* in 1934. There was praise and condemnation for the book from commercial popular reviewers as well as from the intelligentsia. But the unlucky book was too serious a piece of literature to enter the successful ranks of popular reading, and the categorical receptions generated by its setting and materials denied it compensatory enthusiasm from highbrow sources. Furthermore, ever conscious as he was of St. Paul, Fitzgerald (and his St. Paul sales) had to have been hurt by the viciously hostile review in the St. Paul *Daily News* ("Mr. Fitzgerald Displays His Little White Mice," included here), which dismissed the novel as one more Fitzgerald story about lost generation rich kids ("the soul-heavings and 'weltschmertz' of leisured cosmopolites in the play places of the world"). The number of reviews insisting on the subject matter as decadent and retrogressive is less important than the places in which such reviews appeared, and even if one wishes to settle for quantitative measurement, such responses were not infrequent. Given the context of the times, the atmosphere, the sense Fitzgerald had of his book and his own politics, the political responses were more consequential for Fitzgerald and for the reception of *Tender Is the Night* than Mr. Bruccoli's quantifying corrective implies.

However, when we turn to the two major objections raised by the reviews of the thirties (the mysteriousness of Dick's destruction and a structural confusion of point of view occasioned by the switch from Rosemary to Dick), Bruccoli is closer to the mark than Cowley.[17] In his introduction to the revised version, Cowley suggests that "in spite of knowing so much about . . . [Dick], we are never quite certain of the reasons for his decline."[18] However, the quantity and variety of criticism in the nineteen sixties and seventies more than abundantly indicate that in either the original or the revised version readers have no trouble identifying what Fitzgerald had made dramatically clear. On the level of psychology and personality, Dick contained the inner flaws of his nation's transcendent idealism, part of which is the eternal youth's need to be loved, part of which is the generous heart's need to be used, and part of which is altruistic illusion, self-deception, and foolishness. On the professional level, Dick had subordinated his entire career to one case. On the level of history, Dick's self-sacrifice was naively made for a world that socially and morally was not worth saving in the first place, a world that used him badly and used him up, and in so doing, threw him away. Fitzgerald knew that he was creating a hero who was "an 'homme épuisé,' not only an 'homme manqué'."[19] From the vantage point of the 1980s, it seems strange that fifty years earlier, sophisticated and experienced readers should reiterate their bewilderment about what destroys Dick. Their claim seems to be not so much a matter of the structure, chronology, or prose as it appears to be one of the ephemeral and immediate conventions of response that reviewers seemed to set up, reading and being influenced by each other's reviews. One applauds John Chamberlain's sharp annoyance with his colleagues ("Books of the Times," April 16, 1934, included here).

As for confusions occasioned not by Dick but by structure, any discussion of the beginning of *Tender Is the Night* inevitably involves arguments of preference for the original or the revised version. That argument cannot occupy any of the limited space in this "Introduction," for the problem is important enough to require a separate investigation.[20] And that argument, of course, was impossible for the early reviewers, whose claims that the Rosemary opening was confusing remain a source of mild surprise. The 1934 edition of *Tender Is the Night* did not introduce flashbacks for the first time in literary history, after all, and in any event, Fitzgerald's flashback obscured nothing.[21]

The reviews of the thirties, then, may be summed up as a very mixed response at every level of reviewing, in which praise and disapproval were about equally mixed. Most of the notices concerned themselves with the material of the novel and very few identified the directions of the book's basic themes. The decade was content to be puzzled by the book, tentatively attempting to define the nature of the beast, although as the representative selections included here demonstrate, there was nothing tentative about the judgments that were made. In the nineteen thirties there were no full critical essays on Fitzgerald's *oeuvre* or on *Tender Is the Night*. Fitzgerald was headed into obscurity, and although the reader of the present day might be amused or puzzled by some of the aspects of the book that bothered contemporary reviewers, it is useful to remember that the Fitzgerald criticism of the decade was neither retrospective nor comprehensive, but was entirely confined to review-articles written by people who had many books to consider and report on in brief compass in any given week. If there was one general observation that emerged more frequently than any other, it was the judgment that *Tender Is the Night* is a book of patches of brilliant, powerful, moving writing that does not come together for a sustained triumph.

Poor Zelda Fitzgerald, writing from an institution with all the pathos of ill-controlled prose, struck an admonitory and adumbrative note for the decade:[22]

> Dear — The book is grand. The emotional lift sustained by the force of a fine poetic prose and the characters *subserviated* to forces stronger than their interpretations of life is very moving. It is tear-provoking to witness individual belief in individual volition succumbing to the purpose of a changing world. That is the purpose of a good book and you have written it — Those people are helpless before themselves and the prose is beautiful and there is manifest an integrity in the belief of both those expressions. It is a reverential and very fine book and the first literary contribution to what writers will be concerning themselves with some years from now.
>
> Love
> Zelda

III

The paucity of materials from the 1940s in this volume is a reflection of the critical reputation of both *Tender Is the Night* and its author. What criticism there was in the decade began to tug away at the shroud of obscurity that had enwrapped Fitzgerald by the time he died in the last

month of 1940. As a matter of course, the early notices of the decade were
obituary. Also as a matter of course, the post-obituary period saw attempts
at retrospective summary. Uneasily aware that perhaps Fitzgerald had
been unduly neglected, the decade tried to come back to him, but it was
too largely taken up with the hot war and the politics of the early cold
war. As Theodore Adams' essay, "A Noble Issue" (which was to have been
included in this volume but was deleted for lack of space—it touches on
almost all the major themes of the novel and foreshadows most of the
explicative criticism that was to follow in more fully developed pieces),
indicates, there was finally the beginning of full length explorations of
Tender Is the Night, but relatively little was written about Fitzgerald or
his book.[23] The brief essays, most of which tried to sum up Fitzgerald,
were divided in their views,[24] but the general tone that emerges is one of
condescension: Scott Fitzgerald was not a perennially important writer,
and *Tender Is the Night* was, as John Berryman representatively said, a
slight book that will not last, "diffuse, lush, uncertain, and badly
designed."[25] Symptomatic of the persistent element of ambivalence, however, is the fact that the same *Kenyon Review* that contained Berryman's
pronouncement in the winter carried an essay in the spring in which
Arthur Mizener asserted that *Tender Is the Night* is "surely Fitzgerald's
most important novel for all its manifest flaws of construction."[26] The
extent to which the forties were a critical continuation of the thirties
becomes manifest in one of the central issues of the debate: what makes
Dick break? The question indicates the continuing, widespread concern of
readers with the structure of the original version. For instance, Arnold
Gingerich, the editor of *Esquire* and sympathetic to Fitzgerald, insisted on
the problem in his obituary essay. He called *Tender Is the Night* "a
magnificent failure," "the malformed twin embryo of two books, one of
which might have been a masterpiece . . . [and should have been] titled
simply *Richard Diver*."[27]

There is very little opening up or opening out in Fitzgerald criticism
during the 1940s. Rather the opposite. One senses in the post-mortem
concentration on biography a closing down, a quality of quick and final
summation which was generally disapproving because the commentators
continued to identify Fitzgerald's books and their themes with his life and
materials. We are used to assuming for the 1930s a critical emphasis on
social consciousness, political conscience, and the literary requirements of
anti-fascism. When one looks at book reviewing in the 1940s, one becomes
aware that what we assume for the thirties became a fixture for more than
half of the forties, partly as established convention, partly because of
World War II. The general judgment on Fitzgerald as voice of and prime
actor in the decadent spree of the nineteen twenties, and on his books as
essentially biographical celebrations of the Jazz Age, persisted in blinding
many commentators to the uses he made of his materials. He was, for

many of them, a marvelously evocative creator of beautifully poetic prose that never added up to anything serious for a mature world.

Nevertheless, the biographical focus of the 1940s on Fitzgerald, the desire to total him up, did result in an underlying consciousness that there was more here than could be summed neatly in the categories that had been established in the reviews of the nineteen thirties. The stirring of the counter-summary is best expressed by Stephen Vincent Benet's obituary notice of Fitzgerald and of *The Last Tycoon*:[28]

> When Scott Fitzgerald died, a good many of the obituaries showed a curious note of self-righteousness. They didn't review his work, they merely reviewed the Jazz Age and said that it was closed. Because he had made a spectacular youthful success at one kind of thing, they assumed that one kind of thing was all he could ever do . . . And they were one hundred percent wrong . . . *The Last Tycoon* shows what a really first-class writer can do with material — how he gets under the skin . . . Wit, observation, sure craftsmanship, the verbal facility that Fitzgerald could always summon — all these . . . [and] a richness of texture, a maturity of point of view . . . [show] us what we all lost in his early death . . . the evidence is in. You can take your hats off, now, gentlemen, and I think perhaps you had better. This is not a legend, this is a reputation — and, seen in perspective, it may well be one of the most secure reputations of our time.

Benet's warning cut across a decade of criticism that otherwise, for the most part, does seem like an obituary. The apparent worthlessness of Fitzgerald's work was summed up in the mid-forties by an item in the New York *Times*: a tiny paragraph at the bottom of the next to the last column of page 10 in the November 23, 1946 issue announced that the film rights for *Tender Is the Night* were sold to Vanguard Films, Inc., for $17,500, proceeds to go to Mr. Fitzgerald's wife, Zelda, and his daughter, Mrs. F. Lanahan. Fitzgerald and his work seemed lost and gone, as in the reminiscences in the 1970s of Marie Revello, the caretaker of what used to be Gerald and Sara Murphy's Villa America, the model for the Divers' Villa Diana. Revello did not remember Hemingway or even Fitzgerald, although she did recall the "fada" Zelda, "the most beautiful woman there," always laughing and dancing and being looked at a little bit strangely by the others. Like something out of the nationalities motif in *Tender Is the Night*, the Villa America became the Villa Fiamma, owned by a Hungarian-born West German stereo magnate, Edmond Uher. Talking about the times of the Fitzgeralds and the Murphys, Uher explained that "very little if anything remains from their day . . . and now Villa America is just another place that has disappeared with time. It's like Villa Diana in the Fitzgerald book. It's something that makes for pleasant conversation."[29]

IV

The nineteen fifties are marked in the very first year of the decade by the two most significant events in the development of Fitzgerald criticism and the study of *Tender Is the Night*. One is the appearance of Malcolm Cowley's edition of the revised version of *Tender Is the Night*[30] and the other is the publication of Arthur Mizener's *The Far Side of Paradise*.[31] The first critical biography of Fitzgerald, and still the best, Mizener's book was the first original book-length study of any kind to be published on F. Scott Fitzgerald. There had been one collection of essays by and about Fitzgerald, Edmund Wilson's edition of *The Crack-Up* in 1945 (the first book-length publication of any kind devoted entirely to Fitzgerald),[32] and it was joined in the annus mirabilis of 1951 by the first book-length collection of essays entirely about Fitzgerald, Alfred Kazin's edition of *F. Scott Fitzgerald: The Man and His Work*.[33] These books stimulated a re-examination of Fitzgerald that created a sharp increase in critical publication about him. Two years later, when Scribner's reissued *The Great Gatsby* and *Tender Is the Night* (revised version), both edited by Malcolm Cowley, and *The Last Tycoon*, edited by Edmund Wilson, in one volume,[34] "the Fitzgerald revival" became an accomplished fact. There has been a continuous flow of Fitzgerald criticism ever since.

In the early and mid 1950s criticism of *Tender Is the Night* turned upon arguments about the original and revised versions, but by the end of the decade investigation began to turn away from brief review judgments and biography to analysis. Arguments about the versions continued and continue, but analysis and interpretation remained the center of criticism in the 1960s, and by the early 1970s *Tender Is the Night* enjoyed a full and coherent body of criticism. What had begun to be repetitive—so full and constant did critical production become—in the 1960s and was consolidated in the early 1970s became burdensomely repetitive by the mid-nineteen seventies, and, with a few outstanding exceptions, has continued so.

But even tediousness has its uses. The repetitions permit some freedom—and impose some obligation—on future commentators. Never again need one quote the passage describing Nicole's shopping spree, quote as though it were new Hemingway's remark about *Tender*, quote Doctor Dohmler's insistence on professionalism, quote Baby's remark about what Dick was educated for, quote Dick's, Rosemary's, and Abe's visit to the battleground, describe the Divers' garden-party dinner, quote Tommy's remark about Nicole's money, quote the references to white crook's eyes, quote the last paragraph, quote the description of Daddy's Girl on the screen, explain the sequence in Rome,[35] trace the incest motif, or summarize the plot (a method done to death before the nineteen forties were over).

Throughout the nineteen fifties, although the decade finally was building a foundation for an eventual acceptance of *Tender Is the Night* as a lasting, major work, criticism continued to display some of the same ambivalence that characterized the thirties and forties. There was as yet no clear consensus. There was only one other full, book-length critical study in the fifties, James E. Miller's *The Fictional Technique of Scott Fitzgerald*,[36] and Miller did not see the novel or its main characters as creations of heroic identity. Periodical literature was split, the most hostile being an essay by Kingsley Amis, who, read from the distance of twenty-five years, sounds antagonistic to the point of jealousy.[37] The *Times Literary Supplement* concluded that *Tender Is the Night* is a magnificent failure (a judgment which by then had become a fashionable critical commonplace),[38] and Leslie Fiedler pronounced Fitzgerald to be an able writer about the rich, an honest writer who was capable of glowing prose but who never mastered point of view.[39] Alfred Kazin thought *Tender* a good book,[40] but John Aldridge claimed that it didn't all come together.[41] One commentator allowed *Tender Is the Night* a "slender but secure" existence as literature,[42] and one found the book to be a total bluff that can compel no one's belief.[43] Probably as representative a reading as any in the nineteen fifties is John R. Kuehl's sympathetic essay on the novel as Fitzgerald's major foray into realism.[44] As the essays included in this volume indicate, the nineteen fifties had begun to identify the major areas of fruitful investigation: Fitzgerald's relationship to his past and to its values, his moral perceptions of wealth, the novel as history, the Romantic imagination endangered by historical reality, and incest as a paradigmatic manifestation of corruption in the modern world. (An essay by Richard Schoenwald which was to have been included here but was deleted for lack of space, adumbrates all criticism on Fitzgerald and Keats. Although Doherty's essay, included here, claims that no one had paid attention to the subject, Schoenwald anticipated most of what Doherty had to say.)[45] By the time the nineteen sixties inherited the complete legacy of "the Fitzgerald revival" of the fifties, the shape and scope of the novel was beginning to emerge fully in the critical mind.

So copious was that critical legacy that once we arrive at the 1960s and 1970s, there are more examples than can be discussed within the limits of this introduction. Happily, however, there are scholarly and critical aids that obviate the need for full discussion here. The major bibliographer of Fitzgerald criticism, Jackson Bryer, has provided an overview and summary of Fitzgerald criticism in his books and essays, and Sergio Perosa has written a useful, if problematical, essay on the criticism of the nineteen seventies. (Consult footnote 14 below — this introduction, which scouts the repetitious nature of unwinnowed criticism of *Tender Is the Night*, need not itself repeat superficially what has been provided fully by Bryer and Perosa.) There are, however, two patterns in the criticism of the sixties and seventies that have not been noted and that deserve attention because they not only define the emerging shape of *Tender* in the eighties, but they also illustrate the profound connection between critical perceptions and the historical times.

Dick Diver is, among other things, an old fashioned gentleman. That endangered species is joined in Dick with the quintessential American dreamer. The "gentleman," *sui generis*, is easy to identify with the wealthy, aristocratic W.A.S.P. Princetonian snobbery with which Fitzgerald and his heroes are mistakenly confused. The confusion is a mistake because for all the attraction that the world of established wealth and power had for Fitzgerald—and it had—it is exactly that world by which Fitzgerald's heroes are victimized. It is exactly that world by which Fitzgerald measured every debasement and betrayal of the American Dream. Fitzgerald was the chronicler, not the champion, of the world whose appearances he punctured.

The quintessential American Romantic—*the* American—*sui generis* was certain that the America of promises would save the world. To be the ideal American, in Fitzgerald's Romantic but bitterly ironic view, was to be the redeemer, the one who realizes the Dream. The centrality of the remembrance of the youthful dream gives Fitzgerald's work its lastingly potent chord of nostalgia. The chord becomes discord in Fitzgerald's fiction: both the dream and every meaningful lesson of history become lost when being American means an identification through money and power, of counting what one has as if it were counting what one is. The "gentleman" and "the American" merge in Fitzgerald's story of the American Dream. Fitzgerald's dramatization of that story is always one in which the best of that merged identity, with all its flaws of naïveté and self-indulgent innocent enthusiasm, but also with all its enormous creative energies and dedication and discipline and sense of possibilities (how else can one understand Gatsby and Diver?), is destroyed by the worst of that merged identity, with all its moral shallowness, its belonging, and its tremendous, established power (how else can one understand Tom Buchanan and the Warrens?).

In the 1960s and early 70s, the Viet Nam War divided America as had nothing since the Civil War. Those who supported the war saw nothing but good in American power; those who opposed it saw nothing but ill. Although this stark statement might require modification for any given individual, it is not a misleading indication of the intensity with which the American population was politicized into a deep and bitter division. More than any sector of American society at home, the university was thrown into the turmoil of the division. Fearful of the draft and sickened by the nature of the war, students and faculty generally opposed the war as an apocalyptic exposé of the realities beneath the appearances and illusions of American wealth, power, possibility, and redemption. Beginning in the late sixties, students found Dick Diver hard to understand, hard to take. Critics, almost all of them in the academy, began to find him retrograde. Times of deep division are not apt to be times of fine distinctions, and there grew up in the sixties and seventies a strain of criticism that held Dick to be at best a fool and at worst a villain.

As the criticism of the thirties and forties indicated, there had always been at least a small strain of confusion about Dick in the general body of commentary; but that confusion had not been one of sympathy so much as it had been one concerning causes of his breakdown. In the sixties and seventies, the confusion did not arise from uncertainties about his break-down, but centered on the question of sympathy. The division in Fitzgerald's fiction between the victim-hero who represented the best of America and the triumphant characters who represented its worst became lost for some readers in the deep American divisions of war. As the representative American, Dick became indiscriminately identified for some as the embodiment of Romantic self-deceptions that eventuated in the destructively indiscriminate uses and abuses of American power. As one observer put it, "Over the years . . . readers have easily seen that the many more or less discrete reasons for Diver's collapse can be arranged under two broad categories. The first is socioeconomic: an idealistic, middleclass hero is used and discarded by a rich and careless leisure class. But Fitzgerald was more subtle and more honest than to confine himself to such a baldly dialectical motivation, and provided a second, psychological category of motivation by ascribing to Dick some flaw of character which made him extraordinarily susceptible to the fate which overtook him."[46] In the nineteen fifties, criticism could take for granted the ideal of America as the accepted, albeit Romantic, definition of goodness beset by evil actualities. In the extreme, one critic, after appropriately detailing the novel as a story about the abuse of human talent by voracious and rapacious wealth, could even conclude that Dick experiences salvation in upper New York state: Dick struggles to attain "the solid values taught by his father through serving the weak and the suffering," and "Fitzgerald allows the human spirit, crushed by acquisitive society, hope of redemp-tion through personal reformation."[47] In Hornell, presumably.

But in the nineteen sixties and seventies the problem for criticism became more intricate, for the idealistic sense of America, acceptable as a goal even for the restive thirties and forties, itself came into doubt. As the essays on the Keatsian element in *Tender Is the Night*, especially those included here, indicate, there is a chronologically developing sense of Romantic assumptions as inadequate, a sense of the ineluctable and inescapable morning-after of history, moving from a yearning for the realm of Dream to a nightmare vision of Dream as vampirism. (William Doherty's essay and James Tuttleton's essay should be read in tandem.) The best example of the repudiation of Diver's very idealism is John F. Callahan's *The Illusions of a Nation*, a pertinent section of which is included here. Although by no means all of the repudiations of Diver recognized the core of the problem, and although some were merely in a mode that oversimply found Dick to be a bad man,[48] it is significant that it is Dick's Romanticism that begins to emerge as his own contribution to his own demise. (William Doherty's 1966 essay is one of the best examples of this view in the periodical literature of the time.)

Hostility to Dick also reflected the sexual revolution and women's liberation movement that were complex and inextricable parts of the re-examination of values occasioned by Viet Nam.[49] Part of the effect of the revolution is felt, again, in the responses of students reading *Tender Is the Night* in the nineteen eighties. The change in the nature of sexual identification, of sexual activity, and of expectations concerning marriage and career, makes it difficult for many to understand why there is so much angst associated with Dick's and Rosemary's relationship. Many more young readers in the 1980s than in the 1950s think that Dick is merely stuffy and foolish and that too much is being made of his gentlemanly obligations. They neither sympathize nor identify with Dick. That observation seems to argue against the enduring interest and value of *Tender Is the Night*, but what it really indicates is one more demonstration of the extent to which this book is unlucky. Dick had to wait to be understood in the first place. He had to wait just a shade too long, for just as criticism in the fifties began to catch up with the dimensions and contexts of *Tender Is the Night*, the United States underwent an epochal change in perspectives, obscuring the contexts in which the book is best understood. The novel's own contexts of Dick's idealism and an earlier American Dream of redemption and moral obligation are clear when explained and remain perennially important. This is not to say that the book cannot be understood without special pleading. But this *is* to say that if the novel and the readers of the 1930s, 40s, and 50s shared the same context, the decade of 1965–75 introduced a distance between the context of the novel and that of the reader under thirty in the nineteen eighties. It is this consideration that gives point to the inclusion here of an essay like Henry Dan Piper's examination of Fitzgerald's father's world.

There is another current in Fitzgerald criticism in the sixties and seventies, one inseparable from the first and one that leads toward the conclusion that *Tender Is the Night* is not an anachronistic curio. This emerging pattern is a consensus that the novel is about history, about the lasting interactions of power and morality, of love, temptation, and limitation, both individual and national. More and more, criticism centers not upon the facts of marriage or the formulae of this psychological perspective or that, but upon myth and history, upon the development of America as paradigmatic of western history. In response to the recognition that *Tender Is the Night* requires understanding of its cultural context, for instance, one can justly say that *Hamlet* requires similar special attention: how much does one know about Elizabethan assumptions about life in medieval Danish castles? The historical comprehension is only ancillary to the emergence of worthwhile literature into its own universality and greatness. It seems jarring, but young students force the realization that

Tender Is the Night already has begun to pass down the corridor of time just enough to require of the reader an educated sense of its own context in order to be appreciated most fully in its brightly living relevance to the young reader's contexts. The dovetailing of essays such as those in this volume by Cowley, Fussell, Light, Wasserstrom, Trachtenberg, Callahan, and Grenberg, (which like the Doherty and Tuttleton pieces should be read as a developmental whole) demonstrate both the pattern of growing appreciation of *Tender Is the Night* as a great novel about history and also the beautiful symmetry of good critical perceptions in complex relation to one another when they are lifted out of the welter of wearisome repetition that unhappily characterizes much of the commentary on the book.

V

The relationship of critical perceptions can be glimpsed here because one of the intentions behind this volume has been not only a sampling of some of the most interesting periodical criticism about *Tender Is the Night* but also a representative taste of the diversity of opinions and conclusions. As a highly selected assemblage, this volume has been designed to be as useful as possible for teachers and students as well as for interested general readers. Therefore the first section provides a discussion of the text, including Matthew Bruccoli's invaluable do-it-yourself kit for anyone who wishes to annotate his own copy of *Tender Is the Night* into a correct edition in either version. The last section is Joseph Wenke's very full, probably complete, bibliography of criticism on *Tender Is the Night* from 1934 to 1980, although a few items are included beyond 1980.

There is one principle of selection to be kept in mind in the use of this volume. The quantity of writing on *Tender Is the Night* makes it no longer possible to put into book length all of the best or most representative pieces. By now there are too many first choices, and inevitably too many have to be left out. Except for the Callahan piece, chosen because it is so useful in discerning critical pattern, there are no selections in this volume from book-length studies of Fitzgerald. For one thing, the best book-length criticisms are organic wholes, and as good as a chapter on *Tender Is the Night* might be, it is not as fully revelatory as it is within the context of the ideas that are incrementally and interweavingly developed in the book from which it would be taken. Also there is the very important consideration that usually the chapters are longer than separate essays in periodicals.

But no recapitulation of the criticism of *Tender Is the Night* would be rounded out without at least a few words about the books. On the simplest, the quantitative level, the proliferation of Fitzgerald criticism can be seen in the fact that in the 1950s there were three books of biography or criticism devoted entirely to Fitzgerald; but even if we exclude the many books written about Fitzgerald that do not contain an extended statement about *Tender Is the Night*, and limit ourselves in the two decades from 1960 to 1980 to only those books with sections concerned with *Tender Is the Night*, we find that there were thirty-eight books published! Thirteen were essentially concerned with biographical materials,[50] four were collections of Fitzgerald's correspondence,[51] two were volumes of bibliography,[52] and nineteen were critical studies.[53] Bruccoli's *The Composition of "Tender Is the Night"* remains the definitive study of the text. The five critical books that remain most instructive for an understanding of the novel are Sergio Perosa's *The Art of F. Scott Fitzgerald* (1965) for a general overview; Richard D. Lehan's *F. Scott Fitzgerald and the Craft of Fiction* (1966), especially for the influence of Spengler; Robert Sklar's *F. Scott Fitzgerald: The Last Laöcoon* (1967), especially for the influence of the genteel tradition; Milton R. Stern's *The Golden Moment: The Novels of F. Scott Fitzgerald* (1970), for a long general explication and an analysis of composite characterization, sexual identities, and national identities; and John F. Callahan's *The Illusions of a Nation: Myth and History in the Novels of F. Scott Fitzgerald* (1972), especially for a discussion of American assumptions. Stern and Callahan are particularly illustrative of the view of *Tender Is the Night* as a history of America.

In addition to the Adams and Schoenwald essays previously mentioned, essays by Martin Kallich ("F. Scott Fitzgerald: Money or Morals?" 1949); John Lucas ("In Praise of Scott Fitzgerald," 1963); and Scott Donaldson (" 'No, I Am Not Prince Charming': Fairy Tales in *Tender Is the Night*," 1973) were to be included in this volume but were deleted for lack of space. For full citation information, see Joseph Wenke's bibliography for these pieces and for those mentioned in notes 50 through 54. There are those other first choice essays excluded by the limitations of space. They are too numerous to be treated separately, but a special note[54] will at least serve to identify some of them. The size of the note, like the size of Wenke's bibliography, suggests that perhaps *Tender Is the Night* is not totally unlucky after all. The job of winnowing gives shape that is lacking in the raw quantity of criticism. But both shape and quantity reveal clearly that Fitzgerald has taken his place among America's classic authors and that *Tender Is the Night*, in any context, has emerged and remains as one of the great books, one of the most beautiful and significant major novels in the history of American literature.

MILTON R. STERN

Notes

1. Alexander Cowie, *The Rise of the American Novel* (New York: American Book Co., 1948), p. 747.

2. See Arthur Mizener, "F. Scott Fitzgerald, 1896–1940: The Poet of Borrowed Time" in this volume.

3. Arthur Mizener, *F. Scott Fitzgerald: A Collection of Critical Essays* (Englewood Cliffs, N.J.: Prentice Hall, 1963).

4. D. W. Harding, "Mechanisms of Misery," included in this volume.

5. Kenneth E. Eble, *F. Scott Fitzgerald: A Collection of Criticism* (New York: McGraw-Hill, 1973).

6. Marvin J. LaHood, *Tender Is the Night: Essays in Criticism* (Bloomington and London: Indiana University Press, 1969).

7. See the discussion of composite characters in M. R. Stern, *The Golden Moment: The Novels of F. Scott Fitzgerald* (Urbana: University of Illinois Press, 1970), pp. 289–330, ff.

8. Riley Hughes, "F. Scott Fitzgerald: The Touch of Disaster," in *Fifty Years of the American Novel, A Christian Appraisal*, ed. Harold C. Gardiner (New York: Charles Scribner's Sons, 1951), pp. 135–49.

9. See James Thurber's recollections in *Credos and Curios* (New York: Harper and Row, 1962), p. 159; see also Fitzgerald's important letter to John Peale Bishop, April 7, 1934, in Andrew Turnbull, ed., *The Letters of F. Scott Fitzgerald* (New York: Charles Scribner's Sons, 1963), p. 363.

10. There have been several discussions of Spenglerian patterns of history in Fitzgerald's work. Two useful commentaries are Richard Lehan, *F. Scott Fitzgerald and the Craft of Fiction* (Carbondale: Southern Illinois University Press, 1966) *passim*; and, especially, Joan Kirkby, "Spengler and Apocalyptic Typology in F. Scott Fitzgerald's *Tender Is the Night*," *Southern Review* 12 (November 1979). 246–261. This is one of the excellent essays not included here only because of space limitations and is recommended to the reader.

11. Matthew Bruccoli, *The Composition of "Tender Is the Night,"* (Pittsburgh: The University of Pittsburgh Press, 1963). Bruccoli's book is the definitive study of the manuscripts of the novel in its various stages.

12. Charles Poore, *New York Times*, Thursday, November 15, 1951, p. 27: "When 'Tender Is the Night' was first published in 1934 some (but by no means all) critics were haring hotly after proletarian novels, the wild-westerns of the intellectuals. They looked sternly down their noses at Fitzgerald's story of the heart's splendor. Others used it as a stick to beat the expatriates. It would be preposterous, however, to think that was the reason for 'Tender Is the Night's' failure to be an immense success. The public spent its shrinking dollars even more sparingly on the Ph.D.'s to-the-barricades novels. In 1934 it was reading Stark Young's 'So Red the Rose' and James Hilton's 'Good-Bye, Mr. Chips' in quantities."

13. A revision of pp. 1–16 of *The Composition of Tender Is the Night*. See Matthew J. Bruccoli, ed., *Profile of F. Scott Fitzgerald* (Columbus, Ohio: Charles E. Merrill Publishing Co., 1971), pp. 93–4.

14. There are rich bibliographical aids for a study of *Tender Is the Night*. As Bruccoli is the primary textual scholar and compiler of facts and memorabilia concerning Fitzgerald, Jackson Bryer is the primary bibliographer. See Bryer's *The Critical Reputation of F. Scott Fitzgerald: A Bibliographical Study* (Hamden, Connecticut: Archon Books, 1967); his *Supplement* to the *Critical Reputation* (Archon, 1984); his *F. Scott Fitzgerald, The Critical Reception* (New York: Burt Franklin & Co., 1978); and his "Four Decades of Fitzgerald Studies: The Best and the Brightest," *Twentieth Century Literature* 26 (Summer 1980) 247–67. See also Sergio Perosa, "Fitzgerald Studies in the 1970s," *Twentieth Century Literature* 26 (Summer 1980) 222–46.

15. Amy Loveman, for instance, in her article on the spring list of new books for the *Saturday Review*, spared only two sentences for *Tender Is the Night*, concluding that "it is not a good novel." 10 (April 7, 1934), 610.

16. September 26, 1934. *Correspondence of F. Scott Fitzgerald*, eds. Matthew Bruccoli and Margaret M. Duggan (New York: Random House, 1980), p. 386.

17. Bruccoli: "The critic who finds Dick Diver an unconvincing or confusing character

will not be persuaded otherwise by any amount of argument – or by a detailed reconstruction of the composition of *Tender Is the Night*. For the record, this reader believes that Dick Diver is a satisfying character, that the causes of his deterioration are sufficiently probed, that his fall is moving, and that the novel is unified by Fitzgerald's view of his hero. A study of the manuscripts supports some of these beliefs. Although Fitzgerald did not write long, detailed analyses of his work, the preliminary sketch of Dick Diver prepared in 1932 indicates that he knew the causes of Dick's decline. The first holograph draft for the published version of *Tender Is the Night* reveals that Fitzgerald felt he thoroughly understood his hero." "*Tender Is the Night* – Reception and Reputation," p. 101.

18. See the concluding paragraph of Cowley's "Introduction" to the revised version, included in this volume.

19. To Edmund Wilson, March 12, 1934. *Letters*, p. 346.

20. For an introduction to the problem see the section of "The Text Itself" in this volume.

21. In either version, structure is not a problem for meaning. As Bruccoli asserts, "readers recognized that the revised structure did not really have a significant effect on the essential qualities of *Tender Is the Night*." "*Tender Is the Night* – Reception and Reputation," p. 99. Bruccoli argues that if there is confusion in the novel, it results from chronology rather than structure. See "Material for a Centenary Edition of *Tender Is the Night*" in this volume.

22. April, 1934. *Correspondence*, p. 341.

23. Theodore Adams, "A Noble Issue," *Gifthorse* (Ohio State University, 1949), pp. 35–43.

24. Early in the decade, Oscar Cargill's unfavorable – and ignorant – review was typical. See *Intellectual America* (New York: Macmillan, 1941), pp. 342–46, esp. p. 344. In 1943, Maxwell Geismar thought *Tender Is the Night* a good book badly focussed: see *The Last of the Provincials* (Boston: Houghton Mifflin Co.), pp. 327–37. J. Donald Adams thought it a bad novel: *The Shape of Books to Come* (New York: The Viking Press, 1944), pp. 89–90. Arthur Mizener said that the novel was Fitzgerald's best ("The Poet of Borrowed Time," 1946, reprinted here).

25. John Berryman, "F. Scott Fitzgerald," *Kenyon Review* 8 (Winter 1946); 107.

26. Arthur Mizener "The Portable F. Scott Fitzgerald," 8 (Spring 1946); 342.

27. Arnold Gingerich, "Salute and Farewell to F. Scott Fitzgerald," *Esquire* (March, 1941), 6. It is moving to see that a Pat Hobby story runs in the same issue.

28. Stephen Vincent Benet, "Fitzgerald's Unfinished Symphony," *Saturday Review of Literature* 24 (December 6, 1941); 10.

29. Jeffrey Robinson, "Fitzgerald's Riviera – Disappeared," *Christian Science Monitor* (April 8, 1975), p. 10.

30. Malcolm Cowley, ed., *Tender Is the Night*, (New York: Scribner's, 1951).

31. Arthur Mizener, *The Far Side of Paradise*, (Boston: Houghton Mifflin, 1951).

32. Edmund Wilson, ed., *The Crack-Up* (New York: New Directions, 1945).

33. Alfred Kazin, *F. Scott Fitzgerald: The Man and His Work*, (New York: The World Publishing Company, 1951).

34. *Three Novels of F. Scott Fitzgerald* (New York: Scribners, 1953).

35. Another excellent essay that would have been included had space allowed is Robert Roulston's "Dick Diver's Plunge into the Roman Void: The Setting of *Tender Is the Night*," *South Atlantic Quarterly* 77 (Winter 1978): 85–97.

36. James E. Miller, *The Fictional Technique of Scott Fitzgerald* (The Hague: Martinus Nijhoff, (1957).

37. Kingsley Amis, "The Crack-Up," *Spectator* (London) 203 (November 20, 1959): 719.

38. "Power Without Glory" *Times Literary Supplement* (January 20, 1950), p. 40.

39. Leslie Fiedler, "Notes on F. Scott Fitzgerald," *New Leader* 34 (April 16, 1951): 23–24.

40. Alfred Kazin, introduction to *F. Scott Fitzgerald: The Man and His Work.*

41. John Aldridge, *After the Lost Generation* (New York: McGraw-Hill, 1951): pp. 52–55.

42. A. H. Steinberg, "Fitzgerald's Portrait of a Psychiatrist," *University of Kansas City Review* 21 (March 1955): 219–22.

43. Dan Jacobson, "F. Scott Fitzgerald," *Encounter* 14 (June 1960): 71–77.

44. John R. Kuehl, "Scott Fitzgerald: Romantic and Realist," *Texas Studies in Literature and Language* 1 (Autumn 1959): 412–26.

45. Richard L. Schoenwald, "F. Scott Fitzgerald as John Keats," *Boston University Studies in English* 3 (Spring 1957): 12–21.

46. George D. Murphy, "The Unconscious Dimension of *Tender Is the Night*," *Studies in the Novel* 5 (Fall 1975): 314. Unfortunately, Murphy devotes the rest of his essay to a dismissal of the "socioeconomic" in a revelation of the "real" psychological motivation, which becomes a formulaic reduction of *Tender Is the Night* to an allegory of the relation of the son (Dick, the ego) to the father (all the fathers, the superego).

47. W. F. Kennedy, "Are Our Novelists Hostile to the American Economic System?" *Dalhousie Review* 35 (Spring 1955): 32–44.

48. For instance, Vincent Robson, "The Psychosocial Conflict and the Distortion of Time: A Study of Diver's Disintegration in *Tender Is the Night*," *Language and Literature* 1 (1972): 55–64. Robson sees Diver motivated and ruined by greed and insecurity.

49. Madonna C. Kolbenschlag, for instance, asserted that "Fitzgerald, mystified by the competitive and erratic 'animus' of Zelda, seems also to have failed to fully comprehend the dimensions of 'anima' in himself – in effect, he never successfully demythologized the sexual stereotypes of masculinity and femininity in his sensibility." By implication, the dimension and center of *Tender Is the Night* are one of sexual stereotypes. See "Madness and Sexual Mythology in Scott Fitzgerald," *International Journal of Women's Studies* 1 (May–June 1978): 270. Following an earlier lead from Leslie Fiedler, who, in effect, exonerates the Warren world by making Nicole a victim of Dick ("Some Notes on F. Scott Fitzgerald," in *An End to Innocence: Essays on Culture and Politics*, Boston: The Beacon Press, 1955, pp. 174–82), Milton Hindus ignores the novel's stated facts and goes so far as to assume that Nicole was never raped by Daddy, that it was all in her mind, and that Dick was a sexually stupid psychiatrist foolish enough to believe her. See *F. Scott Fitzgerald: An Introduction and an Interpretation* (New York: Holt, Rinehart, and Winston, 1968), pp. 50–69. See also Coleman, Martin, and McNichols, note 54.

50. Andrew Turnbull, *Scott Fitzgerald* (1962); William Goldhurst, *F. Scott Fitzgerald and His Contemporaries* (1963), on literary crosscurrents; Henry Dan Piper, *F. Scott Fitzgerald: A Critical Portrait* (1965); Matthew J. Bruccoli and Jackson R. Bryer, eds., *F. Scott Fitzgerald in His Own Time: A Miscellany* (1971); Matthew J. Bruccoli, ed., *Profile of F. Scott Fitzgerald*, (1971); Aaron Latham, *Crazy Sundays* (New York: Viking Press, 1971); Sara Mayfield, *Exiles from Paradise* (New York: Delacorte Press, 1971); Arthur Mizener, *F. Scott Fitzgerald and His World* (1972); Matthew J. Bruccoli, Scottie Fitzgerald Smith, and Joan P. Kerr, eds., *The Romantic Egoists* (1974); Tony Buttita, *After The Good Gay Times* (1974); Sheilah Graham, *The Real F. Scott Fitzgerald* (1976); Matthew J. Bruccoli, *Scott and Ernest: The Authority of Failure and the Authority of Success* (1978); Matthew J. Bruccoli, ed., *The Notebooks of F. Scott Fitzgerald* (1979). It must be remembered that this list does not include biographical books on Fitzgerald which do not contain any developed reference to *Tender Is the Night* nor does it include biographical work (Bruccoli's *Some Sort of Epic Grandeur*) that appeared after 1980.

51. Andrew Turnbull, *The Letters of F. Scott Fitzgerald* (1963); John Kuehl and Jackson R. Bryer, eds., *Dear Scott/Dear Max: The Fitzgerald-Perkins Correspondence* (1971); Matthew J. Bruccoli, ed., *As Ever, Scott Fitz —: Letters Between F. Scott Fitzgerald and . . . Harold Ober* (1972); Matthew J. Bruccoli and Margaret M. Duggan, eds., *Correspondence of F. Scott Fitzgerald* (1980).

52. Jackson R. Bryer, *F. Scott Fitzgerald: The Critical Reception* (1978); and Jackson R. Bryer, *The Critical Reputation of F. Scott Fitzgerald* (1967).

53. Charles E. Shain, *F. Scott Fitzgerald* (1961); Kenneth Eble, *F. Scott Fitzgerald* (1963); K. G. W. Cross, *F. Scott Fitzgerald* (1964); James E. Miller, Jr., *F. Scott Fitzgerald: His Art and His Technique* (1964); Sergio Perosa, *The Art of F. Scott Fitzgerald* (1965); Richard D. Lehan, *F. Scott Fitzgerald and the Craft of Fiction* (1966); Edwin M. Mosely, *F. Scott Fitzgerald: A Critical Essay* (1967); Robert Sklar, *F. Scott Fitzgerald: The Last Laocoon* (1967); Milton Hindus, *F. Scott Fitzgerald: An Introduction and Interpretation* (1968); Milton R. Stern, *The Golden Moment: The Novels of F. Scott Fitzgerald* (1970); John F. Callahan, *The Illusions of a Nation: Myth and History in the Novels of F. Scott Fitzgerald* (1972); William A. Fahey, *F. Scott Fitzgerald and the American Dream* (1973); Howard Greenfeld, *F. Scott Fitzgerald* (1974); Eugen Huonder, *The Functional Significance of Setting in the Novels of F. Scott Fitzgerald* (1974); Joan M. Allen, *Candles and Carnival Lights: The Catholic Sensibility of F. Scott Fitzgerald* (1978); Rose A. Gallo, *F. Scott Fitzgerald* (1978); M. Sivaramkrishna, *Icarus of the Jazz Age: A Study of the Novels of F. Scott Fitzgerald* (1978); Thomas J. Stavola, *Scott Fitzgerald: Crisis in an American Identity* (1979); Brian Way, *F. Scott Fitzgerald and the Art of Social Fiction* (1980).

54. In addition to the Robert Roulston and Joan Kirkby essays mentioned above (notes 10 and 35), there are several that would have been added among the first choices were there space. These additional essays do not include among them any of the many excellent general essays on Fitzgerald, such as Wright Morris's splendid piece in *The Territory Ahead*: only articles that concentrate entirely on *Tender Is the Night* are allowed among these additions. There are too many interesting reviews from the nineteen-thirties to be named separately here. If there were to be an addition from the nineteen forties (besides Kallich and Adams), it would be Arthur Mizener's "A Note on 'The World's Fair' " (1948). Two interesting essays from the nineteen-fifties are by John W. Bicknell, "The Waste Land of F. Scott Fitzgerald" (1954) and by A. H. Steinberg, "Fitzgerald's Portrait of a Psychiatrist" (1955). Five essays to be added from the nineteen-sixties are William F. Hall's "Dialogue and Theme in *Tender Is the Night*" (1961); A. Wilber Stevens's "Fitzgerald's *Tender Is the Night*: The Idea as Morality" (1961); John Grube's "*Tender Is the Night*: Keats and Scott Fitzgerald" (1965); James Ellis's "Fitzgerald's Fragmented Hero: Dick Diver" (1965); and William Nestrick's section on *Tender* in "F. Scott Fitzgerald's Types and Narrators" (1967). Pieces worth including from the nineteen-seventies are by Tom C. Coleman III, "The Rise of Doctor Diver" (1970); Frank Kinahan, "Focus on F. Scott Fitzgerald's *Tender Is the Night*" in David Madden, ed., *American Dreams, American Nightmares* (1970); Tom C. Coleman, III, "Nicole Warren Diver and Scott Fitzgerald: The Girl and the Egoist" (1971); John Stark, "The Style of *Tender Is the Night*" (1972); Richard Foster, "Time's Exile: Dick Diver and the Heroic Idea" (1975); Marjory Martin, *Fitzgerald's Image of Women: Anima Projections in "Tender Is the Night"* (1976), 17 pp.; Judith Wilt, "The Spinning Story: Gothic Motifs in *Tender Is the Night*" (1976); Maria DiBattista, "The Aesthetic of Forbearance: Fitzgerald's *Tender Is the Night*" (1978); and Sr. Mary Verity McNichols, "Fitzgerald's Women in *Tender Is the Night*" (1977).

The Text Itself

Tender Is the Night: The Text Itself

As the drafts, versions, rewritings, and revisions of *Tender Is the Night* indicate, Fitzgerald worked on the shape of the novel right up to its publication.[1] As Fitzgerald's correspondence indicates, many readers judged the book from a perusal of the four serial installments of the *Scribner's Magazine* version in 1934. Others read negligently or incompletely: one reader, the novelist Joseph Hergesheimer, opined that a good novel about a movie star can't be written, revealing his own failure to read beyond the Rosemary section that opened the book. And Fitzgerald kept fussing with methods to reorganize the novel even after it was published.

The reviews intensifed his own uneasiness about the book's structure, chronology, and transitions, making him wonder about the possibility that Rosemary's point of view was overemphasized.[2] Just as the composition of *Tender Is the Night* was an endless process of painstaking revision up to the moment it was presented to the world on April 12, 1934, so Fitzgerald continued to work on yet more revisions beyond that date. He tried a few times to get the book republished and suggested transition-pages with new headings indicating the chronology of the action. Sometime around 1938 he developed his own "Analysis of *Tender*" in a notebook. Also, he ripped apart one of his own copies of the novel, refitting the sections so that the tale proceeded chronologically, beginning not with Rosemary, but with Dick Diver at the beginning of his career. Fitzgerald annotated this copy and wrote in it that it was the structure he preferred. He never completed the revision down to the last detail, but apparently until the day he died, he wished he could have published the revised version as his final choice. A decade after Fitzgerald's death, Malcolm Cowley said to Scribner's, "Let him have his wish,"[3] and with Cowley as editor the revised version finally was published in 1951. In effect, F. Scott Fitzgerald left the world two *Tender Is the Nights.*

In the 1950s, most reviewers favored the original edition, although the response was mixed.[4] Among influential critics, for instance, Frederick

*This essay was written specifically for this volume and appears here with the permission of the author.

21

J. Hoffman was unhappy with the Rosemary beginning of the first edition,[5] but Walter Allen favored the original version.[6] But in 1963, with Matthew Bruccoli's announced preference for the original version, the preponderance of critical opinion became more pronounced in favor of the first edition.[7] Wayne Booth, in 1961, had made an argument for the revised version in his influential *The Rhetoric of Fiction*;[8] but except for a countercurrent in the early 1970s generated by my own book[9] and by John F. Callahan's *The Illusions of a Nation*,[10] the mainstream of critical opinion has remained a small tide of disapproval for the revised version.

At first the disagreements among readers were relatively quiet and unmarked by partisan nastiness, like Arthur Mizener's gentle contemplation of his own change from being "a convinced revisionist" to being "not so sure now."[11] However, more recently, opposition to the revised version has taken on pronounced tones of angry bibliocide. In an apparent desire to see the revised version buried forever, antirevisionists have begun to dismiss it by first referring to Bruccoli's *The Composition of "Tender Is the Night"* as scriptural proof that there is to be the original version only, and then by abusing Malcolm Cowley.

Two fairly recent examples will suffice. One is "Sober Second Thoughts: Fitzgerald's 'Final Version' of *Tender Is the Night*," by Brian Higgins and Hershel Parker;[12] the other is "*Tender Is the Night*," chapter six in *F. Scott Fitzgerald and the Art of Social Fiction* by Brian Way.[13] Here are Higgins and Parker: "For the most part, Bruccoli contented himself with laying out evidence which other critics could — but in fact did not — use to argue against the revised edition." But although Higgins and Parker quote Bruccoli's judgments and conclusions and preferences, they too do not specify the evidence; they too summarize Bruccoli's opinions in favor of the first version. They characterize Cowley as barely aware of even "superficial critical questions" (136), as an "inattentive" (135) and "insensitive" (136) dolt "guilty of neglect" (137), who "trampled on or blithely sidestepped a hoard of problems involving biography, textual and aesthetic theory, and criticism" (136), and who "blundered his way" (135) into the creation of an edition which is "bad luck" (135) that must be exorcised lest its rising from Scribner's crossroads, wooden stake and all, "bedevil professors of American literature still again" (135). Higgins and Parker characterize their own essay as an "attempt to lay the [revised] edition to rest as a historical curiosity" (135).

Similarly, Brian Way invokes Bruccoli, stating that all the stages of composition up to the 1934 edition show that "the structure of the novel remained absolutely unchanged," as "Matthew Bruccoli has shown conclusively" (124). Like Higgins' and Parker's essay in tone and manner, Way's dicta consign Cowley's work to nonexistence: "Cowley's edition no longer stands in the way" (125). "No one now attaches any importance whatever to Cowley's edition" (124), Way says, and one is overcome with resonances of the moment when Rosemary hears that Dick Diver is not received anywhere anymore. Although the condescending hostility to Cowley is shameful, there is a real foundation for Way's certitude that the revised version will disappear: except for an English edition (Penguin) not easily obtained, there is no large-printing paperback reissue of the revised version. Scribner's has not proved to be a conscientious custodian of Fitzgerald's books. In its reprintings of the original version, Scribner's never took advantage of Bruccoli's kit of instructions for a fair edition (reprinted as the next essay in this volume), and after its reprinting of the revised version in *Three Novels of F. Scott Fitzgerald* (1953 — also a foul edition), Scribner's reprinted the revised version only by careless accident in 1970: it had intended to reprint the original version! Thereafter, Scribner's destroyed the plates of the Cowley revision, so to all intents and purposes, those who would let Fitzgerald "have his wish" are out of luck.

In the controversy about the two versions, there is one constant: at the center of both Fitzgerald's original structure and his revision was his clear and announced determination to make his object the "dying fall" that he explained in his correspondence, especially to Hemingway. What he wanted to emphasize in the swift fade-out ending was the diminishment, the impact in suffocating quietness, of the main character as he disappears into insignificance — a main character who once had all the greatness of being that made him the center of light, life, hope, and excitement. It was the impact of that effect on the reader that Fitzgerald always and constantly held to as his goal and purpose.

> The first part [of the 1934 edition, Fitzgerald wrote to H. L. Mencken eleven days after the book was published], the romantic introduction, was too long and too elaborated largely because of the fact that it had been written over a series of years with varying Plans, but everything else in the book conformed to a *definite intention* and if I had to start to write it again tomorrow I would adopt the same plan, irrespective of the fact of whether I had in this case brought it off or not brought it off. That is what most of the critics fail to understand (outside of the fact that they fail to recognize and identify anything in the book): that the motif of the "dying fall" was absolutely deliberate and did not come from any diminution of vitality but from a definite plan.[14]

Arguments about the two versions will have to take into account the effect of each version on the "dying fall," which is dramatized in Dick's life, in the idea of the "older America," in Abe North's life and death, in various patterns throughout the novel, and which culminates in the overwhelming three final paragraphs.

The Higgins-Parker essay (which would have been included here had there been space for a full section on "The Text Itself") offers a long discussion of objections to the revised edition. They are listed below, and following each item there is my bare statement in parentheses of at least one possible rebuttal that should be explored. The list and the parenthetical countersuggestions indicate the spectrum of the argument, and most of them relate, in one way or another, to the "dying fall."

1. Fitzgerald revised his novel only because he was desperate and wanted to make the book more appealing for acclaim and sales. (At the very end of his life, when he was more serene, he still wanted the revision.) 2. The revision sacrifices dramatic tension and suspense—and it should be noted that although Higgins and Parker use Miller, Piper, Sklar, and Hindus to voice this complaint on page 133, on pages 148–49 they are upset because the revised version retains elements of suspense and mystery. (Are mystery and suspense central to the nature of this novel?) 3. Nostalgia aroused by the original Book Two for the materials of the original Book One disappears in the revision. (To the extent that nostalgia is the criterion, doesn't the revision intensify it by showing us the transcendent goals of the young Dick Diver at the very beginning, unknowable to Rosemary, who can't see, as the reader now can, all that is beginning to disintegrate?) 4. The revision ominously intensified the foreshadowing and the inexorability of the career leading to the dying fall. (But isn't that just exactly the point?) 5. The revision doesn't allow us to think as well of Dick as the original does. (Is this in fact true for any given good reader, and is there a possibility that the revision's chronological development of plot sharpens one's identification of Dick's necessary flaws?) 6. The parallel between Abe and Dick is made more pointed in the revision. (Is that not an improvement?) 7. The revision lengthens the period of steady destruction between the heroic Dick and the ruined Dick, thereby losing the shock of contrast. (Is that contrast in the revised version not as shockingly clear as any good reader could wish? Isn't the steady, incremental destruction particularly appropriate to the ending's dying fall?) 8. The revision diminishes the differences between the Diver set and the McKisco set in the beach scenes. (Are not those differences strong and sufficient for any good reader? And are not hints of similarity part of the incremental foreshadowing with which the revised version presages the absorption of both groups into the sameness of the triumphant post-war world?) 9. The revised version does not tell us more about "the kind of relationship that Dick and Nicole achieve" than does the original version, and this is a sign of "lack of logical development" (p. 147). (But because the original version does not tell us anything more or different about the Divers' "relationship," what is to be said about the original version?) 10. The revised version delays too long a presentation of Dick's resentment of the Warrens, their world, their manner, their ways. (But too long for what? The revised version develops Dick's resentments exactly as they happen, in developmental relationship to what has come before in chronological increment. And in either version, is there really any problem about understanding Dick's resentment of the Warrens?) 11. Throughout the essay, Higgins and Parker provide instances in which the changes made in the revision upset nuances, relationships of parts, and the success of the section. But, again,

one can agree or disagree with any given conclusion and can argue for improvements in the revision.

By now the point is clear. One need agree with neither the objections raised by Higgins and Parker as representative of the consensus of antirevisionism nor with my countersuggestions raised in parentheses. The point is that the arguments are matters of perspective and perception, not of fact. Furthermore, the arguments are suggested here necessarily only in their barest and therefore crudest outline: they expand and refine in development. In sum, it is totalitarian to declare as a matter of fact or as a matter of settled opinion that one or the other version is the only version that should be considered. And because it is almost as difficult to find support for the revision as it is to find a copy of it, it is appropriate here to develop very briefly two of the considerations that should be thought about in defense of the revision's life.

1. The most constantly revived argument against the revision is that it loses suspense and mystery and therefore evokes a devitalized emotional response. But the emotional context of the book is the dying fall, not mystery and suspense. Whatever *Tender Is the Night* is, it is not a suspense thriller, and one must keep in mind that the "mystery" and "suspense," after all, are a matter for rather superficial curiosity: what did Violet McKisco see in the bathroom of the Villa Diana? The argument to be considered is that the revision replaces that curiosity with the more powerful and infinitely more central emotion generated by the intensification of the dying fall.

The revision does intensify the dying fall. The chronological, inexorable development of Dick Diver's struggle and defeat, from the heights of his promise at the beginning to the depths of his oblivion at the end, in one incremental, long, slanting dive, sets up the dying fall perfectly. It is an odd objection to fault Fitzgerald for this. In an essay which is largely a verbatim version of the introductory portions of his "Notes Toward a Centenary Edition of *Tender Is the Night*," Bruccoli includes a passage deleted from the "centenary" article. Fixing on chronology, not flashback, as a problem for readers, Bruccoli observes that "*Tender Is the Night* is Dick Diver's novel: the reader who cannot calculate the velocity of Dick's dive loses much of the meaning of that novel."[15] Exactly so. The velocity. The rate. The steadiness. Not even the chronology is as important, for it makes less difference that one places an action in 1925 or 1926, 1928 or 1929 — even though it is helpful to clear up some of the confusions of dates that Fitzgerald left in the novel — than if one misses the steadily increasing pressures that create the sharp and woeful change from Dick Diver in 1917 to Dick Diver at the end of the book. Fitzgerald never took his eye from that change and worried and worried about the presentation of it. He knew what the center of his book was at least as well as those who comment on it, and his decision to revise in order to strengthen that center has to be honored.

At the end of Hemingway's *The Old Man and the Sea*, when the languid and safely comfortable tourists, sipping their drinks at their beach-terrace tables, see the skeleton of Santiago's fish lashed to his boat, they ignorantly and incorrectly comment in bland assurance on the species of the fish and the worth of the catch. Precisely because the reader has gone from the beginning, step by step, through the ordeal of catching and landing the fish, the extent to which the obtuse tourists diminish the heroic feat creates in the reader a powerful recoil, a strong contempt and revulsion for the tourists and an immediate and final insight into their worthlessness and limitations. The other magnetic pole of the reader's response is attraction to the hero, an intensified retrospective recognition of the hero's magnificent dimensions.

Similarly, the Warren-Barban-McKisco world's miscomprehension of Dick Diver belittles him in its blithe ignorance of his long day-by-day battle, his self-sacrificial victory in his "case," and his bitter defeat in his life. The reader recoils in contempt and revulsion from the world that dismisses him exactly because the reader knows Dick's greatness as none of the book's characters do. Sadness and sympathy for Dick—a chokingly grieving sense of all that has been lost and of the total reduction of greatness that has been made—are one with our repudiation of the world that drops him into oblivion. Like Santiago, but in far greater complexity and dimension, Dick has also done, all alone, what is misunderstood or unrecognized. By affecting us through a negation of Dick, the inexorable decline of Diver into the dying fall confirms us in our sense of his lost greatness. Both versions create the dying fall. Both versions create our sense of Dick. But the revision sacrifices momentary curiosity for a seamless merger with the central intention of the dying fall: the impact on the reader of the loss of the old idea of young America, with all its naive dreams of salvation, its discipline, its morality, its self-destructive, foolish and self-indulgent generosities, its idealism, its great virtues, all the power and yearning of its early transcendental expectations and ineffable certainties—that, all that, is lost, derided, used up, cast away, and dwindles into tawdry distances, locked away in one grubby nowhere after another, each one shabbier and more lost than the last. What the revision does is sharpen our placement of Dick, and this helps us understand both the nature and energy of his own flaws and the power of the destructive external forces acting upon him.

2. The other point to be considered concerns meaning. There is no question that changes in the position of words and chapters can change meaning. There can hardly be anyone interested in literature who by now still requires instruction in that fact. Clearly, there are shifts of nuance and emphasis created by some of the differences between the two versions. But it is a mistake to think that *the* book is lost or even really different if one reads the original version rather than the revised or the revised rather than the original.[16] For all the changes, the two versions are essentially the same

Tender Is the Night. The choice remains one of preference, not a choice between *the* "real" book and something else. Anyone who has taught the two versions learns that although interesting, complex, and sophisticated critical observations can arise from the difference between the two versions, either version yields the same "real" Fitzgerald, the same "real" meaning, whatever one sees it to be. But this does not mean that the argument of opinion about the two versions will not continue forever. There is no final *fact* that regulates one version to life eternal and the other to death everlasting.

As for evidence of fact against the revised edition, since everyone rightly refers to Bruccoli as the source of factual evidence, it is appropriate to look at his own words: "Again the evidence is mainly negative: there is no other discarded structure, and there is no indication that Fitzgerald had any doubts about his narrative plan while he was writing the novel."[17] If there had been an alternative structure that Fitzgerald had discarded, that indeed would have been factual proof that Fitzgerald preferred the 1934 version to the one he had discarded. He could hardly have discarded the structure he came to prefer but had not yet created. The negative evidence as *fact* can lead only to a tautological conclusion: Fitzgerald wrote the structure he wanted in 1934; the structure that he wrote and wanted in 1934 was the structure he published in 1934; the structure he published in 1934 was the structure he wrote to publish in 1934. The fact is that the first edition version was the version Fitzgerald saw through the press; that is the version he published, that is the version he hoped the world would say is "good, good, good," and — conclusion — therefore that is the version that should be republished. There is no question that the 1934 version should be republished — in a fair edition, one hopes. Beyond this vision of factual evidence, all other points are not matters of fact but of interpretation, conclusion, taste, judgment, perspectives, explications: they are, as I have insisted in this essay, matters of preference.

One cannot argue a matter of fact. The fact is the overwhelming reason that I agree that the original version should continue to be republished, that the partisans of the original version have a secure basis for their preference, and that the republication should be done according to the notes provided by Bruccoli in his "Material for a Centenary Edition of *Tender Is the Night."*

But once one comes past the facts of composition leading to acceptance of the 1934 version, the drawing of conclusions against the revised version is as much a matter of impression and judgment — no matter who pronounces it — as anything in the copious secondary literature surrounding this novel. For better or worse, the arguments are derived from readings; the facts *for* the 1934 version are not also facts *against* the 1951 version.

For there are other facts and other evidence. One basic fact I have already outlined: the composition of *Tender Is the Night* did not stop on

April 12, 1934, and critics who act as though it did are not willing to accommodate the facts. Bruccoli's evidence is superb up to April 12, 1934, and accounts for the version of that date; it does not unmake the years and events that went into post-publication revision; it does not unwrite the revised version, created by Fitzgerald himself.

The factual history is complex, but can be condensed as follows: the seven blue cardboard boxes of approximately 3500 pages of manuscript in Princeton's Firestone Library contained three major versions of the novel, comprising seventeen drafts *up to* the publication of the first edition. The first version, the story of Francis Melarkey, a young Hollywood technician who was to have killed his mother, was revised in five drafts, with a change in title for almost every draft: *Our Type, The Boy Who Killed His Mother, The Melarkey Case,* and *The World's Fair.* These drafts occupied Fitzgerald from 1925 through 1930. Briefly Fitzgerald interrupted the Melarkey story of matricide in 1929 to begin the second, the Kelly version. But he quickly abandoned his new hero and his new start without a title, without a complete draft, without anything, in fact, but two long and tentative scenes on an ocean liner and the introduction of a young actress named Rosemary. The Melarkey version introduced background characters named, through various christenings, Abe and Mary Grant, later to become the Norths, and Seth and Dina Piper, later to become the Divers. That's six drafts.

The seventh through twelfth drafts were created when the third version developed out of an original set of notes and five revisions; it was revised a sixth time in the galleys for its serial publication in *Scribner's* (the thirteenth draft), a seventh time in pageproof for the serial (the fourteenth draft), an eighth time on tearsheets from the published serial in preparation for publication in book form (the fifteenth draft) a ninth time in the galleys for the book (the sixteenth draft), and a tenth time in the page proofs for the book. That's seventeen.

Given the tortuous continuing labor of doubts and changes — no other of Fitzgerald's books received such treatment — one can see the first edition of *Tender Is the Night* as the culmination of another stage in the ongoing process of revision. For there *was* an eleventh revision of the third version, an eighteenth draft that was created when Fitzgerald began to prepare a final revision for republication of the novel as he would like to see it. He died without completing every detail of that revision, which he called his "final version." If one is to account for *facts,* there is the fact that Fitzgerald repeatedly urged a new edition of *Tender,* and there is the fact of the famous letter to Maxwell Perkins, in which he says that the book's "great fault is that the true beginning — the young psychiatrist in Switzerland — is tucked away in the middle of the book. If pages 151–212 were taken from their present place and put at the start, the improvement in appeal would be enormous. In fact the mistake was noted and suggested by a dozen reviewers. To shape up the ends of that change would, of course, require changes in half a dozen other pages" (December 24, 1938). This letter has been an ineluctable obstacle to critics who would sweep away the revised version. They explain it away in various ways, but none convincingly. Many emphasize the word "appeal" and interpret it to mean that broken and sick, Fitzgerald was thinking only of sales, not of his art. But he was also broken and sick during the composition of most of the drafts of what came to be the 1934 edition, and if we are not to credit his judgment or integrity because he was desperate when he devised a revision, then we have to discredit his choice of the first edition's structure, when he was just as desperate and eager to see his book in print. In fact, as the biographies — particularly Scott Donaldson's *Fool for Love* — indicate, toward the very end of his life, Fitzgerald miraculously managed to attain a small measure of peace and reflective sobriety, more than he had enjoyed while writing the 1934 version, and to the very end, even in his relatively settled steadiness, he continued to prefer his final, unpublished version.

The fact is that as close to publication as February 5, 1934, Fitzgerald had written to Perkins that in revising the four serial installments for book publication, he remained least satisfied with section I, which was to introduce the book. The fact is that just before publication, in his letters of January and February, 1934, his advice about advertising the book had made it abundantly clear that he was uneasy about the beginning, and the fact is that in letters to friends he stated and restated his wish that they had not read the serial because of the extent to which the materials *after* the beginning were polished in the book. The fact that the manuscripts indicate more revisions for the beginning, in relation to what he wrote his friends, suggests even more strongly how worried he was about the beginning. The fact is that Fitzgerald had been uneasy about the book's opening long before it was published; he remained uneasy when he began his efforts in 1936 to revive the book; and he specified his uneasiness in his "true beginning" letter of December 24, 1938. The obdurate fact is that after April 12, 1934, Fitzgerald *did* create an alternative structure, one he did *not* discard, one he called "the *final version* of the book as I would like it." The matters of factual evidence must include the facts after April 12, 1934, as well as before. Because of the facts, the revised version should be republished also.

It is interesting, when one holds fact and preference side by side, that in his essay on a Centenary edition of *Tender*, Bruccoli *does* accept Fitzgerald's "final" revisions for a definitive edition in almost all substantive changes; but he won't accept Fitgerald's restructuring, not on a basis of fact but on *his* judgment that it's not Fitzgerald's best judgment. In short, facts are important only in that they become judgments, and Bruccoli, no less than anyone else, finds that Fitzgerald's judgment is "good" when it accords with his, and that it isn't when it doesn't.[18] In the matter of drawing conclusions from facts, in the case of versions of *Tender Is the Night* there are too many facts on both sides of the argument to allow for one version and one version only. Probably one strong motivation for wishing annihilation of the revision is that critics and teachers prefer to work with familiar materials and do not feel comfortable about the possibility of a textual future that untidily refuses to be ordered and settled into one and only one version of the novel.

The reluctance of some critics to honor Fitzgerald's last wishes is really quite strange, especially when one considers that the established editorial practice is to honor an author's last intent. And there is ample precedent to demonstrate that living with more than one version of a work is hardly destructive of the work, appreciation of the work, or consideration of it, and of the many possible examples, three will suffice. If we want long-standing precedent, there are the folio and quarto versions of Shakespeare, who has managed, somehow, through time. Closer to the twentieth century, one can point to the variant versions of Wordsworth's "Prelude," no inconsiderable piece. And coeval with Fitzgerald, there was W. H. Auden — the reader is recommended to the first two paragraphs of the "Editor's Preface" of the collected poems for a highly apposite statement about last intent and variant editions.[19] Auden himself identified, perhaps, the nervousness of critics when authors revise their works: "Critics," he observed, "are apt to find revisions ideologically significant."[20] He insisted that he did not change his ideologies or meanings from originals to revisions, just as the ideologies and meanings of *Tender Is the Night* do not change from one version to the other. Auden insisted that he understood his own work at least as well as his commentators, and that he understood his own reasons and intentions much better. So too Fitzgerald. But Fitzgerald never had Auden's posthumous luck. It is certainly well past time that he had it.

More than anything else in Fitzgerald scholarship, we need a carefully edited fair edition of each version. But given the cavalier, cynical, corporate aspects of publishing today, we are likely to get neither until the books become available in public domain in 1990. Probably only then shall we have the co-existence that Fitzgerald's original vision and revision both deserve. For in either version, *Tender Is the Night* makes a strong bid to emerge more and more powerfully — and to last — as the great American novel of history in the twentieth century.

Notes

1. The standard and exhaustive study of the subject is Matthew Bruccoli's *The Composition of "Tender Is the Night"* (Pittsburgh: The University of Pittsburgh Press, 1963).

2. One plausible explanation of overemphasis, if it is overemphasis, is given by Arthur Mizener, "A Note on 'The World's Fair,' " *Kenyon Review* 10 (Autumn 1948): 701–04.

3. Malcolm Cowley, "The Fitzgerald Revival," *Fitzgerald / Hemingway Annual* (1974), p. 13.

4. The British reviews offer a good example. In "Echoes of the Jazz Age," the London *Times* (Nov. 19, 1959, p. 15) favored "the first conception"; the writer of "Golden Boy" in the

London *Tablet* (March 5, 1960, p. 230) preferred the revised edition; and the reviewer for the London *Times Literary Supplement* ("The Round-Up," Nov. 27, 1959, p. 695), while asserting that the revised edition must be considered as a serious and lasting version, was glad to have both versions.

5. Frederick G. Hoffman, *The Modern Novel in America, 1900–1950* (Chicago: Henry Regnery, 1951), pp. 127–28.

6. Walter Allen, "An Age and an Image," *New Statesman*, n.s. 59 (January 9, 1960): 48–49.

7. Because of the very useful wealth of factual materials that Bruccoli presented and tirelessly continues to provide, his critical pronouncements had and continue to have a wide effect. In the 1960s, most of the studies touching on this problem favored the original version: James E. Miller, *F. Scott Fitzgerald: His Art and His Technique* (New York: New York University Press, 1964), p. 135; Henry Dan Piper, *F. Scott Fitzgerald: A Critical Portrait* (New York: Holt, Rinehart, and Winston, 1965) p. 226; Robert Sklar, *F. Scott Fitzgerald: The Last Laocoon* (New York: Oxford University Press, 1967), p. 291; Milton Hindus, *F. Scott Fitzgerald: An Introduction and Interpretation* (New York: Holt, Rinehart, and Winston, 1968), pp. 52–53; James Gindin, "Gods and Fathers in F. Scott Fitzgerald's Novels," *Modern Language Quarterly* 30 (March 1969): 64–85, esp. 74–80.

8. Wayne Booth, *The Rhetoric of Fiction*, (Chicago and London: The University of Chicago Press, 1961) pp. 190–95.

9. Milton R. Stern, *The Golden Moment: The Novels of F. Scott Fitzgerald* (Urbana: The University of Illinois Press, 1970), pp. 289–462 *passim*, esp. pp. 374–93.

10. John F. Callahan, *The Illusions of a Nation*, (Urbana: The University of Illinois Press, 1972), pp. 62–70 *et passim*.

11. Arthur Mizener, "An Author's Final Version," *Saturday Review of Literature* 34 (December 8, 1951): 19.

12. Brian Higgins and Hershel Parker, "Sober Second Thoughts: Fitzgerald's 'Final Version' of *Tender Is the Night*," *Proof* 4 (1975). 129–152. References to this essay are given in parentheses.

13. Brian Way, *F. Scott Fitzgerald and the Art of Social Fiction*, (New York: St. Martin's Press 1980), pp. 119–148. References to this essay are given in parentheses.

14. *The Letters of F. Scott Fitzgerald*, ed. Andrew Turnbull (New York: Charles Scribner's Sons, 1963), p. 510.

15. Matthew Bruccoli, " 'A Might Collation': Animadversions on the Text of F. Scott Fitzgerald," *Editing Twentieth Century Texts*, ed. Francis G. Halpenny (Toronto: University of Toronto Press, 1972), p. 34.

16. In another essay that would have been included here had there been room for a developed section on "The Text Itself," one can find an example of the assertion that the two versions are "two quite different novels, each with a different focus, each with a different theme." See Lucy M. Buntain, "A Note on the Editions of *Tender Is the Night*," *Studies in American Fiction* 1 (Autumn 1973): 212. But see also the conclusion that although one might prefer the original version, it really doesn't matter *essentially* which version one prefers: see Theodore L. Gross, "F. Scott Fitzgerald: The Hero in Retrospect," *South Atlantic Quarterly* 67 (Winter 1968): 64–77.

17. Matthew Bruccoli, *The Composition of "Tender Is the Night*," (Pittsburgh: The University of Pittsburgh Press, 1963), p. 14.

18. Matthew Bruccoli, "Material for a Centenary Edition of *Tender Is the Night*," *Studies in Bibliography* 17 (1964): 177–93.

19. Edward Mendelson, ed, *W. H. Auden: Collected Poems* (New York: Random House, 1976), p. 11.

20. *W. H. Auden: Collected Poems*, p. 16.

Material for a Centenary Edition
of *Tender Is the Night*   Matthew J. Bruccoli*

The pre-publication history of F. Scott Fitzgerald's *Tender Is the Night* is fascinating; the post-publication history of the text is distressing. As I have shown in *The Composition of Tender Is the Night*,[1] the novel had twelve drafts of three different versions before it was serialized, and then it was heavily revised for book publication.[2]

As published in April 1934 the first printing included more than 100 substantive errors. One correction was made in the 1934 third printing of the first edition, and one in the 1951 fourth printing.[3] The Scribner Library edition of 1960, the second Scribners edition of the 1934 text, introduced six corrections and thirteen errors—even though Malcolm Cowley and his 1951 revised edition were both available for consultation.[4] Collation of eighty-four pages of the English first edition against the American shows twenty-four changes—of which eleven are English spellings, nine are corrections, and four are fresh errors.

Obviously, most of the blame for the sloppy text of *Tender Is the Night* belongs to Fitzgerald. Even at his best he was weak on the mechanical details of writing, and he read proof on this novel during a period of great personal strain. Moreover, his wholesale revising in proof would have made the job of copy-editing *Tender Is the Night* difficult for even the most skilled editor. The books galleys were set directly from the unrevised *Scribner's Magazine* serial, and then Fitzgerald proceeded to prepare the book text by covering these galleys with revisions. Although all the book galleys have not survived, it is demonstrable that they had to be reset.[5] As Cowley notes, Maxwell Perkins was not the plodding editor this novel needed. Perkins "had an aristocratic disregard for details so long as a book was right in its feeling for life. Since Fitzgerald was regarded as one of his special authors, the manuscript was never copy-edited by others."[6]

In 1951 Malcolm Cowley edited a new edition for Scribners, "The Author's Final Version," based on Fitzgerald's marked dummy in which the story is re-arranged into straight chronological order.[7] Fitzgerald seems to have remained unaware of the concentration of errors in the text, for he made only four corrections—as opposed to revisions—in his copy. In 1936 when the Modern Library was considering reprinting the original plates Fitzgerald asked for permission to insert explanatory headings, but did not mention correcting the errors.[8] However, Cowley recognized the foul state of the text and undertook to clean it up in his edition. This chore he performed so painstakingly that his edition includes more than 900 variants from the first edition—but less than thirty of these are identified

*Reprinted from *Studies in Bibliography* (Charlottesville: University Press of Virginia, 1964), 17:177–93, with permission of the Press and of the author. The essay has been revised by the author for inclusion in this volume.

in his notes. This edition also introduces thirteen new errors into the text.[9] Cowley is right in suggesting that the errors in the first edition have the cumulative effect of distracting the reader's attention, but he fails to recognize that his liberal position on silent emendation offers the reader something less than straight Fitzgerald. Given the conditions of trade publishing, Cowley probably never had the option of listing all his emendations. Nonetheless, the fact remains that an unwary critic could get into trouble with Cowley's text.

More than spelling, grammar, and punctuation are at stake, for *Tender Is the Night* includes a group of chronological inconsistencies which seriously affect the reader's reaction to the novel. Serious difficulty is caused by the inconsistencies in the ages of the characters; and Fitzgerald's inattention to the time-span of his story confuses Book III, which traces Dick's crack-up and which critics have found unsatisfactory. It is essential that the reader be aware of the pace of Dick's collapse, but from the first edition it is hard to tell whether Book III occupies one or two years. Fitzgerald's preliminary plan reveals that the novel was intended to open with Rosemary's arrival on the Riviera in June 1925 and ends with Dick's departure from the Riviera in July 1929.[10] But Fitzgerald seems to have confused four years with five summers. Thus, on page 276 he gives the year of Dick's Rome meeting with Rosemary as 1928, but on this page and on page 271 he adds an extra year to their ages. If the break-up of the Divers' marriage and Dick's abdication are to occur in the summer of 1929, then Book III occupies one year. At this point four years (but five summers) have passed since Rosemary and Dick first met — not five years, as Fitzgerald states on page 364. That this is the summer of 1929 gives Dick's crack-up an ironic significance in view of what will happen on Wall Street in October. Unfortunately, Fitzgerald's carelessness or confusion blurred this effect. Indeed, Cowley is convinced that Fitzgerald changed the time-scheme of the novel after he drew up the preliminary plan, and that *Tender Is the Night* does in fact cover five years:

> We will be told several times that five years have passed since Rosemary's first visit to the Cap d'Antibes in the summer of 1925. Her second visit, then, was in June, 1930. The date reveals a change in Fitzgerald's plans. . . . There is always a sense of historical events in the background of the novel . . . and many episodes in it have the color of a special year. At this point, however, the author needed more elapsed time to accomplish Dick's ruin — five years instead of four — and actually 1930 was better for the historical background than 1929. It was the year when, in spite of the crash, there were more rich Americans in Europe than ever before and when the summer season on the Riviera was the biggest and maddest.[11]

Although Cowley does not account for the year 1929, his idea is supported by Fitzgerald's statement at the beginning of chapter four of Book III, "The Villa Diana had been rented again for the summer. . . ."[12] which indicates that a full year passes between the Divers' departure from the clinic and their return to the Riviera. But my feeling is that this is another piece of Fitzgerald's own confusion, of which there is ample evidence in the novel. The case for the four-year time-span rests on two points: it is extremely unlikely that Fitzgerald would not have mentioned the crash if it had occurred during the novel; and Tommy's statement on page 353 that his stocks are doing well hardly belongs to the summer of 1930.

Cowley correctly points out that the year 1926 is unaccounted for in the action of the first edition.[13] The trip to Gstaad occurs during December of 1925, and in chapter fourteen of Book II Fitzgerald states that Dick has been at the clinic for eighteen months,[14] which would make the time of this chapter June 1927. But since the Rome chapters that follow are dated 1928, one year must be accounted for. Cowley suggests that the Divers remained on the Riviera during 1926 while the clinic was being renovated. It may be that this is the point where Fitzgerald lost track of his time-scheme. If the Rome chapters are moved back to 1927, then Cowley can have his two years for Book III and the summer 1929 Riviera ending can be retained. I have not suggested this change in a projected edition, though, because Fitzgerald specifies that the Rome chapters take place in 1928.

Since my study of the composition of Tender Is the Night has convinced me that the structure of "The Author's Final Version" does not represent Fitzgerald's best judgment, I believe that the 1934 first edition should be used as the copy-text for a projected critical edition. Thus all page references in the tables are to the first edition.

The list of Emendations to be Made in the First-Edition Copy-Text includes all changes — substantive, accidental, and typographical — that I would make in the first edition. Except in cases where there is a possibility of confusion I have resisted improving Fitzgerald's punctuation. His punctuation by ear and eye is frequently wrong, but it was his system and part of the texture of his work. In this list the first reading is the emendation to be made in the copy-text; the bracket is followed by the rejected reading(s) and its sources. The Emendations list is based on the first edition and records only the changes required in that text. Asterisked entries are discussed in the Textual Notes.

The Historical Collation records only substantive variants among the three editions published by Scribners (1934, Cowley 1951, and Scribner Library 1960). Like the Emendations list, the Historical Collation is based on the first-edition copy-text. The first reading is that of a proposed definitive edition; following the bracket are the rejected readings and their sources. The serial has been used only as a check on variants in these three editions. The Historical Collation does not include all variants between the serial and the first edition, since these would be both voluminous and distracting.

Emendations to be Made in the First-Edition Copy-Text

The following symbols are used: B (Bruccoli — that is, an emendation to be made for the first time), C (Cowley — "The Author's Final Version," 1951), F (Fitzgerald — a revision marked by the author in his copy of the novel), S (Serial — *Scribner's Magazine*, 1934), I (first edition, 1934), II (The Scribner Library edition, 1960).

3.1   the shore] F; the pleasant shore S, I–II

3.2   stood] F; stands S, I–II

3.4   cooled] F; cool S, I–II

3.4   stretched] F; stretches S, I–II

3.5   Now] F; Lately S, I–II

3.6   in 1925] F; a decade ago S, I–II

3.7–8   April; in those days only] F; April. Now, many bungalows cluster near it, but when this story begins only S, I–II; April. Only C

3.17   had come] F; came S, I–II

3.21   had floundered] C; floundered S, I–II

4.8   this] F; one S, I–II

4.10; 19.6   hotel] C; Hotel S, I–II

18.25; 220.2   hotel] S; Hotel I–II

12.6   Antheil] C; Anthiel S, I–II

12.8; 13.5   *Ulysses*] S; Ulysses I–II

16.11; 30.11   *Daddy's Girl.*] C; 'Daddy's Girl.' S, I–II

17.11   the] C; The S, I–II

18.11   "Nice Carnival Song"] B; ∧ ~ ∧ S, I–II, C

18.12   *Le Temps*] S; Le Temps I–II

18.13   *The Saturday Evening Post*] S: Saturday Evening Post I–II; the *Saturday Evening Post* C

18.30   czar] C; Czar S, I–II

19.1   Buddhas'] C; Buddha's, S, I–II

19.5   Eleven years ago] B; Ten years ago S, I–II; Eleven years before C

20.19   was] C; were S, I–II

21.26   swimming.] C; ~ , S, I–II

22.18   the *Paris Herald*] B; The New York Herald I; *The New York Herald* S, II; the Paris edition of the *New York Herald* C

*24.19–23   His eyes . . . . more] stet S, I–II, C

24.23   uninterested] C; disinterested S, I–II

*24.30   Señor] C; Signor S, I–II

28.1   as nearly sulky] S; nearly as sulkily I–II; feeling nearly as sulky C

42.8   Divers'] S; Diver's I–II

42.25   irrelevant] C; irrelative S, I–II

48.20   Iles de Lérins] C; Isles des Lerins S, I–II

60.4   party] C; parties S, I–II

*61.10   words] *stet* S, I–II

68.16   chair. . . .] B; ~ . . . S, I–II, C

70.6   *Daddy's Girl*] C; "Daddy's Girl" S, I–II

71.12   because] C; due to the fact that S, I–II

74.5   Beaumont-Hamel] C; ~ ∧ ~ S, I–II

75.15   *mairie*] S; mairie I–II, C

75.21   *Undine*] S; Undine I–II

75.22   *marraines*] S; marraines I–II, C

75.23   Württemberg] C; Wurtemburg S, I–II

76.26   seven] C; six S, I–II

78.6   Württembergers] C; Wurtemburgers S, I–II

78.8   Old] C; old S, I–II

79.2   Arts] C; Art S, I–II

79.4   Hôtel] C; Hotel S, I–II

97.5   hotel] C; Hotel S; Hôtel I–II

101.9   odyssey] C; Odyssey S, I–II

102.5   Hengist] C; Hengest S, I–II

104.28; 136.15   Champs Élysées] C; ~ ∧ ~ S, I–II

105.1   Saint-Lazare] C; ~ ∧ ~ I–II; St. Lazare S

106.9   on a world] C; on world S, I–II

111.19   Diaghilev] C; Diaghileff S, I–II

111.21   décor] C; decor S, I–II

117.5   friend] S; friends I–II

*119.10,12   100,000 Chemises] C; 1000 chemises S, I–II

*119.30   Canossa] B; Ferrara S, I–II, C

*120.1–122.6   hour it had become] F; hour of standing. . . . It had become S, I–II

120.14   de Saint-Ange] B; des Saintes Anges S; des Saintes-Anges I–II

121.11   through?] S; ~ . I–II, C

122.31   Brizard] C; Brizzard S, I–II

122.31   Fernet-Branca] B; André Fernet ∧ Blanco S, I–II; Fernet ∧ Branca C

122.32   Rocher] C; Rochet S, I–II

125.4   had been awakened] C; had awakened S, I

*128.17   Montmartre] *stet* S, I–II, C

*128.18   Copenhagen] *stet* S, I–II, C

128.22   Why you] *stet* S, I–II

128.23   Évreux] C; Evreux S, I–II

129.26   conservatism] S; conversation I–II, C

131.4   Mosby] C; Moseby S, I–II

132.10   concessionnaire] C; concessionaire I–II

132.23   *Liberty*] C; Liberty S, I–II

133.4,8   *France*] C; France S, I–II

133.15   about] C; of S, I–II

136.2   arrondissement] C; arrondisement S, I–II

136.16   failing] *stet* S, I–II, C

137.21   godlike] C; Godlike S, I–II

139.9   states] C; States S, I–II

139.29   Latin Quarter] C; French Latin quarter S, I–II

142.13   Third] C; third S, I–II

145.32   unexceptionably] B; unexceptionally S, I–II, C

152.18   Damenstiftgasse] C; Damenstiff Strasse S, I–II

153.18   at] F; in S, I–II

153.27   criterion] C; criteria S, I–II

153.31   *The Rose and the Ring*] S; The Rose and the Ring I–II

154.17   yourself. Once] F; yourself — once S, I–II

154.24   subject. No good sense."] F; subject." S, I–II

154.28   people — they were the illusions] F; people; illusions S, I–II

155.7–9   destiny. Best] F; destiny . . . Best S, I–II

156.16   cortex] C; cervical S, I–II

157.2; 158.33   Zürichsee] B; Zurichsee S, I–II

157.7   Kraepelin] F; Krapaelin S, I–II

*157.13–15   You . . . Dick."] *stet* I–II

*157.16   war — you] *stet* S, I–II

158.5   privates] F; private soldiers S, I–II

158.10   "Toward] F; " — toward S, I–II

159.6   plateau] F; eminence S, I–II

159.12   Outside, some] F; Some S, I–II

159.13   one] F; they S, I–II

159.20   room. Pushing] F; room; pushing S, I–II

159.24   first] F; first one S, I–II

160.1   about the] F; about the time of the S, I–II

*162.21   farcical] B; farcicle S, I–II, C

164.3, 4, 5, 8, 13   . . . .] C; . . . S, I–II

*167.7   thirteen] B; eleven S, I–II; twelve C

175.9; 311.26   clinic] C; Clinic S, I–II

175.9   Interlaken] C; Interlachen S; Interlacken I–II

177.4   gladiolus] C; gladiola S, I–II

178.10   Suppé's] C; Suppe's S, I–II

178.19–20   path, where, in a moment, a shadow cut across it — she]
        C; path; where, in a moment, a shadow cut across it —
        she F; path — where in a moment a shadow cut across it.
        She S, I–II

180.10   "A] C; ∧ ~ S, I–II

180.12   down . . . .] B; down . . . S, I–II; down — " C

180.22   shoulder — then apart.] F; shoulder. S, I–II

180.23   record. — Have] C; record," she said. " — Have S, I–II; re-
        cord, — Have F

181.4   table, male eyes] F; table, eyes S, I–II

181.26   service] B; Service S, I–II; army C

183.11   Glas Bier] C; Glas-bier S; Glas–Bier I–II

187.17   Burberry] B; burberry S, I–II, C

192.12   who] S; whom I–II

193.9, 31   Kraepelin] C; Krapaelin S, I–II

193.15   *Extra space after l.15*] F; *no extra space* S, I–II

*193.17   Dent du Midi] C; Jugenhorn S, I–II

193.22   trainbands] C; trained bands S; trained-bands I–II

193.31   sie] C; siz I–II

194.7   down into port] C; down port S, I–II

195.3   Kursaal] C; Kursal I–II

*197.19   four] C; five S, I–II

199.23   *Vanity Fair.*] C; 'Vanity Fair.' S, I–II

199.24   schizoid] S; schizzoid I

200.1   Guards] C; guards' S, I–II

205.12   Rocher] C; Rochers S, I–II

209.23   *camérière*] B; camérière I–II; cameriere C

209.30   Grotto] C; Grotte S, I–II

211.28   Affaires Étrangères] C; *Affaires Etrangères* S, I–II

*212.9   Tommy] *stet* S, I–II

*212.23-4   beach with my husband and two children.] *stet* S, I–II

215.10   "Nice Carnival Song"] C; ∧ ~ ∧ S, I–II

217.23   McBeth] C; MacBeth S, I–II

219.30   into] C; in S, I–II

221.11   menagerie] C; Menagerie S, I–II

223.28   hotel] C; Hôtel I; Hotel S, II

223.29; 353.11   casino] C; Casino S, I–II

*226.5   just over] C; almost S, I–II

226.8   spinster's] C; spinsters' S, I–II

*227.23   Gregorovious] B; Gregorovius S, I–II, C

*230.11   have] C; haven't S, I–II

230.20   Privatdocent] B; Privat docent S, I; Privat-dozent II, C

233.3   Humpty Dumpty] C; Humpty-Dumpty S, I–II

236.5   Prokofiev's *Love for Three Oranges.*] C; Prokofieff's *Love of Three Oranges.* S; Prokofieff's "Love of Three Oranges." I–II

236.8   his bed-lamp and] C; the light and S; his bed-lamp light and I–II

*238.1   seven] C; eight S, I–II

*238.15   ergo] *stet* S, I–II

*239.30   uninstructed] B; instructed S, I–II, C

240.25   as if imprisoned in] C; as imprisoned in S, I; as imprisoned as in II

243.14   with nail scissors] C; with scissors S; with a nail scissors I–II

*246.22   nine] C; six S, I–II

249.20   opposite] C; apposite S, I–II

250.21   schizophrenic] C; "schizophrène" S, I–II

252.10   Émile's] C; Emile's S, I–II

252.10   Émile's] C; Emile S, I–II

254.7   patients'] S; patient's I–II

255.10   *The Century*] B; The Century I–II, the *Century* C

255.10   the *Motion Picture*] C; The Motion Picture I–II

255.10   *L' Illustration*] S; L' Illustration I–II

255.11   and the *Fliegende Blätter*] S; and the Fliegende Blätter I–II; and *Fliegende Blätter* C

256.13   a] C; A S, I–II

257.7   or] C; nor S, I–II

257.7   men's] C; their S, I–II

257.32   inordinately, meanwhile] B; inordinately and S; inordinately ∧ meanwhile I–II; inordinately C

258.2   grand tour] B; Grand Tour S, C; grand Tour I–II

*259.11   stood ready to depart] S; departed I–II; lingered C

259.31   the *Herald*] C; *The Herald* S; The Herald I–II

262.7   Erbsensuppe] B; erbsen-suppe S, I–II; Erbsen-suppe C

262.7   Würtschen] C; würstchen S, I–II

262.8   steins] B; helles S, I–II; seidels C

262.9   Kaiserschmarren.] B; kaiserschmarren. S;
"kaiser-schmarren." I–II Kaiser-schmarren. C

266.16   the income] C; it S, I–II

268.17   the steamer's] C; it S, I–II

270.11   hoofs] C; hoops I–II

270.17   *The Grandeur that was Rome*] C; 'The Grandeur that was
Rome' S, I–II

271.1   *Corriere della Sera*] C; Corriere della Sera I–II

271.1   Sainclair] *stet* S, I–II, C

271.1   *Wall Street*] C; 'Wall Street' I–II

271.3   città] C; citta I–II

*271.14   three] B; four S, I–II, C

*271.16   twenty-one . . . thirty-seven] B; twenty-two . . . thirty-
eight S, I–II, C

274.2   *Daddy's Girl*] C; Daddy's Girl I–II

274.17   now. . . .] C; now . . . S, I–II

274.21   heaven. . . .] B; heaven . . . I–II; heaven. C

276.12   twenty-one] B twenty-two S, I–II, C

288.16   Nazionale] C; Nationale S, I–II

290.5   mousseux] S; mousseaux I–II

*291.12   Birmingham] *stet* S, I–II

294.16,23   saoul] C; sault S; saoûl I–II

296.7   Guards] B; guards' S, I–II, C

301.10   on which] C; whereon S, I–II

*301.18   *sempre diretto*] C; *semper dritte* S, I–II

301.18   *sinistra*] C; *sinestra* S, I–II

301.18   *destra*] C; *dextra* S, I–II

301.22   Piazza di Spagna] C; Piazzo d' Espagna S, I–II

306.18   palpable] *stet* S, I–II

309.28   telegram] C; cable S, I–II
313.6   with] C; to S, I–II

314.3   Wassermanns] B; Wassermans S, I–II, C

314.15   Chilean] C; Chilian S, I–II

316.7, 25; 319.22   Chile] C; Chili S, I–II

*317.3   the late thirties] B; the forties S, I–II; one's late thirties C

*320.17   Devereux] I[c]; Charles S, I[a-b]

320.20 in which] B; wherein S, I–II; where C

320.27 *grata*] S; *gratis* I–II

323.6 the *Paris Herald*] B; The New York Herald S, I–II; the *New York Herald* C

325.5 "The Wedding of the Painted Doll."] S; The Wedding of the Painted Doll. I–II

327.18 cess] C; 'cess S, I–II

*331.2–3 been rented again, so] B; long been rented for the summer, so S; been rented again for the summer, so I–II, C

331.6 are] C; is S, I–II

*331.11 eight and six] B; eleven and nine S, I–II; seven and nine C

332.4 regimen] C; regimentation S, I–II

*332.13 six] B; nine S, I–II; seven C

332.24 Owing] C; Due S, I–II

*332.29–341.11 *stet* S, I–II, C

334.1 Kabyle . . . Sabæan] C; Kyble . . . Sabian S; Kyble . . . Sabaean I–II

336.27 itself] S; herself I–II

*337.11 La] B; El S, I–II, C

342.13 Mouton] C; Moutonne S, I–II

344.7 Salaud] I[a-c]; Salaut S; Saland I[d]

345.8 him, about . . . guess in] C; him, about . . . guess at in I–II; him . . . guess at in S

345.23 bay] C; Bay S, I–II

345.23; 346.6; 349.16; 353.30 *Margin*] S; Margin I–II

347.23 nous autres héros," he said, "il faut] B; nous héros," he said, "Il nous faut S, I–II; nous autres héros il faut C

347.24 héroïsme] S; héroisme I–II, C

*348.6 Légion Étrangère] B; Corps d'Afrique du Nord S, I–II; Bataillon d'Afrique C

349.23 Lady Caroline] C; Lady Sibly-Biers S, I–II

350.24 enfantillage] C; enfance S; enfanterie I–II

351.14 saying, "What] B; saying: ¶"What S, I–II; saying ∧ "What C

353.11 casino] B; Casino S, I–II, C

*352.3 lesion] *stet* S, I–II

353.16 them] C; it S, I–II

354.2 waiting] B; attendant S, I–II; Divers' C

354.13 à] C; a S, I–II

357.17 Niçois] C; Niçoise S, I–II

361.20   expressed] C; personified S, I–II

363.30   hook] S; nook I

*364.5   four] B; five S, I–II, C

*364.8   summers] B; years S, I–II, C

*364.14   four] B; five S, I–II, C

367.1   Baby Gar] *stet* S, I–II

368.33   Abrams's] S; Abram's I–II

369-31   Loos] S; Loos' I–II

369-31   *Faits Accomplis*] S; Faits Accomplis I–II, C

380.18   from what] C; than I–II

382.6   Kornilov] C; Korniloff S, I–II

384.15   to find] C; finding S, I–II

*391.28   Sibly] S; Sibley I–II, C

399.16   the *Herald* . . . the *Times*] C; *The Herald* . . . *The Times*
         S; The Herald . . . The Times I–II

399.20   ouste] C; Ouste S, I–II

*399.24–5   purse. It] C; purse–and Dick recognized it as he saw it.
         It S, I–II

*399.29–33   en," Dick called after him, "When . . . here?"] C; en,"
         Dick identified him as the man who had once hailed
         him in the . . . five years before. ¶"When . . . here?"
         he called after him. S, I–II

399-31   Rue de Saint-Ange] B; Rue de St. Anges; Due de Saints
         Anges I; Rue de Saints Anges II

400.31   victims] C; dupes S, I–II

401.11   principle] S; principal I–II

*401.21   "I . . .Dick.] *stet* I–II

403.5   beach] C; Beach S, I–II

403.10   The AP] B; the A. and P. S, I–II; the AP C

407.9   New York] C; N. Y. S, I–II

408.7   section] C; Section S, I–II

Textual Notes

24.19–23   I have rejected the author's plan for moving this passage to
p. 157 (see list of revisions in Fitzgerald's copy) because the revision seems
based on Fitzgerald's desire to get a good description of Dick near the
front of "The Author's Final Version."

24.30   As Cowley notes, Campion's first name, Luis, is Spanish.

61.10   "I wouldn't miss it for words" is not idiomatic, but I have
retained *words* because it appears in every draft of the passage and it is

possible that Fitzgerald intended to characterize Campion by this word choice.

119.10,12   Cowley notes that the name of the shop was *Aux Cent Mille Chemises.*

119.30   I can discover no appropriate incident associated with Ferrara. Henry Dan Piper has suggested to me that Fitzgerald may have been thinking of the penance performed by the emperor Henry IV before Pope Gregory at Canossa in 1077.

120.1–122.6   See list of revisions in Fitgerald's copy and his "Analysis of *Tender.*" As noted below, this deletion requires additional cuts at 399.24–25, 29–33.

128.17   As Cowley notes, at 139.11 the scene of the dispute is given as Montparnasse. It is difficult to tell whether this contradiction resulted from Abe's condition or Fitzgerald's carelessness.

128.18   As Cowley notes, at 139.2 Peterson's home is given as Stockholm. Again, it is difficult to tell whether the error was Abe's or the author's.

157.13–15   See note on 24.19–23.

157.16   I have rejected the author's insertion of *Dick said* because it is unnecessary to identify the speaker if the change at 157.13–15 is not made (see list of revisions in Fitzgerald's copy).

162.21   Since *farcical* is correctly spelled at 211.6 and 248.17 it is possible — but not very likely — that Fitzgerald deliberately mis-spelled it in Nicole's letter.

167.7   Nicole's mother could not have died when she was eleven because at 72.19 Nicole mentions having been in Berlin with her mother when she was thirteen.

193.17   The Swiss National Tourist Office informs me that there is no Jugenhorn in Switzerland. Cowley emends to *Dent Du Midi,* which Dick could have seen from Montreux.

197.19   Baby can't be twenty-five here because she is twenty-four at 186.18.

212.9, 23–24   I have rejected the author's emendations at these points because they seem designed to provide information for the reader of the "Author's Final Version" (see list of revisions in Fitzgerald's copy).

226.5   Baby must be more than thirty because this is 1925, and she was twenty-four in 1918.

227.23   This is the only place Fitzgerald spells the name *Gregorovius.* Cowley changes the spelling to *Gregorovius* in all appearances on the ground that *Gregorovious* "is highly improbable in German." Nevertheless I have retained *Gregorovious* — as I have resisted changing *Chillicheff* to *Chillichev* — because it is a made-up name.

230.11   The sense here requires Gregorovious to have examined the books. Since *have* appears in the manuscripts and typescripts before the serial, it is probable that *haven't* was a typo Fitzgerald missed.

238.1   Dick is thirty-seven because this is 1928, and Fitzgerald's preliminary plan states that he was born in 1891.

238.15   Cowley emends to *ego*, but Fitzgerald wrote *ergo* in the drafts, which is possible in the sense of "activity-therapy."

239.30   Fitzgerald wrote *instructed* in his manuscript, but the sense of the passage requires *uninstructed*.

246.22   The Divers have been married nine years. This is 1928, and they were married in 1919.

259.11   McKibben speaks on p. 260, so he can't leave on p. 259.

271.14   It has been three years since Dick and Rosemary first met. This is 1928, and they met in 1925.

271.16   Rosemary and Dick were eighteen and thirty-four in 1925; they are twenty-one and thirty-seven in 1928.

291.12   Clay is a Georgian, but it is possible that his father's firm was in Birmingham.

301.18   It is possible—but extremely unlikely—that the Italian words on p. 301 were mis-spelled to show Baby's mispronunciations.

317.3   This is fall-winter 1928, so Dick—who was born in 1891—is not yet forty.

320.17   Charles Marquis Warren has written me (5 August 1959) that Nicole's father was originally named *Charles Warren* after him, but that Fitzgerald changed his mind.

331.2–3   If another summer passes at this point, the novel will occupy an extra year. See the discussion of the time-scheme above.

331.11   Fitzgerald's preliminary plan states that Lanier was born in August 1920 and Topsy in June 1922. This is 1928, and they are eight and six.

332.13   Topsy is six in 1928. See note on 331.11.

332.29–341.11   In his "Analysis of *Tender*" Fitzgerald indicated that he planned to delete the whole visit with Mary; but, as explained below, I have retained this material because Fitzgerald provided no substitute explanation for the bad feeling between Dick and Mary.

337.11   *El* is Spanish masculine.

348.6   I have not found a *Corps d'Afrique du Nord*. There was a *Corps Franc d'Afrique*, but it was a penal unit, as was the *Bataillon d'Afrique*. Since Tommy is apparently referring to the film *Beau Geste*, the general term for the French Foreign Legion seems best here.

352.3   Although *lesion* does not seem quite right here, it is the word Fitzgerald wrote in his manuscript. Cowley's emendation to *lessening* alters the meaning of the sentence.

364.5,8,14   This is the summer of 1929. It has been four years or five summers since Dick and Rosemary met in the summer of 1925.

391.28   Cowley changes the spelling to *Sibley* in all appearances.

399.24–25,29–33   If Dick's earlier encounter with the news-vendor is cut from 120.1–122.6, then these passages in which Dick recognizes him must also be cut.

401.21   In 1936 when the novel was being considered for the Modern Library, Fitzgerald wrote Bennett Cerf, "There is not more than one complete sentence that I want to eliminate, one that has offended many people and that I admit is out of Dick's character: 'I never did go in for making love to dry loins.' It is a strong line but definitely offensive" (Cowley, p. 356). The present editor cannot bring himself to kill this sentence.

Special Note: One class of error has not been dealt with in the Emendations list, and this is the repetition of phrases which resulted from Fitzgerald's habit of salvaging phrases from his stories into his novels. There are three instances of this repetition in *Tender Is the Night:* at pp. 33 and 89 the description of Nicole's hair; at pp. 35 and 69 the words "compromises of how many years"; and at pp. 138 and 204 the description of a kiss.

Historical Collation

The following symbols are used: C (Cowley – "The Author's Final Version," 1951), F (Fitzgerald – a revision marked by the author in his copy of the novel), S (Serial – *Scribner's Magazine*, 1934), I (first edition, 1934), II (The Scribner Library edition, 1960).

3.1   the shore] the pleasant shore S, I–II

3.2   stood] stands S, I–II

3.4   cooled] cool S, I–II

3.4   stretched] stretches S, I–II

3.5   Now] Lately S, I–II

3.6   in 1925] a decade ago S, I–II

3.7-8   April; in those days only] F; April. Now, many bungalows cluster near it, but when this story begins only S, I–II; April. Only C

3.17   had come] came S, I–II

3.21   had floundered] floundered S, I–II

4.8   this] one S, I–II

7.21   raft, and who] raft who C

10.28   water, followed] water. He was followed C

10.29   followed] waded after them C

12.6   Antheil] Anthiel S, I–II

15.21-2   One of her husbands had been a cavalry officer and one an army doctor] Her first husband, Rosemary's father, had been an army doctor and her second a cavalry officer C

16.1   Rosemary] Rosemary Hoyt C

16.4   felt that it was time she were] felt it was time that she was C

19.5   Eleven years ago] Ten years ago S, I–II; Eleven years before C

19.6   were] had been C

19.7   were] had been C

19.27   the] that C

20.19   was] were S, I–II

22.18   the *Paris Herald*] The New York Herald I; *The New York Herald* S, II; the Paris edition of the *New York Herald* C

24.23   uninterested] disinterested S, I–II

24.30   Señor] Signor S, I–II

28.1   as nearly sulky] nearly as sulkily I–II; feeling nearly as sulky C

29.32   and that] and one that C

35.16   fascinated] fascinating C

35.24   destinies buried under the compromises of how many years.] destinies. C

36.7   To resume Rosemary's point of view it should be said that, under] Still under S; Under C

36.9   she and her mother] they S; Rosemary and her mother C

36.28   arrived, discovering] arrived and discovered C

42.11   everyone] eveyone II

42.25   irrelevant] irrelative S, I–II

46.17   him – this led up to the trouble in which he presently found himself.] him. C

48.20   Iles de Lérins] Isles de Lerins S, I–II

55.9   *immejetely] immejitly* C

55.33   coo-coo] cuckoo C

56.17   McKisco] Kisco C

57.19   the latter] he C

60.4   party] parties S, I–II

61.10   words] worlds C

63.16   rabbit] rabit II

63.17   second – the latter] second, who C

66.3–5 that in a few hours she would see the person whom she still referred to in her mind as "the Divers" on the beach.] that a few hours later on the beach she would see the person whom she still referred to in her mind as "the Divers." C

69.22   onto] to C

71.12   because] due to the fact that S, I–II

72.19   thirteen] twelve C

75.23   Württemberg] Wurtemburg S, I–II

76.26   seven] six S, I–II

78.6   Württembergers] Wurtemburgers S, I–II

78.8   Old] old S, I–II

79.2   Arts] Art S, I–II

80.8   when] then C

85.32   afterwards] afterward C

90.14   Georgian] Gerogian II

90.12   Films, to be] Films. They were C

91.15   aviation port] airport C

92.6   not] sot II

95.6   the aforementioned qualities] the qualities C

96.2   gracefully about above] gracefully above C

97.5   whither] to which C

102.5   Hengist] Hengest S, I–II

104.4   and] and the C

104.14   him] Dick C

105.19   upon] at C

106.2   he asked] he had asked C

106.9   on a world] on world S, I–II

108.13   No] Not II

109.10   faces] facees C

111.19   Diaghilev] Diaghileff S, I–II

117.5   friend] friends I–II

119.10,12   100,000 Chemises] 1000 chemises S, I–II

119.30   Canossa] Ferrara S, I–II, C

120.1-122.5   hour it had become] hour of standing. . . . It had
              become S, I–II

120.14   de Saint-Ange] des Saintes ∧ Anges S; des Saintes-Anges
              I–II

122.6   had become] became C

122.31   Brizard] Brizzard S, I–II

122.31   Fernet-Branca] André Fernet ∧ Blanco S, I–II; Fernet ∧
              Branca C

122.32   Rocher] Rochet S, I–II

125.4   had been awakened] had awakened S, I

125.10   he is here] is he here C

127.5   over] more than C

128.22   Why you] Why are you C

129.26   conservatism] conversation I–II, C

130.13   whereon] at which C

131.4   Mosby] Moseby S, I–II

132.10   concessionnaire] concessionaire I–II

133.15   about] of S, I–II

133.21   step] drop C

136.2   arrondissement] arrondisement S, I–II

136.7   Ashamed] He was ashamed C

138.6–7   mouth, her face getting big as it came up to him; he] mouth. He C

139.29   Latin Quarter] French Latin quarter S, I–II

141.5   advised] told C

145.8   blanket] blankets C

145.32   unexceptionably] unexceptionally S, I–II, C

147.17   doors] door C

152.2   bier] beer C

152.16   aeroplane] airplane C

152.18   Damenstiftgasse] Damenstiff Strasse S, I–II

153.18   at] in S, I–II

153.27   criterion] criteria S, I–II

154.17   yourself. Once] yourself – once S, I–II

154.24   subject. No good sense."] subject." S, I–II

154.28   people – they were the illusions] people; illusions S, I–II

155.5   lolling] looling II

155.7–9   destiny. Best] destiny. Moreover it is confusing to come across a youthful photograph of some one known in a rounded maturity and gaze with a shock upon a fiery, wiry, eagle-eyed stranger. Best S, I–II

156.16   cortex] cervical I–II

157.7   Kraepelin] Krapaelin S, I–II

157.9   If] Though C

157.13–15   You have the same stupid and unaging American face, except I know you're not stupid, Dick."] You are still a carrot top. You have the same unaging American face." C <You are still a carrot-top." ¶Dick's eyes were of a bright, hard blue. His nose was somewhat pointed and there was never any doubt at whom he was looking or talking – and this is a flattering attention, for who looks at us? – glances fall upon us, curious or disinterested, nothing more. F>

157.16   war – you] war," Dick said. "You C; war" Dick said, "You F

158.5   privates] private soldiers S, I–II

158.13   Krenzegg] Kreuzegg II

159.6   plateau] eminence S, I–II

159.12   Outside, some] Some S, I–II

159.13   one] they S, I–II

159.20   room. Pushing] room; pushing S, I–II

159.24   first] first one S, I–II

160.1   about the] about the time of the S, I–II

160.1   of] of a C

160.3   thence] there C

160.16   (2)] [page] 2 – Follow this form with the breaks here F;
[page] 2 – C

160.23   (3)] [page] 3 – (ect) F; 3 – C

161.18;   162.12; 162.27; 163.29 (2)] [page] 2 – C

161.31   in] on C

162.21   farcical] farcicle S, I–II, C

167.7   thirteen] eleven S, I–II; twelve C

175.9   Interlaken] Interlachen S; Interlacken I–II

175.22   horizons] horizon C

177.4   gladiolus] gladiola S, I–II

178.19–20   path, where, in a moment, a shadow cut across it – she]
path; where, in a moment, a shadow cut across it – she
F; path – where in a moment a shadow cut across it.
She S, I–II

180.22   shoulder – then apart.] shoulder. S, I–II

180.23   record. – Have] record," she said. " – Have S, I–II; record, – Have F

181.4   table, male eyes] table, eyes S, I–II

181.19   obsession] obsessions C

181.26   service] Service S, I–II; army C

182.3   but Dick] but one day at luncheon Dick C

184.4   morning] day C

188.7   it] is C

192.12   who] whom I–II

193.9,31   Kraepelin] Krapaelin S, I–II

193.17   Dent du Midi] Jugenhorn S, I–II

193.22   trainbands] trained bands S; trained-bands I–II

193.31   sie] siz I–II

194.7   down into port] down port S, I–II

195.3   Kursaal] Kursal I–II

197.19   four] five S, I–II

199.24   schizoid] schizzoid I

200.1   Guards] guards' S, I–II

203.27   all so] also C

205.12   Rocher] Rochers S, I–II

207.19   afterward] after that C

208.19   over] more than C

209.30   Grotto] Grotte S, I–II

212.9   Tommy] Abe North F, C

212.23-4   beach with my husband and two children.] beach near my home above the Mediterranean with my husband and two children and our dear friends. F, C

212.31-2   Yes . . . people."] *omitted* C

213.14   written:] written from Paris: C

217.23   McBeth] MacBeth S, I–II

218.9   aeroplanes] airplanes C

218.10   mighty] might II

219.30   into] in S, I–II

220.6   Topsy's birth, he] the birth of Topsy, their second child, he C

223.18   this] the C

226.5   just over] almost S, I–II

227.23   Gregorovious] Gregorovius S, I–II, C

228.32   twenty-four hours] two days C

230.11   have] haven't S, I–II

230.20   Privatdocent] Privat docent S, I; Privat-dozent II, C

232.1   pair] pairs C

236.1   Dick] One July morning Dick C

236.5   Prokofiev's *Love for Three Oranges.*] Prokofieff's *Love of Three Oranges.* S; Prokofieff's "Love of Three Oranges." I–II

236.8   his bed-lamp and] the light and S; his bed-lamp light and I–II

238.1   seven] eight S, I–II

238.15   ergo] ego C

239.24   workshop] workshops C

239.30   uninstructed] instructed S, I–II, C

240.25   as if imprisoned in] as imprisoned in S, I; as imprisoned as in II

243.14   with nail scissors] with scissors S; with a nail scissors I–II

244.19   Though it was couched] Couched C

245.3   upon] at C

246.22   nine] six S, I–II

247.7   and started] and he started C

248.1   crowd, a crowd which] crowd, which C

249.20   opposite] apposite S, I–II

250.8   ah] et C

250.9   Madame] Dame C

250.21   schizophrenic] "schizophrêne" S, I–II

256.13; 257.24; 258.7,24; 260.14 Chillicheff] Chillichev C

257.7   or] nor S, I–II

257.7   men's] their S, I–II

257.32   inordinately, meanwhile] inordinately and S; inordinately ∧ meanwhile I–II; inordinately C

259.11   stood ready to depart] departed I–II; lingered C

262.8   steins] helles S, I–II; seidels C

263.9   nine] eight C

265.8   rolled up through] rolled through C

266.16   the income] it S, I–II

268.17   the steamer's] its S, I–II

269.13   couturières] couturiers S, C

269.31   After] Early in the morning, after C

270.11   hoofs] hoops I–II

270.28   two] one C

270.31   Nazionale] Nationale S

270.33–271.1   discovered from . . . that] read . . . and learned about C

271.14   three] four S, I–II, C

271.16   twenty-one . . . thirty-seven] twenty-two . . . thirty-eight S, I–II, C

276.12   twenty-one] twenty-two S, I–II, C

276.13   eight] nine C

285.5   sniffling] sniffing C

288.16   Nazionale] Nationale S, I–II

289.27   for the] the C

290.5   mousseux] mousseaux I–II

291.12   Birmingham] Atlanta C

294.16,23   saoul] sault S; saoûl I–II

296.7   Guards] guards' S, I–II, C

301.10   on which] whereon S, I–II

301.18   *sempre diretto*] *semper dritte* S, I–II

301.18   *sinistra*] *sinestra* S, I–II

301.18   *destra*] *dextra* S, I–II

301.22   Piazza di Spagna] Piazzo d'Espagna S, I–II

306.18   palpable] palatable C

309.28   telegram] cable S, I–II

311.19   ship] trip C

313.6   with] to S, I–II

313.14   such a rate] such rate C

314.3   Wassermanns] Wassermans S, I–II, C

314.15   Chilean] Chilian S, I–II

317.3   the late thirties] the forties S, I–II; one's late thirties C

316.7,25; 319.22   Chile] Chili S, I–II

320.17   Devereaux] Charles S, I[a-b]

320.20   in which] wherein S, I–II; where C

320.27   *grata*] *gratis* I–II

323.6   the *Paris Herald*] The New York Herald S, I–II; the *New York Herald* C

327.18   cess] 'cess S, I–II

328.8–9 But what absorbed Dick after the disappearance of the caravan was the question as to what] But the question that absorbed Dick after the disappearance of the caravan was to what C

331.2–3 been rented again, so] long been rented for the summer, so S; been rented again for the summer, so I–II, C

331.6   are] is S, I–II

331.11   eight and six] eleven and nine S, I–II; seven and nine C

332.4   but content] but were content C

332.4   regimen] regimentation S, I–II

332.13   six] nine S, I–II; seven C

332.24   Owing] Due S, I–II

333.6–7 For example with the great quantity of heavy baggage — presently] Presently C

334.1   Kabyle . . . Sabæan] Kyble . . . Sabian S; Kyble . . . Sabaean I–II

336.27   itself] herself I–II

337.11   La] El S, I–II, C

342.13   Mouton] Moutonne S, I–II

344.7   Salaud] Salaut S; Saland I[a-c]

345.8   him, about which she could only guess in] him which she could only guess at in S; him, about which she could only guess at in I–II

346.11   playing] plaing C

346.29   dress, the] dress and the C

347.23   nous autres héros," he said, "il faut] nous héros," he said, "il nous faut S, I–II; nous autres héros il faut C

348.6   Légion Étrangère] Corps d'Afrique du Nord S, I–II; Bataillon d'Afrique C

349.8   bear] hear C

349.23   Lady Caroline] Lady Sibly-Biers S, I–II

350.24   enfantillage] enfance S; enfanterie I–II

351.19   here] there C

352.3   lesion] lessening C

353.16   them] it S, I–II

354.2   waiting] attendant S, I–II; Divers' C

357.17   Niçois] Niçoise S, I–II

361.16   killed, that] killed and that C

361.20   expressed] personified S, I–II

362.1   drink] drinking C

362.13   the wrench it was] it was the wrench C

363.30   hook] nook I

364.5   four] five S, I–II, C

364.8   summers] years S, I–II, C

364.14   four] five S, I–II, C

365.1   Last summer] Summer before last C

365.5   afterwards] afterward C

365.8   thought] think C

367.26   "Château"] the Mexican C

368.33   Abrams's] Abram's I–II

380.18   from what] than I–II

382.6   Kornilov] Korniloff S, I–II

383.32   arose] rose C

384.15   to find] finding S, I–II

388.30   up putting] up to him and, putting C

389.12   "Profession] "My profession C

389.31   bottles, empty] bottles, the empty C

391.28   Sibly] Sibley I–II

395.22   Monsieur] M. C

398.18   "Ça va."] omitted C

399.24   purse. It] purse — and Dick recognized it as he saw it. It S, I–II

399.29–33   en," Dick called after him, "when . . . here?"] en," Dick identified him as the man who had once hailed him in the . . . five years before. ¶"When . . . here?" he called after him. S, I–II

399.31   Rue de Saint-Ange] Rue de St. Anges S; Due de Saints Anges I; Rue de Saints Anges II

400.31   victims] dupes S, I–II

401.11   principle] principal I–II

401.21   "I never did go in for making love to dry loins," said Dick.] *omitted* C

403.2   high] righ II

403.10   The AP] the A. and P. S. I–II; the AP C

407.9   New York] N. Y. S, I–II

Revisions in Fitzgerald's Copy

3.1   the shore] the pleasant shore

3.2   stood] stands

3.4   cooled] cool

3.4   stretched] stretches

3.5   Now] Lately

3.6   in 1925] a decade ago

3.7-8   April; in those days only] April. Now many bungalows cluster near it, but when this story begins only

3.17   had come] came

4.8   this] one

24.19   Dick's] His

24.19–23   Shift this forward.] His eyes . . . more.

75   *At the top of this page Fitzgerald drew a Greek key design.*

120.1–122.6   hour it had become] hour of standing. . . . It had become

153.18   at (L.)] *in*

154.17   yourself. Once] yourself — once

154.24   subject. No good sense."] subject."

154.28   people — they were the illusions] people; illusions

155.7–9   *deleted*] Moreover . . . stranger.

157.7   Kraepelin] Krapaelin

157.13–15   You are still a carrot-top" Here insert description from page 24 old numbering] You have the same stupid and unaging American face, except I know you're not stupid, Dick." *It is impossible to be sure what Fitzgerald intended here because he seems to have revised this passage twice.*

157.16   war" Dick said, "You] war — you

158.5   privates] private soldiers

158.10   "Toward] " — toward

159.6   plateau] eminence

159.12   Outside, some] Some

159.13   one] they

159.20   room. Pushing] room; pushing

159.24   first] first one

159.29   etc. etc.] etc, etc.

160.1   about the] about the time of the

160.16   [page] 2 — Follow this form with the breaks here] (2)

160.23   [page] 3 — (ect)] (3)

160   *This is my mark to say I have made final corrections up to this point.

178.19-20   path; where, in a moment, a shadow cut across it — she] path — where in a moment a shadow cut across it. She

179.33   Bye-and-bye (?)] By and by

180.22   shoulder — then apart.] shoulder.

180.23   record, — Have] record," she said. " — Have

181.4   table, male eyes] table, eyes

193.15   *Extra space after line 15.*

193.   Lester begin here & go to end of Chapter (2 pages)

212.9   Abe North] Tommy

212.23-4   beach near my home above the Mediterranean with my husband and two children and our dear friends] beach with my husband and two children.

362   This is DULL

362   You lay down the book & never pick it up —

369   Tiresome stuff! True but why?

The following entry from Fitzgerald's notes shows the revised structure of "The Author's Final Version" and indicates that he planned to omit two passages: Dick's encounter with the news-vendor in Paris (actually pp. 120–122), and the Divers' visit to Mary North Minghetti (pp. 322–341).[15] I have followed Cowley in deleting the first of these which necessitated making two other deletions on page 399 (see Textual Notes). I have also followed Cowley in retaining the Minghetti material. (There is no *moon* on page 212.[16])

Analysis of *Tender:*

I	Case History	151–212	71 pps.	(change moon)		p.212
II	Rosemary's Angle	3–104	101 pps.	P. 3		
III	Casualties	104–148,	213–224	55 pps.	(-2)	(120 & 121)
IV	Escape	225–306	82 pps.			
V	The Way Home	306–408	103 pps.	(-8)	(332–341)	

Editions of *Tender is the Night*
Original Version

1.a.–c. New York: Scribner's 1934. Three printings. 1.d. New York: Scribners, 1951. Fourth printing.

2. London: Chatto & Windus, 1934

"The Author's Final Version," ed. *Malcolm Cowley*

1. a. New York: Scribners 1951

   b. *Three Novels of F. Scott Fitzgerald.* New York: Scribners 1953

2. London: Grey Walls, 1953

3. Harmondsworth: Penguin, 1955

POSTSCRIPT: The 1982 Penguin edition edited by Arnold Goldman provides an emended text partly based on this study.

Notes

1. University of Pittsburgh Press, 1963.

2. *Tender Is the Night* was serialized in four installments in *Scribner's Magazine,* January–April 1934. There are 183 differences between the serial and the first six chapters of the book.

3. There were three printings in 1934; 2 April 7,600; 11 April 5,075; and 4 May 2, 520. The first printing is easily identified by the A on the copyright page; the third printing has one plate alteration at 320.17; and the fourth printing of 1951 has one plate alteration at 344.7. See Bruccoli, *F. Scott Fitzgerald: A Descriptive Bibliography* (University of Pittsburgh Press, 1972).

4. The errors in the Scribner Library edition are: 32.31 eveyone; 49.6 rabit; 68.19 Gerogian; 69.33 now. ∧; 69.38 sot; 82.29 Not; 118.5 looling; 120.7 Kreuzegg; 167.3 might; 168.20 Gausses; 261.30 person-; 311.28 righ; 314.17 "As. None of these was corrected by the fifth printing of August 1961.

5. See *The Composition of Tender Is the Night* for a description of the book galleys.

6. *Tender Is the Night,* ed. Malcolm Cowley (1951), p. xiii, Hereafter referred to as Cowley.

7. This copy is in the Princeton University Library.

8. Cowley, pp. x-xi.

9. The errors in Cowley are: 72.11 invitaion.∧; 93.24 dears—'∧; 93.27 house.'∧; 101.16 Kisco; 131.4 stage.∧; 145.21 facees; 166.9 arm.; 22.34 horizon; 34.24 is; 47.29 also; 258.2 Dick?'∧; 287.14 plaing; 289-29 hear. Only 145.21 was corrected, but in the separate edition and not in the Modern Standard Authors volume.

10. Fitzgerald's "General Plan" is with the *Tender Is the Night* manuscripts at the Princeton University Library. It contains contradictory information about the time-span of

the novel. The ages of Dick and Nicole are reckoned in four and five-year spans, and the ages of Rosemary and Tommy only in five-year spans. In two places Fitzgerald states that the story ends in July 1929. But in 1935 he inscribed a copy of the novel: "F. Scott Fitzgerald requests the pleasure of Laura Guthrie's company in Europe 1917–1930" (Bruccoli: Collection).

11. Cowley, p. 355.

12. P. 331.

13. Cowley, p. 352.

14. P. 238.

15. Fitzgerald's notebooks are in the Princeton University Library.

16. My thanks are due to the following impressed crewmen: Alexander Clark, Mrs. F. R. Hart, Donald Hutter, Paul Jureidini, Paul Kann, Mrs. H. W. Kritzer, Horst Kruse, Henry Dan Piper, and H. E. Solomon.

The 1930s

The Psychopathic Novel

Mary M. Colum*

. . . At least three of the writers whose new books are before me —
Scott Fitzgerald, Morley Callaghan, and William March — are approaching their forties, and it is well to consider how their minds and brains
burn, and how their futures appear. The restlessness and originality in
their minds is seen in their choice of material; all three take a plunge into
that latest of literary interests, the study of the psychopathic personality,
the personality which is either on the borderland of insanity, or which
some happening in life can drive over that borderland.

. . . Scott Fitzgerald has been longer before the public than either of
these [other] writers. He has a far more varied talent and a brilliance that
has not dimmed. It simply has not grown more profound nor does it seem
to have drawn any fresh sustenance from life. More complex excitements
than were rife in his previous books are found in *Tender Is the Night*, but
all of them are on too shallow a level of experience, and his mental
nutriment seens to have been a trifle too jazzy and lacking in some of those
more solid vitamins which give a writer sympathy with the characters he is
creating. . . .

In the three novels previously mentioned the most remarkable psychologic study is certainly that of Morley Callaghan's Father Dowling,
whose character is drawn with such subtlety and insight that it is
powerfully convincing to readers, whether or not they have any special
knowledge. It is the study of a type whose outstanding characteristics are
goodness, benevolence, and self-sacrifice, beginning at a certain point of
eccentricity which, like the initial mistake of a single figure in a long
calculation, finally throws out the total. The case of Father Dowling
would, I think, seem authentic to any psychiatrist, and it never becomes
merely distressing, as does the bathroom scene in Scott Fitzgerald's story,
where the breakdown is not sufficiently prepared for. Father Dowling
remains an attractive person, lovable and pathetic in everything he does;
his gradual sinking into mental confusion, after an emotional upset and
bewilderment at the injustice of the world, is done with such beauty and

*Reprinted from *Forum and Century* 91 (April 1934): 219–23.

reality that the man remains as he was at the beginning, a kind of saint without weakness or milksoppery.

On the other hand, Scott Fitzgerald's chief woman character, Nicole, in her insane passages seems more like a case history from a textbook than a novelist's study of a real character. It is, indeed, a study of the disease rather than a study of that type of personality which may be subject to the disease. Considerable knowledge of psychiatry and its history is shown, and psychiatric terms are scattered lavishly through the pages, along with the names of great mental experts like Kraepelin and Bleuler. There is far too much external documentation and too little of the novelist's intuitive knowledge of the character he is creating. The heroine, Nicole, can pass for long periods as a normal wife and mother and as an entertaining member of a social set. But she is a psychopath, afflicted with that baffling mental disease which, because it often begins between the ages of fifteen and twenty-five, used to be called dementia præcox. It also breaks out in people up to the age of fifty and is often unaccompanied by dementia, and for this reason Bleuler found the term inexact; he named it schizophrenia, or split personality, thereby indicating that the disease destroys the cohesion of the personality, causes the will to deteriorate and the affective power to diminish so that ideas of death or love or liberty lose all meaning. In such cases, the previous attachments of patients are changed into hatreds when they do not sink into indifference, living in a dream detached from all reality.

A number of these traits in some form can be observed in people we consort with every day who we think are normal — people who have no feeling or who feel only in patches or people who live forever in a sort of dream, who have what is called shut-in personalities. There are others, apparently living a normal life, who have achieved hardly as much consciousness as an intelligent animal. Most authorities on the subject say that the disease in a simple form is widespread, but that many touched by it are capable of living a moderately normal life. But how disastrous they can be for the people they live with!

In the old classic novel the character was always depicted as the normal integrated human being, able to impose a unity on himself and his actions and actuated on the whole, if he was the hero, by distinguished principles. Now there is coming into literature this other type which may, after all, be as common — the people who are unreliable, lying, subject to fears; who are treacherous; who cannot keep a secret; who, if they have any affections at all, have them for one person; who are full of jealousies and terrors; and who, above all, are alone and lonely.

The chief character, Chester, in William March's *Come in at the Door*, is a man who had received in childhood what psychologists call a trauma, in this instance a result of witnessing the hanging of a negro whom he himself had treacherously betrayed. . . .

There is a deeply intuitive quality about the revelation of this character that may elude the general reader. It is, as is Scott Fitzgerald's Nicole, the study of the schizophrenic personality, and there are therefore certain points in common between the two characters to which it is necessary to draw attention. Both have suffered a psychic injury in childhood, the effect of which eventually causes the breakdown of their minds — Chester, because he witnessed the hanging, Nicole because of what seems to be an incestuous attack, though this has the air of an incident tacked on to the character by the author, rather than a happening woven into her subconsciousness, as the psychic injury to Chester is woven into his subconsciousness.

There is in both books a wild running scene, but the one in Fitzgerald's is the more dramatic, authentic, and memorable. The heroine, feeling an attack coming on, begins to run suddenly and madly through the crowd at the fair, eluding her husband. She is eventually found, revolving in a boat on a Ferris wheel and laughing hysterically as the astonished bystanders gaze at her. This episode is beautifully and revealingly done, and could have been written only by a man of high gifts. But always the personality is revealed from the outside, whereas William March, with a less brilliant mind than Fitzgerald's, reveals his hero from the inside and from the character he has created. We get the sensation that we have met a man so constructed by nature and inheritance that under the buffets of fate his mind must break.

How, it may be asked, can a sane and normal person depict the personality of one who is abnormal? Nearly everybody under some strain in life has felt sufficiently near breaking to understand how a neurotic can lose his balance. But even the inventive mind of the novelist needs some first-hand observation of a broken mind before he can begin to create one. At that, no matter how realistic his data may be, he must have that power, which all the great creators of character had, whether they were creating beggar, king, pimp, or madman, of first discovering the beggar, king, pimp, or madman in themselves. This is the quality in which Scott Fitzgerald's creation of Nicole is inferior to March's Chester and to Callaghan's Father Dowling. Among the multiple creatures that people every novelist's mind Morley Callaghan was able to discover, not only the lovable and eccentric priest, who ascetically loved the two prostitutes, but also the prostitutes themselves, the bishop, and the respectable parishioners. And William March was able to find in the creatures of his mind, not only the Chester who betrayed Baptiste, but also Baptiste himself and the negro woman Matty.

The only character in *Tender Is the Night* who has life like these is Dick Diver, Nicole's husband. Fitzgerald, however, in sheer writing power is superior to both Callaghan and March, and this book, despite the impression it gives of being slung together, rather than constructed, shows its author's distinctive gifts — a romantic imagination, a style that is often brilliant, a swiftness of movement, and a sense of enchantment in people and places, all of which combine to give his books the great merit of being always entertaining. Nevertheless, nearly all his early faults remain: his male characters are still as they were over a decade ago, prankish sophomores; his female characters are bright, brittle, and young, with all the material sophistications, and those of the social sophistications understood, in a jazzy and superficially cultivated society. He can summon up terror and pathos, but what pity and tragedy are he does not know, for he has never really meditated on life. Yet he has expressed very well indeed a section of the life of his time, a section that may perhaps seem totally crazy to our descendants. And because he is its chronicler and because there is that sort of personality in his writing that there is in the memoir writers, he may last a trifle longer than his superiors in profundity — than, for example, Callaghan, who is a profounder writer, but a less interesting one, and who has a style which is too often queerly pedestrian. . . .

Page after Page   Michael March*

It hardly seems so long as fourteen years ago that F. Scott Fitzgerald caught the shrill spirit of the jazz age in *This Side of Paradise*, and followed it quickly with *Flappers and Philosophers*, *The Beautiful and Damned*, and *Tales of the Jazz Age*. The world was on fire then with a new generation that had sprung loose, helter-skelter, as if out of the mouths of tired cannon in the Argonne. It was the beginning of the debauch after the war, a kind of danse macabre compounded of joy and heartbreak, frayed nerves cut loose in the harsh dissonances of saxophone and clarinet. The muted violins of another time had disappeared with romance in the limbo of the days before the war. The world was new and raw, and Fitzgerald, fresh from the battlefields, after having quit Princeton to join Democracy's army, caught its tempo in his tales. He became famous over night with *This Side of Paradise*, a novel which is still important as documentary, not to say artistic, evidence of those mad times.

In 1926 *The Great Gatsby* made its appearance and the new generation had come into maturity arm-and-arm with Fitzgerald, the artist. It was a brilliant performance, more so than his fondest admirers had expected from the author of *This Side of Paradise*. Gatsby was the archetype of the new bootleg era, and beneath the far-flung and bejewelled gaiety of Gatsby's world, the sprawling parties, the high power of its motorcars, its recklessness, lay the fetid miasma of futility. The mad youngsters of *This Side of Paradise* had grown up and it was, to the sensitive, a pretty awful sight. Heartbreak again lay at the core, a brittle

*Reprinted from the *Brooklyn Citizen*, 11 April 1934, p. 11.

kind of break that merely snapped under the pressure, and Fitzgerald proved himself an artist of the first importance in laying hold of the sorry mess, solidifying it, unifying the experience of it, with remarkable mastery.

After Gatsby, with the exception of a negligible volume of short stories called *All the Sad Young Men*, Fitzgerald escaped to France and remained more or less silent, an ex-patriate, living, apparently, in the ease afforded by an income. In those ten years many things have happened in the world and in literature and it is doubtful if many of the new generation know very much about F. Scott Fitzgerald. The lost generation of the war remembers him, perhaps, with nostalgia and a vague unease. Some of us have been wondering what has happened. *The Great Gatsby* was so exciting a job, so full not of promise, but of greater things to come, that we were beginning to fear that a great artist had got himself lost in the soft beauties of the Mediterranean.

Now, ten years later, in *Tender Is the Night* (published tomorrow by Scribners, $2.50), assurance comes that Fitzgerald has not fallen into the Mediterranean of indulgence, but remains probably the finest American writer of our time. Whatever disappointment may be found in his latest novel must rest with its subject matter, but certainly not with its manner. He is still the conscientious artist, still the brilliant writer of prose that is so rich in color and insight, but he writes, alas, of a world with which most of us here in this depression-ridden America are unfamiliar. Because of this, but for no other reason, I am sure, *Tender Is the Night* may fail of as wide an audience as it most certainly deserves.

Fitzgerald is in for a sound trouncing by the left-wingers among the critics. When Gatsby came upon the horizon there was nothing apparently the matter with the economic world. The ground was being laid for the boom years to follow and the class struggle was at least confined to very small corners of the earth. But the pinnacle was reached in 1929, capitalism tottered, though it has not yet altogether fallen, and the chemistry of the mass mind changed. In the interim Fitzgerald escaped and *Tender Is the Night*, having nothing whatever to do with the struggle of the proletariat, shows its lack of relationship to the contemporary American scene.

The scene of *Tender Is the Night* is the Riviera and Zurich in Switzerland. It concerns, in its main structure, the marriage of Dr. Richard Diver, a promising young psychiatrist, and the daughter of a wealthy American, a girl whom he helped out of the darkness of an incestuous psychosis. The marriage, which springs from a beautiful idyll of romantic love, eventuates in the ultimate dissolution of Dr. Diver's genius. It is a depressing tale, a modern tapestry into which Fitzgerald weaves his story, and any attempt to outline the plot and its ramifications must prove futile. I can only hint, which is about all that is possible with a genuine work of art. The world of Dick Diver and his wife, Nicole, on the shore of the French Riviera is first revealed in 1925 through the eyes of a pretty, young American motion picture star. It is all glitter and color, such glitter and color and charm as Fitzgerald depicts with breath-taking mastery. It is, to say the least, bewitching; but soon the pathological foundation upon which this deceptive beauty rests, seeps through the crevices, bit by bit, which is Fitzgerald's way of suspense, of impending disintegration and doom.

When we are given a vague glimpse of the decay under the surface the tale shifts back to the end of the war, when Dick Diver, full of promise as a brilliant psychiatrist, discharged from the army, visits his friend at a Zurich sanitarium. It is here he falls in love with Nicole, still a patient there. This crisis in his life is so masterfully contrived that one hears the inevitable drums of fate rumbling in the distance. Dick could no more have escaped than he could have escaped his birth. From then on the story concerns the painful, insidious growth and decay of this marriage, in which the octopus of Nicole's weakness (her pathological past) and her strength (her fabulous wealth) fastens itself upon Richard Diver and drains him of all hope and aspiration. In the end they part, she with new strength and new hope, drawn from him, and he, broken, last heard of as the book closes, practicing medicine in the small town of Galena, N.Y. [sic].

Reading Tender Is the Night, one is struck by the sheer brilliance of F. Scott Fitzgerald, before which practically everything written in America pales and is dwarfed. The prose is beautiful, full of subtle color and sound; it is prose at its very best, which is to say magical. And the depths of his probing into character, mood and emotion is, I think, unmatchable in our country. Tender Is the Night is by all odds the finest novel to have come my way in ten years.

Scott Fitzgerald Re-enters, Leading Bewildered Giant

James Gray*

Re-enter, after many years, Scott Fitzgerald leading by the hand a bewildered giant.

His new book, to which the zealous champions of The Great Gatsby have been looking forward with the greatest eagerness, like a giant is formidable in its bulk and intimidating in its attitudes. But since Mr. Fitzgerald himself is in a highly scientific frame of mind, it is appropriate to examine the medical definition of giantism in order to understand what

*Reprinted from the St. Paul Dispatch, 12 April 1934, sec. 1, p. 8, with permission of the St. Paul Dispatch.

he has produced. As the doctors in their grim, unfanciful way put it, giantism means a "development to abnormal size accompanied by various stigmata such as disproportionately large extremities or marked facial asymmetry and usually by constitutional weakness." That, I think, is an accurate clinical description of the giant in novel form that Fitzgerald brings us.

This is a big, sprawling, undisciplined, badly coordinated book. It is very far from being uninteresting. The very faults of such a novel are engrossing. The mass of material is tremendous. There is enough for four books, a dozen essays and a treatise or two on psychoanalysis beside. On almost every page one comes upon a passage of great literary brilliancy, a little masterpiece of characterization, an extremely witty and cleverly recorded bit of dialogue. But the parts are not well integrated. It is not necessary to be an expert to observe the asymmetry and the disproportion. I think the constitutional weakness is also evident. The pituitary gland simply did not function normally.

The essential tragedy is that of Richard Diver who sacrifices his individual integrity and his career to the protection of a rich, psychopathic wife. But the sacrifice is foredoomed from the start. The circumstances of a violent and hysterical way of life batter at the flimsy shelter of the marriage and finally destroy it. Richard Diver, divorced at last, tries to return to his career, but it is too late. The end of the book finds him retreating deeper and deeper into the obscurity of medical practice in a succession of American towns each smaller and more remote than the one before.

It is a pathetic human story containing some of the elements of inevitable tragedy. But what alienates sympathy and finally interest is the fact that two people, trying to create a destiny for themselves out of such unpromising emotional materials, should have chosen to live in so mad and chaotic a world.

The backgrounds of *Tender Is the Night* are Paris, Zurich and the towns of the Riviera. The incidental characters are the psychopathic wrecks of the sanitarium set and the decadent playboys of the cafes. The incidents include orgies of the peculiarly sinister sort invented by postgraduate adolescents — duels, race riots. The intellectual interest centers upon such topics as homosexuality, chronic alcoholism, and schizophrenia (divided personality). There are three quite casual murders. Into this symphony of violence the motif of illicit love comes with the overtone of pastoral sweetness and it is in that vein that Fitzgerald treats it.

I think it should be obvious that this is not the milieu for a woman the prognosis of whose mental illness is not good. Sterner intellects than that of Nicole, wife of Dr. Diver, might have reeled under the impact of so distressful a routine.

There is no one in the book strong enough to have held together under any circumstances such an undisciplined world. Richard Diver has sensitiveness, charm and good will, but Fitzgerald is never able to suggest that there was about him any ruggedness of temperament worthy to receive such a grave responsibility.

The book would have been better if a substantial man had failed under more nearly normal circumstances. The novelist's conclusions are all so hazily suggested that his own attitude toward the central character is never clear. But it seems almost equally pointless to blame either fate or Dr. Diver for the failure of his life. Fate did not arrange the bizarre succession of catastrophes which *Tender Is the Night* records. It took an ingeniously misguided human intellect to do that. And from the beginning Dr. Diver is so obviously inadequate that one could just as reasonably reproach a scarecrow for not being equal to the emergency when birds declining to be intimidated, defiantly fly into the field.

With Fate and Dr. Diver acquitted there seems to be no indictment to return. And yet if none results out of all this social outlawry, the record seems more bewildering and pointless than ever.

Quite as serious is the technical fault of poor organization. Fitzgerald is never the aloof observer interpreting the bitter and cruel course of his story. He is in the heat of the struggle. The violence engulfs him, distracts, sends him scurrying this way and that in the mad confusion of one quite unable to maintain order in such a crisis.

It is strange that he should, after all these years, have written such an immature book. It has all the faults from which he so triumphantly escaped in *The Great Gatsby*. That novel, too, had its tempestuous melodrama, its undisciplined characters. But Fitzgerald, standing aside, understood the pathos of the impulse that carried his central character stubbornly toward a quite unobtainable goal. The quality of compassion which he got into that admirable record was completely touching and persuasive.

I think that he could have done it again in *Tender Is the Night* but for the fact that this time he was not willing to submit himself to the stern self-discipline which made him rewrite and rewrite *The Great Gatsby* many times until he had eliminated all its irrelevances. Fitzgerald's chief fault is his facility. It makes him clutter his pages with a tremendous amount of amusing and entirely unimportant material which obscures the view of his theme.

Tender Is the Night is a very great disappointment because it comes from one of our most brilliant writers who has already provided one witness to the fact that he is capable of expert craftsmanship and fastidiousness of feeling. But the night to which he now calls our attention is more murky than tender.

True to Type—Fitzgerald Writes
Superb Tragic Novel

Gilbert Seldes*

About ten years ago I met Scott Fitzgerald because he wanted to meet anyone who thought as little of his work as I did. It was the time when we were getting up lists of people and marking them plus and minus.

Fitzgerald had published *This Side of Paradise* and *The Beautiful and Damned* and one of two volumes of short stories and was generally the top boy of young American letters—and I gave him minus 90 per cent.

No explanations went with the ratings, but in my own mind I said that he had more talent—more positive genius—than anyone else writing in America and was throwing it away on everything trivial and insignificant.

Three years or so later Fitzgerald wrote *The Great Gatsby*, the turning point in his career, the first novel which indicated that he could control all his powers and would eventually write a great novel.

Now he has written the great novel: *Tender Is the Night*.

The publishers, Scribners, sent me an advance copy about two weeks ago and I read this beautiful and profoundly tragic story at once. It has been in my mind ever since. You feel, as you read it, that you will never forget it.

This is exactly the reverse of the feeling made famous by reviewers, that you "cannot lay the book down." I haven't met many of these and don't care if I never do again.

The great books are the ones you have to put down because they bring life to you so intensely that you are compelled to stop, to think and to feel. Reading *Tender Is the Night* was for me the satisfaction of an appetite; a long, deep satisfaction.

The book begins with a group of people on the French Riviera seen through the innocent eyes of a young American girl, a movie actress, as it happens. They seem to her the most attractive human beings in the world.

All Fitzgerald's romantic talent is expended on this overture to his dark tragedy. Bizarre, absurd, half desperate events occur: quarrels, drunkenness, a duel, a murder which accidentally touches the lives of the principal people. Then the book takes hold of its principal theme.

Below the surface of the lives of Richard and Nicole Diver lies the tragedy of Nicole's recurrent madness. How the madness came, how Doctor Diver met and married Nicole, how their lives went on, and how their lives separated, form the material of the book.

Fitzgerald's triumph is that without a trace of symbolism or allegory, he makes this special story universally interesting. The emotions are not special; they are devotion, exasperation, love, hatred, despair. The people

*Reprinted from the *New York Evening Journal* 12 April 1934, p. 23

are men and women, of tremendous passions, doing fine things and ignoble things; living.

Gertrude Stein said that Fitzgerald "really created for the public the new generation." It is easy to say that in his new book he has shown to what that generation tended. But I think he has done more. He has gone behind generations, old or new, and created his own image of human beings. And in doing so has stepped again to his natural place at the head of the American writers of our time.

Books of the Times   John Chamberlain*

As one who would rather have written *The Great Gatsby* than any other American novel published in the Twenties, we approached F. Scott Fitzgerald's *Tender Is the Night* with anticipation and trepidation. *The Great Gatsby* was so perfect in its feeling and its symbolism, such a magnificent evocation of the spirit of a whole decade, so great an improvement over Mr. Fitzgerald's second novel, *The Beautiful and Damned* (which might have been, as Jerome Hill once called it, "an American 'Madame Bovary,' " were it not for its diffuse quality), that one could hardly see Mr. Fitzgerald striking the same high level twice in succession. As the years went by, recurrent surges of gossip had it that Mr. Fitzgerald was unable to bring his unfinished post-*Gatsby* novel to any satisfactory conclusion. He had been a child of boom America; had the lean years after 1929 sapped his artistic vitality by stealing from him his field of reference?

After having read *Tender Is the Night*, we now know that the gossip was — just gossip. Mr. Fitzgerald has not forgotten his craftsmanship, his marvelous sense of what might be called social climate, his sheer writing ability. Judged purely as prose, *Tender Is the Night* is a continually pleasurable performance. From a technical point of view, it is not as perfect as novel as *The Great Gatsby*, but once the reader has gotten past the single barrier to complete appreciation of the book, it proves to be an exciting and psychologically apt study in the disintegration of a marriage.

Seemingly, Mr. Fitzgerald begins well. He introduces us to a fledgling film actress, Rosemary Hoyt, a girl with the dew still on her, who is taken up by Richard and Nicole Diver during a summer stay at the Riviera. For some eighty pages or more we constantly expect Rosemary to develop, to become more and more important in the story. And then suddenly, we realize that this innocent and as yet entirely plastic girl is introduced

*Reprinted from the *New York Times*, 13 April 1934, p. 17. Copyright 1934 by the New York Times Company. Reprinted by permission.

merely as a catalytic agent. When Dick Diver, who is a psychiatrist without a practice, falls in love with Rosemary, his marriage to Nicole commences to founder. But, Rosemary, having started a chain of developments, is dismissed almost completely from the novel, and the reader pauses, at page 100, in rueful bewilderment.

In the critical terminology of Kenneth Burke, Mr. Fitzgerald has violated a "categorical expectancy." He has caused the arrows of attention to point toward Rosemary. Then, like a broken field runner reversing his field, he shifts suddenly, and those who have been chasing him fall figuratively on their noses as Mr. Fitzgerald is off on a new tack.

At this point one could almost guarantee that *Tender Is the Night* is going to be a failure. But, as a matter of fact, the novel does not really begin until Rosemary is more or less out of the way. What follows is a study of a love affair and a marriage between doctor and mental patient that is as successful a bit of writing as it must have been difficult to create in dramatic terms. Mr. Fitzgerald set himself an incredibly confused problem, but he draws the lines clearly as he works the problem out in terms of two human beings.

Tender Is the Night is not, as might be thought, a story of post-war degeneracy. The story has nothing much to do with the famous "lost generation," although many playboy Americans figure on the periphery as Mr. Fitzgerald's drama moves through Europe, from the Riviera to Paris, and thence to Switzerland and Rome. Nicole Warren could have been psychologically violated by the attack by her father in any decade. She might not have found psychiatrists to take her case before Jung commenced practicing and before Freud commenced writing, but that is not germane to the "lost generation." Dick Diver himself is a brilliant young man; Nicole saves herself by transferring her outraged affection for her father to the young psychiatrist with his "cat's face" and his air of being a good, solid bulwark for distress.

What follows is dimly prefigured in the first hundred pages of the book, when Rosemary is seemingly the star attraction. We know that some horror lurks behind the facade of happiness that Dick and Nicole present to the world. But it is not until Mr. Fitzgerald suddenly cuts back to Nicole's years at the Swiss neurological hospital that we know much about the circumstances. And, given the circumstances, it is a foregone conclusion that Nicole will remain in love with Dr. Diver only so long as she needs him. The fact that she is in love with him is predicated on sickness; when she ultimately comes to feel that she can stand by herself, her love for him collapses. Mr. Fitzgerald, in nervous scenes of great skill, traces the forces leading to this collapse. And Dr. Diver is ruined in the process. We see him, at the end, pursuing a meaningless career as a general practitioner in upper New York State, where he had lived as a boy. Any love he may have had for Rosemary, the precipitant of the solution, has been smothered by events. And when he ceased to be Nicole's physician, he ceased also to be her lover. He has been mentally corrupted, too, by living for many years on Nicole's money, and by absence from active work as a psychiatrist taking many and all cases.

Beyond the story, there is Mr. Fitzgerald's ability to catch the "essence of a continent," the flavor of a period, the fragrance of a night and a snatch of old song, in a phrase. A comparison of *Tender Is the Night* as it ran in *Scribner's Magazine* and as it appears in book form gives a measure of the author's artistic conscience. He has made many deft excisions, many sound reallocations of conversation. If, with Rosemary, he presents nothing much beyond an unformed girl, that must lie within the conception of his novel. Rosemary was evidently intended to be meaningless in herself, an unknown quantity projecting itself into a situation that merely required leverage, any leverage, to start its development toward a predictable end. The story is the story of the Divers, husband and wife, how they came together, and how they parted. As such as it is a skillfully done dramatic sequence. By the time the end is reached, the false start is forgotten.

Stale; Unprofitable
Edith H. Walton*

There is danger in rousing expectations over too long a period. For years, it seems, people have been waiting around for a successor to *The Great Gatsby* and have been predicting that, with the jazz age behind him, Mr. Fitzgerald would do great things. Because, as a novelist, he has been silent for so many seasons, a spotlight beats unfairly on *Tender Is the Night*. One tends to judge it too hardly — to make a final reckoning of what Fitzgerald's brilliant talents have profited him in the end.

When the score is added up, unfortunately, one's hopes are left cheated. In a certain sense Mr. Fitzgerald has matured. He is, now, a writer with a soberer purpose, a wider range of material, and a firmer grasp of technic. His gilded sophisticates have learned what suffering is and are aware of being foredoomed. Essentially, however, they are the flappers and philosophers of a decade ago grown tired and a little tarnished. They remain supremely unimportant — and Mr. Fitzgerald, although it is clear that he condemns them, has failed to evoke their full tragic significance. . . .

It would be easy to overemphasize the psychopathic aspects of Mr. Fitzgerald's story — as, for example, Mary Colum has done in the Forum in an article on the psychopathic novel. Actually, despite all the accurate terminology and analysis, the abnormality of the Divers' tragedy is irrelevant to the real theme of *Tender Is the Night*. The point is that these

*Reprinted from the *New York Sun*, 14 April 1934, p. 30.

people are self-destroyed—that they are pampered, shallow, barren, essentially soft and diseased at core. They are kin to Hemingway's Brett, victims of a general social malady rather than of specific neuroses.

A failure to recognize this fully, though he does so in part, is responsible for the weaknesses of Mr. Fitzgerald's book. One does not believe in the destruction of Dick's brilliant promise as the result of Nicole's demands on him. One knows that there was some deeper and more fundamental trouble at work—and at work on Nicole as well. One feels that by stressing the psychopathic he has evaded the real reason for their failure and has muffed the real clew to their immaturity. After all, his other characters, Rosemary, the Norths, Nicole's sisters, are quite as thoroughly damned without the excuse of abnormality.

Better than any one, perhaps, except Ernest Hemingway, Mr. Fitzgerald knows the psychology of those wealthy, hard-drinking expatriates who seem, today, to be a vanishing tribe. Certainly his perception of their predicament is superior to Hemingway's and his judgment of them more mature. His pictures of their life on the Riviera are superb. However garish and fantastic they may be, his drinking parties, duels, fights, murders have an uncanny air of truth. What one looks for, and misses, is some adequate background for all this hysteria. *Tender Is the Night* shares the shallowness, and some of the attitudes, of its characters. It does not go far enough nor deep enough, and by substituting terror for tragedy—as William Faulkner, also, has done—Fitzgerald has missed his chance to write a first-rate novel of a decadent society.

Decadence: Fitzgerald Again Tells a Sinful, Ginful Tale

Anonymous*

Francis Scott Key Fitzgerald is the young man who fourteen years ago, according to Gertrude Stein, "created for the public the new generation."

While many readers have lost interest in just how depraved boys and girls became after the World War, Mr. Fitzgerald is still wrestling with the old problem of gin and kisses. His first book, *This Side of Paradise*, revealed how the youth of St. Paul, Minn., and Princeton, N.J., learned to sin in the gin-and-tea-dance era of the early 1920s. His latest effort shows the same kind of people doing the same kind of things. A little older and more sophisticated, they now pursue decadence on the Riviera.

Tender Is the Night is the story of Richard Diver, modern psychiatrist,

*Reprinted from *News-Week* 3 (14 April 1934): 39–40. Copyright 1934 by Newsweek, Inc. All rights reserved, reprinted by permission.

and his wife, Nicole, who had been a "mental case." In a hotel near Cannes they meet the 18-year-old Rosemary Hoyt, who has just become a movie star under the watchful guidance of her mother, and who so disturbs Richard's equanimity that he announces: "I want to give a really bad party. I mean it. I want to give a party where there's a brawl and seductions and people going home with their feelings hurt and women passing out in the cabinet de toilette." The party and its consequences live up to expectations.

Later, the scene shifts back and forth between the Riviera and the post-war Paris of drunken Americans.

Richard has fallen in and out of love so many times that he has lost his early ambition. The unhappy group is still "This Side of Paradise" when the story ends.

There is some good descriptive writing in this book, and the first part is plotted adroitly enough to produce excitement. But the atmosphere is stale. For purposes of fiction, the wiles of Freud seem as familiar as those of Sherlock Holmes; and it is a long time since the decay of American expatriates on the Riviera was hot news.

A Generation Riding to Romantic Death
Horace Gregory*

We have been a long time waiting for this new novel by F. Scott Fitzgerald, the novel that was to supersede his remarkable performance in *The Great Gatsby*. In 1931 he had said goodbye to those post-war years on which he had set his trade-mark with the name, "Jazz Age," across the page. This epitaph was written in the form of a short essay which appeared in *Scribner's Magazine* and it proved again that Fitzgerald had lost none of that self-consciousness, that awareness to the life of his time which had made *The Great Gatsby* an important item in contemporary literature. This essay was reinforced as recently as last fall by a tribute to Ring Lardner, which was published in *The New Republic*. As a last word for a friend it ranks among the best of our modern elegies, and to evaluate the qualities of its prose we must turn to poetry for comparison. Beyond these we have the present novel with its deliberately ironic title clipped from Keats's "Ode to the [sic] Nightingale."

From the bright sunlight on the French Riviera we are prepared to walk in darkness, a deeper darkness, I think, than Fitzgerald himself anticipated, for, when we remember his great talents and his ability to control them, the book is not all that it should have been. There is an air of

*Reprinted from the *New York Herald Tribune Books*, 15 April 1934, p. 5.

dangerous fatality about it, as though the author were sharing the failure of his protagonist, charming Dick Diver, and here there is no cure for the disease which had entered their blood and made them what they were.

Let us turn then to the story, a not-too-simple arrangement of the familiar triangle, two women and a man. The setting is on the French Riviera, and the people in it are of that fast-drinking, hard-driving set of rich Americans that Fitzgerald has made his own. One is Rosemary Hoyt, a picture actress; another is Dick Diver, a psychiatrist; another is Nicole, Diver's ex-patient, but now his wife — and with them are two minor characters, McKisco, a social-climbing novelist, and Abe North, a dipsomaniac. All are on holiday, a kind of extended sick-leave, in which there is nothing to do but make love in the corrosive sunlight or drink too much at night, or buy fine clothes or travel. A certain doom is written across their handsome faces; the holiday cannot last forever, nor can they remain, transfixed upon that border-line between youth and middle age. We witness Nicole spending money, she, the daughter of a Chicago millionaire: "For her sake trains began their run at Chicago and traversed the round belly of the continent to California; chicle factories fumed and link belts grew link by link in factories; men mixed toothpaste in vats and drew mouthwash out of copper hogsheads; girls canned tomatoes quickly in August or worked rudely at the five-and-tens on Christmas Eve; half-breed Indians toiled on Brazilian coffee plantations and dreamers were muscled out of patent rights in new tractors — these were some of the people who gave a tithe to Nicole, and as the whole system swayed and thundered onward it lent a feverish bloom to such processes of hers as wholesale buying."

I quote this passage because it indicates Fitzgerald's awareness of the materials which have gone into the making of his book and why we are asked to judge it by higher standards than those which apply to the usual novel. Incidentally this quotation represents, I think, the higher levels of writing in the book; the ironic intention behind it is obvious, for Nicole is a neurotic, whose periods of near-insanity contribute much toward Diver's disintegration. From such people in the environment Fitzgerald recreates one is led to expect violence and violence follows. Under the glass of wealth and at high noon there is murder and the intrusion of hysteria; a generation is riding to its death and is possessed by a romantic will to die.

We know that somehow Fitzgerald is circling round the actual subject of his book; we know he sees as clearly as any one can see that under the surface of his familiar story lies a criticism of the entire system which has made such creatures as his people possible. Yet he has slightly miscast each of his characters. We don't believe that Dick Diver was a good psychiatrist or that Nicole was unhinged by incest. We accept Diver as a well-to-do American, whose career, whatever it might have been, is shattered. We see him as a once-attractive person now gone rotten — but we are not so sure that his wife was the cause, because we are given no evidence of the fact that Diver had done more than read the titles of books in medical libraries. This distrust of his abilities weakens a number of our convictions about him.

As for Rosemary, she might well be the daughter of any wealthy American and not a motion-picture heroine. These doubts distract attention from Fitzgerald's purpose and diminish the importance of what he has to say. What is real in Fitzgerald's novel is a sense of terror. The world in which his people live to die has all the instability of a society that sees no reason for existence. These children of the very rich had been children too long, and all they can salvage from the wreckage of their lives is the futile wisdom of the damned. They are deeply wounded (or corrupted), and for a moment, Fitzgerald reveals that unsounded depth with the erratic touch of wisdom that runs throughout the book.

Closing the book we feel a sense of loss, not so much because each character (with the exception of McKisco, who remains a bounder) is slated for destruction, but because Fitzgerald has failed to carry his own responsibility. There is but one consolation — though Fitzgerald fails to realize the larger scheme of his novel, the book is a grand affair, a storehouse of all the ills that doomed an entire colony of young Americans away from home. A number of isolated scenes in this novel have extraordinary power: Nicole screaming in the bathroom; a nameless Englishman shot dead upon a railway platform; Dick Diver, stripped of his will to live, drinking alone, dying by inches on the Riviera, and the last scene where Diver, betrayed by Nicole, vanishes to America, his address fading into small-town postoffice stations in New York State. All this is terror beyond death, that once revealed, even in fragmentary fashion, will not be soon forgotten.

Fitzgerald's Novel a Masterpiece   Cameron Rogers*

A novel from F. Scott Fitzgerald, silent since 1925 save for short stories of a variety acceptable to the better popular magazines, is a major event in contemporary American letters. Fitzgerald placed his talent before an international reading public at so early an age (he was 24 when *This Side of Paradise* held spellbound a whole generation now not so young) and displayed so rapid a mastery of his profession that for the past nine years his readers might have likened him to a rocket which imperiously soared to a point defined by the publication in 1925 of *The Great Gatsby*, but which then exploded into stars and streamers of brilliance too

*Reprinted from the *San Francisco Chronicle*, 15 April 1934, p. 4D. Copyright 1934 by the *San Francisco Chronicle*. Reprinted by permission.

delicate to survive. For while everything he has written in, say, the *Saturday Evening Post*, has been informed by his talent, in it the sinews of his greater powers have been lacking.

We have waited for almost a decade, but *Tender Is the Night* is so well worth it that Fitzgerald's silence during that time seems natural and explicable. For in the characterization in this story of a few Americans forming a shifting, dissolving and reassembling group in Europe in the years following the war, there is so much beauty, so much compassion and so much understanding that it seems as though it could only have sprung from a mind left wisely fallow. Fitzgerald's style was always admirable; deft, delicate, flexible and essentially his own. Wedded in *Tender Is the Night* to those other qualities of mind, it achieves a final significance as a medium of expression in English which hereafter should be difficult to overestimate.

To a very definite degree a psychopathic novel, an amazingly competent study of schizophrenia, the term applied by Bleuler to cases of split personality, *Tender Is the Night* owes to the description and cure of this mental disease in the girl, Nicole, many of its most beautiful and touching passages. Daughter of one of those fabulously rich Americans, Nicole, apparently doomed by what seems to have been an incestuous attack, to a swift decline into hopeless dementia, falls in love with Dr. Diver, a young American completing in Europe at the conclusion of the war his studies in psychopathia. Diver, unwillingly at first, succumbs to a helplessness and a beauty memorably described and for some ten years devotes his life to the cure of Nicole, who becomes his wife. It's about these two figures that the action develops to Paris, and from Switzerland to Italy and back again to the Cote d'Azur.

Such in the barest outline, is the story of *Tender Is the Night*. Of the unforgettable balance of the dramatis personae there is no space here to speak, but each is developed with a skill in observation and description which is notable and their reactions to each other and to the circumstances of their lives when together or when alone read so convincingly as to remind one of the explanation of an exact science.

Tender Is the Night is a profoundly moving, beautifully written story, and it should assure Fitzgerald's stature as an American author when the brutal improvisations on police blotter themes of currently better known writers are forgotten.

Books of the Times

John Chamberlain*

The critical reception of F. Scott Fitzgerald's *Tender Is the Night* might serve as the basis for one of those cartoons on "Why Men Go Mad." No two reviews were alike; no two had the same tone. Some seemed to think that Mr. Fitzgerald was writing about his usual jazz age boys and girls; others that he had a "timeless" problem on his hands. And some seemed to think that Doctor Diver's collapse was insufficiently documented.

With this we can't agree. It seemed to us that Mr. Fitzgerald proceded accurately, step by step, with just enough documentation to keep the drama from being misty, but without destroying the suggestiveness that added to the horror lurking behind the surface. Consider Doctor Diver's predicament in being married to a woman with a "split personality" deriving from a brutal misadventure in adolescence. He had married Nicole against his better judgment, partially because she brought him memories of home after years spent abroad. He was drawn into accepting her money, for reasons that living up to a certain income and "cushioning" existence were bound up with the cure. His husband-physician relationship to Nicole, involving constant companionship, cut him off from his practice, and he thought wistfully at times of how the German psychiatrists were getting ahead of him.

With all these factors preparing the ground, it would merely take the sight of an uncomplicated girl (Rosemary) to jar him into active unrest. And when Nicole, subconsciously jealous of Rosemary, comes to a new phase of her disease, and attempts to throw the car off the road when Dick is driving with her and the two children, it is enough to give any one the jitters. Weakness indeed! The wonder to us is that Dick didn't collapse long before Mr. Fitzgerald causes him to break down. And when he does collapse, his youth is gone, it is too late to catch up with the Germans who have been studying new cases for years. This seems to us to be a sufficient exercise in cause-and-effect. Compared to the motivation in Faulkner, it is logic personified.

Mr. Fitzgerald Displays His Little White Mice

H. A. MacMillan**

When one tries to find words with which to label Mr. Fitzgerald's new, "mature" novel, a few much-used tags present themselves, such as "Hemingway," "lost generation," and one's first swift revulsion on learning

*Reprinted from the *New York Times*, 16 April 1934, p. 15. Copyright 1934 by the New York Times Company. Reprinted by permission.

**Reprinted from the *St. Paul Daily News*, 22 April 1934, magazine section, p. 4.

what the book is about is, "Kind heaven! am I again to be asked to view with pity and horror the soul-heavings and 'weltschmerz' of leisured cosmopolites in the play places of the world."

For here it is again — the now-so-familiar group of decadents, near-decadents of French, British, American, Italian extraction coming together on the Cannes sands, a "bright tan prayer rug of a beach," and mingling while the author of their being makes the reader aware, in mysterious and enigmatic reference, of their inter-relationships, their pasts, their probable future. One is asked to look upon them, their charm, their occasional beauty, their superior breeding, their apparent carefree existence, and shudder because beneath their smooth facades lie envy, jealousy, hatred, greed, disillusion, abnormalities which accord ill with their supposed civilization.

One can politely be compassionate, of course, but it is a little too much to ask the reading world to go on and on, shedding oh-the-pity-of-it tears over a relatively unimportant class of bluebloods with not enough to do who find the world a cage and themselves little white mice running round and round, aimlessly seeking a way out.

With the inability (peculiar to the Hemingway school) to write a story chronologically, Mr. Fitzgerald in *Tender Is the Night* plunges his audience into an already-created situation upon which Rosemary Hoyt, Hollywood actress, vacationing in a Cannes hotel bursts with the stupidity of the outsider who feels hostile and suspicious because he does not understand what preceded the mood of his fellow-companions. She finds that the group to which she wants to belong, that led by the young Divers who have a permanent home in Cannes, is difficult to penetrate, but her beauty and her reputation open doors and she keeps them open by force when she falls in love with Dr. Richard Diver, American psychiatrist with a European reputation, who is inseparable from his rich and lovely wife, Nicole. Attracted to Rosemary he remains for a long time stubbornly faithful to his wife. Only gradually (and when half the book is completed) does Rosemary learn the 'tragic' story of the gifted young doctor and the girl he has married, a 'split personality' case to whom he is at once lover, husband and healer. He has given the best of his talents to making a normal being of her, identifying himself with her until after an emotional crisis between them completely cures her and she no longer needs him, he is only a shell without her. Separated from her he disintegrates, is last heard of as an itinerant, unsuccessful small town doctor in the States.

Granted an unusual story of a psychological abnormality, the book nevertheless suffers from the obscure manner in which the narrative is developed, and from the introduction in the first half of the novel, of matter which has no real and intimate connection with the main theme, and little enough interest for its own sake. The entire character of Rosemary Hoyt, for instance, strikes one as having no legitimate reason for being.

You Can't Duck Hurricane Under
a Beach Umbrella
Philip Rahv*

F. Scott Fitzgerald made a name for himself in the literature of the past decade as the voice and chronicler of the jazz age. This, in a sense, was his strength, as he showed himself capable of quickly responding to features of American life that other writers assimilated rather slowly; but it also proved to be his greatest defect, since he failed to place what he saw in its social setting. He himself was swept away by the waste and extravagance of the people he described, and he identified himself with them. Hence the critics who, at his appearance on the literary scene, saw in him a major talent in post-war American literature, soon realized that here was another creative promise petering out. The fever of the boom days settled in his bones. In the end he surrendered to the standards of the *Saturday Evening Post.*

In these days, however, even Fitzgerald cannot escape realizing how near the collapse of his class really is. In his new work he no longer writes of expensive blondes and yachting parties, lavish surroundings and insane love-affairs from the same angle of vision as in the past. These things are still there, but the author's enthusiasm for them has faded, giving way to the sweat of exhaustion. The rich expatriates who trail their weary lives across the pages of the novel breathe the thin air of a crazy last autumn. The author is still in love with his characters, but he no longer entertains any illusions concerning their survival. Morally, spiritually, and even physically they are dying in hospitals for the mentally diseased, in swanky Paris hotels and on the Riviera beaches. Yet, having immersed himself in the atmosphere of corruption, Fitzgerald's eye discerns a certain grace even in their last contortions. The morbid romance of death sways his mind, and signs are not wanting that instead of severing the cords that bind him to their degradation, he prefers to stick out with them to the end. Even while perceiving their doom, he still continues to console and caress them with soft words uttered in the furry voice of a family doctor pledged to keep the fatal diagnosis from his patients.

A number of things happen in *Tender Is the Night.* First, let us introduce Mr. Warren, a Chicago millionaire who rapes his sixteen-year-old daughter Nicole. This non-plebeian act drives the girl out of her mind, and she is sent to a sanatorium in Switzerland, where she is partially cured and where she meets Dick Diver, a young American psychologist who marries her. Nicole is extremely wealthy and the Divers lead a model parasitic life, flitting from one European high spot to another, accompanied by a varied assortment of neurotics and alcoholics. Wherever they go

*Reprinted from the *Daily Worker*, 5 May 1934, p. 7, by permission from the *Daily World.*

they are intent on smashing things up. Dick Diver's strength and charm fall apart in the insufferable atmosphere of sophisticated brutality. In the course of time he realizes his role as a live commodity bought by the Warren family to act as husband-doctor to their crazy daughter. And Nicole, sensing Dick's growing despair, flies from him to the arms of Tommy Barban, the stylized young barbarian who is potentially an ideal leader of a Nazi storm-troop.

When the plot is thus bluntly stated, stripped of its delicate introspective wording, of its tortuous style that varnishes rather than reveals the essential facts, we can easily see that the book is a fearful indictment of the moneyed aristocracy. But Fitzgerald's form blunts this essence, transforming it into a mere opportunity for endless psychologizing. And on account of it many a reader will let himself float on the novel's tender surface, without gauging the horror underneath.

The reviewer is inclined to think that in creating the figure of Dick Diver, Fitzgerald has created — perhaps unconsciously — the image of a life closely corresponding to his own. The truth is that Nicole can be understood as a symbol of the entire crazy social system to which Fitzgerald has long been playing Dick Diver.

And lastly, a not too private postscript to the author. Dear Mr. Fitzgerald, you can't hide from a hurricane under a beach umbrella.

Scott Fitzgerald a Modern Orpheus
Mabel Dodge Luhan*

To the Editor of *Books*:

Here are some thoughts about *Tender Is the Night*. Max Eastman says I don't know how to think and maybe that is true, so perhaps these will not be thoughts, really, so much as approximations of my impressions, perceptions of a manly performance, set down with great respect.

When Orpheus first went down into the underworld to bring back Eurydice it was not so risky an excursion as in these days we live in. It took then, apparently, rather a simple courage and it was more cut and dried for there was a stout surface to his world and a more definite descent and emergence. He went down and he returned.

But now the whole surface is worn thin. Everywhere the social tissue is giving way, ominous cracks appear upon the pleasant rink of our conscious life where we skim to and fro upon the thin thin ice.

Once in a while, quite frequently, as compared with Orpheus's day, some one sinks under and disappears and Orpheus is not there to save.

*Reprinted from the *New York Herald Tribune Books*, 6 May 1934, p. 21.

Neither love nor courage is available to many and for the few there is only the cold sport of science frisking delicately in the dangerous stream, trying to hook these fish.

The greater number, then, disappear with the vast undifferentiated gray underworld and are seen no more. They are engulfed in the ancient reservoir where good and evil are all one and nothing matters yet, but where the eager unnamed elements wait for a chance to rise and be; for while the children of this world are sinking through these terrible exits, the powers of the undisclosed world make their entrances.

Now, it seems to me, Scott Fitzgerald is a man who knows about all this — and what realizations has he gazed at and accepted before he could tell of it? In the wrack and ruin of his environment he ponders and smiles. Even while the waters close over him he smiles and tells of life as it has come to him, tells about his experience that was the experience of Orpheus, with this vast difference between them, that Orpheus didn't know what he was doing nor what happened to him. Some one else had to tell about him while here is one who can and does tell his own story. This makes people murmur about "taste." Is it "taste"? Well, has life taste? Because this writing is as actual as talking, the critics are confused. They are habituated to art forms and here is something that does not fit into them. Here is something real and confused and no more a novel than life is. Yet readers talk about it "as a novel" and compare it with *The Great Gatsby,* and they debate whether or no the author has fulfilled his earlier promise. Why can't they see that this is stern stuff and not to be mixed up with just books? But no — they are disappointed and they cover that up as best they can by calling it "brilliant" — which is their way of condoning it for its lack of this and that!

Do they realize, I wonder, that here is a book that is very close to being a live, organic resume of present reality and that that is something rare? I don't believe they do or they would drop their little measures and realize that something important, more important than a novel, has happened.

Here is an objective grasp of the conditioned, mechanical activity of oneself, the picture taken of oneself upon a journey, the lens directed and the shutter clicked at the moment of submersion, at the opening of the waters.

In these days it is Orpheus who must be saved. The roles are reversed but Eurydice is not aware yet of her predestined importance for still she is not strong enough to endure. She is still unstable although he has brought her through. Again and again she sinks into those grey depths where the amorphous things wait for birth. Each time she rises they come too, clinging about her unseen. She is, all unbeknownst, a carrier of forces that are evil when set loose — she is, as Gilbert Seldes said, a kind of "Typhoid Mary," and where she passes in her pleasant places, things happen. Her neighborhood is lively with potential battle, murder and sudden death.

The gulf is open beneath her and ghastly eventualities attend her. Yet she is saved herself because Orpheus has taken over her account. With ignorance and loving blindness he will atone for an old, old mistake: that of touching with love those who are lost. He has not learned to save by the cold and scientific methods of modern salvation. Sacrifice is all he knows — that and knowing himself. He is the child of transition wandering in no man's land, between two worlds, one dead, the other not yet born. But he creates the future for us. He is not inactively resigned, nor passively submissive. With dreadful endurance and clarity he attempts to tell us — "this is how it is" — and by adding his portion to consciousness he changes the present.

I am afraid I have been clumsy and inadequate in trying to show how much I admire this mature act. The book doesn't need defense or interpretation. Of its own vitality it will make its own way, and gathering momentum it will cover long spaces and I hope I may be excused for seeming to think it needs any one to defend it.

The Worm i' the Bud   William Troy*

To label Mr. Fitzgerald's new novel a study in psychological degeneration is not strictly accurate, for such degeneration presupposes an anterior dignity or perfection of character, and none of the characters in this book is made sufficiently measurable at the beginning to give to his later downhill course anything more than a mildly pathetic interest. None of them is even what one might call, in the loosest sense, mature. Richard Diver, young American war veteran turned psychiatrist, is too perfect a specimen of the Yale man of his generation to seem quite plausible as a surgeon of souls. Nicole recovers from her schizophrenia, the effect of an incestuous assault in childhood, only to acquire the neuroses of the frivolous, luxurious, and empty-pated society to which she is restored. And Rosemary Hoyt, that incredible flower of the Hollywood studios, begins, and ends, as hardly more than a glamorous moron. Yet the effect of the novel as a whole is quite as depressing as that of any authentic study in moral and psychological degeneration. The vague depression that hovers over the opening chapters increases in intensity as the book moves on to its sordid termination. It increases, as a matter of fact, in an exact ratio to the growth of our confusion as to the precise reason for the hero's disintegration. Is it that once Nicole is cured of her disease she no longer has need of his kind of love — the old story of the physician unable to heal himself? Is it that her money has acted like a virus to destroy his personality and with it

*Reprinted from the *Nation* 138 (9 May 1934):539–40. Copyright 1934 by the *Nation*. Reprinted with permission from Nation Associates, Inc.

his life-work? Or is it simply that he is a man of weak character, unable to resist temptation and concealing the fact from himself through immersion in alcohol? All these causes are indicated, and any one of them might be made sufficient, but the author's own unwillingness to choose between them, his own uncertainty communicated to the reader, continues to the last. And the result is depressing in the way that confusion in a work of literature is always depressing.

Glamor is here as elsewhere one of the most frequently used words in Mr. Fitzgerald's vocabulary, and because this very abstract word so obviously sums up much important feeling, constituting perhaps a key to Mr. Fitzgerald's sensibility, it may be worth while to submit it to that process of "dissociation" which Rémy de Gourmont recommended for cases of this kind. Now the word glamor, in Mr. Fitzgerald's writing, is usually applied to people or things or ways of living represented as being, in some total and general sense, attractive. It stands for a whole imponderable compound of desirable qualities — youth, beauty, gaiety, romantic charm. Daisy in *The Great Gatsby* possessed glamor, and so do the two heroines in the present book. But it should be noted that in the case of each of these exquisite creatures to the possession of glamor is added another and more palpably attractive possession — money. In *The Great Gatsby*, the narrator, fumbling for an exact description of Daisy, is told by Gatsby himself, "Her voice is full of money . . . That was it. . . . It was full of money — that was the inexhaustible charm that rose and fell in it, the jingle of it, the cymbals' song of it. . . . High in a white palace the king's daughter, the gold[en] girl. . . ." And now again, in this new book, we find Nicole's lover reminding her, "You've got too much money. That's the crux of the matter." In other words, for Mr. Fitzgerald's heroes youth and wealth, romance and luxury, love and money become somehow identified in the imagination. "Glamor" becomes a compound of glittering opposites. And because it consists for them in a confusion of essentially irreconcilable elements their surrender to it leads, in the end, either to inglorious death in Long Island swimming pools or to slow deterioration on foreign sands.

This conflict, since that is what it really amounts to, is probably the thing that makes Mr. Fitzgerald an artist, the very distinguished artist that he revealed himself to be in *The Great Gatsby*. But the time has come when we must demand a more clean-cut recognition of its elements and a more single-minded effort toward its resolution. The biographer of Gatsby, weary of his riotous excursions into the human heart, returned to the Middle West wanting the whole world to be "in uniform and at a sort of moral attention forever." But Dick Diver turns out to be Jay Gatsby all over again, another poor boy with a "heightened sensitivity to the promises of life" betrayed by his own inability to make the right distinctions. And the repetition of the pattern turns out to be merely depressing. It is time now for Mr. Fitzgerald, with his remarkable technical mastery of his craft, to give us a character who is not the victim of adolescent confusion, who is strong enough to turn deaf ears to the jingling cymbals of the golden girl.

Breakdown

Malcolm Cowley*

Tender Is the Night is a good novel that puzzles you and ends by making you a little angry because it isn't a great novel also. It doesn't give the feeling of being complete in itself.

The theme of it is stated in a conversation among the three principal characters. "What did this to him?" Rosemary asks. They are talking about Abe North, an American composer who became prominent shortly after the War. He was shy and very talented; often he came to stay with Dick and Nicole Diver in their villa near the Cap d'Antibes and they scarcely knew he was there—"sometimes he'd be in the library with a muted piano, making love to it by the hour." But for years now he hadn't been working; his eyes had a hurt look; he got drunk every day as if trying to escape from nobody knew what. And Rosemary wondered, "Why does he have to drink?"

> Nicole shook her head right and left, disclaiming responsibility for the matter: "So many smart men go to pieces nowadays."
> "And when haven't they?" Dick asked. "Smart men play close to the line because they have to—some of them can't stand it, so they quit."
> "It must lie deeper than that. . . . Artists like—well, like Fernand don't seem to have to wallow in alcohol. Why is it just Americans who dissipate?"
> There were so many answers to this question that Dick decided to leave it in the air, to buzz victoriously in Nicole's ears.

The question remains victoriously buzzing in the reader's ears long after the story has ended. Fitzgerald tries to answer it, but obliquely. He tells us why Dr. Richard Diver went to pieces—because he married a rich woman and became so dependent on her money that his own work seemed unimportant and he no longer had a purpose in living; that is the principal reason, although he is also shaken by his love for Rosemary and by Nicole's recurrent fits of insanity, during one of which she came near killing not only her husband and herself but also their two children. Dick's case seems clear enough—but what about Abe North, whose wife was poor and sane and devoted? What about the other nice people who ended as lunatics or drunkards? Fitzgerald is continually suggesting and reiterating these questions that he leaves in the air.

*Reprinted from the *New Republic* 79 (6 June 1934):105–6.

The Divers and their friends are, in reality, the characters he has always written about, and written well. They are the richer members of his own generation, the young women who learned to smoke and pet in 1917 and the Yale and Princeton men who attended their coming-out parties in new uniforms. In his early books, especially in *This Side of Paradise*, he celebrated the youth of these people in a tone of unmixed pride — "Here we are," he seemed to be saying, "the children of the conquerors, the free and beautiful and very wicked youngsters who are setting the standards for a nation." Later, when he described their business careers and their life in great country houses on the north shore of Long Island, his admiration began to be mixed with irony and disillusionment. In the present novel, which chronicles their years of exile, the admiration has almost completely vanished; the prevailing tone is one of disillusionment mixed with nostalgia. "We had good times together," Fitzgerald seems to say, "but that was a long time ago." Dick Diver is now an unsuccessful drunken country doctor, divorced and living somewhere in central New York State. Rosemary is an empty and selfish movie star; Abe North is dead, killed brawling in a speakeasy — all the kind and sensitive people of their circle have gone to pieces, and there remain only the "wooden and onanistic" women like Nicole's sister, only the *arrivistes* like Albert McKisco and the cultivated savages like Tommy Barban. A whole class has flourished and decayed and suddenly broken into fragments.

Here is a magnificent subject for a novel. The trouble is that Fitzgerald has never completely decided what kind of novel he wanted to write — whether it should center round a single hero or deal with a whole group. Both types of approach are present, the individual and the collective, and they interfere with each other. We are conscious of a divided purpose that perhaps goes back to a division in the author himself.

Fitzgerald has always been the poet of the American upper bourgeoisie; he has been the only writer able to invest their lives with glamor. Yet he has never been sure that he owed his loyalty to the class about which he was writing. It is as if he had a double personality. Part of him is a guest at the ball given by the people in the big house; part of him has been a little boy peeping in through the window and being thrilled by the music and the beautifully dressed women — a romantic but hard-headed little boy who stops every once in a while to wonder how much it all cost and where the money came from. (Fitzgerald says, "There is a streak of vulgarity in me that I try to cultivate.") In his early books, this divided personality was wholly an advantage: it enabled him to portray American society from the inside, and yet at the same time to surround it with an atmosphere of magic and romance that exists only in the eyes of people watching at the carriage entrance as the guests arrive in limousines. Since those days, however, the division has been emphasized and has become a liability. The little boy outside the window has grown mature and cold-eyed: from an enraptured spectator he has developed into a social historian. At the same time, part of Fitzgerald remains inside, among the dancers. And now that the ball is ending in tragedy, he doesn't know how to describe it — whether as a guest, a participant, in which case he will be writing a purely psychological novel; or whether from the detached point of view of a social historian.

There is another reason, too, for the technical faults of *Tender Is the Night*. Fitzgerald has been working on it at intervals for the last nine years, ever since he published *The Great Gatsby* in 1925. During these years his attitude has inevitably changed, as has that of every other sensitive writer. Yet no matter how much he revised his early chapters, he could not make them wholly agree with those written later — for once a chapter has assumed what seems to be a final shape, it undergoes a process of crystallization; it can no longer be remolded. The result is that several of his characters are self-contradictory: they don't merely change as living creatures change; they transform themselves into different people.

If I didn't like the book so much, I wouldn't have spoken at such length about its shortcomings. It has virtues that deserve more space than I can give them here. Especially it has a richness of meaning and emotion — one feels that every scene is selected among many possible scenes and that every event has pressure behind it. There is nothing false or borrowed in the book: everything is observed at first hand. Some of the minor figures — especially Gausse, the hotel keeper who was once a bus boy in London, and Lady Caroline Sibley-Biers, who carries her English bad manners to the point of viciousness — are more vivid than Rosemary or Dick; and the encounter between Gausse and Lady Caroline is one of those enormous episodes in which two social castes are depicted melodramatically, farcically and yet convincingly in a brief conversation and one gesture.

Fitzgerald says that this book is his farewell to the members of his own generation; I hope he changes his mind. He has in him at least one great novel about them, and it is a novel that I want to read.

[Untitled Review]   C. Hartley Grattan*

Scott Fitzgerald's new novel has called forth more than the usual quota of discussion allowed these days for the works of writers definitely identified with the dead and gone pre-depression era. This alone should serve to indicate that it is an uncommonly interesting piece of work and one which makes plain, strange as it may seem to those who remember only the frothy brilliance of *This Side of Paradise*, that Fitzgerald has

*Reprinted from the *Modern Monthly* 8 (July 1934):375–77.

grown steadily and now definitely promises to emerge as one of the really important interpreters of the upper middle class in our time. Unusually sensitive to the charm and excitement of the life of the idle and semi-idle rich and near-rich and the vast army of hangers-on they attract to them, he has slowly moved toward a position which allows him to abate very little his sympathetic attitude while definitely taking up the position of an observer rather than a participant in their revels. *Tender Is the Night* exploits to the full the feverish beauty of a class in decay, the polished charm of a decadence that is not yet self-conscious, the exciting insecurity of our betters.

The integral significance of the opening pages of the book has been missed by most reviewers. Almost to a man they have complained that the stress laid upon Rosemary, the beautiful cinema star, is unjustified by the future action of the story, that the pages devoted to building her up are really wasted effort, and that they "throw the reader off." Rather I should say that in these pages Fitzgerald is presenting the type of girl who, in the past, has always been foreordained to absorption into the world of his characters. She is the typical outsider who, moonstruck by glamor, can be quite sure that some man will select her from the host of the beautiful and innocent as his particular contribution to the seraglio of physically charming females. She is obviously not a female hairy ape, excluded, downtrodden, and exploited. She can and will belong. For it is indisputable that this process of absorbing beautiful women from the outside has been going on from time immemorial and is a characteristic of all the "aristocracies" of history. It always goes on to the end. Not gifted with insight into social processes (and why on earth should she be anyhow?) Rosemary does not realize that she has come a bit too late and that on penetrating the world she will find it already in decay and dissolution. Seen through her eyes, however, what glamor remains can legitimately be exploited and by the same token, the tragedy of its actuality can be all the more accentuated.

And so we come to the central characters, Dr. Richard Diver and his wife Nicole, beautiful daughter of a wealthy household whose life has been distorted and made precarious by incestuous relations with her father. Fitzgerald has tried to use this situation, this extreme (according to our tabus) example of decadence, to symbolize the rottenness of the society of which Nicole is a part. This is well-nigh impossible. It is always difficult to argue from the individual to the social and when the social issues are so tremendous as they are here, the chances are that any individual will turn out to be an inadequate symbol. Nevertheless Fitzgerald has done as well as possible. Dr. Diver's relation to his wife is more than that of a man to a woman he has loved enough to marry; it is also that of a psychiatrist to a patient. First encountering her in a sanitorium, he is gradually persuaded by his emotions and his technical interest and against his better judgment, to undertake her cure as her husband as well as her physician. He is, therefore, in much the same relationship to her as the reformer is to the sick society which he wishes to cure because he cannot bring himself to abandon it and which in the end forces him either to accept it on its own terms or reject it and with it his life. That the reformer should fail and in the process be corrupted by the poisons flowing through the social veins, is as inevitable as the slow corruption of the charming Dick Diver. And when he finally abandons the task, the chances are as good that he will plunge into an even more complete obscurity than overtakes those who reject the task from the first in favor of the more drastic cure of revolution as that he will go over to the masters and become at one with them in the tacit or self-conscious support of the corrupt values. Dick Diver when he finally realizes that his task of rehabilitating Nicole is accomplished and that he can do no more without abandoning the few remnants of physician's values he retains and accepting all those of her world, chooses the way to obscurity, the corruption that follows on the realization of a wasted life, and death from the cultivation of that corruption. He is divorced by Nicole and disappears into upper New York State. No one knows what has become of him but "in any case he is almost certainly in that section of the country, in one town or another." This fate is so close to that of unstable personalities in any place and time that it has been perversely misread by those critics anxious to avoid the implications of the whole book.

For it would be folly to ignore the fact that society always produces its misfits and no-goods and that many of them can and do move in leisured society until the inevitable disintegration takes place and they disappear into obscure saloons, shabby rooming houses and out of the way towns, there to nurse their vices to the death. It is even possible that no higher percentage of each college generation today goes down to obscurity and extinction than heretofore. But if this were all that Fitzgerald had intended to say he would not have been so careful to introduce overtones of a larger purpose into his book. In the light of the plainly indicated larger purpose, we are not straining the facts of the narrative to see in these miscellaneous and sometimes highly entertaining ascents and descents, mere symbolic reflections of a larger corruption. One passage which makes that perfectly clear is the following:

> Nicole was the product of much ingenuity and toil. For her sake trains began their run at Chicago and traversed the round belly of the continent to California; chicle factories fumed and link belts grew link by link in factories; men mixed toothpaste in vats and drew mouthwash out of copper hogsheads; girls canned tomatoes quickly in August or worked rudely at the Five-and-Tens on Christmas Eve; half-breed Indians toiled on Brazilian coffee plantations and dreamers were mus-cled out of patent rights in new tractors — these were some of the people who gave a tithe to Nicole, and as the whole system swayed and thundered onward it lent a feverish bloom to such processes of hers as wholesale buying, like the flush of a fireman's face holding his post

before a spreading blaze. She illustrated very simple principles, containing in herself her own doom, but illustrated them so accurately that there was grace in the procedure, and pleasantly Rosemary would try to imitate it.

This is perceptive writing and I should like to stress for the benefit of those austere individuals who see in the bourgeois world nothing but filth and corruption the significance of the words "feverish bloom" and "grace." Only a person utterly insensitive to the grace and beauty of the way of life open to the leisured will fail to see that even in decay these people are infinitely charming, insidiously beguiling to all but sea-green incorruptibles.

Mechanisms of Misery   D. W. Harding*

Many of the features that go to making *The Great Gatsby* as fine as it is are also present in this latest novel of Scott Fitzgerald's.[1] There is still his power of seeming to lose himself in incident and letting the theme emerge by itself, there is his sensitiveness (occasionally touching sentimentality) and his awareness of the brutalities in civilized people's behavior, and there is simultaneously his keen appreciation, not entirely ironic, of the superficies of the same people's lives. This last is the feature that is most nearly lost in the new book. Here there is no more gusto, but right from the start an undercurrent of misery which draws away even the superficial vitality of the Euramerican life he depicts.

The story is the acutely unhappy one of a young psychiatrist, brilliant in every way, who gradually deteriorates. In place of plot there is a fine string of carefully graduated incidents to illustrate the stages of the descent. Rather than tragedy, however, the book appears to me to be one variety of the harrowing, if this can be taken to mean that as we read it our feelings are of misery and protest, and that, unlike tragedy, it can give no satisfactions to those who wish to go on living. On the other hand, it is so effectively and sincerely harrowing that its mechanisms deserve close examination.

In the first place the doomed hero is offered as the most admirable kind of modern man we can reasonably ask for, and throughout the novel he is made to stand out as superior to all the other personae. This being so we look for some explanation of his collapse, and the first mechanism of misery appears in the ambiguity here. Various possible explanations are hinted at but none is allowed to stand. His wife's wealth, with its heavy burden of smart leisure, Dick deals with like a disciplined artist; he shows

*Reprinted from *Scrutiny* 3 (December 1934):316–19, by permission from Cambridge University Press.

himself heroically adequate to the strain of her recurrent mental trouble; and he has as full an insight into himself and the strains his work imposes as he has into his patients. Everything that we could hope to do he is shown doing better, and — apparently as a consequence — he cracks up. The gloomy generalization is made by Dick himself in commenting on a man who precedes him to ruin: "Smart men play close to the line because they have to — some of them can't stand it, so they quit." But the pessimistic conviction of the book goes deeper than that, and its puritan roots are suggested by Dick's misgivings over his good fortunes and achievements in his heigh-day. He soliloquises: " — And Lucky Dick can't be one of these clever men; he must be less intact, even faintly destroyed. If life won't do it for him it's not a substitute to get a disease, or a broken heart, or an inferiority complex, though it'd be nice to build out some broken side till it was better than the original structure." Scott Fitzgerald sees to it that life *will* do it for him.

But in addition to the puritan conviction, there is also present a curious mingling of a childish fantasy with an adult's attempt to correct it, and much of the harrowing effect of the book depends on this. On the one hand, Dick is the tragic fantasy hero who is so great and fine that everyone else expects to go on taking and taking from him and never give back; and so he gets tired, so tired; and he breaks under the strain with no one big enough to help him, and it's terribly pathetic and admirable. The vital point of this childish fantasy is that he should remain admirable and (posthumously) win everyone's remorseful respect. But the story is too obviously sentimental in those terms. To try ruthlessly to tear out the sentimentality, Scott Fitzgerald brings in a much more mature bit of knowledge: that people who disintegrate in the adult world don't at all win our respect and can hardly retain even our pity. He gets his intense painfulness by inviting our hearts to go out to the hero of the childish fantasy and then checking them with the embarrassment which everyone nearest him in the story, especially Nicole his wife, feels for the failure.

The question is whether the situation could in fact occur. Not whether the main events could be paralleled in real life, but whether all the elements of action and feeling could co-exist in the way they are presented here, whether we are not being trapped into incompatible attitudes toward the same events. In short, is an emotional trick being played on us?

There seem to me to be several tricks, though without extensive quotation they are hard to demonstrate. Chief among them is the social isolation of the hero, isolation in the sense that no one gives him any help and he has no genuinely reciprocal social relationships; he remains the tragic child hero whom no one is great enough to help. Even towards the end he is made to seem superior to the others so that they are inhibited from approaching him with help. That this should be so is made plausible by the continual returns of his old self amongst the wreckage, returns of self-discipline and willingness to shoulder responsibility that amounts almost to alternations of personality. He explains it himself: "The manner remains intact for some time after the morale cracks." But it seems highly doubtful whether anyone could remain so formidable spiritually during a process of spiritual disintegration, especially to someone who had been as close to him as Nicole had been. But here another trick appears in the interests of plausibility: the patient-physician relationship between the two of them is now emphasized, and Nicole's abandonment of Dick is interpreted as an emergence from fixation, whereas much of the misery of the collapse springs from its wrecking what has earlier been made to seem a genuine and complete marriage.

Once achieved, Dick's isolation permits of the further device of making his suffering dumb. Reading the aquaplane episode in particular is like watching a rabbit in a trap. The story begins to become less harrowing and more like tragedy when, once or twice, Dick is articulate about himself. This happens momentarily when he comments on the manner remaining intact after the morale has cracked: but no other persona is allowed to be big enough to hear more, and " 'Do you practise on the Riviera?' Rosemary demanded hastily." At one point the cloud of dumb misery lifts again for a moment, when he thinks he is unobserved and Nicole sees from his face that he is going back over his whole story, and actually feels sympathy for him; but this episode only introduces the final harrowing isolation. His position at the end is the apotheosis of the hurt child saying "Nobody loves me," but the child's self-pity and re-proaches against the grown-ups have largely been rooted out and in their place is a fluctuation between self-disgust and a fatalistic conviction that this is bound to happen to the nicest children.

The difficulty of making a convincing analysis of the painful quality of this novel, and the conviction that it was worth while trying to, are evidence of Scott Fitzgerald's skill and effectiveness. Personal peculiarities may of course make one reader react more intensely than another to a book of this kind, and I am prepared to be told that this attempt at analysis is itself childish — an attempt to assure myself that the magician didn't really cut the lady's head off, did he? I still believe there was a trick in it.

The 1940s

The Talk of the Town Anonymous*

It is our guess that very young men wrote the obituaries for F. Scott Fitzgerald. Not only were they somewhat uninformed (note to the New York *Times*: *The Beautiful and Damned* is not a book of short stories, and it isn't called *The Beautiful and the Damned*, either) but they were also inclined to be supercilious. He was the prophet of the Jazz Age, they wrote patronizingly, who never quite fulfilled the promise indicated in *This Side of Paradise*. As an approximate contemporary of Mr. Fitzgerald's and, we suppose, a survivor of the Jazz Age ourself, we find this estimate just a little exasperating. He undoubtedly said and did a great many wild and childish things and he turned out one or two rather foolish books; he also wrote, however, one of the most scrupulously observed and beautifully written of American novels. It was called, of course, *The Great Gatsby*. If Jay Gatsby was no more than could be expected of Amory Blaine, Manhattan Island has never quite come up to Peter Stuyvesant's early dreams.

The Great Gatsby was always accepted as his best book, but we have a feeling that Fitzgerald may have preferred *Tender Is the Night*, which he wrote very near the end, perhaps when the end was sometimes too clear to him. It was probably as close to autobiography as his taste and temperament would allow him to come. We read it again the other day when we heard that he was dead, and somehow or other we can't forget the last sentence: "Perhaps, so she liked to think, his career was biding its time, like Grant's in Galena; his latest note was postmarked from Hornell, New York, which is some distance from Geneva and a very small town; in any case he is almost certainly in that section of the country, in one town or another." Scott Fitzgerald knew better than that. The desperate knowledge that it was much too late, that there was nothing to come that would be more than a parody of what had gone before, must have been continually in his mind the last few years he lived. In a way, we are glad he died when he did and that he was spared so many smaller towns, much further from Geneva.

*Reprinted from the *New Yorker* 16 (4 January 1941):9. © 1941, 1969, The New Yorker Magazine, Inc. Reprinted by permission.

F. Scott Fitzgerald, 1896–1940:
The Poet of Borrowed Time
Arthur Mizener*

. . . After *The Great Gatsby* Fitzgerald set himself a task which, as Edmund Wilson once remarked, would have given Dostoevski pause. It was to be a story of matricide, and though an immense amount of work was done on it, he was never able to complete a novel on this subject. As if to mock his failure, and perhaps too his deep concern for the subject, Fitzgerald wrote a comic ballad about matricide which he used to perform with great effect as a parlor trick.

In 1930 Zelda, who had been working for several years with all her energy to become a ballet dancer, broke down, and late in 1931 the Fitzgeralds returned to America and settled in a rambling old brown house at Rodgers Forge, between Baltimore and Towson. Here they remained until Fitzgerald went to Hollywood in 1937. Meanwhile Fitzgerald had been struggling with *Tender Is the Night*; he managed, by a furious effort in the latter part of 1933, to get it into shape for publication in *Scribner's* in 1934; he revised it considerably again before book publication, and there is in existence a copy of the book with further revisions in which Fitzgerald has written: "This is the *final version* of the book as I would like it."

Much of this revision appears to have been the result of his having felt his theme everywhere in his material without always seeing a way to draw these various aspects of it together in a single whole. The war, the ducal perversion and ingrown virginity of the Chicago aristocracy which the Warrens represent — stronger and so more terrible than the corruption of the English Campions and Lady Sibley-Bierses; the hardness and lack of moral imagination of the rich in general, the anarchic nihilism represented by Tommy Barban, the self-indulgence of Abe North, destroyed, beyond even an awareness of his own destruction, as Dick will be destroyed; all these forces are beautifully realized. But, though their general bearing on the situation is clear enough, their exact incidence and precise relation to each other sometimes is not.

The result is that *Tender Is the Night*, though the most profoundly moving of all Fitzgerald's novels, is a structurally imperfect book. To this difficulty must be added the fact that its central theme is not an easy one. We believe overwhelmingly in the collapse of Dick Diver's morale because we are made to see and hear, in the most minute and subtly shaded detail, the process of that collapse. It is very like the collapse of Fitzgerald's own morale as he describes in in "The Crack-Up." But it is not easy to say in either case what, in the immediate and practical sense, happens to cause

*Reprinted from Willard Thorp, ed., *Lives of Eighteen from Princeton* (Princeton: Princeton University Press, 1946), pp. 333–353. Copyright 1946, © renewed 1974 by Princeton University Press. Reprinted by permission of Princeton University Press.

the collapse. As do many romantics with their horror of time and age, Fitzgerald tended to think of spiritual resources — of courage and generosity and kindness — as he thought of physical resources, as a sum in the bank against which a man draws. When, in his own life, he realized "with finality that in some regard [he would] never be as good a man again"; when he began to feel that "every act of life from the morning tooth-brush to the friend at dinner had become an effort . . . that my casual relations — with an editor, a tobacco seller, the child of a friend, were only what I remembered I *should* do, from other days"; then he knew the sum in the bank was nearly exhausted and that there was nothing to do but to reduce his scale of living accordingly. "In a really dark night of the soul," he wrote in "The Crack-Up," "it is always three o'clock in the morning, day after day"; and though the dazzling Mediterranean sun blazes everywhere in *Tender Is the Night*, the passage Fitzgerald choose to quote along with the title line from Keats' poem is: "But here there is no light,/ Save what from heaven is with the breezes blown/Through verdurous glooms and winding mossy ways."

As always, however, Fitzgerald began not with a theme but with a body of material. Describing the life portrayed in *Tender Is the Night* in an earlier essay, he had written: "Charm, notoriety, good manners, weighed more than money as a social asset. This was rather splendid, but things were getting thinner and thinner as the eternal necessary human values tried to spread over all that expanse." With this world in all its variety of corruption, hardness, sterility, and despair Fitzgerald confronts his hero and the fundamentally simple "necessary human values" which his father had given him — " 'good instincts,' honor, courtesy, and courage." At the very beginning Dick Diver has to chose between becoming a great psychologist and a fully human being when Nicole, beautiful and schizophrenic, falls in love with him:

> "As you think best, Professor Dohmler," Dick conceded. "It's certainly a situation."
> Professor Dohmler raised himself like a legless man mounting a pair of crutches.
> "But it is a professional situation," he cried quietly.

But for Dick it is a human situation; "wanting above all to to be brave and kind, he . . . wanted, even more, to be loved." So he accepted the responsibility of being loved by Nicole and, gradually, of being loved by all the others whom his life drew around him. To them he gave lavishly of his strength, of his ability to translate into their terms the necessary human values and so remind them of their best selves. "My politeness," as he says, "is a trick of the heart." But the people he worked this trick for had no energy of their own, and gradually he exhausted his supply, spun out all his strength for other people until he had none left: "If you spend your life sparing other people's feelings and feeding their vanity, you get so you can't distinguish what *should* be respected in them."

Because he is proud and sensitive, Dick deliberately breaks Nicole's psychological dependence on him, aware that Nicole's love for him is bound up with her dependence and will cease with it, has already declined with the decline of her need for him; knowing that he has exhausted even his own power to love her in the process of making her psychologically whole again. By a terrible irony it comes about that what he had refused to treat as a merely professional situation is just that. "Dick waited until she was out of sight. Then he leaned his head forward on the parapet. The case was finished. Doctor Diver was at liberty again."

"That," says Baby Warren, speaking for them all, even for Nicole, "is what he was educated for."

Whether one accepts Fitzgerald's conception of the cause of this spiritual death or not, *Tender Is the Night* remains his most brilliant book. All his powers, the microscopic observation of the life he describes, the sense of the significance and relations of every detail of it, the infallible ear, and the gift of expression, all these things are here in greater abundance than ever before. And as never before they are used for the concrete, dramatic presentation of the inner significance of human experience, so that all the people of his book lead lives of "continual allegory" and its world is a microcosm of the great world. Its scope is such as to make *The Great Gatsby* seem small and simple, for all its neatness and perfection, and its dramatic realization so complete that Fitzgerald need not ever say what is happening: we always see. . . .

Mr. T. S. Eliot once remarked that "art never improves, but the material of art is never quite the same." But this is a dangerous way for a writer to look at the matter, however useful it may be to the critic, because it tends to separate in his mind the material from the form and meaning; and whenever the meaning is not something that grows out of the particular circumstances which are the occasion for writing, meaning tends to become abstract, to develop independently of the circumstances, and in some sense to violate their integrity. The safest attitude for the writer seems to be a single-minded desire to realize his material, so that the meaning of the circumstances, the permanent values which emerge for the critic from the representation, are for the writer merely such a further penetration of the particular circumstances as will allow him to realize them more completely. Fitzgerald's difficulty was always of course that his characters and their circumstances were likely to be too much individuals and local habitations, too little what Dr. Johnson approvingly referred to as "general nature." But what general nature there is in Fitzgerald's books — and there is always some and sometimes a great deal — is there because he had found it a part of his knowledge of his world. Such an undistorted imaginative penetration of the particular American world Fitzgerald knew had hardly been made before. Like James, Fitzgerald saw that one of the central moral problems of American life was raised in an acute form among the rich, in the conflict between the possibilities of their life and — to give it no worse name — their insensitivity. So long, therefore, as one realizes that Mr. Eliot is not comparing the two men in stature, it is not too much to say of Fitzgerald's best work what Mr. Eliot wrote him about *The Great Gatsby*: "In fact it seems to me to be the first step that American fiction has taken since Henry James."

After *The Great Gatsby* Fitzgerald produced only two books in fifteen years, one technically less perfect than *The Great Gatsby* and one unfinished. He did, of course, produce a large number of short stories, some of them as good as anything he ever wrote, but a considerable number of them only more or less skillful hackwork. All his life he worried about the hackwork and repeated over and over again a remark he made in 1924: "I now get 2,000 a story and they grow worse and worse and my ambition is to get where I need write no more but only novels." It is easy to condemn him for not having realized this ambition; there was much extravagance in his life and, at the end, debts and unavoidable expenses. But the ambition was there to the end and, in 1939, sick, tired, and under the ceaseless pressure of tragedy, he was writing an editor to whom he proposed to sell *The Last Tycoon*: "I would infinitely rather do it, now that I am well again, then take hack jobs out here." The wonder really is, given his temperament and upbringing, the social pressures of his times and the tragic elements in his personal life, that Fitzgerald did not give in entirely to hackwork, as so many of his contemporaries did, but returned again and again, to the end of his life, to the self-imposed task of writing seriously. For all its manifest faults and mistakes, it was in some ways an heroic life. But it was a life of which Fitzgerald himself, writing to an old friend, a lawyer, could only say rather sadly: "I hope you'll be a better judge than I've been a man of letters."

It is not easy at this close range to separate our opinion of the man from our opinion of the writer, particularly since circumstances combined to make the man a legendary, eponymous figure. But as the accidents of the man's life — and the lies about it — gradually fade, we may well come to feel about the writer, with his purity of imagination and his imperviousness to the abstract theories and intellectual fads which have hag-ridden our times, as Stephen Vincent Benét did when he remarked after Fitzgerald's death: "You can take off your hats, now, gentlemen, and I think perhaps you had better. This is not a legend, this is a reputation — and, seen in perspective, it may well be one of the most secure reputations of our time."

The 1950s

F. Scott Fitzgerald and the Image
of His Father

Henry Dan Piper*

In his serious writings Scott Fitzgerald was a stern and uncompromis-
ing moralist. The two earliest and probably the most important moral
influences in his life were the Roman Catholic Church and his father,
Edward Fitzgerald. By the time he was twenty-two, and had finished
writing his first novel, *This Side of Paradise*, he had left the Church;
thereafter the Catholicism in his work became more and more diffuse. But
his father continued to be a sort of "moral touchstone" for him all his life.
"Always deep in my subconscious," as he says in his hitherto unpublished
fragment "The Death of My Father," "I have referred judgments back to
him, [to] what he would have thought or done."

In *The Great Gatsby* and *Tender Is the Night* the fathers of Nick
Carraway and Dick Diver serve their sons in this same capacity. More than
that, they furnish the moral frames of reference against which the tragic
implications of each novel's story are made explicit. It is his father's code of
right conduct that enables Nick Carraway to attain, at the end of *The
Great Gatsby*, a mature and tragic sense of life. He has grown up; and in
the process of growing up he has been forced to recognize, somewhat
unwillingly, the corruption in his glamorous wealthy cousins, Tom and
Daisy Buchanan, and to acknowledge the fundamental decency of
Gatsby—"who represented everything for which I have an unaffected
scorn."

Tender Is the Night is a more formal tragedy. In the scene (pp.
262–266) where Dick Diver recognizes his own moral corruption, it is by
his father's standards (the "good instincts—honor, courtesy, courage") that
he judges himself and, in acknowledging his guilt, thereby becomes a
genuinely tragic character. In this crucial episode Dick's fall from grace is
suggested first by his fumbling attempt at a rather sordid seduction
(Fitzgerald built it up even more elaborately in the earlier versions of the
novel) and then is appropriately symbolized by memories of his father, and
by the unexpected news of his father's death. Like Fitzgerald, "Dick loved

*Reprinted from the Princeton University *Library Chronicle* 12 (Summer 1951): 181–86,
with permission of the Princeton University Library.

his father—again and again he referred his judgments to what his father would probably have thought and done."

In these two novels both fathers are portrayed as the remote and rather abstract symbols of an ideal moral order. Scott Fitzgerald's relations with his own father were much more ambiguous. Still, out of this very ambiguity came one of his most notable themes. Edward Fitzgerald was a genuine tragic figure, a man of divided loyalties, resembling Nick Carraway and, particularly, Dick Diver, much more than he resembled either of their fathers. In a sense, Mr. Fitzgerald was the prototype of both these heroes, and *The Great Gatsby* and *Tender Is the Night* were efforts on the part of his son to explore and dramatize in fiction the reasons for his father's defeat by life. For, in spite of his son's affection for him, he was always, in Fitzgerald's eyes, a "failure."

Like his fictional counterparts, Edward Fitzgerald taught his son the important things—good manners, good morals, and good taste. He read aloud to him his first poetry, "The Raven" and "The Prisoner of Chillon," and told him the Civil War reminiscences that his son later made into magazine stories. More than this, he supported his son's precocious literary inclinations against the opposition of his wife's more prosperous and pragmatic family. And some years later, when Fitzgerald failed to catch a pass and lost an important prep school football game, it was his father who consoled him and restored his self-confidence by his delight over a poem his son had just written for the school magazine. It was a lesson that stayed with Fitzgerald all his life. Now he could always know that, with his talent for writing, he would win some measure of that acclaim and "success" he coveted so avidly, but which he could rarely attain in the world of vigorous action.

In spite of his sensibility and fine manners, however, Edward Fitzgerald was a failure so far as the bustling, success-worshiping everyday world was concerned. To his ambitious son growing up in the prosperous commercial city of St. Paul, Minnesota, this fact was a source of recurring humiliation. The high point of his father's career seems to have been his marriage to Miss Annabelle McQuillan. Her father had come to St. Paul as a penniless immigrant from Ireland, had established a successful grocery business, and had died suddenly at the age of forty-four leaving a fortune of between a quarter- and a half-million dollars. But Mr. Fitzgerald, in spite of his literary tastes and genteel Maryland connections, never managed to measure up to the McQuillan standards of success. Unfitted by temperament for business, he moved from one unsatisfactory job to another until he was finally fired in 1908 and thereafter lived almost entirely on his wife's money. By this time he was also drinking excessively. Everyone in the neighborhood, and even his children's teachers at school, knew about his tippling. His son never forgot humiliating episodes like the time his father came home drunk and tried to play baseball in the backyard, or the afternoon when he lost his salesman's job and Scott had to give back to his mother the money she had just given him to go swimming.

What was he to make of this father of whom he was both ashamed and proud? Perhaps, at first, it was easier to accept the prevailing judgment of outsiders. But the older Fitzgerald grew, the more reasons he found to justify his father's position in society. It was not an easy problem, and it continued to trouble him all his life, yet it was one that he must solve if he himself was to effect any kind of a reconciliation with life.

It also provided him with important material for his writing. Just how vital his father's position was to him can be seen in the story "Shadow Laurels," Fitzgerald's first really serious piece of work and his first contribution to *The Nassau Literary Magazine* at Princeton. He was eighteen when it appeared in April, 1915. In the competence of its technique and in the implications of its theme, it is a major advance over any of his earlier schoolboy plays and sketches. Written entirely in dialogue, it tells of a young American, "his manner . . . that of a man accustomed only to success," who returns to France, the land of his birth, seeking his father. In a Paris wineshop he is shocked to learn that his father became a disreputable drunkard and finally was murdered in a café brawl. But when, in his humiliation, he speaks of his father disparagingly, he is sharply reprimanded by his father's old drinking companions:

> He was a wonderful talker. . . . He knew everything . . . he used to tell me poetry . . . [of] roses and the ivory towers of Babylon and about the ancient ladies of the court and about "the silent chords that flow from the ocean to the moon." That's why he made no money. He was bright and clever — when [he] worked, he worked feverishly hard, but he was always drunk, night and day.
> Don't you see, he stood for us as well as for himself. . . . how shall I say it? — he expressed us. . . . [He] was everything to me.[1]

Never again, in the novels and stories that Fitzgerald published after this early piece, was he to write so transparently of his feelings toward his father. Several similar allusions crept temporarily into an early manuscript version of *The Beautiful and Damned*, where he described Anthony Patch's lonely boyhood, his sense of isolation from his mother, and his adoration of his rather disreputable father. Anthony's earliest memories of Mr. Patch were always associated with "the pungency of whiskey," and one day, in a disagreeable scene, his father came to dinner drunk and, before the seated family, was ordered from the table by Anthony's grandfather. Afterward the boy went off to bed, "lonely and depressed." But all of this material was carefully deleted by Fitzgerald from later versions of the novel.

Possibly, when he removed these passages from his manuscript, Fitzgerald planned to tell his father's story at even greater length in his next novel. Not long after finishing *The Beautiful and Damned* he wrote

Maxwell Perkins that his next book would be a story of the Middle West in the 1880's (the Gilded Age, when his own father had come west to St. Paul). What he wrote, instead, was *The Great Gatsby*. This, of course, is also a story of Middle Westerners, though the setting has now been moved to Long Island, that most eastern extension of Middle Western wealthy suburbia. And it tells of another postwar Gilded Age, Fitzgerald's own rather than his father's. Besides, his father is no longer the central protagonist, although there are resemblances to him in both Carraway and Gatsby. Rather, he remains dimly in the background, the story's remote but ever-present moral arbiter.

His son was still at work on his next novel, *Tender Is the Night*, when Mr. Fitzgerald died in January, 1931. When the news came, Scott and Zelda were in Europe, and it was one in a succession of shattering blows. Less than a year earlier Zelda's mind had given way, and now she was slowly convalescing in a Swiss sanatorium. And there were other troubles. Fitzgerald was making little headway with the novel of American expatriate life that he had been trying to finish for the past half-dozen years. Most of his creative energy during this time had been dissipated on the hasty but well-paying magazine stories that helped him to meet his exorbitant living expenses. Since Zelda's collapse he had been under even greater financial pressure, and now the novel had been put aside indefinitely. But he was irritable, chafing to get at it again. Hemingway and his other literary friends had been advising him to stop wasting his talent on hasty potboilers and to get his book done. Besides, his magazine stories were growing thinner and thinner as the wells of inspiration ran dry. Even the magazine editors were beginning to grumble. To make things worse, Fitzgerald was drinking harder than ever and had quarreled seriously with most of his intimate friends.

In this depressed state of mind he came home in January for his father's funeral, but it was a confused trip and turned out to be a disappointment in every possible way. Now that his father was gone, he felt more lonely and insecure than ever, and after a few unhappy weeks in America he was eager to return to Zelda. "I'm damn glad to be going back to Europe, where I am away from most of the people I care about and can think instead of feel," he wrote to his favorite cousin from the "Olympic" after a few days at sea.[2]

Some time after this, probably not very long afterward, Fitzgerald wrote his fragmentary sketch of reminiscence, "The Death of My Father." Just what purpose it was intended to serve we do not know. Perhaps Hemingway had something to do with it. "Hope to read your account [of his father's death] between board covers rather than in the *Post*," he had written in a letter of sympathy, admonishing Fitzgerald not to fritter away "such fine material" in a trashy magazine story. Like so many romantic writers, Fitzgerald wrote best of those events which had hurt him most deeply, as Hemingway had already told him before. "Remember," he now wrote, "we writers have only one father and one mother to die."[3]

Not until a year and a half after his father's death did life become orderly enough for Fitzgerald to settle down to work again on his novel. Now he completely replotted his story, building it around the moral and emotional disintegration of a young American expatriate, very much like himself, married to a lovely young schizophrene resembling Zelda. And on pages 455–456 of his manuscript he inserted a considerable part of the text of "The Death of My Father." in the published version of *Tender Is the Night*, where it appears "between board covers," Fitzgerald has omitted some of the more personal portions of these reminiscences. Still, sufficient has been retained to establish his identification of his own father with Dick Diver's.

Even more impressive are the resemblances between Edward Fitzgerald and Dick Diver himself. Like his wife, Diver is a schizophrenic personality; but where her disease is mental, his is spiritual. And like Mr. Fitzgerald, his loyalties are divided between the "good instincts" in which he has been bred ("honor, courtesy, courage") and the gross, wasteful but leisurely world of parvenu wealth into which he has married. Dick's wife also came from Middle Western money made from selling food — but we must not press the parallels too far. They would have turned up in one guise or another whether Fitzgerald consciously intended them or not.

In the beginning, every son is cast in his father's image. To mature and become an individual in his own right, he must at first reject his father and his father's values, and go out into the world to forge his own. But, as he soon learns, the world is a rather chaotic place, and lasting standards are hard to come by. In the long run, every father is judged at last by the values he has taught his son.

The intensity of Fitzgerald's immersion in his own sensuous experience, the accuracy of his dialogue, and the brilliant concreteness of his imagery, are a measure of his preoccupation with the external world in which he came of age. He readily accepted its more superficial values — money, popularity, success — as well as its judgment of his father as a "failure." Yet when he came to write about that world, to deal with it imaginatively and to find values which would give his experience of it meaning, he returned constantly to the old standards, the "good instincts," which he had learned from his father. Whatever story he has to tell, from "Shadow Laurels" to his last full-length novel, *Tender Is the Night*, in all its ambiguities and complications, is identified in some way with this father image. Perhaps the reason that Fitzgerald was at last able to free himself from it in his unfinished novel, *The Last Tycoon*, was because he had gotten his problem out into the open and had explored its tragic implications more fully in *Tender Is the Night* than in any other earlier work. It is here that his use of "The Death of My Father" is central to an understanding of that book. And we see now that Edward Fitzgerald's failure and the standards by which he was willing to fail were, by all odds, his greatest legacy to his son.

Notes

1. *The Nassau Literary Magazine*, LXXI, No. 1 (Apr., 1915), 6–8.
2. Fitzgerald to Mrs. Richard C. Taylor, February 23, 1931 (Princeton University Library).
3. Hemingway to Fitzgerald, April 12, 1931 (Princeton University Library).

[Introduction to the Revised Edition]
Malcolm Cowley*

To the end of his life Fitzgerald was puzzled by the comparative failure of *Tender Is the Night*, after the years he spent on it and his efforts to make it the best American novel of his time. He had started it when he was living on the Riviera in the late summer of 1925. At first he had worked in bursts and had put aside the manuscript for months at a time while he wrote his profitable stories for the *Saturday Evening Post*; but early in 1932 he had found a more ambitious plan for it and had gone into debt to work on it steadily until the last chapters were written and the last deletions made in proof. He had watched it grow from a short dramatic novel like *The Great Gatsby* to a long psychological or philosophical novel on the model of *Vanity Fair*, and then, as he omitted scene after scene, he had watched it diminish again to a medium-length novel, but one in which he was sure that the overtones of the longer book remained. Nine years of his life had gone into the writing and into the story itself. Reading closely one could find in it the bedazzlement of his first summer at the Cap d'Antibes—for he could picture himself as Rosemary Hoyt in the novel, besides playing the part of Dick Diver; then his feelings about money and about the different levels of American society; then his struggle with alcoholism and his worries about becoming an emotional bankrupt; then his wife's illness and everything he learned from the Swiss and American doctors who diagnosed her case; then the bitter wisdom he gained from experience and couldn't put back into it, but only into his stories; then darker things as well, his sense of guilt, his fear of disaster that became a longing for disaster—it was all in the book, in different layers, like the nine buried cities of Troy.

When another writer went to see him at Rodgers Forge, near

*Reprinted from *Three Novels of F. Scott Fitzgerald* (New York: Charles Scribner's Sons, 1953), pp. iii–xii. The revised edition appeared first in 1951.

Baltimore, in the spring of 1933, Fitzgerald took the visitor to his study and showed him a pile of manuscript nearly a foot high. "There's my new novel," he said. "I've written four hundred thousand words and thrown away three-fourths of it. Now I only have fifteen thousand left to write and — " He stood there with a glass in his hand, then suddenly burst out, "It's good, good, good. When it's published people will say that it's good, good, good."

Tender was published in the spring of 1934 and people said nothing of the sort. It dealt with fashionable life in the 1920s at a time when most readers wanted to forget that they had ever been concerned with frivolities; the new fashion was for novels about destitution and revolt. The book had some friendly and even admiring notices, but most reviewers implied that it belonged to the bad old days before the crash; they dismissed it as having a "clever and brilliant surface" without being "wise and mature." Nor was it a popular success as compared with Fitzgerald's first three novels, which had been easier to write; in the first season it sold twelve thousand copies, or less than one-fourth as much as *This Side of Paradise*. In the following seasons the sale dwindled and stopped.

Fitzgerald didn't blame the public or the critics. It was one of the conditions of the game he played with life to accept the rules as they were written; if he lost point and set after playing his hardest, that was due to some mistake in strategy to be corrected in the future. He began looking in a puzzled fashion for the mistake in *Tender Is the Night*. There must have been an error in presentation that had kept his readers from grasping the richness and force of his material; for a time he suspected that it might merely be the lack of something that corresponded to stage directions at the beginning of each scene. In 1936 the book was being considered for republication by the Modern Library. The new edition, if it appeared, would have to be printed from the plates of the first edition in order to reduce the manufacturing costs, but Fitzgerald begged for the privilege of making some minor changes. These, he said in a letter to Bennett Cerf, "would include in several cases sudden stops and part headings which would be to some extent explanatory; certain pages would have to be inserted bearing merely headings. . . .

"I know what printing costs are," he added humbly. "There will be no pushing over of paragraphs or disorganization of the present set-up except in the aforesaid inserted pages. I don't want to change anything in the book but sometimes by a single word change one can throw a new emphasis or give a new value to the exact same scene or setting."

The new edition didn't appear and *Tender* seemed to be forgotten, although it really wasn't; it stayed in people's minds like a regret or an unanswered question. "A strange thing is that in retrospect his *Tender Is the Night* gets better and better," Ernest Hemingway told Maxwell Perkins, of Scribners, who was the editor of both novelists. In scores of midnight arguments that I remember, other writers ended by finding that they had the same feeling about the book. Fitzgerald continued to brood about it. In December 1938, when he was in Hollywood and was drawing near the end of his contract with Metro-Goldwyn-Mayer, he wrote to Perkins suggesting that three of his novels might be reprinted in one volume. *This Side of Paradise* would appear with a glossary that Fitzgerald planned to make of its absurdities and inaccuracies. *Gatsby* would be unchanged except for some corrections in the text. "But I am especially concerned about *Tender*," he added, "—that book is not dead. The *depth* of its appeal exists—I meet people constantly who have the same exclusive attachment to it as others had to *Gatsby* and *Paradise*, people who identified themselves with Dick Diver. Its great fault is that the *true* beginning—the young psychiatrist in Switzerland—is tucked away in the middle of the book."

The first edition of the novel had opened with the visit to the Cap d'Antibes of a young moving-picture actress, Rosemary Hoyt, and her meeting with the circle that surrounded the Richard Divers. It was the summer of 1925 and Antibes was enjoying its days of quiet glory. Rosemary had been entranced with the Divers and their friends, had fallen in love with Dick in a pleasantly hopeless fashion, and had become aware that there was some mystery about his wife. Then, on pages 151–212, the story had gone back to wartime Switzerland in order to explain the mystery by telling about Doctor Diver's courtship and marriage. Fitzgerald now proposed to rearrange the book in chronological order. "If pages 151–212 were taken from their present place and put at the start," he said in his letter to Perkins, "the improvement in appeal would be enormous."

It must have been about the same time that Fitzgerald made an entry in his notebook, outlining the changed order and dividing the novel into five books instead of three. The entry reads:

Analysis of *Tender:*

I	Case History	151–212	61 pps.	(change moon)	p. 212
II	Rosemary's Angle	3–104	101 pps.	P. 3	
III	Casualties	104–148, 213–224	55 pps.	(−2)	(120 & 121)
IV	Escape	225–306	82 pps.		
V	The Way Home	306–408	103 pps.	(−8)(332–341)	

I haven't been able to find the moon that was to be changed in Book I; perhaps Fitzgerald gave some special meaning to the word, and in any case it doesn't occur on 212. That was of course the last page of "Case History" and it had to be revised in order to prepare the reader for 3, which was the first page of Book II and also needed minor revisions. The page numbers in parenthesis— (120 & 121), (332–341) — were passages that the author planned to omit. All these changes were made in Fitzgerald's personal copy of *Tender Is the Night*, which is now in the manuscript room of the Princeton University Library. In that copy the pages are cut loose from the binding and rearranged as suggested in the notebook; but Fitzgerald had some afterthoughts while working over them. Pages 207–212, instead of being the last chapter of Book I, are now the beginning of Book II. The necessary small revisions are made on pages 3 and 212. Book III, the one he thought of as "Casualties," begins on 74, with the Divers' visit to the battlefield of the Somme — and it is a good beginning, too, since it sets the tone for what will follow. There are many small changes and corrections in the text, especially at the beginning of Book I. On the inside front cover Fitzgerald has written in pencil: "This is the *final version* of the book as I would like it."

The words "final version" are underlined, but they have to be taken as a statement of intention rather than as an accomplished fact. It is clear that Fitzgerald had other changes in mind besides his rearrangement of the narrative and the minor revisions already mentioned: he also planned to correct the text from beginning to end. One can see what he intended to do if one reads the first two chapters of the Princeton copy. There he has caught some of his errors in spelling proper names, has revised the punctuation to make it more logical, has sharpened a number of phrases, and has omitted others. Small as the changes are, they make the style smoother and remove the reader's occasional suspicion that the author had hesitated over a word or had failed to hear a name correctly. Near the end of Chapter II there is a pencilled asterisk and a note in Fitzgerald's handwriting: "This is my mark to say that I have made final corrections up to this point." Beyond the mark are a few other corrections but only of errors that happened to catch his eye.

It is too late now to make the changes in a phrasing that, as he said, "can throw a new emphasis or give a new value to the exact same scene or setting." It is not too late, however, to correct the mistakes in spelling and punctuation, and sometimes in grammar and chronology, that disfigure the first edition of *Tender.* On this mechanical level the book was full of errors; in fact, a combination of circumstances was required to get so many of them into one published volume. Fitzgerald had a fine ear for words, but a weak eye for them; he was possibly the worst speller who ever failed to graduate from Princeton. His punctuation was impulsive and his grammar more instinctive than reasoned. Maxwell Perkins, his editor, was better in all these departments but had an aristocratic disregard for details so long as a book was right in its feeling for life. Since Fitzgerald was regarded as one of his special authors, the manuscript was never copy-edited by others. The author received the proofs while his wife was critically ill. He worked over them for weeks, making extensive changes and omitting long passages, but he was in no state to notice his own errors of detail. Scores of them slipped into the first edition and, though they were unimportant if taken separately, I suspect that they had a cumulative effect on readers and ended by distracting their attention, like flaws in a window through which they were looking at the countryside. That the novel continued to be read in spite of the flaws was evidence of its lasting emotion and vitality.

Now that it is being reissued with Fitzgerald's changes I have tried to give it the sort of proofreading that the first edition failed to receive. I used dictionaries and Baedekers and consulted several of the author's friends; two or three of them had made their own lists of errors in the text. For a long time I hesitated over the two passages that Fitzgerald had marked for omission. One was the episode of the American newspaper vendor, on pages 120–121 of the first edition, and I ended by feeling that the pages could be dropped without much loss (although the newspaper vendor reappears on page 399 and once again serves as a herald of disaster). A longer omission was the Divers' visit to Mary Minghetti on pages 332–341. That change was not so easy to make, because it would have required an explanation in a later chapter of how the former Mary North had become very rich and a papal countess; besides, the episode is good in itself and that was a further reason for retaining it. Except in this instance I have tried to follow Fitzgerald's wishes at all points and to provide, so far as possible, the permanent text of a book that will continue to be read for a long time.

The question remains whether the final version as Fitzgerald would like it is also the best version of the novel. I was slow to make up my mind about it, perhaps out of affection for the book in its earlier form. The beginning of the first edition, with the Divers seen and admired through the innocent eyes of Rosemary Hoyt, is effective by any standards. Some of the effectiveness is lost in the new arrangement, where the reader already knows the truth about the Divers before Rosemary meets them. There is a mystery-story element in the earlier draft: something has passed between Nicole Diver and Mrs. McKisco that is shocking enough to cause a duel, and we read on to learn what Nicole has done or said. There is also the suggestion of a psychoanalytical case study: it is as if we were listening behind the analyst's door while his two patients, Nicole and Dick, help him to penetrate slowly beneath their glittering surfaces. But the mystery story ends when Rosemary discovers — on page 148 of the first edition — what Violet McKisco had seen in the bathroom at Villa Diana. The psychoanalytical case study is finished by page 212, when the reader has all the pertinent information about the past life of the Divers; but meanwhile half of the novel is still to come. The early critics of *Tender* were right when they said that it broke in two after Rosemary left the scene and that the first part failed to prepare us for what would follow. By rearranging the story in chronological order Fitzgerald tied it together. He sacrificed a brilliant beginning and all the element of mystery, but there is no escaping the judgment that he ended with a better constructed and more effective novel.

One fault of the earlier version was its uncertainty of focus. We weren't quite sure in reading it whether the author had intended to write about a whole group of Americans on the Riviera—that is, to make the book a social study with a collective hero—or whether he had intended to write a psychological novel about the glory and decline of Richard Diver as a person. Simply by changing the order of the story and starting with Diver as a young doctor in Zurich, Fitzgerald answered our hesitation. We are certain in reading the final version that the novel is psychological, that it is about Dick Diver, and that its social meanings are obtained by extension or synecdoche. Dick is the part that stands for the whole. He stands for other Americans on the Riviera, he stands for all the smart men who played too close to the line, he even stands for the age that was ending with the Wall Street crash, but first he stands for himself. The other characters are grouped around him in their subordinate roles: Rosemary sets in operation the forces waiting to destroy him, Abe North announces his fate, and Tommy Barban is his stronger and less talented successor. From beginning to end Dick is the center of the novel.

All this corresponds to the plan that Fitzgerald made early in 1932, after working for years on other plans and putting them aside. At first he had intended to write a short novel about a young man named Francis Melarky, a movie technician who visited the Riviera with his possessive mother. He met the Seth Pipers, a couple much like the Divers; he fell in love with the wife, followed them to Paris, went on a round of parties, and lost control of himself. The last chapters of this early draft are missing—if Fitzgerald ever wrote them—but it seems that Melarky was to kill his mother in a fit of rage, run away from the police, and then meet his own death—just how we aren't certain. In later versions of the story Melarky was somewhat less the central figure, while Abe Grant (later Abe North) and Seth Piper moved into the foreground. Then, at the beginning of 1932, Fitzgerald drew up the outline of a more ambitious book. "The novel should do this," he said in a memorandum to himself that was written at the time: "Show a man who is a natural idealist, a spoiled priest, giving in for various causes to the ideas of the haute bourgeoisie, and in his rise to the top of the social world losing his idealism, his talent and turning to drink and dissipation. Background one in which the leisure class is at their truly most brilliant and glamorous. . . ." In finishing the book Fitzgerald changed and deepened and complicated his picture of Dick Diver, but his statement of purpose is still the best short definition of the finished novel. His final revision brings the book even closer to the plan made in 1932.

It has to be said that Fitzgerald could never have revised *Tender* into the perfect novel that existed as an ideal in his mind. He had worked too long over it and his plans for it had changed too often, just as the author himself had changed in the years since his first summer on the Riviera. To make it all of a piece he would have had to start over from the beginning and invent a wholly new series of episodes, instead of trying to salvage as much as possible from the earlier versions. No matter how often he threw his material back into the melting pot, some of it would prove refractory to heat and would keep its former shape when poured into the new mould. The scenes written for Francis Melarky, then reassigned to Rosemary or Dick, would retain some marks of their origin. The whole Rosemary episode, being rewritten from the oldest chapters of the book, would be a little out of key with the story of Dick Diver as witnessed by himself and by his wife. But a novel has to be judged for what it gives us, not for its defects in execution, and *Tender* gives us an honesty of feeling, a complexity of life, that we miss in many books admired for being nearly perfect in form.

Moreover, in Fitzgerald's final revision it has a symmetry that we do not often find in long psychological novels. All the themes introduced in the first book are resolved in the last, and both books are written in the same key. In the first book young Doctor Diver is like Grant in his general store in Galena, waiting "to be called to an intricate destiny"; meanwhile he helps another psychiatrist with the case of Nicole Warren, a beautiful heiress suffering from schizophrenia, and learns that the Warrens have planned to buy a young doctor for her to marry. In the last book he finishes her cure, realizes that the Warrens have indeed purchased and used him — "That's what he was educated for," Nicole's sister says — and is left biding his time, "again like Grant in Galena," but with the difference that his one great adventure has ended. The Rosemary section of the novel no longer misleads our expectations; coming in the middle it simply adds fullness and relief to the story.

Although the new beginning is less brilliant than the older one, it prepares us for the end and helps us to appreciate the last section of the novel as we had probably failed to do on our first reading. That is the principal virtue of Fitzgerald's new arrangement. When I read *Tender* in 1934 it seemed to me as to many others that the Rosemary section was the best part of it. The writing there was of a type too seldom encountered in serious American fiction. It was not an attempt to analyze social values, show their falseness, tear them down — that is a necessary attempt at all times when values have become perverted, but it requires no special imaginative vitality and Fitzgerald was doing something more difficult: he was trying to discover and even create values in a society where they had seemed to be lacking. Rosemary with her special type of innocence offered the right point of view from which to reveal the grace and manners and apparent moral superiority of the Diver clan. The high point of her experience — and of the reader's — was the dinner at Villa Diana, when "The table seemed to have risen a little toward the sky like a mechanical dancing platform, giving the people around it a sense of being alone with each other in the dark universe, nourished by its only food, warmed by its only lights." Then came the underside of the Divers' little world, as revealed in Abe North's self-destructiveness and in what Violet McKisco had seen in the bathroom at Villa Diana, and everything that followed seemed a long anticlimax or at best the end of a different story.

Coming back to the novel long afterward and reading it in the new arrangement I had a different impression. The Rosemary section had its old charm and something new as well, for it now seemed the evocation of an age first condemned, then forgotten, and finally recalled with pleasure in the midst of harsher events; but the writing seemed to be on a lower level of intensity than the story of the hero's decay as told in the last section of the novel. That becomes the truly memorable passage: not Dick as the "organizer of private gaiety, curator of a richly incrusted happiness"; not Dick creating his group of friends and making them seem incredibly distinguished — "so bright a unit that Rosemary felt an impatient disregard for all who were not at their table"; but another Dick who has lost command of himself and deteriorates before our eyes in a strict progression from scene to scene. At this point Fitzgerald was right when he stopped telling the story from Dick's point of view and allowed us merely to guess at the hero's thoughts. Dick fades like a friend who is withdrawing into a private world or sinking to another level of society and, in spite of knowing so much about him, we are never quite certain of the reasons for his decline. Perhaps, as Fitzgerald first planned, it was the standards of the leisure class that corrupted him; perhaps it was the strain of curing a psychotic wife, who gains strength as he loses it by a mysterious transfer of vitality; perhaps it was a form of emotional exhaustion, a giving of himself so generously that he went beyond his resources, "like a man overdrawing at his bank," as Fitzgerald would later say of his own crack-up; or perhaps it was something far back in his childhood that could only be discovered by deep analysis — we can argue about the causes as we can argue about the decline of a once-intimate friend, without coming to any fixed conclusion; but the point is that we always believe in Dick and in his progress in a circle from obscurity to obscurity. With our last glimpse of him, swaying a little as he stands on a high terrace and makes a papal cross over the beach that he had found and peopled and that has now rejected him, his fate is accomplished and the circle closed.

Fitzgerald's Brave New World   Edwin Fussell*

Think of the lost ecstasy of the Elizabethans. "Oh my America, my new found land," think of what it meant to them and of what it means to us.

(T. E. Hulme, *Speculations*)

I

The source of Fitzgerald's excellence is an uncanny ability to juxtapose the sensibilities implied by the phrase "romantic wonder" with the most conspicuous, as well as the most deeply significant, phenomena of American civilization, and to deprive from that juxtaposition a moral critique of human nature. None of our major writers is more romantically empathic than this avatar of Keats in the era of Harding; none draws a steadier bead on the characteristic shortcomings, not to say disasters, of the most grandiose social experiment of modern times. Thence the implacable moralist with stars (Martinis) in his eyes: worshipper, analyst, judge, and poet. But it is not very illuminating to say that Fitzgerald wrote the story of his own representative life, unless we are prepared to read his confessions — and then his evaluation of those confessions — as American history; and unless we reciprocally learn to read American history as the tale of the romantic imagination in the United States.

Roughly speaking, Fitzgerald's basic plot is the history of the New World (ironic *double entendre* here and throughout); more precisely, of the human imagination in the New World. It shows itself in two predominant patterns, quest and seduction. The quest is the search for romantic wonder (a kind of febrile secular beatitude), in the terms proposed by contemporary America; the seduction represents capitulation to these terms. Obversely, the quest is a flight: from reality, from normality, from time, fate, death, and the conception of *limit*. In the social realm, the pattern of desire may be suggested by such phrases as "the American dream" and "the pursuit of happiness." Fitzgerald begins by exposing the corruption of that dream in industrial America; he ends by discovering that the pursuit is universally seductive and perpetually damned. Driven by inner forces that compel him towards the personal realization of romantic wonder, the Fitzgerald hero is destroyed by the materials which the American experience offers as objects and criteria of passion; or, at best, he is purged of these unholy fires, chastened, and reduced.

In general, this quest has two symptomatic goals. There is, for one,

*Reprinted from Frederick J. Hoffman, ed., *The Great Gatsby: A Study* (New York: Charles Scribner's Sons, 1962), pp. 244–62. This selection is taken from pp. 244–47, 254–62 and is included among works of the 1950s because it appeared originally in slightly different form in *English Literary History* 19 (December 1952): 291–306.

the search for eternal youth and beauty, what might be called the historic myth of Ponce de Leon. ("Historic" because the man was really looking for a fountain; "myth" because no such fountain ever existed).[1] The essence of romantic wonder appears to reside in the illusion of perennial youth and grace and happiness surrounding the leisure class of which Fitzgerald customarily wrote; thus the man of imagination in America, searching for the source of satisfaction of his deepest aesthetic needs, is seduced by the delusion that these qualities are actually to be found in people who, in sober fact, are vacuous and irresponsible. But further, this kind of romantic quest, which implies both escape and destruction, is equated on the level of national ideology with a transcendental and Utopian contempt for time and history, and on the religious level, which Fitzgerald (whose Catholic apostasy was about half genuine and half imagined) persistently but hesitantly approaches, with a blasphemous rejection of the very conditions of human existence.

The second goal is, simply enough, money. The search for wealth is the familiar Anglo-Saxon Protestant ideal of personal material success, most succinctly embodied for our culture in the saga of young Benjamin Franklin. It is the romantic assumption of this aspect of the "American dream" that all the magic of the world can be had for money. Both from a moral, and from a highly personal and idiosyncratic Marxist standpoint, Fitzgerald examines and condemns the plutocratic ambitions of American life and the ruinous price exacted by their lure. But the two dreams are, of course, so intimately related as to be for all practical purposes one: the appearance of eternal youth and beauty centers in a particular social class whose glamor is made possible by social inequality and inequity. Beauty, the presumed object of aesthetic contemplation, is commercialized, love is bought and sold. Money is the means to the violent recovery or specious arrest of an enchanting youth.

In muted contrast, Fitzgerald repeatedly affirms his faith in an older, simpler America, generally identified as pre-Civil War; the emotion is that of pastoral, the social connotations agrarian and democratic. In such areas he continues to find fragments of basic human value, social, moral, and religious. But these affirmations are for the most part subordinate and indirect; Fitzgerald's attention was chiefly directed upon the merchandise of romantic wonder proferred by his own time and place. Like the narrator in *Gatsby*, he was always "within and without, simultaneously enchanted and repelled by the inexhaustible variety of life." Through a delicate and exact imagery, he was able to extend this attitude of simultaneous enchantment and repulsion over the whole of the American civilization he knew. His keenest perception, and the one that told most heavily for his fiction, was the universal quality of the patterns he was tracing, his greatest discovery that there was nothing new about the Lost Generation except its particular toys. The quest for romantic wonder and the inevitable failure were only the latest in a long series. . . .

Tender Is the Night (1934) restates the essential theme and complicates it. If this novel seems somehow less successful than *Gatsby*, that is perhaps because the greater proliferation of thematic statement is not matched by a corresponding gain in clarity and control. But beneath the additional richness, and apparent confusion, the same general story can be made out. Dick Diver is like Gatsby the American as man of imagination. His chief difference from Gatsby is that he dispenses romantic wonder to others, in addition to living by and for it himself. Gatsby tries to purvey dreams, but doesn't know how. But to Rosemary Hoyt (of whom, more later) Dick's "voice promised that he would . . . open up whole *new worlds* for her, unroll an endless succession of magnificent possibilities" (my italics). Diver is the man with the innate capacity for romantic wonder, temporarily a member of the American leisure class of the 'twenties, and "organizer of private gaiety, curator of richly incrusted happiness." His intellectual and imaginative energies have been diverted from normal creative and functional channels and expended on the effort to prevent, for a handful of the very rich, the American dream from revealing its nightmarish realities.

Although Dick is given a more specific background than Gatsby, he is equally a product of his civilization and shares its characteristic deficiencies: "the illusions of eternal strength and health, and of the essential goodness of people; illusions of a nation, the lies of generations of frontier mothers who had to croon falsely that there were no wolves outside the cabin door." (The lies also of generations of American politicians, historians, publicists, fireside poets, and similar confidence-men, who had no such easy excuse). This inherent romantic has been further weakened, though not quite destroyed, by the particular forms of sentimentality of his own generation: "he must press on toward the Isles of Greece, the cloudy waters of unfamiliar ports, the lost girl on shore, the moon of popular songs. A part of Dick's mind was made up of the tawdry souvenirs of his boyhood. Yet in that somewhat littered Five-and-Ten, he had managed to keep alive the low painful fire of intelligence."

Such is the man, potentially noble like Gatsby, but with the fatal flaw of imagination common to and conditioned by the superficial symbols and motivations of his culture, who is brought against the conditions of temptation represented by Nicole. She is the granddaughter of a "self-made American capitalist" and of a German Count, and her family is placed in perspective by Fitzgerald's frequent analogies with feudal aristocracy. "Her father would have it on almost any clergyman," such as Dick's father; "they were an American ducal family without a title—the very name . . . caused a psychological metamorphosis in people." Yet behind this facade of glamor and power lies unnatural lust and perversion. Nicole's father, this "fine American type," has committed incest with his daughter—the very incarnation of the American vision of youth, beauty, and wealth — and made of her a psychotic for young Dr. Diver to cure. As Nicole says, " 'I'm a crook by heritage.' "

Through Nicole Fitzgerald conveys, as he had with Daisy, all that is sexually and socially desirable in youth and beauty: "there were all the potentialities for romantic love in that lovely body and in the delicate mouth. . . . Nicole had been a beauty as a young girl and she would be a beauty later." Apparently she is eternally youthful, and only at the end of the novel is it discernible that she has aged. Her face, which corresponds in sensuous utility to Daisy's voice, is lovely and hard, "her eyes brave and watchful, looking straight ahead toward nothing." She is an empty child, representative of her social class, of the manners and morals of the 'twenties, and of the world of values for which America, like Diver, was once more selling its soul. But it is chiefly Nicole's semblance of perpetual youth that allows Fitzgerald to exploit her as a central element in the narrative correlative he is constructing for his vision of American life. Occasionally he handles her in a way that goes beyond social criticism, entering, if obliquely and implicitly, the realm of religious apprehension:

> The only physical disparity between Nicole at present and the Nicole of five years before was simply that she was no longer a young girl. But she was enough ridden by the current youth worship, the moving pictures with their myriad faces of girl-children, blandly represented as carrying on the work and wisdom of the world, to feel a jealousy of youth.
>
> She put on the first ankle-length day dress that she had owned for many years, and crossed herself reverently with Chanel Sixteen.

(So Diver, at the end of the novel, but with full consciousness of the blasphemy, "blesses" the Riviera beach "with a papal cross," immediately before returning to the obscurity of small-town America. The malediction may by a later generation of readers be taken as Fitzgerald's also, whose equally obscure end was ironically to come in the most notorious of American small towns. Hollywood.) But while Fitzgerald could upon occasion thus extend the significance of his narrative, he never neglected to keep it firmly grounded in a specific social and economic world, and it is in this realm that most of his correspondences are established:

> Nicole was the product of much ingenuity and toil. For her sake trains began their run at Chicago and traversed the round belly of the continent to California; chicle factories fumed and link belts grew link by link in factories; men mixed toothpaste in vats and drew mouthwash out of copper hogsheads; girls canned tomatoes quickly in August or worked rudely at the Five-and-Tens on Christmas Eve; half-breed Indians toiled on Brazilian coffee plantations and dreamers were muscled out of patent rights in new tractors — these were some of the people who gave a tithe to Nicole, and as the whole system swayed and thundered onward it lent a feverish bloom to such processes of hers as wholesale buying, like the flush of a fireman's face holding his post

before a spreading blaze. She illustrated very simple principles, containing in herself her own doom, but illustrated them so accurately that there was grace in the procedure.[2]

Yet even here religious nuance continues ("Christmas Eve," "tithe"); the simple principles Nicole illustrates are not only Marxian but also Christian. Still, if her principles are simple, their illustration is epic in scope and intention. The social ramifications of Fitzgerald's great novels are broad indeed; at their base are criminal injustice and inhuman waste, on a world-wide scale, and at their apex the American girl, the king's daughter, beautiful, forever young, and insane.

In the central scenes of temptation (Book II, chapter V, in the original form), Fitzgerald quite deliberately allows Nicole to assume her full symbolic significance, thereby revealing unmistakably that the central action of *Tender Is the Night* must be read against the broadest background of American life. Throughout this chapter runs the *leitmotif* of the author's generalizing commentary, beginning with the passage: "the impression of her youth and beauty grew on Dick until it welled up inside him in a compact paroxysm of emotion. She smiled, a moving childish smile that was like all the lost youth in the world." This mood of pathetic nostalgia is quickly objectified in the talk of Dick and Nicole about American popular songs; soon Dick feels that "there was that excitement about her that seemed to reflect all the excitement of the world." So ends the first of the two scenes that comprise this chapter. The second meeting opens on a similar key: "Dick wished she had no background, that she was just a girl lost with no address save the night from which they had come." This time they play the songs they had mentioned the week before: "they were in America now." And Fitzgerald drives the point home in his last sentence: "Now there was this scarcely saved waif of disaster bringing him the essence of a continent. . . ."

At first Dick laughs off the notion that Nicole's family has purchased him, but he gradually succumbs, "inundated by a trickling of goods and money." Once again, Nicole is the typifying object of her class and society, especially in the terms she proposes for the destruction of her victim's moral and intellectual integrity: "Naturally Nicole, *wanting to own him, wanting him to stand still forever*, encouraged any slackness on his part" (my italics). Although the pattern is more complex than in *Gatsby*, practically the same controlling lines of theme can be observed. The man of imagination, fed on the emotions of romantic wonder, is tempted and seduced and (in this case, nearly) destroyed by that American dream which customarily takes two forms: the escape from time and the materialistic pursuit of a purely hedonistic happiness. On the historical level, the critique is of the error of American romanticism in attempting to transcend and thus escape historical responsibility. On the economic level, the critique is of the fatal beauty of American capitalism, its destructive charm and recklessness. Thematically, the lines come together when

Nicole attempts to own Dick and therefore to escape time — keeping him clear of it, too — as when Gatsby tries to buy back the past. On the religious level, if indeed there is one, the critique must be defined more cautiously: perhaps one can say that Fitzgerald intermittently insinuates the possibility that human kind are inveterately prone to befuddle themselves with the conspicuous similarities between the city of man and the city of God, paying scant attention to their more radical difference.

In Rosemary Hoyt, who brings from Hollywood to Europe the latest American version of the dream of youthful innocence, Fitzgerald has still another important center of consciousness. It is through her eyes, for instance, that Fitzgerald gives us his first elaborate glimpses of the Divers, and their hangers-on, at the Americanized Riviera. Because of Rosemary's acute but undisciplined perceptions, Fitzgerald can insist perpetually on the ironic tensions between the richest texture of social appearance and the hidden reality of moral agony: her "naïveté responded whole-heartedly to the expensive simplicity of the Divers, unaware of its complexity and its lack of innocence, unaware that it was all a selection of quality rather than quantity from the run of the world's bazaar; and that the simplicity of behavior also, the nursery-like peace and good-will, the emphasis on the simpler virtues, was part of a desperate bargain with the gods and had been attained through struggles she could not have guessed at." (Nursery-like peace and good will" is a good example of how Fitzgerald's subtly paradoxical prose style incessantly supplies the kind of religious-secular befuddlement alluded to above).

Rosemary manifests the effects of Hollywood sentimentality and meretriciousness on the powers of American perception and imagination. The image-patterns that surround her movements are largely concerned with childhood; she is "as dewy with belief as a child from one of Mrs. Burnett's vicious tracts." Immature and egocentric, she provides one more symbol of the corruption of imagination in American civilization; both deluded and deluding, she is without resources for escape such as are available to Nick Carraway and, to a considerably lesser extent, Dick Diver. It is Diver who sounds the last important note about her: " 'Rosemary didn't grow up.' " That she is intended as a representative figure Fitzgerald makes amply clear in his embittered account of her picture "Daddy's Girl": "There she was — *so* young and innocent — the product of her mother's loving care . . . embodying all the immaturity of the race, cutting a new cardboard paper doll to pass before its empty harlot's mind."

Nicole and Rosemary are for this novel the objectified images of Fitzgerald's "brave new world." Only occasionally, and only in pathos, does Dick Diver escape the limits of this terrifying world. Once, the three of them are sitting in a restaurant, and Dick notices a group of "gold star mothers": "in their happy faces, the dignity that surrounded and pervaded the party, he perceived all the maturity of an older America. For a while the sobered women who had come to mourn for their dead, for something they could not repair, made the room beautiful. Momentarily, he sat again on his father's knee, riding with Moseby while the old loyalties and devotions fought on around him. Almost with an effort he turned back to his two women at the table and faced the whole new world in which he believed." Only as this illusion fades, to the accompaniment of an almost unbearable "interior laughter," does Dick Diver achieve a minimal and ambiguous salvation, a few shattered fragments of reality, including the anonymity of professional and social failure.

For purposes of corroboration, one can add a certain amount of documentation from Fitzgerald's non-fictional writings, as collected in the posthumous volume *The Crack-Up* (1945). The point that most needs buttressing, probably, is that Fitzgerald saw in the quest for romantic wonder a recurrent pattern of American behavior. Such an attitude seems strongly implied by the works of fiction, but of course it is additionally reassuring to find Fitzgerald writing his daughter: "You speak of how good your generation is, but I think they share with every generation since the Civil War in America the sense of being somehow about to inherit the earth. You've heard me say before that I think the faces of most American women over thirty are relief maps of petulant and bewildered unhappiness" (p. 306). A brief sketch of a "typical product of our generation" in the *Note-Books* indicates further what qualities were involved in this "sense of being about to inherit the earth": "her dominant idea and goal is freedom without responsibility, which is like gold without metal, spring without winter, youth without age, one of those maddening, coo-coo mirages of wild riches" (p. 166). That this personal attitude, translated into the broader terms of a whole culture, represented a negation of historical responsibility, is made sufficiently clear in another *Note-Book* passage: "Americans, he liked to say, should be born with fins, and perhaps they were — perhaps money was a form of fin. In England, property begot a strong place sense, but Americans, restless and with shallow roots, needed fins and wings. There was even a recurrent idea in America about an education that would leave out history and the past, that should be a sort of equipment for aerial adventure, weighed down by none of the stowaways of inheritance or tradition" (p. 109). Still another passage, this time from one of the "Crack-Up" essays, makes it equally clear that Fitzgerald habitually saw the universal applicability of all he was saying about the ruling passions of America: "This is what I think now: that the natural state of the sentient adult is a qualified unhappiness. I think also that in an adult the desire to be finer in grain than you are, 'a constant striving' (as those people say who gain their bread by saying it) only adds to this unhappiness in the end — that end that comes to our youth and hope" (p. 84).

Fortunately, by some kind of unexplained miracle (perhaps nothing more mysterious than his deep-seated integrity as a writer), Fitzgerald did not have it in himself to be a cynic. For all the failure and futility he found in the American experience, his attitude was an attitude of acceptance, remarkably free of that sense of despair with Kierkegaard correctly prophesied as the typical sin of the moderns. There was always in him something of Jimmy Gatz's "extraordinary gift of hope," which enabled him to touch the subjects he touched without being consumed by them. (The tragedies of his personal life are another matter; I am speaking only of his heroism and integrity as an artist.) The exhaustion of the frontier and the rebound of the post-war expatriate movement marked for him the end of a long period in human history and it was really this entire period, the history of the post-Renaissance man in America, that he made the substance of his works. After exploring his materials to their limits Fitzgerald knew, at his greatest moments, that he had discovered a universal pattern of desire and belief and behavior, and that in it was compounded the imaginative history of modern, especially American, civilization. Thus (again from the *Note-Books*):

> He felt then that if the pilgrimage eastward of the rare poisonous flower of his race was the end of the adventure which had started westward three hundred years ago, if the long serpent of the curiosity had turned too sharp upon itself, cramping its bowels, bursting its shining skin, at least there had been a journey; like to the satisfaction of a man coming to die — one of those human things that one can never understand unless one has made such a journey and heard the man give thanks with the husbanded breath. The frontiers were gone — there were no more barbarians. The short gallop of the last great race, the polyglot, the hated and the despised, the crass and scorned, had gone — at least it was not a meaningless extinction up an alley (p. 199).

There are dozens more such passages, in the non-fictional prose as in the fictional; naturally, for Fitzgerald's subject, however broadly he came to understand it, was in the first instance his own journey. He was by nature almost incredibly sympathetic. He was also more knowledgeable — both morally and intellectually — than he is generally credited with being. To such an extent that his more enthusiastic readers are almost tempted to say: if the polyglot gallop is not a meaningless cancellation of itself, that is chiefly because Fitzgerald — and the few Americans who by virtue of their imaginative grasp of our history can rightly be called his peers — interposed a critical distance between his matter and his expression of it. There is perhaps more difference between an ordinary understanding of America and Fitzgerald's than between the gaudy idealizations of the Elizabethans and the equally comfortable cynicism of twentieth-century London.

Notes

1. It is a curious but far from meaningless coincidence that Frederick Jackson Turner used the image of "a magic fountain of youth" to evoke the creative and restorative powers of

the unexhausted Western frontier. I am inclined to think Fitzgerald knew what he was about when he called *The Great Gatsby* "a story of the West." Traditionally in American writing "the West" means both the Western part of the United States and the New World, and especially the first as synecdoche of the other.

2. Cf. Gatsby as seismograph. Probably it is dangerous to take too literally Fitzgerald's remark that he was "essentially Marxian"; it seems to me equally dangerous to ignore it altogether.

"Daddy's Girl": Symbol and Theme in *Tender Is the Night*   Robert Stanton*

Francis Scott Fitzgerald has come a long way from the limbo into which some of his obituaries tried to thrust him in 1941; his return has been marked and encouraged by several important editions of his stories, novels, and articles, an outstanding biography, and a gradually increasing supply of critical articles. Fortunately, although the interest in his writing still stems largely from the excitement of the 1920's and the glamour and pathos of the author's life, his critics have become increasingly willing to view him — as they must, if his reputation is not to decline again — as an artist and craftsman.

The purpose of this article is to examine one of the major artistic devices used in *Tender Is the Night*. It will show that the novel contains a large number of "incest-motifs," which, properly understood, take on symbolic value and contribute to the thematic unity of the novel. The term "incest-motifs" may seem ill-chosen at first, since most of these passages allude, not to consanguineous lovers, but to a mature man's love for an immature girl. I have used the term chiefly because the first of these passages concerns Devereux Warren's incestuous relation with his fifteen-year-old daughter Nicole, so that whenever Fitzgerald later associates a mature man with an immature girl, the reader's reaction is strongly conditioned by this earlier event. Devereux's act is the most obvious, and the only literal, example of incest in the novel. It is of basic importance to the plot, since it causes Nicole's schizophrenia and thus necessitates her treatment in Dr. Dohmler's clinic, where she meets Dick Diver. Nicole's love for Dick is in part a "transference" caused by her mental disorder; the character of their marriage is dictated largely by the requirements of her condition.

In spite of the importance of Devereux' act, the use of incest as *motif* is more evident in the fact that Dick, Nicole's husband and psychiatrist, falls in love with a young actress whose most famous film is entitled

*Reprinted from *Modern Fiction Studies* 4 (Summer 1958): 136–42. © Purdue Research Foundation. Reprinted with permission.

Daddy's Girl. As this coincidence suggests, Fitzgerald deliberately gives an incestuous overtone to the relationship between Dick Diver and Rosemary Hoyt. Like Rosemary's father, Dick is of Irish descent and has been an American army doctor, a captain. At his dinner-party on the Riviera, he speaks to Rosemary "with a lightness seeming to conceal a paternal interest."[1] He calls her "a lovely child" just before kissing her for the first time, and in the Paris hotel he says, again with a "paternal attitude," "When you smile . . . I always think I'll see a gap where you've lost some baby teeth" (124, 125). Dick is thirty-four, twice Rosemary's age, and to emphasize this, Fitzgerald continually stresses Rosemary's immaturity. When she first appears in 1925, her cheeks suggest "the thrilling flush of children after their cold baths in the evening" (58–59); "her body hovered delicately on the last edge of childhood—she was almost eighteen, nearly complete, but the dew was still on her" (59). She and her mother are like "prize-winning school-children" (59). Even Nicole pointedly refers to Rosemary as a child (161).

By the time of Abe North's departure, Dick admittedly loves Rosemary; now, "he wanted to . . . remove the whole affair from the nursery footing upon which Rosemary persistently established it"; but he realizes that Rosemary "had her hand on the lever more authoritatively than he" (146, 147). Helpless as is, he remains conscious—even over-conscious—of the incongruity of the situation; he tells Rosemary, "When a child can disturb a middle-aged gent—things get difficult" (154). Finally he tells Nicole that Rosemary is "an infant. . . there's a persistent aroma of the nursery" (179).

After Rosemary leaves the Riviera, Dick begins to exaggerate the immaturity of *other* women as well. He is uneasy when Nicole suggests that he dance with a teen-age girl at St. Moritz, and protests, "I don't like ickle durls. They smell of castile soap and peppermint. When I dance with them, I feel as if I'm pushing a baby carriage" (188). He looks at a pretty woman, and thinks, "Strange children should smile at each other and say, 'Let's play'" (219). Gradually an obscure sense of guilt appears. When Nicole accuses him, falsely and irrationally, of seducing a patient's daughter—"a child," she says, "not more than fifteen"—he feels guilty (206). When he is being taken to court after the taxi-driver fight, a crowd boos him, mistaking him for a man who has raped and slain a five-year-old child; later that day Dick cries, "I want to make a speech. . . . I want to explain to these people how I raped a five-year-old girl. Maybe I did—" (253).

As his decline continues, Dick's attitude toward his own children, Topsy and Lanier, begins to change. In Rome, he decides that Rosemary "was young and magnetic, but so was Topsy" (225). When Nicole realizes that his aquaplaning at the Riviera is inspired by Rosemary's "exciting youth," she remembers that "she had seen him draw the same inspiration from the new bodies of his children. . . ." (301). Earlier, Dick has exclaimed, "What do I care whether Topsy 'adores' me or not? I'm not bringing her up to be my wife" (276), apparently assuming that the love of a child does not differ essentially from the love of an adult; he jokes with Lanier about "a new law in France that you can divorce a child" (283). Finally, late in the novel Nicole notices his "almost unnatural interest in the children" (286).

The presence of these incest-motifs may be explained in several ways. First, they may have been suggested, if only slightly and indirectly, by Fitzgerald's own ambivalent attitudes toward his mother and his daughter. He vacillated between being ashamed of his mother and devoted to her;[2] one of the early titles for *Tender Is the Night* was *The Boy Who Killed His Mother*. According to his biographer, with his daughter Scottie, Fitzgerald was alternately "the severe father, the difficult alcoholic, and the man who loved his child intensely."[3] But opposing this explanation is the fact that incest is not mentioned in his other works, and only "Babylon Revisited" and "The Baby Party" concern the love of father for daughter.

In any case, the incest-motifs may be fully accounted for by *Tender Is the Night* itself. Most of them grow logically out of Dick's relationship to Nicole. When Nicole first begins writing to Dick, she still pathologically mistrusts all men; her first letter to him speaks of his "attitude base and criminal and not even faintly what I had been taught to associate with the rôle of gentleman" (10). Gradually Dick begins to take the place once occupied by her father, as a center of trust and security. As a psychiatrist, Dick realizes the value of this situation; he also realizes that Nicole must eventually build up her *own* world. After her psychotic attack at the Agiri fair, for example, he says, "You can help yourself most," and refuses to accept the father-role into which she tries to force him (207). But this sort of refusal costs him a difficult and not always successful effort of will. First, loving Nicole, "he could not watch her disintegrations without participating in them" (207). Second, he is by nature a "spoiled priest," the father for all of his friends; he creates the moral universe in which they live. His nature and his love oppose his profession. It is therefore plausible, once his character begins to crumble, that he compensates for his long self-denial by falling in love with a girl literally young enough to be his daughter; that after the crowd has booed him for raping a five-year-old girl, he makes a mock-confession; and that when Nicole accuses him of seducing a patient's fifteen-year-old daughter, "He had a sense of guilt, as in one of those nightmares where we are accused of a crime which we recognize as something undeniably experienced, but which upon waking we realize we have not committed" (206).

Ironically, although Dick's fascination with immaturity gives him an opportunity to be both lover and father, it also reveals his own fundamental immaturity. Like Nicole, who responds to Tommy Barban because she sees her own hardness and unscrupulousness reflected in his character, and like Rosemary, who responds to Dick at first because of his "self-control and . . . self-discipline, her own virtues" (75), Dick is attracted to Rosemary's immaturity partly because of a corresponding quality within himself. Behind his facade of self-discipline, this central immaturity appears in the obsessive phrase, "Do you mind if I pull down the curtain?" Rosemary calls him "Youngster" (171, 227), "the youngest person in the world" (154), and while he waits for Rosemary outside her studio, he circles the block "with the fatuousness of one of Tarkington's adolescents" (152). When Abe North talks to Nicole in the railroad station, Fitzgerald says, "Often a man can play the helpless child in front of a woman, but he can almost never bring it off when he feels most like a helpless child" (143); similarly, when Dick talks to Mary Minghetti just before leaving the Riviera, "his eyes, for the moment clear as a child's, asked her sympathy. . . ." (332).

The significance of the incest-motifs is not limited to Dick's personal disaster. After all, they do not all *issue* from him. It is not of Dick's doing that a patient accuses him of seducing her fifteen-year-old daughter or that a crowd boos him for raping a five-year-old girl. And except for Devereux Warren's act, the most conspicuous incest-motif in the novel is the motion picture for which Rosemary is famous, *Daddy's Girl*. Everyone, we are told, has seen it; and lest we miss the point of the title, we are given Dick's reaction to the final scene of the picture, "a lovely shot of Rosemary and her parent united at the last in a father complex so apparent that Dick winced for all psychologists at the vicious sentimentality" (131). As the universal popularity of *Daddy's Girl* suggests, the incest-motifs symbolize a world-wide situation. In 1934, C. Hartley Grattan wrote of the relation between Nicole and her father, "Fitzgerald has tried to use this situation, this extreme (according to our tabus) example of decadence, to symbolize the rottenness of the society of which Nicole is a part."[4] But the meaning of the repeated motif is both broader and more precise than this.

During the 1920's, the relationship between the prewar and post-war generations was curiously reversed. In Mark Sullivan's words, "The Twenties, reversing age-old custom, Biblical precept and familiar adage, was a period in which, in many respects, youth was the model, age the imitator. On the dance-floor, in the beauty parlor, on the golf course; in clothes, manners, and many points of view, elders strove earnestly to look and act like their children, in many cases their grand-children."[5] And Frederick Lewis Allen notes that "the women of this decade worshipped not merely youth, but unripened youth. . . ."[6] That Fitzgerald agreed with this interpretation of the period is evident from a late essay in which he described the Jazz Age as "a children's party taken over by the elders. . . . By 1923 [the] elders, tired of watching the carnival with ill-concealed envy, had discovered that young liquor will take the place of young blood, and with a whoop the orgy began."[7]

Here, on a world-scale, is Dick Diver's fascination with immaturity;

and since the younger generation is the child of the elder, here is a situation to which the incest-motifs are relevant. Dick Diver's generation is older than Rosemary's, and he is the product of an older generation still, his minister-father's, with its stress upon " 'good instincts,' honor, courtesy, and courage."[8] Rosemary is the product of Hollywood, with its emphasis upon the future, and we are told that in *Daddy's Girl* she embodies "all the immaturity of the race" (130). In embracing Rosemary, therefore, Dick Diver is a symbol of America and Europe turning from a disciplined and dedicated life to a life of self-indulgence, dissipation, and moral anarchy — a symbol of the parent generation infatuated with its own offspring. Dick's collapse, appropriately, occurs in 1929.

Even aside from Dick's relationship with Rosemary, there are many hints that he is gradually shifting allegiance from the past culture of his father to an unworthy future. In the beginning, he exhibits dignity and self-discipline, unfailing courtesy, and a firm (if unexpressed) moral code; before the novel is over, he has been beaten in a brawl with taxi-drivers, has insulted his friend Mary Minghetti, and, at the very end, has been forced to leave Lockport, New York, because he "became entangled with a girl who worked in a grocery store" (334). To clarify this change, Fitzgerald underlines it in several passages. The most memorable example is Dick's remark at his father's grave, "Good-bye my father — good-bye, all my fathers"; later, as he enters the steamship to return to Europe, he is described as hurrying from the past into the future (222). But this is only his formal farewell to something he has long since left behind. Most of the allusions to the shift occur four years earlier, during the episode in which Dick falls in love with Rosemary. At the battlefield near Amiens, he tells Rosemary that the "whole-souled sentimental equipment" of the past generations was all spent in World War I (118). Next day, he takes her to the Cardinal de Metz's palace: the threshold of the palace connects the past without (the stone facade) to the future within (blue steel and mirrors), and crossing that threshold is an experience "perverted as a breakfast of oatmeal and hashish" (133). Just after leaving the palace, Dick admits for the first time that he loves Rosemary. Next day, his attempt to visit Rosemary at her studio is explicitly labelled "an overthrowing of his past" (152). And on the following day, in the hotel dining room, although Dick sees in the gold-star mothers "all the maturity of an older America," and remembers his father and his "old loyalties and devotions," he turns back to Rosemary and Nicole, the "whole new world in which he believed" (162). It is worth noticing that at both the beginning and end of this episode, Fitzgerald emphasizes Rosemary's significance by placing her beside the memory of World War I.

One reason for the broad applicability of the incest-motif is its inherent complexity: it simultaneously represents a situation and expresses Fitzgerald's judgment of it. First, it suggests how appealing youth can be (whether as person or as quality) to the adult in whom the long-opposed edges of impulse and self-restraint have begun to dull. He longs not only for youth's vitality but for its innocence, which apparently confers moral freedom. In the first flush of love, Dick and Rosemary seem to share "an extraordinary innocence, as though a series of pure accidents had driven them together, so many accidents that at last they were forced to conclude that they were for each other. They had arrived with clean hands, or so it seemed, after no traffic with the merely curious and clandestine" (136). Similarly, most of the rebels of the Twenties sought not merely to discard the Victorian morality but to do so without any aftermath of guilt—to recapture the amorality of youth. But the incest-motif also suggests decadence and the violation of a universal taboo—particularly since in *Tender Is the Night* it appears first as the cause of Nicole's insanity—and thus indicates that the unconscious innocence of youth is forever lost to the adult, and that in searching for it he may find disaster: "that madness akin to the love of an aging man for a young girl."[9]

The purpose of this study has been to give a glimpse to Fitzgerald's artistry by examining one of the major patterns in *Tender Is the Night*. The incest-motifs, as we have seen, help to unify the novel on several levels, as well as to show how those levels are interrelated. First, these motifs function literally as one result of Dick's relationship to Nicole; they are symptoms of his psychological disintegration. Second, they both exemplify and symbolize Dick's loss of allegiance to the moral code of his father. Finally, by including such details as *Daddy's Girl* as well as Dick's experience, they symbolize a social situation existing throughout Europe and America during the Twenties. Fitzgerald's ability to employ this sort of device shows clearly that he not only felt his experience intensely, but *understood* it as an artist, so that he could reproduce its central patterns within the forms and symbols of his work. His experience transcends the historical Fitzgerald who felt it and the historical Twenties in which it occurred, and emerges as art.

Notes

1. *Tender Is the Night*, in *Three Novels of F. Scott Fitzgerald* ed. Malcom Cowley & Edmund Wilson (N.Y., 1953), p. 85.

2. Arthur Mizener, *The Far Side of Paradise: A Biography of F. Scott Fitzgerald* (Cambridge, Mass., 1951), p. 8.

3. Mizener, *The Far Side of Paradise*, p. 261.

4. *F. Scott Fitzgerald: The Man and His Work*, ed. Alfred Kazin (Cleveland, 1951), p. 105.

5. *Our Times: The United States 1900–1925*, Vol. VI: *The Twenties* (N.Y., 1935), pp. 385–86.

6. *Only Yesterday* (N.Y., 1931), p. 108.

7. "Echoes of the Jazz Age," *The Crack-Up*, ed. Edmund Wilson (N.Y., 1945), p. 15.

8. P. 221. Arthur Mizener discusses Dick as inheritor of the past in *The Far Side of Paradise*, pp. 243–44; for a discussion of the extent to which Fitzgerald's image of Dick's

father as the "symbol . . . of an ideal moral order" was based upon his own father, see Henry Dan Piper, "F. Scott Fitzgerald and the Image of His Father," *PULC*, XII (1951), 181–86.

9. *The Last Tycoon*, in *Three Novels*, p. 116.

The 1960s

The "Intricate Destiny" of Dick Diver
Eugene White*

The usual reading of F. Scott Fitzgerald's *Tender Is The Night* makes the hero, Dr. Richard Diver, something less than heroic and considerably less than a tragic figure. He is a brilliant psychiatrist whose life is ruined because he falls in love with the wrong woman and because his vitality is sapped by the abundance of the Warren money.[1] It seems to me, however, that another and more satisfying reading is possible and that careful attention to certain key passages in the novel makes such a reading plausible, if not inevitable. Therefore, I should like to offer support for the theory that Dick Diver is a man who because of his deep love for Nicole Warren makes a deliberate choice with full realization of the dilemma which it will eventually force upon him. And when the dilemma must be resolved, he chooses what is best for Nicole even though it brings heartbreak to him.

As a psychiatrist he knows the pattern which Nicole's life will follow, he knows what marriage to her would mean. Moreover, to make certain that there is no illusion, his colleagues and mentors Franz and Dohmler are there to tell him bluntly that he must break with her. When they force him to face the fact that Nicole is in love with him and that this "transference" must be terminated if she is to be spared what might appear as a tragedy to her, he admits that he is half in love with her, that the question of marrying her has passed through his mind (p. 153).[2] Franz exclaims: " 'What! And devote half your life to being doctor and nurse and all — never! I know what these cases are. One time in twenty it's finished in the first push — better never see her again!' " (p. 154). Dohmler agrees and they work out a plan for what Dick must do — "he must be most kind and yet eliminate himself."

Dick attempts the break but cannot go as far with it as he had intended because of the agony of watching the stricken girl as her "flimsy and scarcely created world" goes to pieces. He is puzzled and distraught as he leaves the hospital and returns to Zurich, and the next weeks are filled

*Reprinted from *Modern Fiction Studies* 7 (Spring 1961):55–104. © Purdue Research Foundation. Reprinted with permission.

with vast dissatisfaction: "The pathological origin and mechanistic defeat of the affair left a flat and metallic taste. Nicole's emotions had been used unfairly—what if they turned out to have been his own?" (p. 159).

At sight of her once in a car as he walked down the street in Zurich, "the air around him was loud with the circlings of all the goblins on the Gross-Münster." He goes home and tries "to write the matter out of his mind in a memorandum that went into detail as to the solemn régime before her," but it is a "memorandum that would have been convincing to any one save to him who had written it." He knows how deeply his emotions are involved. He attempts to find antidotes. He is all too aware that "the logic of his life tended away from the girl." But after encountering her on a trip to the mountains and riding back to Zurich with her on the train from Caux, he knows that "her problem was one they had together for good now" (p. 173).

All of this detailed analysis of his emotional involvement and his resistance to it shows two things, of course: his powerful love for Nicole and his realization of what marriage to her will mean to his future. One might simply say that it is a battle between reason and emotion and that emotion wins. If Diver had been a stronger man, he would not have ruined his life. But this is only part of the truth. It may well be that he is a greater man because he does have the capacity for great love, for sacrificial love that knows what it is sacrificing.

The love which Dick has for Nicole must not be underestimated. Indeed, Fitzgerald will not let us underestimate it. Over and over again he insists upon it, never more so than in the scenes with Rosemary, the symbol of what he has renounced for it: the dreams, the ambitions, the creative energy of his youth. Rosemary is a romantic dream. In reality she has nothing for him as he has nothing for her. And in his yearning away from the difficult path which he has chosen he never really fools himself.

Early in their relationship, when Rosemary begs Dick to take her and he refuses, he attempts to tell her something of what his love for Nicole means, an attempt foredoomed to failure. "Active love," he says, "—it's more complicated than I can tell you" (p. 81). And four years later, after he meets her in Rome and "what had begun with a childish infatuation on a beach was accomplished at last," he thinks of his feeling for Rosemary: "He supposed many men meant no more than that when they said they were in love—not a wild submergence of soul, a dipping of all colors into an obscuring dye, such as his love for Nicole had been. Certain thoughts about Nicole, that she should die, sink into mental darkness, love another man, made him physically sick" (p. 239).

It is only if we understand the greatness of his love that we can understand the tragic proportions of the dilemma with which he is faced. If he is to save her, he must give her up. This is the knowledge which Dick Diver the psychiatrist must carry with him perhaps from the moment he decides to marry Nicole. Certainly it is a knowledge which he must face squarely long before the break is accomplished.

We get one clear indication of the professional side of his relationship to Nicole following her collapse in Paris as a result of the murder of the Negro and the appearance of his body in Rosemary's room:

> It prophesied possibly a new cycle, a new *pousse* of the malady. Having gone through unprofessional agonies during her long relapse following Topsy's birth, he had, perforce, hardened himself about her, making a cleavage between Nicole sick and Nicole well. This made it difficult now to distinguish between his self-protective professional detachment and some new coldness in his heart. As an indifference cherished, or left to atrophy, becomes an emptiness, to this extent he had learned to become empty of Nicole, serving her against his will with negations and emotional neglect. (p. 185)

And we should not forget that it is against his will that he continues to serve her by forcing her step by painful step to a completeness that can come only with independence of him. His love for her cries out to him to protect her, to shield her, to support her. At the same time his love is great enough to make him do what he knows he must do if she is ever to be a whole person again: "Many times he had tried unsuccessfully to let go his hold on her . . . but always when he turned away from her into himself he left her holding Nothing in her hands and staring at it, calling it many names, but knowing it was only the hope that he would come back soon" (p. 198).

This is the torment which racks him as he continues in his double role of Dick Diver, husband, and Dr. Richard Diver, psychiatrist. It is stated explicitly after Nicole's running away from him and the children at the Agiri Fair. Recovering, she begs, " 'Help me, help me, Dick!' A wave of agony went over him. It was awful that such a fine tower should not be erected, only suspended, suspended from him" (p. 210). It is Tommy Barban who becomes the final instrument of release. And Dick knows it even before Nicole does, knows it, fights his inward battle and comes out the victor and the loser.

Nicole is vaguely aware that something beyond her understanding and beyond her control is developing. She senses that it is willed by her husband and forced inexorably to its conclusion as he drains his own heart's blood to give her life. "It was as though an incalculable story was telling itself inside him, about which she could only guess at in the moments when it broke through the surface" (p. 292).

It comes close to the surface when they board the Golding yacht and Nicole meets Tommy Barban. "In the moment of meeting she lay on his bosom, spiritually, going out and out. . . . Then self-preservation reasserted itself and retiring to her own world she spoke lightly" (p. 294). The evening goes badly. Dick fights with the vicious Lady Caroline Sibly-Biers. For a moment alone on the deck his despair brings him almost to the point of carrying Nicole with him in a suicidal leap into the water below, and she yields to him "in one moment of complete response and abnegation." Instead, he lets her go, Tommy joins them, and never again is she completely his.

Next morning Nicole is happy knowing that two men, Dick and Tommy, are in a sense in combat for her: "She did not want anything to happen, but only for the situation to remain in suspension as the two men tossed her from one mind to another; she had not existed for a long time, even as a ball" (p. 301). She begins to think of an affair with Tommy. "If she need not, in her spirit, be forever one with Dick as he had appeared last night, she must be something in addition, not just an image on his mind, condemned to endless parades around the circumference of a medal" (p. 302). She has reached the first real point of independence. For the first time she can defy Dick, as she does a few moments later when, against Dick's express command, she tosses the whole jar of camphor-rub to the departing Tommy and then turns "to take her own medicine."

Following him upstairs, where he lies down on his own bed without saying anything, she asks if he wants lunch brought up:

> He nodded and continued to lie quiescent, staring at the ceiling. Doubtfully she went to give the order. Upstairs again she looked into his room — the blue eyes, like searchlights, played on a dark sky. She stood a minute in the doorway, aware of the sin she had committed against him, half afraid to come in. . . . She put out her hand as if to rub his head, but he turned away like a suspicious animal. Nicole could stand the situation no longer; in a kitchen-maid's panic she ran downstairs, afraid of what the stricken man above would feed on while she must still continue her dry suckling at his lean chest. (p. 304)

How dark the sky on which his blue eyes played Nicole can not guess. It is a sky darkened by a loss which only Dick foresees and must not stop. She has only an "apprehension that Dick was contriving at some desperate solution."

> Since the evening on Golding's yacht she had sensed what was going on. So delicately balanced was she between an old foothold that had always guaranteed her security, and the imminence of a leap from which she must alight changed in the very chemistry of blood and muscle, that she did not dare bring the matter into the true forefront of consciousness. . . . For months every word had seemed to have an undertone of some other meaning, soon to be resolved under circumstances that Dick would determine. (p. 305)

Dick, the physician, is certainly aware of this delicate balance and aware that he controls it. The torture, the disintegration of these last months is fully understandable only if we are aware of the agony of such dread control.

As Nicole comes gradually to a realization that she can stand alone, a new sense of freedom develops within her:

> She had a sense of being cured and in a new way. Her ego began blooming like a great rich rose as she scrambled back along the labyrinths in which she had wandered for years. She hated the beach, resented the places where she had played planet to Dick's sun.
> "Why, I'm almost complete," she thought. "I'm practically standing alone, without him." And like a happy child, wanting the completion as soon as possible, *and knowing vaguely that Dick had planned for her to have it* [italics mine], she lay on her bed as soon as she got home and wrote Tommy Barban in Nice a short provocative letter.
> But that was for the daytime—toward evening with the inevitable diminution of nervous energy, her spirits flagged, and the arrows flew a little in the twilight. She was afraid of what was in Dick's mind; again she felt that a plan underlay his current actions and she was afraid of his plans—they worked well and they had an all-inclusive logic about them which Nicole was not able to command. (p. 316)

But the cure is not yet complete, the darkest hour has not yet arrived for Dick. It follows swiftly after Nicole's rendezvous with Tommy Barban.

As she wanders about the house remembering the details of the day before and trying to arrive at some kind of justification of her action, "remorse for this moment of betrayal, which so cavalierly belittled a decade of her life, turned her walk toward Dick's sanctuary."

> Approaching noiselessly she saw him behind his cottage, sitting in a steamer chair by the cliff wall, and for a moment she regarded him silently. He was thinking, he was living a world completely his own and in the small motions of his face, the brow raised or lowered, the eyes narrowed or widened, the lips set and reset, the play of his hands, she saw him progress from phase to phase of his own story spinning out inside him, his own, not hers. Once he clenched his fists and leaned forward, once it brought into his face an expression of torment and despair—when this passed its stamp lingered in his eyes. For almost the first time in her life she was sorry for him—it is hard for those who have once been mentally afflicted to be sorry for those who are well, and though Nicole often paid lip service to the fact that he had led her back to the world she had forfeited, she had thought of him really as an inexhaustible energy, incapable of fatigue—she forgot the troubles she caused him at the moment when she forgot the troubles of her own that had prompted her. That he no longer controlled her—did he know that? Had he willed it all? (p. 329)

Nicole has unknowingly been present at Gethsemane. Through her eyes we have seen Dick in the struggles of his darkest hour, the hour when he knows that he has saved Nicole and must now try to save himself. He rebuffs her tentative gesture toward him. He forces her to anger. She struggles to free herself from the power she still responds to in him:

> And suddenly, in the space of two minutes she achieved her victory and justified herself to herself without lie or subterfuge, cut the cord forever. Then she walked, weak in the legs, and sobbing coolly, toward the household that was hers at last.
>
> Dick waited until she was out of sight. Then he leaned his head forward on the parapet. The case was finished. Doctor Diver was at liberty. (p. 330)

At liberty for what? Can the doctor of ten years ago, the doctor with the brilliant future, take up again where he left off, as if those intervening years had not taken their toll? Of course not. The toll has been too much. He is sapped, drained emotionally. His energy, his strength, his love have been expended in the one passion of his life. "The layer of hardness in him, of self-control and of self-discipline" which Rosemary had felt in him at their first meeting had served him well. It will serve him still as he moves from one small town practice to another, but it can not wipe out what has been or compensate for what can never be again.

Such a reading obviously makes Dick Diver a more admirable character and a more heroic one. His story assumes the dimensions of tragedy if one accepts his choice to marry Nicole and his choice to free her as deliberately made because of his love for her. But Fitzgerald is too good a writer to make it quite that simple. He is aware of the complexities of human motivations and personal relationships. He makes his character believable by showing the less admirable qualities in him and the selfish motives which complicate the altruistic.

A conscious decision to marry a mental patient, to devote one's life to her cure; a calculated plan to force her to completion by forcing her to renounce her savior—this is too cold, too incredible, too inhuman. The choices must be blurred, must be softened, must be less starkly rational. The plan of "redemption" must not be conceived in its entirety but must evolve from the partly unforeseeable circumstances which arise. In attempting to trace a dimension of the novel which I believe has been neglected and which I believe to be essential to a recognition of its real merit, I have presented it more baldly than it appears in the total work and removed it from the qualifying colorations which act to soften its edges and humanize it.

We are told before Dick knows whether he will marry Nicole or not, before he has to make any decision about her, something about his nature which is crucial to an understanding of his subsequent actions: "In the dead white hours in Zurich staring into a stranger's pantry across the upshine of a street lamp, he used to think that he wanted to be good, he wanted to be kind, he wanted to be brave and wise, but it was all pretty difficult. He wanted to be loved, too, if he could fit it in" (p. 145). And in a passage which comes, significantly, immediately after the final break with Nicole, the passage in which she gains completeness and with it independence of Dick, he receives a telephone call at two o'clock in the morning and responds to it by going to Antibes to help get Mary North and Caroline Sibly-Biers out of jail — two women whom he despises and who have publicly humiliated him. His response is described in these words:

> He got up and, as he absorbed the situation, his self-knowledge assured him that he would undertake to deal with it — the old fatal pleasingness, the old forceful charm, swept back with its cry of "Use me!" He would have to go fix this thing that he didn't care a damn about, because it had early become a habit to be loved. . . . On an almost parallel occasion, back in Dohmler's clinic on the Zürichsee, realizing this power, he had made his choice, chosen Ophelia, chosen the sweet poison and drunk it. Wanting above all to be brave and kind, he had wanted, even more than that, to be loved. (p. 331)

This is the selfish element, this is the fatal weakness which underlies the pattern of his life. There is an incompleteness in him which is covered over by the charm which he has cultivated and used to draw people to him, to sweep them up and manipulate them, to use himself to attempt their fulfillment. "He was condemned to carry with him the egos of certain people, early met and early loved, and to be only as complete as they were complete themselves" (p. 268).

During his studies in Vienna, sharing a flat with Ed Elkins, "who would name you all the quarterbacks in New Haven for thirty years," he begins to doubt that his mental processes are in any profound way different from the thinking of Elkins. And he has a vague perception of the incompleteness within him:

> "— And Lucky Dick can't be one of these clever men; he must be less intact, even faintly destroyed. If life won't to it for him it's not a substitute to get a disease, or a broken heart, or an inferiority complex, though it'd be nice to build out some broken side till it was better than the original structure."
>
> He mocked at his reasoning, calling it specious and "American". . . .
> He knew, though, that the price of his intactness was incompleteness. (p. 126)

Mingled thus with the elements in his character which make for greatness, for love and sacrifice and discipline and control, are the elements of weakness and insufficiency, the elements which blur the actions of love and selflessness and confuse them with suggestions of self-gratification and deep-seated need. But it is this very complexity of character and of motive that enriches the story and raises it to the level of the tragic. Dr. Richard Diver is a man who "is ready to be called to his intricate destiny."

Notes

1. This is essentially the interpretation accepted by most of the members of a Danforth Seminar on Literature and Religion at the University of Chicago in the summer of 1959. See also articles by Arthur Mizener, Alfred Kazin, John Chamberlain, and C. Hartley Grattan in

F. *Scott Fitzgerald, The Man and His Work*, ed. Alfred Kazin (Cleveland and New York: The World Publishing Co., 1951); Malcolm Cowley's introduction to *Tender Is the Night* in *Three Novels of F. Scott Fitzgerald* (New York: Charles Scribner's Sons, 1953); Arthur Mizener, *The Far Side of Paradise* (New York: Vintage Books, 1959). Mr. Mizener says that "what really destroys Dick is emotional bankruptcy. . . . Dick uses up the emotional energy which is the source of his personal discipline and of his power to feed other people." While I agree with this statement, my purpose is to examine the cause of this bankruptcy in order to show the conscious element in the expenditure.

2. This and all subsequent references are to the Bantam edition.

Political Conscience in the Novels of F. Scott Fitzgerald
James F. Light*

In March 1922 F. Scott Fitzgerald's close friend Edmund Wilson asserted that Fitzgerald was ". . . little concerned with the general affairs of the world: like a woman he is not much given to abstract or impersonal thoughts. Conversations about politics or general ideas have a way of snapping back to Fitzgerald." In 1931, Fitzgerald himself commented, in "Echoes of the Jazz Age," that though the May Day riots of 1919 ". . . alienated the more intelligent young men from the prevailing order . . . ," the outbreak of moral indignation was short-lived, for the Jazz Age was tired of "Great Causes" and characteristically had ". . . no interest in politics at all."

Such remarks as these have led to the common critical assumption that Fitzgerald and his art lack a political conscience. That Fitzgerald himself might not have agreed whole-heartedly is evident from a passage in "Handle with Care." In that ruthless self-analysis, Fitzgerald lamented, in March 1936, that ". . . my political conscience had scarcely existed for ten years save as an element of irony in my stuff. When I became again concerned with the system I should function under, it was a man much younger than myself who brought it to me." The implication of such a passage would seem to be that before 1926 and after 1936 Fitzgerald considered himself as a man and an artist with a political conscience. Since only one of his novels, *Tender Is the Night*, was published in the period between 1926 and 1936, and even that novel may manifest a political conscience as ". . . an element of irony in my stuff . . . ," there seems some justification in emphasizing an aspect of Fitzgerald's work that hitherto has been neglected. To emphasize the political man and artist is not to claim that Fitzgerald was nothing other than that. He had many

*Reprinted from *Ball State Teacher's College Forum* 4 (Spring 1963):13–25. This selection is taken from pp. 13–15, 19–22. Reprinted with permission of Ball State Teacher's College Forum and the author.

sides, and he knew it well. As he said in one of his notebooks: "There never was a good biography of a good novelist. There couldn't be. He's too many people if he's any good."

As Malcolm Cowley and Arthur Mizener have said, Fitzgerald was a Keatsian romantic, and certainly his novels convey the irony of youth and beauty consumed by the time which nourishes them. Fitzgerald was something other than a Keatsian romantic too. His more ambitious works are novels of ideas, and among the most important of his concerns is the system he felt he ". . . should function under." Always in his art, Fitzgerald felt he was unlike such people as Cole Porter and Rodgers and Hart. Instead, Fitzgerald claimed, as he wrote to his daughter in 1939, that he was ". . . a moralist at heart . . ." who wanted to ". . . preach at people in some acceptable form rather than to entertain." As a moralist he recognized that the only lasting way to improve the world was to improve the individuals in it, but in addition his discontent with American social inequities made him constantly hostile to an American aristocracy of wealth and privilege. That he was fascinated by the fetes and gracious living which wealth made possible did not lessen, but only made more complex, his hostility to the very rich. Quite possibly it was his awareness of this enmity in himself and the lack of it in D. H. Lawrence that made Fitzgerald write cryptically in his notebooks that Lawrence was ". . . essentially pre-Marxian . . . ," while he himself was ". . . essentially Marxian."

Fitzgerald's discontent with the way wealth was distributed in America existed throughout his life. As a student at Newman school he was constantly aware, or so his roommate asserted, that he ". . . was one of the poorest boys in a rich boy's school." In early adulthood, Fitzgerald almost lost Zelda Sayre because of a lack of money, and his quarrel with the very rich was exacerbated by this painful memory. Though Fitzgerald wrote a novel, and so got money enough for everything to turn out all right, Fitzgerald still felt aggrieved, as he noted in "Handle with Care":

> It came out all right for a different person. The man with the jingle of money in his pocket who married the girl a year later would always cherish an abiding distrust, an animosity toward the leisure class—not the conviction of a revolutionist but the smoldering hatred of a peasant. In the years since then I have never been able to stop wondering where my friends' money came from, nor to stop thinking that at one time a sort of droit de seigneur might have been exercised to give one of them my girl.

The dislike of the very rich had not left in Fitzgerald's later life. Around 1937 he wrote to his daughter about Groton school: "They are very democratic there—they have to sleep in gold cubicles and wash at old platinum pumps. This toughens them so they can pay the poor starvation wages without weakening."

In addition to his hostility toward the rich, Fitzgerald showed considerable receptivity throughout his life to the ideas of intellectual and social non-conformists. In his last year of college he was especially friendly with Henry Strater, who led the 1917 revolt against the aristocratic eating clubs of Princeton and who then reaffirmed his reputation as Princeton's leading crack-pot by following Tolstoyan pacifistic principles during World War I. Though Fitzgerald did not agree with all the idealistic principles for which Strater stood, Fitzgerald did assert, in August 1921, that Strater was the dominant influence in his writing until after the completion of *The Beautiful and Damned*. Strater's influence undoubtedly waned during the later 1920's, to be replaced by that of the Gerald Murphys, to whom Fitzgerald dedicated *Tender Is the Night*, but by 1932 the charm of the Murphys and of "many fêtes" had palled for Fitzgerald. To a friend who still treasured the memory of the gay irresponsibility of those days, Fitzgerald wrote in September 1932:

> . . . [you] insist on a world which we will willingly let die, in which Zelda can't live, which damned near ruined us both, which neither you nor any of our more gifted friends are yet sure of surviving; you insisted on its value, as if you were in some way holding a battle front and challenged us to join you. If you could have seen Zelda, as the most typical end-product of that battle during any day from the spring of 1931 to the spring of 1932 you would have felt about as much enthusiasm for the battle as a doctor at the end of a day in a dressing station behind a blood battle.

By 1932 Fitzgerald was so absorbed in Marx that Zelda Fitzgerald wrote to John Peale Bishop: "Scott reads Marx — I read the cosmological philosophers. The brightest moments of our day are when we get them mixed up." The stimulation of Marx led Fitzgerald to curiosity about contemporary communism so that for a while the Fitzgeralds' home was overrun with radicals. Though Fitzgerald soon became disillusioned with the actuality of Stalinist communism, he never lost his awe for the idealism and dedication of some communists. To him they seemed inspired, though fanatic, men; in 1940 he wrote to his daughter: "Poetry is . . . something that lives like fire inside you — like music to the musician or Marxism to the communist." In addition, Fitzgerald always retained his belief in the essential truth of the Marxian indictment of the exploitation of labor by capital. When in 1940 Fitzgerald's daughter wrote him lecturingly about his excessive sympathy for communism, he answered apologetically, but at the end of his reply he added some lecturing of his own: "You must have some politeness toward ideas. . . . Some time . . . read the terrible chapter in *Das Kapital* on *The Working Day*, and see if you are ever quite the same."

In his novels even more than in his life, Fitzgerald showed his discontent with some of the weaknesses of the system under which he functioned . . .

Tender Is the Night was published in 1934, in that period in which Fitzgerald felt he had no ". . . political conscience . . ." save as it manifested itself as ". . . an element of irony in my stuff." Certainly Fitzgerald's estimate is largely valid. Struggling as he was with debt, drunkenness, and Zelda's ill health, he had little time left over for a political conscience, not in his personal life at any rate. Despite this, to say he had *no* political conscience is an exaggeration, made in the depths of his personal despair, full of the hyperbole that made him also say in the same article that Edmund Wilson was his ". . . intellectual conscience . . ." and Ernest Hemingway his ". . . artistic conscience . . ." and nothing was left of Scott Fitzgerald himself: ". . . there was not an 'I' any more—not a basis on which I could organize my self respect." Factually, the renewed stirrings of political conscience are evident in 1932 in Fitzgerald's concern with Marxism and contemporary communism. Artistically, Fitzgerald continues to expose the grossness and the corruption beneath the glittering facade of life among the leisure classes.

Tender Is the Night tells a story which verges on the mythopoeic. A psychiatrist, Dr. Richard Diver, falls in love with a wealthy but schizophrenic girl, Nicole Warren. Nicole is a member of an American ". . . ducal family . . . ," but she has been raped by her father and has slowly retreated from the world. Dr. Diver marries Nicole, and slowly she sucks strength ". . . at his lean chest . . ." until she is cured, and he, who has once been a source of happiness and life, is an emotional bankrupt without strength or balance. To Baby Warren, the sister of Nicole, the sacrifice of Dr. Diver seems part of an accepted order of things: the ducal family has bought a doctor, and his service to Nicole is ". . . what he was educated for." That is the system Baby Warren understands, and it is similar in its philosophy to the botanical theory that a hundred rosebuds may justifiably perish in order to make one perfect bloom. Fitzgerald felt differently, and in *Tender Is the Night* he suggested this when he compared the source of Nicole's wealth to that of the self-made actress, Rosemary Speers:

> Rosemary spent money she had earned—she was here in Europe because she had gone in the pool six times that January day with her temperature roving from 99° . . . to 103°. . . .
>
> . . . Nicole was the product of much ingenuity and toil. For her sake trains began their run at Chicago and traversed the round belly of the continent to California; chicle factories fumed and link belts grew link by link in factories; men mixed toothpaste in vats and drew mouthwash out of copper hogsheads; girls canned tomatoes quickly in August or worked rudely at the Five-and-Tens on Christmas Eve; half-breed Indians toiled on Brazilian coffee plantations and dreamers were muscled out of patent rights in new tractors—these were some of the people who gave a tithe to Nicole, and as the whole system swayed and thundered onward, it lent a feverish bloom to such processes of hers as wholesale buying. . . . She illustrated very simple principles, containing

in herself her own doom, but illustrated them so accurately that there was grace in the procedure.

The ducal Warren family, though the capitalistic system it represents is in decay, can buy a doctor, but it cannot buy moral decency. Read as myth, *Tender Is the Night* is a nightmare, the latent meanings of which are more important than the manifest ones. As myth, the novel asserts that Nicole's youthful moral sense has been offended by the nature of her father's crime. She must become her father's daughter, and to do so she must lose her puritanic squeamishness about his nature and embrace the things he stands for. These things she does; she becomes rapacious and uncivilized and able to hear the word *father* without flinching. By so doing, she accepts her moral inheritance as fully as the money her father has left her. "Cured" of her moral compunctions, she can discard Dick Diver, make her ". . . person into the trimmest of gardens . . ." and accept the barbaric code and martial, fleshly, wolf-like love of Tommy Barban. Being "cured," she can accept the depravity of her father and the exploitative system which makes both him and her possible. When Tommy Barban asserts that she has changed, that she now has ". . . white crook's eyes," she agrees, and then adds: ". . . well perhaps I've gone back to my true self—I suppose my grandfather was a crook and I'm a crook by heritage." To herself, Nicole makes her own justification: ". . . better a sane crook than a mad puritan." She and her new crowd inherit and pervert the beach to which Dick Diver had once brought warmth and grace, civilization and joy. Hers is now a code and a gang which see the world as spoil; they embody the decline of a culture, and in miniature they foreshadow Spengler's prophecy of the decline of the West. In their barbarism and narcissim, Nicole and her gang can be forgiven only because they know not what they do. They are careless drivers, selfish children who are what they are because civilization has taught them nothing better. Because of this, Dr. Diver can forgive them, just as Nick Carraway forgives the Buchanans, and bless them with the sign of the cross. The blessing is ironic, for as Fitzgerald wrote in a memorandum to himself, Dick Diver was to be portrayed as ". . . a spoiled priest . . ." who has given in ". . . for various causes to the *haute bourgeoisie.*" As a life source, as a priest, he has been destroyed, and his blessing no longer will bring life or any semblance of it to the gay corpses who have perverted his beach.

Fitzgerald's original intent in *Tender Is the Night* was to emphasize the social criticism in the novel. He planned, according to his notes for the novel, to make Dick Diver a character ". . . pretending to a stability and belief in the current order he does not have, being in fact a communist–liberal–idealist, a moralist in revolt." Dick was, however, to have become "spoiled" by his life among the bourgeoisie; he was to have become ". . . a quack . . ." to whom ". . . nothing matters but survival as long as possible with the old order." Despite his own defeat, he was to have sent ". . . his neglected son into Soviet Russia to educate him . . . ," so that Dick was at least to have accomplished ". . . his ideals in the case of his son." That Fitzgerald did not follow his original intent completely shows his wisdom as an artist, for though he did have a political conscience, and shows it more than has been recognized in his novels, he was always less concerned with causes than with people. For him, as he asserted in "The Crack–Up," "Life . . . was largely a personal matter," and that concern for individuals forever baffled by the tragedy of time which destroys youth and love and life and civilizations — that irony of clocks which never run down dominates the novels of Fitzgerald and gives them their lyric, Keatsian, poetic timelessness. Granted, however, that it was the tragedy of individuals and not the propaganda of proletarianism that most moved Fitzgerald, that fact should not obscure another one: Fitzgerald was strongly concerned with the system he ". . . should function under." The ". . . awful secret . . ." of Thomas Wolfe, Fitzgerald wrote his daughter, was that ". . . he did not have anything particular to say!"

In "The Rich Boy," Fitzgerald once commented that the ". . . very rich are different from you and me," and he added that ". . . unless you were born rich," you could hardly hope to understand the difference. In *The Beautiful and Damned, The Great Gatsby*, and *Tender Is the Night*, Fitzgerald dramatized unforgettably the evils of a system based on privilege. Emphasizing the morally debilitating influences of the system on the very rich rather than the very poor, he worked with implication and irony to assert his discontent with the system. A part of his dissatisfaction may have stemmed from his feeling that the system was evil in its effects upon science and the scientist, art and the artist: Dick Diver's talent and idealism are destroyed by the *haute bourgeoisie* (and his own weakness), just as Fitzgerald felt, in his most bitter moments, that his own talent had been betrayed through the dissipation encouraged by a *haute bourgeoisie* code of irresponsible, careless driving . . . .

Fitzgerald was indifferent neither to human decancy nor to mankind's need for security. Where these needs were betrayed by individuals or governments, Fitzgerald protested in his art. He demurred bluntly at times and more subtly at others, but he never forgot that his art should preach as well as entertain. Criticism has largely ignored Fitzgerald's political conscience. To assert that he had such a conscience is not to affirm that it is the only thing of importance in his work. It is to assert that an awareness of Fitzgerald's political conscience is helpful in illuminating some important aspects of his art.

The Strange Case of F. Scott Fitzgerald and A. Hyd(Hid)ell: A Note on the Displaced Person in American Life and Literature   William Wasserstrom[*]

It occurred to one for the first that Kennedy's middle name was . . . Fitzgerald, and the tone of his crack lieutenants, the unstated style, was true to Scott. The legend of Fitzgerald had an army at last.

— Norman Mailer, *The Presidential Papers*, 1963

The resources of fantasy were endless. A scrapper and an expatriate and a hunter, he was therefore a writer, therefore entitled to compare himself with E. Hemingway. . . . Later he was a counteragent, a jungle man pursued but ferocious, equipped with beard and gun. Still later, he found comfort in an assumed name with a reserved patrician sigh in its sound. A. Hydell, A. Hidell.

— Benjamin De Mott, *The New York Review of Books*
December 26, 1963: Kennedy Memorial Issue

When A. Hyd(Hid)ell killed the President, when Jack Ruby murdered Lee Oswald, these men in concert manifested that Strangelove snarl of agonies which underlies the life and literature of our generation. We are members of a generation whose lives are molded by the imagination not of mere disaster but of utter ruin: the ruin of whole peoples, of whole nations, of the whole earth. Ruin, in turn, is a consequence of human criminality so outrageous that not even Genet's art can rival the real facts of ordinary life. No literary action, however queer, can encompass grotesquerie of the kind we confront each day: assassination in Texas, judicial murder and maneuver in Mississippi, white and black cannibalism in the Congo. Never before has the experience of iniquity been joined with the arts of turbulence in so baleful a union.

Consider Hyd(Hid)ell: Moscovite cowboy with an Italian rifle, a Russian wife, a Marine badge and Fidel's cause; living in a permanent city of night, another country, "Interzone," where the post of president is thought to be so ignominious that "few presidents live out their term of office"; playing get the guests, collecting severed heads at the academic depository. A schlemiel paid with blood money out of the international Zionist oil depletion allowance fund, he shuttles between the Bronx and New Orleans, Dallas and Mexico City. A sexless ginger man, he emerges from the barricades on the fifth floor of his own fancy and is killed by a Jew, self-appointed to the role of scapegoat and savior.

*Reprinted from the *Columbia University Forum* 8 (Fall 1965):5–11, with permission of the author.

Askew as these sentences are, their coherence relies not on a procession of ideas, but on a conjunction of literary details taken from noxious or extraordinary works by John Rechy, James Baldwin, William Burroughs, J. P. Donleavy, Edward Albee, Harold Pinter, Iris Murdoch, Thomas Pynchon. Link this group with Mary McCarthy and Vladimir Nabokov, discern connections, however tenuous, between Fitzgerald and Kennedy, between Jack Rubenstein and André Schwarz-Bart, between Schwarz-Bart and Robert Louis Stevenson and one discovers that the most monstrous of literary plots is tidy in comparison with real outrage in our time. Such an association of persons, however spooky, is not unnatural. If we assent to Mailer's notion that the legend of F. Scott Fitzgerald is somehow inherent in John Fitzgerald Kennedy's style, and if we regard Kennedy's life as a stylization of Fitzgerald's agonized art, then we are led back to the novel, *Tender Is the Night*, in which legend, agony and ruin coalesce.

No theory of social or psychologic or literary action can account for our present catalogue of woe, but for a time, in the late fifties, one school of plausible opinion contended that Jews and Negroes were best equipped to preserve the arts from anarchy. If modern drama and fiction represented brilliant but hysteric exercises in wretchedness, in human alienation, then the time had come for a certain kind of writer, a Jew, to muster his genius and assume his ancient task: to crystallize woe yet preserve grace.

It is of course impossible to locate the exact origins of this belief. Perhaps André Schwarz-Bart's novel, *The Last of the Just*, in 1959, either caused or coincided with a sudden but sustained impulse to self-inquiry among Jewish writers or writers on Jewish subjects. Under our very eyes, Diana Trilling said, we see the Wandering Jew "become wandering man, the alien Jew generalizing into the alienated human being." And the alienated human being, Edgar Rosenberg maintained in *From Shylock to Svengali* (1960), was invented by Proust and Kafka and Joyce, who removed "the Jew as symbol" from the periphery to the center of our attention. Entrenched there, this symbol "reflects the problems and pressures of Western man." Symbolism of a far less general kind led Kenneth Rexroth, in *Bird in the Bush* (1959), to specify some ways in which particular pressures in the modern American community are resolved by jazz. Invoking Martin Buber's Hasidic idea of communion ("Only men who are capable of truly saying *Thou* to one another can truly say *We* to one another"), Rexroth argued than an "ecstatic Hasidic heritage" was ingrained in those East Side and Brooklyn Jews, "musicians from Avenue A and Maxwell Street and Williamsburg," who met Negroes halfway and proceeded to restore "social music to the role it has played in all human societies from time immemorial." In his view, therefore, Jews and Negroes together have sought to create a "revolution in basic human relationships."

Rexroth's appraisal of semitism in jazz was of course less diffuse than talk about the Jew as symbol. But it was considerably less blunt than Leslie

Fiedler's claim: a Jewish writer must assume a unique vocation. In *Jewish Heritage* (1961), Fiedler said that no one on earth "at this moment of history . . . does not feel alienated, in exile, a stranger." The outsider is therefore the man best placed to portray the "human condition of the twentieth century." Ticking off a list of distinguished, gifted, literary American Jews—Delmore Schwartz, Bellow, Salinger, Roth, Shapiro, Mailer, Malamud, Ginsberg—Fiedler claimed that these are the men best-equipped to assume the prophetic role, a role suited to writers who are perforce one step ahead of the moral order in which they live. The Jewish "prophetic writer is driven to blast and excoriate and caricature the community."

But those carefully chosen words, blast, excoriate and caricature, simply don't describe the aims of all Fiedler's choice Jews however aptly the words invoke Fiedler's splendid, lordly thunder. If you attended Fiedler, Rexroth, and Mrs. Trilling (and more recently Irving Malin's book, *Jews and Americans*, in which there is modest dissent from these notions) you derived a perplexing lesson. As entertainers and prophets, Jews composed a tight community of outsiders driven to instruct insiders, Gentiles, in the meaning of disorder, homelessness, and isolation. What was troublesome was not only an infidelity to fact; even more disconcerting was the discourtesy done to artists and critics everywhere, of whatever religious bias, American and European, who had long stood against parochialism of all sorts. *Ship of Fools* is fairly new. But its gist—that alienated men of our age, Bostonians and Jews and Texans, Mexicans and Germans and Spaniards, are fools, gulls of history, of culture, of temperament, of unholy folly itself—is older, Miss Porter says, than Hieronymus Bosch.

Not until summer 1962, at a writers' conference in Edinburgh, were some grander proposals made to rescue our views of current literary art. There, Stephen Spender reported in *Encounter* (October), Mary McCarthy contended that a new kind of novel was being written, fiction based on statelessness not nationality: "She thought that the future lay perhaps with the novels of exile, of wanderers over the earth, whose predecessors were Joyce and Lawrence." Distinguishing between the novel of exile and the novel of expatriation (between Nabokov and Durrell), Miss McCarthy said that the latter exalts a particular place whereas, in the former, roaming across the face of the earth becomes itself the issue. And it is the spokesmen for exile who speak "in the voice of the future."

Although her thoughts were welcome, they did not account for those big novels in which outcast persons roam everywhere, are exiled but not stateless or are stateless but are not homeless. I've already mentioned *Ship of Fools; Dr. Zhivago* is another. Even Nabokov, to whom Miss McCarthy usually gives the highest marks, doesn't fit: in exile, living on an American passport, he's the most suitably settled person in the world for he's wholly at home in its leading languages. Indeed, neither Miss McCarthy's speculations nor the opinion of Jewish critics account for the triad of terrors, tyranny and exile and grief, that preoccupies writers such as Burroughs and Genet, Camus and Nabokov, Malamud and Ellison, or even one as well situated as Flannery O'Connor was. Black, brown, blond and olive, gay or straight, modern writers examine and treat those bruises of body and abrasions of mind suffered by victims of every imaginable kind of displacement in spheres remote and near. No matter how uncommon or monstrous the literary structure, it accommodates a displaced person.

"I'm not responsible for the world's misery," Mrs. McIntyre says in Miss O'Connor's story, "The Displaced Person." She is speaking to Guizac, a Pole who has been settled on her farm by the local priest. Guizac has just told her that he hopes to bring to America a cousin who will marry one of her Negro workmen. "Your cousin," she said in a positive voice, "cannot come over here and marry one of my Negroes." After a second he shrugged and let his arms drop as if he were tired. "She no care black," he said, "She in camp three year." Mrs. McIntyre, who threatens to dismiss Guizac though he has saved her farm from falling apart, complains to the priest: "He didn't have to come in the first place." And the priest replies, "absently," that he came to redeem us. Guizac is sacrificed when Mrs. McIntyre allows one of her men to flatten him with a tractor, allows this to happen although impulsively she had begun to warn Guizac but had held her tongue. In the end, her eyes and her overseer's eyes and the Negro's eyes come together in a single look that "froze them in collusion forever."

Frozen in Satanic collusion, Christians destroy one another. In exile from God, they exile God from earth: He is the ultimate Displaced Person, Miss O'Connor's story says. A far more intricate version of similar matters, Camus' *The Fall*, naturally includes the biblical reference, but the book turns on no mere theology of expulsion and instead stresses the psychology and history of displaced persons in the post-Christian era: exiled from France and from reason, maddened by delusions of absolute power over other men, Clamence exists in a community of one, talking in endless communion with himself alone. *The Fall* is a remarkable work, but I slip it in — and slip past it — because it introduces and exploits the prototypical malaise of displaced men, masters and martyrs, in our wild world: madness. So wild indeed is our world, so alien is the use of reason in the conduct of affairs among alienated men and so insane are the effects of unreason, that the mind itself becomes a wilderness, an imaginary swamp with real reptiles in it, a weird place whose chief chronicler, Vladimir Nabokov, combines the playfulness of Pushkin with the passion of Dostoyevsky.

Like Dostoyevsky's *Notes from the Underground*, where the exile-victim equates toothache with the unremitting pain of consciousness, Nabokov's fiction is customarily rooted in neuralgia. Unlike Dostoyevsky, Nabokov treats torment as a proper pathology of everyday life on a planet where insanity is normal. And in those stories and novels written during the thirties and forties, Nabokov recounts the kinds of remorseless misery inflicted on decent men wrenched from home and tormented to the point of madness by those heroic soldiers of fortune who lovingly built Dachau. In "Cloud, Castle, Lake," Vasili Ivanovich, a Russian exile in Germany during the late thirties, decides to take a summer trip in preference to the impenetrable routines of Nazi life. It is conducted by an official who insists that the group sing, march, drink, eat, sleep together. Escaping one afternoon, he discovers an inn with a "view, beautiful to the verge of tears," a "lake with its cloud and its castle, in a motionless and perfect correlation of happiness." There, in a room overlooking that lake, "life would at last be what he had always wished it to be." He would be home at last. Denied permission to stay, he is carried by force onto the train where everyone "began to beat him." It "occurred to them . . . to use a corkscrew on his palms, then on his feet. The post-office clerk, who had been to Russia, fashioned a knout out of a stick and belt and began to use it with devilish dexterity. Atta boy!" "I have a right to remain where I want," Vasili Ivanovich had said in that moment before they seized him. "Oh, but this is nothing less than an invitation to a beheading."

And this is surely the point, the very issue Nabokov developed in detail in the novel called *Invitation to a Beheading* (1938). To be born into our time is to receive an invitation to a beheading whereby we are separated from ourselves by executioners who say they're concerned only for our well-being. A comic version of such pursuits informs *Lolita*: Humbert, that "deep-voiced D. P.," is both victim and instrument of those highly refined forms of violation which pervert the spirits of our bodies. Although laughter is Nabokov's anodyne, the dark side of his moon is not laughter but lunacy. In "Signs and Symbols," which picks up where "Cloud, Castle, Lake" left off, a European refugee in America imagines that the whole universe shadows him wherever he goes. "Clouds in the staring sky transmit to one another, by means of slow signs, incredibly detailed information regarding him." And he must be constantly on guard, devote every minute to decoding these messages, which is to say that he suffers a neuralgia of the brain: madness. The victim, beheaded but still alive, he has learned to outwit his executioners.

Having set the scene I turn now to the novel around which all my arguments circle, and to its author, F. Scott Fitzgerald, the writer who first diagnosed the disease which infects the world's body, who first connected madness to barbarism, barbarism to tyranny, tyranny to exile, and exile to grief and ruin beyond comfort and cure. Suddenly, too, we are amidst another Fitzgerald revival, and critics begin to say that *Tender Is the Night* is "one of the great novels written in America in the past 50 years"—Robert Sklar's comment in *The New Republic*—a deeper, more penetrating and more radical book than other fiction of our era. But the reasons given to bolster this shift of opinion on that novel are usually honorific or, as in John Lucas' essay for *The Critical Quarterly* (Summer, 1963), ambitious but imprecise. Lucas argues that breakdown is Fitzgerald's theme: "For all that Tommy may want to see himself as a soldier and lover on an heroic scale," his affair with Nicole expresses a reduction not an expansion of sexual and social energy, a diminution of virtue in a "world of compromised possibilities."

For all that Tommy Barban represents, Lucas' paraphrase is too cramped. *Tender Is the Night* is a prophetic novel precisely because Fitzgerald, recording the process which leads Dick to take a dive rather than to accept an invitation to a beheading, correlates this action with Nicole's movement away from Diver toward Barban. As the plot unfolds these twin actions, its theme grows portentous and the novel as a whole becomes a work of vast social resonance, of revelation. Tracing the transmission of worldly power from civilized men to barbarians, *Tender Is the Night* helps us to account for Eichmann in Jerusalem and Hyd(Hid)ell in Dallas.

Diver's "moment" had begun in 1919, Fitzgerald says, when, having been in 1914 a Rhodes Scholar from Yale, having taken a medical degree at Hopkins, having managed in 1916, despite war, to get to Vienna for study with Freud, Diver had ended the years of apprenticeship. All during that time of private triumph and public catastrophe, he is serene at his tasks: he imagines that the war doesn't "touch him at all." And only much later does he realize that he's suffered what he calls noncombatant shell-shock. In 1919 he comes to maturity bearing fewer "Achilles' heels than would be required to equip a centipede," but just the right number to hamstring him utterly in the "broken universe of the war's ending." For he's a marked man. His family, friends, teachers mark him as a man of genius: "of all the men who have recently taken their degrees," Dick is the most brilliant. But Fitzgerald has him pegged for doom. With no better training than "the lies of generations of frontier mothers who had to croon falsely that there were no wolves outside the cabin door," Diver believes in all the "illusions of a nation" itself determined to glorify man's "eternal strength and health," his essential goodness. These are the naivetés which render him vulnerable to disaster in the new world. For a short time, sustained in faith, he undertakes to perform his professional and historic duty — to instruct profane persons in sacred learning: he tries to teach the very rich some "ABC's of decency." By the time he decides that this is fruitless work, he is a philanderer and an alcoholic, unfit for work of any kind, expert in the XYZ's of indecency. "Dick is no longer a serious man," says his colleague Dr. Gregorovius.

Most critics, having arrived at this stage of argument turn to Fitzgerald's customary explanation of all human nastiness — money. Realizing that Fitzgerald had a small vocabulary of moral ideas, they conceive Diver's victimization, as physician and husband, to result from the corrosions of cash in an acquisitive society. Dick is infected by the disease of absolute egoism epidemic in the very rich, a disease which breaks down the very tissues of love it was formerly his task as a man of science to repair. My view is that this opinion is far too narrow: it may account for personal deterioration; it doesn't do much for the decay of war. One day, sitting between his two women, Rosemary and Nicole, the one still perfectly innocent and the other thoroughly depraved, Diver sees a group of gold star mothers "come to mourn for their dead, for something they could not repair." And in an instant he "sat again on his father's knee" hearing all the old paternal lessons, loyalties, pieties, his father's nine-teenth-century romantic certainties about the final triumph of honor, courtesy, courage.

But of what use are honor and courtesy in Dr. Diver's psychiatric career? In truth, it's a profession for which Dick is no longer qualified. No longer is he the most decent man in the world, the person whose national traditions are suffused by that form of training best suited to bring high civilization to birth among men. On the contrary, he dishonors himself. The turning point of the novel comes in Rome where, following a spasm, a flash of violence which leads him to fight taxi drivers and policemen, Dick is imprisoned. But the spasm is all he can muster; he's not really a man of violence in the new style. After this, Diver's situation is little different from the condition of those he is called on to treat. There is, for example, Senor Pardo y Cuidad Real, a man of wealth and power, whose son Francisco is an incorrigibly corrupt homosexual. The father tells Dick: "I have tried everything . . . a tour of Spain" during which every evening "Francisco had an injection of cantharides" then was sent to a "reputable bordello . . . but the result was nothing. Finally . . . I made Francisco strip to the waist and lashed him with a whip." These are, of course, forms of therapy which before long would become popular for the treatment of every sort of malaise. Diver's last act in the service of vile people is to help two women of his former circle who, having dressed in the costume of French sailors, had picked up two young girls and been jailed. "I have never seen women like this sort of women," an old European remarks as he and Diver leave together. "I have known many of the great courtesans of the world, and for them I have much respect often, but women like these women I have never seen before."

They are unfamiliar not because they are decadent, not because they're outrageously selfish and rich, but because they belong to a new race. Theirs is style of an age in which a weak man like Abe North is beaten to death in a speakeasy while a strong man, all relaxed for combat, pieces of skull knitting under his hair, helps White Russians escape the Bolsheviks and assists at revolutions in which men are twisted into forms the rulers select. I refer to Tommy Barban's occupation in the novel, a form of work that does not distinguish among causes and merely seeks out tests of courage. Barban's ferocious courage enables him to serve as the perfectly villainous hero in the new time. Fitzgerald contrasts Barban, the expert in brutality, and Diver, former expert in the psychology of humaneness, a man whose work was not to force men and women into contours conceived by despots, but to enable individual persons to discover their own best form. This contrast is the deep radical issue in the novel as a whole. For it reports, in 1934, the shape of a world in the throes of death, not breakdown—The Age of Diver; and etches the shape of a world in the process of birth—The Age of Barban. This is the issue, therefore, that informs the rebirth of Nicole from the maddest of puritans to the sanest of pagans: she's all new like a baby, Barban tells her. But in order to become all new, she must have a love affair with Tommy and must fight her husband-doctor with all the resources of the new age. Using "her unscrupulousness against his moralities," she finds strength even in her weakness, in her psychosis. "I think Nicole is less sick than anyone thinks," Frau Gregorovius had said earlier; she "only cherishes her illness as an instrument of power." Nicole's final display of power is to accede to Diver's dissolution in order to live as Tommy Barban's perfect dynastic mate, villainous lovely heroine in the new age of barbarism.

The new age will have many uses for Diver. Within a few years he might have been invited to rejoin Jung at Zurich in order to develop an Aryan not a Jewish psychiatry. Or he might have joined the staff at Dachau and engaged in studies of the psychopathology of intensely chilled D. P.'s. But he prefers to exile himself from the world. Beginning his adult life as an expatriate from America, he ends as an exile in upstate New York, somewhere between Buffalo and Hornell. Dick Diver is the first displaced person in American literature, created by the one member of a generation—not the lost but the displaced generation—who foresaw which exact causes would turn this globe into a barbaric place populated by refugees.

If we take Diver's career to typify the experience of all exiles expelled from communities controlled by executioners of one persuasion or another, we may see that to speak of modern writing as a Jewish thing, to refer to "the Jew as symbol" of alienation, is to reduce vast matters to a communal affair. And to stress, as Miss McCarthy does, the theme of statelessness alone is to treat segment as if it were integument. For if convulsion in the world is the stupefying social fact implicit in our arts of absurd and gratuitous violence, and if usurpation and abuse of power constitute the presiding political and moral state, then obviously all men are victims in our time. Surely European Jews can serve to incarnate these dark things. But the general condition is reported with equal intensity by persons from Lowndes County to Capetown.

Although we must repudiate cant, the particular role of Jewish writers, neither traduced nor glorified, must be weighed and esteemed. For Jewish displaced persons preserve an endowment of being, retain a bearing that, Hannah Arendt aside, enables them to relinquish their lives without acquiesing in their fate. This bearing and that fate compose the subject of *The Last of the Just*, a novel in which Jewish legends of *ches-yud* (*chesed*: piety and chosenness), of the *lamed vov* (a complex mystic numerology attesting the fact and weighing the cost of chosenness) are adapted to current affairs. The legends are intricate but their drift is plain: Jews, killing Christ, acted according to the general will but selflessly assumed the Romans' and the world's guilt. In consequence, Jews have served as the villains chosen to suffer heroically in order to redeem all men from sin, however gross, and to absolve men of evil, however foul. Schwarz-Bart, fulfilling both the classic symbolism and the contemporary utility of this myth, presents the last just chosen Jew as a displaced person. And this person, Ernie Levy, before he dies realizes that Jesus too was a man of his own kind, a *Lamed-Vovnik*, chosen to suffer so that men would be reminded of their capacity for selfless love despite their genius for hateful passion. Ernie Levy is executed by Christian barbarians; he dies believing that only Jews are Christians. Schwarz-Bart's novel portrays in quintessence the position cultivated by those Jewish writers whose heroes, displaced persons all, distinguish themselves by displaying a resilience of spirit despite the dominion of gall.

When the President was executed, put to death by a European rifle ordered from Chicago in the name of that metonymous and anonymous man, A. Hyd(Hid)ell, life in the Age of Barban came full circle. The displaced person, convinced of his virtue and fanatic for revenge, for release from pain, himself issued an invitation to a beheading. "Though so profound a double-dealer, I was in no sense a hypocrite; both sides of me were in dead earnest; I was no more myself when I laid aside restraint and plunged in shame, than when I laboured in the eye of day, at the furtherance of knowlege or the relief of sorrow and suffering." Did Oswald, that literary and literal man, recall these lines from Robert Louis Stevenson's story? Did he know that "to cast in with Hyde was to . . . become, at a blow and for ever, despised and friendless?" This is exactly the sort of fiction, the kind of fantasy, of kitsch, he would have absorbed, taken seriously, treated as high literature, but my notion is sheer guess. What is incontrovertible is that Oswald preferred to cast his lot with A. Hyd(Hid)ell and thereby christened the displaced person, exposed his current passion and terror: ". . . within the soft blur of the name fantasy selves whirled like the blades of a fan. Hydell, Hidell, hide, hell, hideous, idle, idol, Fidel, Hyde, Jekyll," said Benjamin De Mott in *The New York Review of Books*. And "next day came the news," Stevenson himself had added, "that the guilt of Hyde was patent to the world," that the "victim was a man high in public estimation."

And next came the news of Jack Rubenstein's heroic deed of piety and self-sacrifice: *chesed*. A Ruby, skull knitted round a metal plate — product of a street fight in 1940, one of his lawyers said — executed A. Hyd(Hid)ell.

In that instant life was turned into a take-off on myth, a parody of art. Two disordered men performed on camera twin acts of tyranny inspired by the experience and shaped by the imagination of displacement in our time.

Tender Is the Night and the "Ode to a Nightingale"

William E. Doherty*

Critics often express a feeling that there is something mysterious about Fitzgerald's *Tender Is the Night*, that there is something unsatisfying in the analyses we have had — a discomfort one does not feel with the more elaborately structured *The Great Gatsby*, or with the intriguing, unfinished *The Last Tycoon*. Searching the critical opinion on *Tender Is the Night* — this "magnificent failure" — one is likely to feel that something *is* missing; one seems to have, as Maxwell Geismar says, "the curious impression at times that the novel is really about something else altogether."[1]

It seems strange that the relationship between the novel and Keats's "Ode to a Nightingale," which supplied Fitzgerald with both title and epigraph, should have received no more than passing attention from the critics. The epigraph reads:

> Already with thee! tender is the night,
>
> . . .
>
> But here there is no light,
> Save what from heaven is with the breezes blown
> Through verdurous glooms and winding mossy ways.

We know that Fitzgerald had a lifelong and deep response to Keats: "for awhile after you quit Keats all other poetry seems to be only whistling or humming." The "Ode to a Nightingale" was especially important to him; he found it unbearably beautiful, confessed he read it always with tears in his eyes.[2]

I

It is true that the title *Tender Is the Night* was chosen late in the extended course of the book's writing; but it seems clear that Fitzgerald was conscious of the "Ode" not merely in the last stages of composition. The title is appropriate, though no one has said why. Yet, a moment's reflection will show that there is a good deal of Keatsian suggestiveness in

*Reprinted from Rima Drell Reck, ed., *Explorations of Literature* (Baton Rouge: Louisiana State University Press, 1966), pp. 100–114. Reprinted by permission of Louisiana State University Press.

Tender Is the Night in both decor and atmosphere—the Provençal summers of sunburnt mirth, the nights perfumed and promising, the dark gardens of an illusory world. But I suggest that there are parallels more significant than those of color and mood. The correspondences I offer in this case, when taken individually, might seem no more than coincidental; but considered in their cumulative weight, they indicate a calculated pattern of allusion beneath the literal surface of the novel which deepens the psychoanalytic rationale and adds context to the cultural analysis the book offers. In addition, the "Ode" appears to provide us with a sort of thematic overlay which clarifies unsuspected symbolic structures, essential to the understanding of the book.

I will begin with an admission that weakens my case. Fitzgerald dropped a reference to the nightingale from his second and subsequent versions of the published novel. In the *Scribner's Magazine* version he wrote of "roses and the nightingales" that had become an essential part of the beauty of that "proud gay land," Provence.[3] Why that observation was dropped, I cannot say; but its appearance, however brief, suggests that like Keats, Fitzgerald associated the south of France with the romantic bird. There is a second and more interesting reference which remained. It too connects the bird and the south of France. To understand its significance, one must consider it in context.

The Riviera, Mediterranean France, came to be, as Maxwell Geismar has pointed out, that apogee of ease and grace, that "psychological Eden" in which Fitzgerald and his heroes took refuge.[4] None of his characters responds more fully to this environment than does Rosemary, coming as she does from the "salacious improvisations of the frontier." At the party at the Villa Diana, no guest is more enchanted by the life that seems promised there; she feels a sense of homecoming, feels drawn as if by magnetic lights. The spell of the party is still on her as she lies awake in her room "suspended in the moonshine . . . cloaked by the erotic darkness." She is disturbed by secret noises in the night: an "insistent bird" sings in the tree outside. She is not sure what bird it is, but the singing and the Divers seem to merge in her mind: "Beyond the inky sea and far up that high, black shadow of a hill lived the Divers. She thought of them both together, heard them still singing faintly a song like rising smoke, like a hymn, very remote in time and far away."[5] But Rosemary is confused by it all; she cannot think as yet except through her mother's mind. Abe North identifies the bird for her:

> "What are *you* doing up?" he demanded.
> "I just got up." She started to laugh. . . .
> "Probably plagued by the nightingale," Abe suggested and repeated, "probably plagued by the nightingale" (42).

The entire chapter, heavy with night imagery, seems to lead up to this identification. Rosemary has been brought up with the idea of work. Now she is on a summer's holiday, an emotionally lush interval between two winters of reality; and what she discovers is a world remote, romantic, something southern, a mysterious dark lure of life to which she responds — symbolized by the night bird. It is unreal; a duel will be fought; "up north the true world thundered by."

What I suggest is that the novel deals with characters who are plagued by the nightingale, those enamored of the romantic illusion. Nicole seems to be the nightingale.

Consider the scene in which Nicole sings to Dick. As she waits for Dick at the sanatorium, singing surrounds Nicole, summer songs of ardent skies and wild shade. The night, the woods, gardens, flowers are associated with Nicole throughout the novel. Here, the unknown seems to yield her up, "as if this were the exact moment when she was coming from a wood into the clear moonlight" (135). Dick responds to that illusion, wishes that she had no other background, "No address save the night from which she had come." She leads him to a secret copse. In this melodious plot she has hidden a phonograph. She plays for him "thin tunes, holding lost times and future hopes in liaison." Through song the two of them are transported out of the copse into another world. The journey is chronicled in ironic song titles. Finally Nicole herself sings to Dick. She supposes he has heard all these songs before. " 'Honestly, you don't understand — I haven't heard a thing.' Nor known, nor smelt, nor tasted, he might have added" (136). Now here was this girl bringing him the essence of a continent, "making him a profound promise of herself for so little. . . . Minute by minute the sweetness drained down into her out of the willow trees, out of the dark world" (136). But there is danger in the promise of this "waif of disaster," in the song of this "young bird with wings crushed."

The brief transport from the world which the "Ode" details, the emotional adventure of climax and decline is suggested in this and in a number of other scenes in *Tender Is the Night*. Indeed, the pattern describes the very rhythm of the novel. The party at the Villa Diana, as Malcolm Cowley suggests, appears to be the high point in the story. The scene marks a change of mood; thereafter, the light romantic atmosphere is dispelled.[6] We see there the Divers at their point of greatest charm — a "vision of ease and grace," commanding all the delicacies of existence. It is a high point for another reason. It is in this scene that the principals of the story make an escape from the prosaic and temporal world. In the rarefied atmosphere of the party a moment is caught in which a delicate triumph over time is achieved.

The party is given out-of-doors in the garden, Nicole's garden. To Rosemary the setting seems to be the center of the world: "On such a stage some memorable thing was sure to happen" (29). The guests arrive under a spell, bringing with them the excitement of the night. Dick now seems to serve Nicole as prop man, arranging the set, dressing the trees with lamps. The guests are seated at Nicole's table:

There were fireflies riding on the dark air and a dog baying on some low and far-away ledge of the cliff. The table seemed to have risen a little toward the sky like a mechanical dancing platform, giving the people around it a sense of being alone with each other in the dark universe, nourished by its only food, warmed by its only lights. And, as if a curious hushed laugh from Mrs. McKisco were a signal that such a detachment from the world had been attained, the two Divers began suddenly to warm and glow and expand, as if to make up to their guests, already so subtly assured of their importance, so flattered with politeness, for anything they might still miss from that country well left behind. Just for a moment they seemed to speak to everyone at the table, singly and together, assuring them of their friendliness, their affection. And for a moment the faces turned up toward them were like the faces of poor children at a Christmas tree. Then abruptly the table broke up — the moment when the guests had been daringly lifted above conviviality into the rarer atmosphere of sentiment, was over before it could be irreverently breathed, before they had half realized it was there.

But the diffused magic of the hot sweet South had withdrawn into them — the soft-pawed night and the ghostly wash of the Mediterranean far below — the magic left those things and melted into the two Divers and became part of them (34–35).

When we consider the care with which Fitzgerald dresses this scene, we sense an emphasis beyond what the mere events of the party would demand. This garden, the fireflies riding on the dark air, the summer evening, the wine-colored lanterns hung in the trees — the Romantic decor is there, and the Keatsian atmosphere: "the diffused magic of the hot sweet South . . . the soft-pawed night and the ghostly wash of the Mediterranean far below. . . ." There is no need to insist that these images have their antecedents in the "Ode" — in its "murmurous haunt of flies on summer eves," or its "warm south," its "tender night," its "charmed magic casements opening on perilous seas"; for the clearest parallel to the poem lies in the brief achievement of the precious atmosphere, achieved through the familiar Romantic formula of escape at the moment of emotional pitch — here ironically, a moment of social ecstasy, but suggesting inevitably the dynamics of the sexual event. The imagery itself reiterates the pattern: the fragile loveliness of Nicole's garden increases "until, as if the scherzo of color could reach no further intensity, it broke of suddenly in mid-air, and moist steps went down to a level five feet below" (26).

It seems unlikely that the material of the "Ode" was so immediate in Fitzgerald's mind that it would come to add to the novel a dimension of allusion of which he was unaware. We are willing to concede unlimited conscious subtlety to his contemporaries in the novel; but Fitzgerald, despite the evidence of his deliberate workmanship, is too often pictured by critics as a somewhat fatuous tool of the muse, whose mind was inferior to his talent. The intricacies of Tender Is the Night would suggest otherwise. Not only is the pattern of the momentary climax a repeated one in the novel; there occurs, too, the *recall to reality* that marks the ending of the "Ode." In the novel it is not the sound of a bell that signals the descent from bliss—or the word "forlorn" striking like a bell, tolling the poet back to his sole self; it is another sound heard three times in the book: when Dick falls in love with Nicole, when Abe leaves on the train from Paris, and when Tommy becomes Nicole's lover. Each time a shot is heard, a loud report that breaks the illusion signifies the end of his happiness and the escape from self.

After Nicole leaves the sanatorium, Dick tries to avoid her; but she fills his dreams. Their chance meeting in the Alps ends in Dick's complete surrender of self: "he was thankful to have an existence at all, if only as a reflection in her wet eyes" (155). As in all her love situations, Nicole is triumphant, self-controlled, cool: "I've got him, he's mine" (155). The scene remains tender; it is raining, the appropriate weather for love in Fitzgerald's novels. But, "suddenly there was a booming from the wine slopes across the lake; cannons were shooting at hail-bearing clouds in order to break them. The lights of the promenade went off, went on again. Then the storm came swiftly . . . with it came a dark, frightening sky and savage filaments of lightning and world-splitting thunder, while ragged, destroying clouds fled along past the hotel. Mountains and lakes disappeared—the hotel crouched amid tumult, chaos and darkness" (155–56).

This is not the storm of passion. Dick has come suddenly to his senses: "For Doctor Diver to marry a mental patient? How did it happen? Where did it begin?" The moment of passion and illusion is over. He laughs derisively. "*Big* chance—oh, yes. My God! —they decided to buy a doctor? Well, they better stick to whoever they've got in Chicago" (156). But Dick has committed himself to Nicole. His clear sight comes too late, and when the storm is over her beauty enters his room "rustling ghostlike through the curtains."

A loud shot sounds the ominous recall another time, in the Paris railway station. Here is departure and farewell; a gunshot cracks the air. Abe, on the train, waves good-bye, unaware of what has happened. The shots do not mark the end of his happiness, for he has long been in misery, though they do forebode his violent death. It is the brief summer happiness of Dick—won in a desperate bargain with the gods—that is ending. It marks the end of a summer mirth for the Divers' group, the beginning of misfortune for Dick. Dick and his friends move out of the station into the street as if nothing had happened. "However, everything had happened—Abe's departure and Mary's impending departure for Salzburg this afternoon had ended the time in Paris. Or perhaps the shots, the concussions that had finished God knew what dark matter, had terminated it. The shots had entered into all their lives . . ." (85).

The third of these recalls to reality occurs just after Tommy possesses Nicole. The entire account from the arrival of Tommy at the Villa Diana to the departure from the hotel presents a curious parallel to the ending of the "Ode." Tommy comes to Nicole like a worshiper before a mystery. His happiness intensifies: "And, my God, I have never been so happy as I am this minute" (294). But the time of joy is brief; the point of greatest happiness is a moment outside of self, a taste of oblivion. The escstasy passes: disappointment and foreboding follow: "The nameless fear which precedes all emotions, joyous or sorrowful, inevitable as a hum of thunder precedes a storm." After the act, things begin to look tawdry to Tommy. He is edgy and apprehensive. Outside there are disturbing noises: "There's that noise again. My God, has there been a murder?" The final recall is heard. As they leave the room "a sound split the air outside: Cr-ACK-Boom-M-m-m! It was the battleship sounding a recall. Now, down below their window, it was pandemonium indeed . . ." (296–97). There is a rush to depart. Cries and tears are heard as the women shout farewells to the departing launch. The last ludicrous moments of the scene, the girls shouting their tearful good-byes from the balcony of Tommy's room, waving their underwear like flags, appear to be Fitzgerald's ironic counterpart to the adieu of the final stanza of the poem. The fading anthem of the "Ode" becomes the American National Anthem: "Oh, say can you see the tender color of remembered flesh? — while at the stern of the battleship arose in rivalry the Star-Spangled Banner" (297).

II

The title of the novel and the epigraph Fitzgerald offers illuminate the significance of "night" and "darkness" in the story. An enquiry reveals a complicated and careful symbolic structure in *Tender Is the Night* involving a contrast between the night and the day, darkness and light. The title of the novel declares that the night is tender. There is in it an implicit corollary about the day.

Early in the story, the sun is established as something harsh and painful, even maddening. The sun troubles the Divers and their group. They seek shelter from it under their umbrellas which "filter" its rays. At the beach the sea yields up its colors to the "brutal sunshine." Rosemary retreats from the "hot light" on the sand. Dick promises her a hat to protect her from the sun and to "save her reason." In the scene in which Nicole lapses into madness at the Agiri Fair, "a high sun with a face traced on it beat fierce on the straw hats of the children." The day scenes are those of pain and fear: "the April sun shone pink upon the saintly face of Augustine, the cook, and blue on the butcher's knife she waved in her drunken hand" (265).

On the other hand, darkness and the night are addressed in fond, in honorific terms: "the lovely night," the "soft rolling night," the "soft-pawed night," the "erotic darkness." Fitzgerald's description of Amiens reveals something of the character and virtue of the night: "In the daytime one is deflated by such towns . . . and the very weather seems to have a quality of the past, faded weather like that of old photographs. But after dark all that is most satisfactory in French life swims back into the picture — the sprightly tarts, the men arguing with a hundred Voilas in the cafés, the couples drifting, head to head, toward the satisfactory inexpensiveness of nowhere" (59). Part of the meaning is here, but the symbolism of the night is not merely opposite in meaning to that of the day; it is more complicated and more intricately woven into the story. The night is the time of enchantment, masking the ugliness of reality that the day exposes. The night, as in the "Ode," is the time of beauty and the time of illusion. Dick and his friends prefer the night: "All of them began to laugh spontaneously because they knew it was still last night while the people in the streets had the delusion that it was bright hot morning" (79). But the night is not entirely superior to the day. The desirable night is the all allowing darkness. It is a dimness preferred, perhaps, by those ineffective in dealing with the practical day-lit reality. If the day is harsh, it has vigor; the night is the time of ease and also weakness. Some hint of these sinister implications may also be detected in the scene in which Baby Warren makes her frustrated effort to aid Dick after he has been beaten and thrown into the Roman jail. She cannot function in the real world: "She began to race against the day; sometimes on the broad avenues she gained but whenever the thing that was pushing up paused for a moment, gusts of wind blew here and there impatiently and the slow creep of light began once more" (227). She cringes at the unstable balance between night and day. The strange creature she encounters in the embassy, wrapped and bandaged for sleep, "vivid but dead," appears an unwholesome figure of the night, incongruous with the day.

It would appear that Fitzgerald has divided his world into two parts — the night and the day. The day is reality, hard, harsh, and vigorous; the night is illusion, tender, joyful, but devitalizing.

The most significant illusion that the night fosters is the illusion of happiness. To the Romantic, happiness consists in preserving the high moment of joy. He has a dread of endings. *Tender Is the Night* is a book of endings: "Things are over down here," says Dick. "I want it to die violently instead of fading out sentimentally" (37–38). Paradoxically, the Romantic dream is that the moment of joy can be embalmed forever in the final night; death then appears to be a welcome extenuation of the night, ending all endings. Both the poem and the novel deal with these lovely illusions; but what they teach is that the fancy cannot cheat so well, that disillusionment is the coefficient of time.

There is a difference in tone between the two works which is due to the fact that Keats emphasizes the swelling dimension of the ecstatic experience, while Fitzgerald deals more with its deflation. Where Keats conveys a sense of disappointment, fond regret, Fitzgerald expresses a Romantic's anti-Romantic argument; for in tracing the grim disenchantment Fitzgerald underscores the sense of deception, trickery, the sense of victimage in the martyring of the dreamer. The "immortal bird" of the "Ode" becomes the "perverse phoenix" Nicole; the deceiving elf becomes the "crooked" Nicole, one of a long line of deceivers, pretending to have a mystery: "I've gone back to my true self," she tells Tommy; " . . . I'm a crook by heritage" (292). We suspect complicity in her father's sin; he tells the doctor, "She used to sing to me" (129).

There are other victims of the Romantic deception—the inmates of the sanatorium where Dick labors without accomplishment. "I am here as a symbol of something" (185), the American woman artist tells Dick. She and the others are there because "life is too tough a game" for them. Unlike the thick-ankled peasants who can take the punishment of the world on every inch of flesh and spirit, these are the fine-spun people suffering private illusions, their "compasses depolarized." They are "sunk in eternal darkness," people of the night, spirits sensitive and weak, now caught in Nicole's garden. For it is Nicole who has designed the means of holding these inmates fast. With floral concealment and deceptive ornament she has created those camouflaged strong points in which they are kept. Outwardly these houses are attractive, even cheerful, screened by little copses; but "even the flowers lay in iron fingers." Perhaps the "Ode" suggested the names: the "Beeches" and the "Eglantine."

III

These inmates are, many of them, the "victims of drug and drink." There is in *Tender Is the Night* what might be called a potion motif, involving liquor, drugs, and poison. As in the "Ode" these are associated with the illusory adventure. Dr. Diver is as much an addict as his patients. In the early parts of the novel, wine is associated with the delicacy of living the Divers maintain and with the sensual qualities of their lives. The enjoyable swim in the ocean is like the pleasure of "chilled white wine." The wine-colored lamps at the Villa Diana give a lively flush to Nicole's face. Nicole is gay-spirited after the "rosy wine at lunch." There is a faint spray of champagne on Rosemary's breath when Dick kisses her for the first time. But wine quickly loses its pleasant character. As Dick's esteemed control begins to slip and he acts for the first time without his customary "repose," he stares at the shelf of bottles, "the humbler poisons of France— bottles of Otard, Rhum St. James, Marie Brizzard. . . ." Dick's Roman debauch recalls Abe's disastrous drunks. At home Dick drinks brandy from a three-foot bottle. He comes to regard liquor as food, descending to the level of the rich ruins he treats. Late in the novel we see that the sinister qualities of these draughts, potions, beakersful are associated with Nicole: in falling in love with her, in marrying her, Dick "had chosen the sweet poison and drunk it." Again Nicole is characterized as the attractive evil, the sinister allurement.

The draught of vintage from the deep delved earth, the dull opiate, the hemlock of Keats's poem may not be the direct sources of Fitzgerald's images; yet the associations of drug, drink, and poison with the Romantic appetencies are interesting and suggest that Keats and Fitzgerald were dealing with a similar psychological syndrome—the urge to "fade away, dissolve and quite forget. . . ."

This urge, as Albert Guerard, Jr., points out in his essay, "Prometheus and the Aeolian Lyre," is really the urge toward loss of self, the impulse toward self-immolation, to the drowning of consciousness—one of the hallmarks of the Romantic temperament—which accepts the myth of a vital correspondence between man and nature, a correspondence demanding the submersion of our rational, coherent selves. In the "Ode to a Nightingale," Mr. Guerard argues, Keats has written a poem about the actual submersion of consciousness, dramatizing the process itself, and presenting in the poem a symbolic evasion of the actual world:

> In one sense this ode is a dramatized contrasting of actuality and the world of the imagination, but the desire to attain this fretless imaginative world becomes at last a desire for reason's utter dissolution: a longing not for art but for free reverie of any kind. . . . This sole self from which Keats escapes at the beginning of the poem, and to which he returns at its close, is not merely the conscious intellect aware of life's weariness, fever, and fret, but truly the sole self: the self locked in drowsy numbness, the self conscious of its isolation. . . .[7]

Mr. Guerard's analysis may be modified, perhaps, to this degree: the "Ode" seems not so much a product of the Romantic myth of a prevailing correspondence between man and nature as it is an acknowledgment that the correspondence does not prevail. This thesis is reiterated in *Tender Is the Night*. What the nightingale symbolizes and promises in the "Ode," Nicole symbolizes and promises too. The ecstatic union with the bird is a taste of oblivion in loss of self.

Dick manifests the symptoms that Mr. Guerard indicates. There is the obsessive awareness of isolation that characterizes Dick even in his student days. He feels separated from his "fathers." He has the feeling that he is different from the rest, the isolation of the scientist and the artist—"good material for those who do most of the world's work"; but it is a loneliness he cannot endure. He wanted to be good, to be kind; he wanted to be brave and wise; but, as we learn toward the end, "he had wanted, even more than that, to be loved" (302). He gives a strange answer to Franz's criticism of his scholarship: "I am alone today. . . . But I may not be alone to-morrow" (138). One by one he burns his books to keep warm. In marrying Nicole he abandons his work in "effortless immobility." The critics have frequently noted the self-sacrificial aspect of Dick's behavior; but too frequently that self-sacrifice has been taken as the very theme of the novel because Dick gives himself so completely in serving others that he is left with nothing in the end. Rather, this self-sacrifice should be understood as one of the paradoxical impulses which constitute the desire to submerge the self. Self-immolation seems to contradict the longing for freedom from burdens and cares, yet both urges are aspects of the desire to abandon individuality. Abe, like Dick, has a strong desire for loss of self, and forgetfulness. Abe wants oblivion and seeks it in drink; he longs for death. Tommy too has inclinations toward the moribund, following death and violence all over the world. Baby Warren "relished the foretaste of death, prefigured by the catastrophes of friends" (172). Dick looks fondly at death in his decline. At the railing of Golding's yacht he comes close to suicide and to taking Nicole with him. The isolation Dick feels as a young man is never relieved. The entire age is alien to him. Dick mourns on the battlefields of World War I: "All my beautiful lovely safe world blew itself up here with a great gust of high explosive love" (57). Coming home to bury his father, he feels the final tie has been broken; there is no identity with his own land; he feels only a kinship with the dead: "Good-by, my father — good-by, all my fathers" (205).

IV

Finally, what does the correspondence between the novel and the "Ode" reveal about the social and cultural analysis Fitzgerald offers in *Tender Is the Night?* The distinction between the night and the day that Fitzgerald establishes symbolically has its significance in the "class strug- gle" he presents; the social antagonisms seem to be aspects of the antipathy which arises between the Romantic and the anti-Romantic disposition.

Fitzgerald, as we have seen, divides things into opposing pairs in *Tender Is the Night.* When Rosemary arrives at the Riviera beach she finds two groups. The McKisco party is made up of McKisco, the *arriviste* who has not yet arrived, his silly ambitious wife, two effeminates, and the shabby-eyed Mrs. Abrams. They are pale, gauche people, unattractive beside the Divers' group. The Divers are rich, cultured, talented, leisured. We get a fuller understanding of what these groups may represent in the scene in which Dick and Rosemary visit the house on the Rue Monsieur. It is a place of incongruities and contrasts. Clearly there is a clash between the past and the present, suggesting, it seems, the evolving future of the Western world: "It was a house hewn from the frame of Cardinal de Retz's palace in the Rue Monsieur, but once inside the door there was nothing of the past, nor of any present that Rosemary knew. The outer shell, the masonry, seemed rather to enclose the future so that it was an electric-like shock, a definite nervous experience, perverted as a breakfast of oatmeal and hashish, to cross that threshold. . ." (71). The people within are an odd mixture. They fit awkwardly into the environment. They lack the command over life that earlier ages managed to exert. Rosemary has a detached "false and exalted feeling" of being on a movie set. No one knew what the room meant because it was evolving into something else. It is important to recognize who these people in the room are:

These were of two sorts. There were the Americans and English who had been dissipating all spring and summer, so that now everything they did had a purely nervous inspiration. They were very quiet and lethargic at certain hours and then they exploded into sudden quarrels and breakdowns and seductions. The other class, who might be called the exploiters, was formed by the sponges, who were sober, serious people by comparison, with a purpose in life and no time for fooling. These kept their balance best in that environment, and what tone there was, beyond the apartment's novel organization of light values, came from them (72).

The room apparently holds the society of the West. We find in it the McKisco group, the sponges, the hard practical people; and there are the Divers' type, the dissipated old "quality" class, the run-down Romantics who are doomed. The sober and serious exploiters set the tone for the future, and in it they will succeed. Rosemary stands between the two groups. Her youth and success separate her from the Divers' crowd, but she inclines toward them by temperament and training. She is a product of her mother's rearing, tutored in the values of the old society. "I'm a romantic too," Rosemary tells Dick. Yet, she is coldly practical, "economically . . . a boy not a girl." The first day on the beach Rosemary does not know which group is hers. She is attracted by the Divers' party; but, "between the dark people and the light, Rosemary found room and spread out her peignoir on the sand" (5–6).

The people of the McKisco type are not the victims of Nicole; they are immune to the Romantic illusion. The "tough minded and perennially suspicious" cannot be charmed. McKisco is the only one at the party at the Villa Diana who remains unassimilated, unaffected by the emotional excursion. In the house on the Rue Monsieur there are others who are likewise immune. The "cobra women" discuss the Divers:

"Oh, they give a good show," said one of them in a deep rich voice. "Practically the best show in Paris—I'd be the last one to deny that. But after all—" She sighed. "Those phrases he uses over and over—'Oldest inhabitant gnawed by rodents.' You laugh once."
"I prefer people whose lives have more corrugated surfaces," said the second, "and I don't like her."
"I've never really been able to get very excited about them, or their entourage either. Why, for example, the entirely liquid Mr. North?" (72–73).

The incapacity for illusion gives these people an advantage in the world. McKisco, for whom the sensual world does not exist, ends successful and honored; his novels are pastiches of the work of the best people of his time. "He was no fool about his capacities—he realized that he possessed more vitality than many men of superior talent, and he was resolved to enjoy the success he had earned" (205). McKisco's duel with Tommy symbolizes the clash between the two groups and underscores the anachronism of the soldier and hero. Tommy is a product of the older civilization, educated in forgotten values. Ironically it is McKisco who is "satisfied" in the duel. He builds a new self-respect from his inglorious performance. Tommy, Abe, and Dick are Romantic remnants, the children of another century, fettered by its illusions — "the illusions of eternal strength and health, and of the essential goodness of people; illusions of a nation, the lies of generations of frontier mothers who had to croon falsely, that there were no wolves outside the cabin door" (117).

They are the salt of the earth — charming, gifted people, but over-matched in the struggle against the cold, shrewd frauds who are inheriting the earth. Tender Is the Night deals with the passing of the old order, with the passing of an attitude toward life, or rather with the last remnants of that life, "the oldest inhabitants gnawed by rodents." The specific content of the illusions which fetter them is less important than how Fitzgerald deals with the attraction to the irrational dream which marks the romantic temperament, a dream which may promise the world, the sustained ecstasy of love, or the satisfactions of oblivion — symbolized by the beautiful, mad woman, Nicole. She is the dream without real referent. She has no existence outside the mind of the dreamer: "When I talk I say to myself that I am probably Dick. Already I have even been my son, remembering how wise and slow he is. Sometimes I am Doctor Dohmler and one time I may even be an aspect of you, Tommy Barban. Tommy is in love with me . . ." (162).

In the end it is Dr. Diver who is "cured" when he releases her from his mind; he returns to the terrible emptiness of the "sole self." Late in the novel Nicole sings to him again in her "harsh sweet contralto." But this time Dick will not listen: "I don't like that one" (290).

The dream and the dreamer are, of course, Fitzgerald's subject matter in fiction; and in treating them he invariably delivers up the dreamer as victim of his own Romantic infatuations. And yet for all his insight, his self-lacerating satire, Fitzgerald leaves the dream and the dreamer somehow inviolable at the end. Gatsby, that most extravagant Romantic, leaking sawdust at every pore, is still intact at the end and dies with his dream intact. "No — Gatsby turned out all right at the end; it was what preyed on Gatsby, what foul dust floated in the wake of his dreams . . ." that defeated him.

The best of the Romantic writers are not vulnerable to their own myths. The "Ode to the Nightingale" declares exquisitely the abandon-ment of faith in the imagination. It is not until Tender Is the Night that Fitzgerald abandons that last comfort of the Romantic, the notion that the botching, the disappointment of the imagination's most cherished ambi-tions may be blamed on the unworthy environment of the dreamer. Tender

Is the Night is a harder, harsher book than *Gatsby*; and it tells us that the super-dream is an internal corruption, a damaging, self-begotten beauty. Dick's final return to his sole self in upstate New York — "almost certainly in that section of the country, in one town or another" — is an utterly unsentimental fade-out; the hero is gone from the stage before we can cover him with our fond sympathy, before we can murmur, "Alas."

Notes

1. Maxwell Geismar, *The Last of the Provincials* (Cambridge, Mass., 1947), p. 333. Reprinted from *Explorations of Literature*, ed. Rima Drell Reck, Louisiana State University Press, 1966, by permission of the publisher.

2. F. Scott Fitzgerald, *The Crack-up* (New York, 1956), p. 298.

3. F. Scott Fitzgerald, "Tender Is the Night, a Romance," *Scribner's Magazine*, XCV (January–June, 1934), 7.

4. Geismar, pp. 290–91.

5. F. Scott Fitzgerald, *Tender Is the Night* (New York, 1962), p. 40. Quotations in the text are from this edition unless otherwise indicated.

6. Malcolm Cowley, "Introduction," *Tender Is the Night* (New York, 1956), p. xvii.

7. Albert Guerard, Jr., "Prometheus and the Aeolian Lyre," *Yale Review*, XXXIII (March, 1944), 495.

Tender Is the Night   Arthur Mizener*

F. Scott Fitzgerald was the first of the gifted American novelists of the 1920's to become famous; he had a Byronic, overnight success with his first novel, *This Side of Paradise*, which was published in the first year of the decade. It was a brash, immature novel that Fitzgerald's lifelong friend Edmund Wilson called "one of the most illiterate books of any merit ever published." Later in life Fitzgerald himself said of it, with the queer impersonality he could always give his considered judgments of himself, "A lot of people thought it was a fake, and perhaps it was, and a lot of others thought it was a lie, which it was not."

The essential quality of Fitzgerald's insight is shown by that comment. Looked at objectively, *This Side of Paradise* was in many ways a fake; it pretended to all sorts of knowledge and experience of the world its author did not in fact have. But it was not a lie; it expressed with accuracy and honesty its author's inner vision of himself and his experience, however false to literal fact that vision might be at certain points. Fitzgerald's reality was always that inner vision, but he had a deep respect

*Reprinted from Arthur Mizener, *Twelve Great American Novels* (New York: New American Library, 1967), pp. 104–19. © 1967 by Arthur Mizener. Reprinted by arrangement with New American Library.

for the outer reality of the world because it was the only place where his inward vision could be fulfilled, could be made actual. The tension between his inescapable commitment to the inner reality of his imagination and his necessary respect for the outer reality of the world is what gives his fiction its peculiar charm and is the source of his ability to surround a convincing representation of the actual world with an air of enchantment that makes the most ordinary occasions haunting.

The success of *This Side of Paradise* did not do Fitzgerald any good. It gave him the fame and money to plunge into the gay whirl of New York parties that in postwar America somehow seemed to be a more significant life than the provincial one prewar America had lived. Fitzgerald and his beautiful wife, Zelda, rode through New York on the tops of taxis, jumped fully clothed into the Pulitzer Fountain in front of the Plaza, and quickly became leaders among the bright spirits of postwar New York. It was all harmless enough in itself, but it left very little time for serious writing, particularly for a man to whom alcohol was very damaging, almost a poison.

Yet all the time Fitzgerald was busy being the handsome hero of the Younger Generation, there was a serious writer inside him struggling to get out. That serious writer got control for a moment when he wrote *The Great Gatsby* (1924). But then the Fitzgeralds fell back into the life of parties—now mostly in Paris and on the Riviera—that gradually became for them a more and more desperate and self-destructive effort to be happy. It ended in 1930, when Zelda became a serious schizophrene and Fitzgerald, pulled up short by this disaster, found himself an alcoholic. He spent the rest of his brief life—he died in 1940, shortly after his forty-fourth birthday—fighting a grim battle to save Zelda, to cure his own alcoholism, and to fulfill his promise as a writer. "I have been a poor caretaker of everything I possessed," he said at this time, "even of my talent." He lost Zelda—she never grew better—and he was only partly successful in his fight against alcoholism. But, sick and discouraged though he was, he managed before he died to write *Tender Is the Night*, published in 1934, and a marvelous fragment of another novel called *The Last Tycoon*.

Tender Is the Night has certain defects traceable to the conditions in which it was written. As Fitzgerald himself said of it with his remarkable honesty, "If a mind is slowed up ever so little, it lives in the individual parts of a book rather than in a book as a whole; memory is dulled. I would give anything if I hadn't had to write Part III of 'Tender Is the Night' entirely on stimulant." Despite these defects, *Tender Is the Night* is the most mature and moving book Fitzgerald ever wrote.

It is not, however, an easy book to understand. Its difficulty is at least partly due to the odd discrepancy in it between the almost frivolous insignificance—by conventional standards anyhow—of the hero's life and the importance Fitzgerald obviously means us to attach to it. This difficulty in *Tender Is the Night* is only a particular instance of the general problem created in American fiction by the subjective novel as distinguished from the objective novel of social history such as Dos Passos wrote. Fitzgerald and Dos Passos were friends, but it is evident that neither could understand what the other was up to. In 1933, the year before Fitzgerald completed *Tender Is the Night*, he wrote a mutual friend, "Dos was here, & we had a nice evening—we never quite understand each other & perhaps that's the best basis for an enduring friendship." As if to prove how right Fitzgerald was, Dos Passos wrote him, when he published the revealing essays called "The Crack-Up" that describe the personal experience underlying *Tender Is the Night*, "I've been wanting to see you, naturally, to argue about your *Esquire* articles—Christ, man, how do you find time in the middle of the general conflagration to worry about all that stuff? . . . most of the time the course of the world events seems so frightful that I feel absolutely paralysed." Clearly, Dos Passos is baffled by Fitzgerald's preoccupation "with all that stuff" about the meaning of his personal experience. Fitzgerald was equally baffled by Dos Passos' obsession with "the course of world events."

There was of course a subjective novelist somewhere in Dos Passos, but Dos Passos relegated this novelist to the Camera Eye passages of *U.S.A.* and he affects the narrative only indirectly. There was also a man with a considerable sense of history in Fitzgerald: as Malcolm Cowley once put it, Fitzgerald lived in a room full of clocks and calendars. But Fitzgerald's knowledge of history, astonishing as his memory for it was, gets into his novels almost entirely as metaphors for the life of his consciousness, for the quality of his private experience. His summary of the year 1927—the year in which the slow decline of Dick Diver, the hero of *Tender Is the Night*, becomes clearly evident—is characteristic: "By 1927 a wide-spread neurosis began to be evident, faintly signalled, like a nervous beating of the feet, by the popularity of cross-word puzzles. I remember a fellow expatriate opening a letter from a mutual friend of ours, urging him to come home and be revitalized by the hardy, bracing qualities of the native soil. It was a strong letter and it affected us both deeply, until we noticed that it was headed from a nerve sanitarium in Pennsylvania."

Fitzgerald tended to notice only those events that had this kind of meaning for him, that came to life for him as images of his personal feelings. The advantage of knowing the world in this way is that anything you notice at all takes on the vividness of your strongest private emotions. But because Fitzgerald knew the world this way, he had little capacity for sharing the common, public understanding of it. For readers to whom a novel is a dramatic representation of the world as that understanding knows it, Fitzgerald often appears to be treating with ridiculous seriousness characters and situations that "everyone knows" are insignificant.

One can frequently see in Fitzgerald's actual life, where conventional judgments are more important — or at least more difficult to ignore — how little such judgments really counted for him. All his life, for instance, he remembered bitterly his failure to achieve social success as an undergraduate at Princeton. The conventional judgment is that undergraduate social life is trivial, but Fitzgerald's failure at Princeton — whatever common sense may say of its circumstances — involved his deepest private feelings. Princeton was his first independent experience of the world, and he threw himself into realizing his ambitions there exactly as if Princeton had been the great world itself. For him the common judgment of Princeton's unimportance did not count; what counted was what he felt. He came very close to succeeding at Princeton, except that he neglected what was to him the trifling business of passing his courses, which seemed to him a great bore, and just as he was about to come into his kingdom as a big man on campus, he was forced to leave the university.

He tried for the rest of his life to tell himself that society always has this power to enforce its own values and that it was foolish of him to ignore the university's academic requirements simply because they were insignificant to him. But he never could really believe it, and gradually this experience at Princeton became for him — despite the objective insignificance of its occasion — one of his two or three major images for the unjust suffering that is the essence of human defeat.

This typical episode makes it evident that Fitzgerald, subjective novelist though he was, was not the kind of man who could commit himself wholly to the life of inner reality or be content as a novelist "with a very slight embroidery of outward manners, the faintest possible counterfeit of real life." In his life Fitzgerald strove to achieve in the actual world the ideal life he could so vividly imagine, and he was intent as a writer on producing the most lively possible counterfeit of real life.

But if this episode shows us that both in his life and his work he was determined to live in the actual world, as he often did quite dazzlingly, it also shows us that for him the meaning and value of the world were something that was determined by his private feelings, which operated independently of the established, conventional understanding of the world, not because he was consciously defying that understanding — his desire to realize the good life as he conceived it made him struggle to conform — but because the subjective life of his imagination was so intense, so overwhelmingly real for him, that even his efforts to conform to conventional ideas transformed them into something personal and queer.

Fitzgerald's first mature novel, *The Great Gatsby*, for example, is a brilliant picture of Long Island society in the 1920's. But that is only one aspect of it, the image Fitzgerald creates for a feeling too complex to be expressed in any other way. *The Great Gatsby* is a fable, marked at every important point by the folklore qualities of fables and charged with meaning by a style that is, despite the sharpness of its realistic detail, alive with poetic force. At the crisis of the story, the heroine, Daisy Buchanan, unintentionally reveals to her husband by the unguarded tone of her beautifully expressive voice that she loves Gatsby. The narrator says anxiously to Gatsby, "She's got an indiscreet voice. It's full of — " and when he hesitates Gatsby says suddenly, "Her voice is full of money." And the narrator thinks, "That was it. I'd never understood before. It was full of money — that was the inexhaustible charm that rose and fell in it, the jingle of it, the cymbals' song of it. . . . High in a white palace the king's daughter, the golden girl. . . ."

This passage is resonant with an irony that echoes back and forth between the gross actual fact of money jingling in the pocket and the romance of beauty adorned, of the golden girl. On the surface Daisy Buchanan is a convincing, historically accurate portrait of the charming and irresponsible upper-class girl of the American twenties. But she is also the princess, high in a white palace, for whom the disregarded younger son longs hopelessly, until the great moment when he astonishes everyone by performing the impossible feat that wins her hand.

One of the things that has certainly helped make *Tender Is the Night* less popular than *The Great Gatsby* of ten years earlier is that the image it uses, its story, is not, as social history, so significant as Gatsby's. Its story describes the life of well-to-do American expatriates on the Riviera during the 1920's, and such people are usually thought to be about as insignificant as Princeton undergraduates. They were especially thought to be so when the novel was published in 1934 at the depth of the Great Depression, and the idea that Fitzgerald was naïvely impressed by rich people became widely accepted. This is one of those foolish ideas put about by people who cannot read. Fitzgerald was no more a mere worshiper of rich people than Henry James was a snob. He was a man who dreamed of actually living the good life men can imagine. He had, as did Jay Gatsby, "a heightened sensitivity to the promises of life," and he had the elementary common sense to see that in real life the rich have an opportunity to live the good life that the rest of us do not.

One consequence of his seeing they do was that he felt the deepest scorn — what he called "the smouldering hatred of the peasant" — for rich people who did not take full advantage of the opportunity their wealth gave them. About rich people of this kind *Tender Is the Night* is devastating. Another consequence of it was his fascination with the intelligent and sensitive among the rich, like Dick Diver, who could see that opportunity. With his Irish sense of the absurd aspect of what he believed most deeply, Fitzgerald could make fun of this ideal as he had formulated it for himself, what he called "the Goethe-Byron-Shaw idea, with an opulent American touch — a sort of combination of Topham Beauclerk, St. Francis of Assisi, and J. P. Morgan"; and in the end he came to feel that the unimaginative brutality and organized chaos of the life of the rich always defeated men like Dick Diver. In Dick's best moments,

Tender Is the Night shows us how beautiful the realized ideal life is; but in the end it shows us that people with the sensitivity and imagination to conceive that life cannot survive among the rich.

Tender Is the Night begins with the arrival of a young movie star named Rosemary Hoyt at Cap d'Antibes on the Riviera.* When Rosemary goes down to the beach she finds herself between two groups of expatriates. The first is an incoherent mixture. There is "Mama" Abrams, "one of those elderly 'good sports' preserved by an imperviousness to experience and a good digestion into another generation." There is a writer named Albert McKisco who, according to his wife, Violet, is at work on a novel "on the idea of Ulysses. Only instead of taking twenty-four hours [he] takes a hundred years. He takes a decayed old French aristocrat and puts him in contrast with the mechanical age. . . ." There is a waspishly witty young man named Royal Dumphry and his companion, Luis Campion, who keeps admonishing Mr. Dumphry not to "be too ghastly for words." The other group consists of Dick Diver and his wife, Nicole, their friends Abe and Mary North, and a young Frenchman named Tommy Barban.

Rosemary is instinctively attracted to the second group but she is quickly picked up by the first group, who cannot wait to tell her they recognize her from her film. It is not a very happy group. For one thing, it is clearly jealous of the second group. "If you want to enjoy yourself here," Mrs. McKisco says, "the thing is to get to know some real French families. What do these people get out of it? They just stick around with each other in little cliques. Of course we had letters of introduction and met all the best French artists and writers in Paris." For another thing, Mr. McKisco is being difficult, as if, in spite of his extensive collection of secondhand attitudes from the best reviews, he does not quite know who he is or where he is going. When his wife makes a harmless joke, he bursts out irritably, "For God's sake, Violet, drop the subject! Get a new joke, for God's sake!" and when she leans over to Mrs. Abrams and says apologetically, "He's nervous," McKisco barks, "I'm not nervous. It just happens I'm not nervous at all."

It is the poverty of ideas and the mediocrity of imagination in these people, the shapelessness of their natures, that depresses and discomforts Rosemary and makes her dislike them. It is her glimpses of the opposite qualities in the second group that attracts her. What Rosemary sees in Dick Diver is his consideration, his grace, his sensitivity to others, and — behind them all — his intense vitality. No wonder she falls in love with him.

At this point Fitzgerald goes back to trace Dick's history. He is the son of a gentle, impoverished clergyman in Buffalo, from whom he had inherited his old-fashioned, formal manners and what Fitzgerald calls " 'good instincts,' honor, courtesy, courage." He has gone to Yale, been a Rhodes Scholar, and been trained as a psychiatrist at Johns Hopkins, in Vienna, and in Zurich. After the war, he returns to Zurich, where he meets again a young mental patient named Nicole Warren, who has clung to their slight relation all through the war and her slow recovery from an illness that is not congenital but has been brought on by her father's seducing her.

Dick falls in love with Nicole, and in spite of his professional knowledge that she may be a lifelong mental problem, despite the unconscious arrogance with which the Warrens make it clear they are buying a doctor to take care of Nicole, he marries her. This act reveals the defect of uncontrollable generosity in Dick's character. "He wanted," Fitzgerald says, "to be good, he wanted to be kind, he wanted to be brave and wise . . . ; [and] he wanted to be loved, too. . . ." He had an "extraordinary virtuosity with people . . . the power of arousing a fascinated and uncritical love." This power was a kind of imaginative unselfishness; "it was themselves he gave back to [people]," as Fitzgerald says, "blurred by the compromise of how many years." This power he could not resist exercising, not merely to give Nicole back her self but to make everyone he came close to feel once more the self he had been at his best.

Dick knows from the start that in taking up his life with Nicole among the Warrens and their kind he is making the task he has set himself as difficult as possible, but with his youthful vitality intact, that seems to him only to make it more challenging and interesting. For five years he meets the challenge effortlessly. Then, at first imperceptibly, his life begins to slip from his control. Something within him, some essential vitality, is beginning to decline, and he slowly realizes that he has exhausted the source of energy for the superb self-discipline that makes it possible for him to perform for others what he calls his "trick of the heart."

This change occurs very deep in his nature. Fitzgerald is careful to prevent the reader from thinking it is some change controllable by the will, some drift into dissipation or the idleness of the rich. Dick does begin to drift in these ways, but that is only a symptom of his trouble, a desperate search for something to fill the time and stave off boredom after the meaning and purpose have gone out of his life. What destroys Dick is something far more obscure and difficult to grasp, some spiritual malaise that is anterior to any rational cause and is—as has become much plainer since Fitzgerald noticed it—as widespread among sensitive people in our time as was accidie in the middle ages or melancholia, the "Elizabethan malady," in Shakespeare's. Dick Diver is, as Fitzgerald put it in one of his notes for the book, not simply an *homme manqué*, but an *homme epuisé*. He is in a state of terrible spiritual ennui that is without visible cause and yet makes men like him—talented, attractive, successful—feel quite literally that *all* the uses of the world are weary, stale, flat, and unprofitable. "I did not manage, I think in retrospect," Fitzgerald once said of Dick Diver, "to give Dick the cohesion I aimed at. . . . I wonder what the hell the first actor who played Hamlet thought of the part? I can hear him say, 'The guy's a nut, isn't he?' (We can always find great consolation in Shakespeare)."

Perhaps he did not manage to give Dick all the cohesion he might have, but the real difficulty is that the source of Dick's disaster is indescribable. It can be shown and felt, but it can no more be analyzed than Hamlet's disaster can. As a result the main action of *Tender Is the Night* is, for all its haunting emotional appeal, as puzzling and unparaphrasable as is the famous passage from Keats's "Ode to a Nightingale" from which its title comes.

What Fitzgerald can — and does — do is to create for the reader a group of characters who, as dramatic parallels or contrasts with Dick, show what he is. The first of these we learn all about is Abe North, a musician who, after a brilliant start, has done nothing for the last seven years except drink. When Mary North says, "I used to think until you're eighteen nothing matters," he says, "That's right. And afterwards it's the same way." And when Nicole, frightened at what he is doing to himself and irritated by his lack of any visible reasons for doing it, says to him, "I can't see why you've given up on everything," he can only say, "I suppose I got bored; and then it was such a long way to go back in order to get anywhere." Dick has understood from the beginning what has happened to Abe, even though he will not know what it feels like until later. "Smart men," he has said of Abe, "play close to the line because they have to — some of them can't stand it, so they quit." Thus, at the very start of the novel, Abe North has reached the point Dick will reach at its end.

About halfway through the novel, just as Dick is beginning his own desperate battle with the impulse to quit, he hears — in fact, he overhears, as a piece of idle, feelingless gossip — that Abe has been beaten up in a New York speakeasy and crawled to the Racket Club to die — or was it the Harvard Club? The gossips' grumbling quarrel over where it was Abe died fades out around Dick as he tries to face the meaning of Abe's death, a death more shocking — more grubby and humiliating as well as more terrifying to him — than anything he had dreamed of.

There is also Tommy Barban, a sophisticated and worldly barbarian of great charm, who stands for everything Dick Diver most disapproves of. The carefully ordered life that Dick first constructed for Nicole and himself because it was necessary to Nicole's health has, as Nicole's need for it has slowly decreased, been gradually transformed to another purpose, until it has become an alert but elaborate, almost ritualized ordering of the pleasures of a highly cultivated existence. The whole business irritates Tommy, party because it is all strictly under Dick's control and holds Nicole, with whom Tommy has been in love for years, a prisoner, but partly too because it represents in itself a way of life that offends him deeply. When he is about to leave the Riviera, Rosemary Hoyt asks him if he is going home. "Home?" he says, "I have no home. I am going to a war," and when Rosemary asks him what war, he says, "What war? Any war. I haven't seen a paper lately but I suppose there's a war—there always is." A little shocked by this, Rosemary asks him if he doesn't care at all about what he may find himself fighting for, and he says, "Not at all—so long as I'm well treated. When I'm in a rut I come to see the Divers, because I know that in a few weeks I'll want to go to war."

The novel's central group of characters consists of Dick, Nicole, Rosemary, and these two. It is surrounded by a larger group of minor characters, each of whom shows us an aspect of the world Dick Diver lives in. There is Lady Caroline Sibley-Biers, the latest wild woman from London, petulant and stupid, whose idea of amusement is to dress up as a French sailor and pick up a girl in Antibes. There is Baby Warren, Nicole's sister, "a tall fine-looking woman deeply engaged in being thirty" who "was alien from touch" and for whom "such lingering touches as kisses and embraces slipped directly through the flesh into the forefront of her consciousness." She is supremely confident that the most dehumanized routines of British social life are the ideal existence and that her series of engagements to socially eligible Englishmen, which even she no longer really expects will come to anything, constitutes a full life. There is Albert McKisco, the confused but proud possessor of a host of secondhand ideas that safely insulate him from experience. Such characters define for us the chic grossness, the neurotic orderliness, the lifeless intellectuality of the world Dick Diver lives in. They are not what they are because they are rich, though, being rich, they are able to be what they are with a freedom and completeness that ordinary people cannot. Still, they are not what they are merely because they are rich; they are so because the world is.

In this world Dick Diver's need to reach out to people, to galvanize them into life by reminding them of the selves they originally were, is like a wound, a "lesion of vitality" as Fitzgerald calls it, from which his spiritual energy slowly drips away until there is nothing left. At the beginning of the novel, "one June morning in 1925" when Rosemary meets Dick, the first faint signs of the loss have begun to show. He is still able to produce for people such enchanted moments as the one on the beach that Rosemary has watched with delight, when he holds a whole group of people enthralled, not by what he does—what he does is almost nothing—but by the quality of his performance, the delicate sense of the tone and feeling of occasion and audience by which he can make a small group of people feel they are alone with each other in the dark universe, in some magically protected place where they can be their best selves. He performs this trick of the heart once again for Rosemary when she goes to dinner with the Divers just after she has met them. At the climax of that dinner, the table seemed just for a moment "to have risen a little toward the sky like a mechanical dancing platform" and "the two Divers began suddenly to warm and glow and expand, as if to make up to their guests, already so subtly assured of their importance, so flattered with politeness, for anything they might still miss from that country well left behind. Just for a moment they seemed to speak to every one at the table, singly and together, assuring them of their friendliness, their affection. And for a moment the faces turned up toward them were like the faces of poor children at a Christmas tree."

But now, each such moment is followed for Dick by a spell of deep melancholy in which he looks "back with awe at the carnival of affection he had given, as a general might gaze at a massacre he had ordered to satisfy an impersonal blood lust." Rosemary catches a glimpse of that melancholy, without recognizing it, her very first morning on the beach when, after all the others have gone, Dick stops to tell her she must not get too sunburned and she says with young cheerfulness, "Do you know what time it is?" and Dick says, "It's about half-past one."

> They faced the seascape together momentarily.
> "It's not a bad time," said Dick Diver. "It's not one of the worst times of the day."

These periods of melancholy are one consequence of his decreasing vitality; another is his inability to maintain the self-discipline he has heretofore exercised almost unconsciously because it is only by not yielding to his momentary impulses that he can fulfill his central need to make the world over for others. The first failure of this discipline—and the major one—is allowing himself to fall in love with Rosemary. Though he cannot control that impulse, he knows that it "marked a turning point in his life— it was out of line with everything that had preceded it—even out of line with what effect he might hope to produce on Rosemary." Then he finds himself drinking just a little too much in a carefully controlled way—"an ounce of gin with twice as much water" at carefully spaced intervals. The book on psychiatry he has been working on for years begins to seem to him stale and unimportant and his work at the clinic tiresome. "Not without desperation he had long felt the ethics of his profession dissolving into a lifeless mass." When Nicole has a third serious breakdown, the long months of "restating the universe for her" leave him exhausted in a way he has never known before.

He goes off alone to try to rest and get himself together and discovers to his horror that he cannot stop yielding to every vagrant impulse of his nature—to charm a pretty girl, to blurt out without regard for his listeners the bitterness in his heart. He sees more clearly than anyone what is happening to him, but since it is happening somewhere below the level of reason, beyond the control of his will, he can only watch helplessly. "He had lost himself—he could not tell the hour when, or the week, the month, or the year. . . . Between the time he found Nicole flowering under a stone on the Zurichsee and the moment of his meeting with Rosemary the spear had been blunted."

The first faint signs of this loss of self had appeared at that first meeting with Rosemary Hoyt on the beach at Antibes. When, five years later, he and Rosemary meet again on the same beach, now crowded with dull, fashionable people, he says to her, "Did you hear I'd gone into a process of deterioration? . . . It's true. The change came a long way back—but at first it didn't show. The manner remains intact after the morale cracks." By a desperate effort he can still force himself at moments to exercise that manner, but these moments come more and more rarely and require him to be drunker and drunker, a condition in which he is as likely to assert the black despair in his heart in some outburst of incoherent violence, as he does when he picks a fight in Rome with a detective and is beaten up and thrown in jail, or when at Antibes he gets into a drunken, confused argument with Lady Caroline Sibley-Biers and even she is able to make him look foolish. These scenes are almost intolerably moving, for Fitzgerald's lifelong habit of giving events the value they have for the person who suffers them rather than their conventional public value makes us feel these trivial misfortunes as what they are, the loose ends of life, as Zelda once said, with which men hang themselves.

Finally Dick accepts the exhaustion of his vitality and its consequences, his inability to control himself to any purpose, his inability to love and be loved by others. He sets himself to cut his losses—his responsibilities for Nicole and the children and his friends—and to bury his dead—himself. The task is made simpler by the fact that Nicole has now recovered completely. Though she still depends on Dick, her dependence is now only old habit, not necessity. As she has recovered she has become more and more the superficially orderly, inwardly anarchic barbarian that has always been her true Warren self. As such, she turns instinctively away from Dick and toward Tommy Barban. Dick therefore sets himself to break her dependence on him and to push her toward Tommy. At the last moment he deliberately provokes a quarrel with her and then watches silently while she struggles to deny him and assert her independence. When she succeeds, "Dick waited until she was out of sight. Then he leaned his head forward on the parapet. The case was finished. Doctor Diver was at liberty."

Dick stays at Antibes just long enough to make sure Nicole is safe in Tommy's hands and then leaves for America, taking with him nothing, least of all himself.

> Nicole kept in touch with Dick after her marriage [to Tommy]. . .
> [He] opened an office in Buffalo, but evidently without success. Nicole did not find what the trouble was, but she heard a few months later that he was in a little town named Batavia, New York, practicing general medicine, and later that he was in Lockport, doing the same thing. . .
> He was considered to have fine manners and once made a good speech at a public health meeting on the subject of drugs; but he became entangled with a girl who worked in a grocery store, and he was involved in a law suit about some medical question; so he left Lockport.

After that he didn't ask for the children to be sent to America and didn't answer when Nicole wrote asking him if he needed money. . . . his latest note was post-marked from Hornell, New York, which is some distance from Geneva and a small town; in any case he is almost certainly in that section of the country, in one town or another.

Note

* There are two versions of *Tender Is the Night* in print, the original one described here and a revision based partly on a letter Fitzgerald wrote his editor late in his life and partly on a copy of the book found among his papers after he died, in which, along with some minor revisions in Book I, he had placed the original Book I after Book II Chapter 2.

The Journey Back: Myth and History in *Tender Is the Night*   Alan Trachtenberg*

Like many American writers, Scott Fitzgerald had considerable difficulty in arriving at a reliable and comfortable form for his novels. Uncertainty about form is usually a sign of crisis in the development of an artist; in the case of novelists the crisis is often in a shifting conception of society, a changing vision of the relations between individual minds and the collective mind. Fitzgerald's entire fiction is an extended meditation on America, its history and its notorious dreams, a meditation all the more remarkable for its multiple moods of elegy, prayer, social analysis, and introspection. But difficulties with form in specific works suggest an underlying hesitation or uncertainty in Fitzgerald about his heroes and their place within American society—an uncertainty rooted in part in profound ambivalence regarding his own popular success and his promise. In the several instances in which his fictions do achieve a balance between reflective subjectivity and objective detachment, as in *The Great Gatsby* and *Tender Is the Night*, the resulting forms are fully convincing embodiments of a complex and difficult vision.

Fitzgerald's meditation often brings into focus a tension between history and dreams, between the corrosive action of time and the illusory nature of myth. If his theme is frequently disappointment in the failure of the American Dream to realize itself within history, then a conflict between history and myth as opposing ways of viewing the world lies at the heart of his vision.

*Reprinted from Roy Harvey Pearce, ed., *Experience in the Novel: Selected Papers from the English Institute* (New York: Columbia University Press, 1968), pp. 133–62. This selection is taken from pp. 133–35, 138–62. © 1968 by Columbia University Press. Reprinted by permission of the publisher.

The relation between history and myth is often confused by the suggestion that one is "true," the other "false." In fact, however, both terms refer to states of mind, to conditions or modes of consciousness, to points of view toward experience. The meaningful difference between them lies elsewhere than in their relation to literal "facts" in the world. The term myth has been subject to a bewildering assault of definitions; perhaps the most useful is that myth refers to experiences timeless in nature — experiences of thought, feeling, and imagination outside a linear chronicle of events. Any recurrent pattern can thus be described as mythic. In an influential essay Allen Tate argues that "literature as knowledge" is knowledge of a "mythical order," an order in which, as Mr. Tate quotes I. A. Richards, "the opposite and discordant qualities in things . . . acquire a form."[1] Myth is accordingly a cognitive mode, a way of knowing.

We need to recognize that history can have the same status, as a way of thinking about the world: not how the world actually organizes itself, but how it gets organized in our minds. Like myth, history is a dimension of consciousness. The distinguishing trait of historical as opposed to mythic awareness is that it accepts the reality of time, irreducibly. Also, a historical awareness accepts the idea that things exist "out there," independent of our perceptions, that they change and organize themselves in certain concrete ways. A sense of history need not imply a specific system of explanation, but it must grant an "out there" with a significant, even if problematic, relevance to "in here." Myth tends to diminish the value of separate moments of experience by bringing them into a pre-existing pattern of coherence, while history tends to enhance the value of time as change, even if, in some troubled periods, it deplores both time and change. Myth and history may stand against each other as ways of knowing the world, but both are relevant to the experience of literature.

For Fitzgerald, history and myth provide perspectives upon each other, mutual contexts in which the opposition is rarely simple. He requires his reader to recognize each perspective, to identify the tension and experience it dramatically. The problem is perhaps clearer to demonstrate in *The Great Gatsby*.

. . . The elegiac tone of the book's ending confirms Nick's final insight, that history, in America at least, is a record of struggles to recover the past in the future, to recapture the fleeting moments of wonder when victory over time seemed possible. But the ongoing currents of time, he realizes, will always defeat such an "orgiastic future."

To a great extent the reader relies on Nick for a balanced perspective — one which locates Gatsby at the intersection of two vectors, the pull of dream and the push of time. In *Tender Is the Night* the perspective does not come as easily; it lies in wait for the reader and requires a different kind of activity from him. The difference is almost entirely a matter of a new emphasis given to the historical perspective. Nick's narrative is retrospective and suggestively static; the actions come to us with the clarity and sharpness of formal postures. The later novel, on the other hand, can be described as a novel of process; its actions appear more fluid and casual. But at the same time its movements are more elaborately and calculatedly subtle and complex. What reaches the reader through the consciousness of Nick in the earlier novel, the reader of *Tender Is the Night* must attain for himself. The experience is more difficult, but the rewards justify the kind of attention the book demands, and too rarely receives.

The larger demands, and the different kind of historical awareness in *Tender*, can be introduced by a brief passage from Book Two. Dick Diver has just buried his father in an old churchyard in Virginia. As he prepares to leave he becomes aware of the other buried souls, "made of new earth in the forest-heavy darkness of the seventeenth century," and takes his farewell: " 'Good-by, my father—good-by, all my fathers.' " This scene marks the final break with his personal American past; it sets the stage for his ill-fated fling in Rome in the next episode. In the passage immediately following "good-by," Dick begins to make his way from his old New World to a new Old one: "On the long-roofed steamship piers one is in a country that is no longer here and not yet there. The hazy yellow vault is full of echoing shouts. There are the rumble of trucks and the clump of trucks, the strident chatter of cranes, the first salt smell of the sea. One hurries through, even though there's time; the past, the continent, is behind; the future is the glowing mouth in the side of the ship; the dim, turbulent alley is too confusedly the present."[2] The imagery of ambiguous time-dimensions on the pier connects the specific narrative moment, Dick's farewell journey, with basic confusions in his sense of time itself. The haze and the echoes in the turbulent vault convey a feeling of literal confusion, of a mixture of tenses (echoes implying the past haunting the present). The sentence, "One hurries through, even though there's time," suggests dislocation, a serious disjunction between time and emotion. The country of the steamship pier defines Dick's condition by objectifying an inner confusion of identities. By means of these images (which have, of course, a yet wider context within the entire narrative), the reader is able to, in fact must, see the concrete fact of Dick's farewell journey in light of the accompanying fact of a confused sense of time. Thus "history" develops two mutually reinforcing meanings: Dick's relation to a specific past, now "behind" him; and his (and our) sense of the disordered structure of the present. The second meaning becomes, in short, the form through which we become aware of the first: the farewell journey becomes equivalent to a dislocated sense of historical time.

The relations among the reader, the imagery, and the action have a different tension here than in *Gatsby*. The difference represents an important shift—as Fitzgerald himself put it, an "advance"—in his understanding of his theme of history and myth in America. In this book, a special kind of historical awareness, created by the reader in the act of reading, becomes the major perspective of the narrative. In order to make this difficult point as clear as possible, we need first to consider more carefully the relevance of "history" to fiction.

"All works of the mind," writes Jean-Paul Sartre, "contain within themselves the image of the reader for whom they are intended." Sartre continues, in "For Whom Does One Write?",[3] to establish an important connection between the imagined reader and the historical dimension of literature. Before considering the implications of that connection, I want to cite a number of instances which demonstrate Fitzgerald's own acute awareness of the intended reader of *Tender Is the Night*. Fitzgerald belongs with Henry James among the most conscious and scrupulous craftsmen in American literature, and his comments upon craft, almost invariably practical and concrete, indicate his ability to think about his work from the point of view of a reader. "The novel should do this," he began his "General Plan" for *Tender* in 1932, an expression which emphasizes his sense of the book as an action upon a reader.

In 1925, fresh from the success of *The Great Gatsby*, Fitzgerald promised impetuously that his next book would be "something really NEW in form, idea, structure—the model for the age that Joyce and Stein are searching for, that Conrad didn't find."[4] It would be, he wrote at the same time, "the most amazing form ever invented." Discussing the finished product in 1934, Fitzgerald had subdued his exuberance somewhat—sobered no doubt by the enormous difficulties of composition—but he insisted in a letter to John Peale Bishop that the book was a definite "advance" over *Gatsby*. His explanation was largely technical; the book's importance, he felt, lay chiefly in its form. "The intention in the two books," he wrote to Bishop, "was entirely different." The compressed, highly compacted method of the first work had come to seem too limited. "The dramatic novel," he continued, "has canons quite different from the philosophical, now called psychological, novel. One is a kind of *tour de force* and the other a confession of faith. It would be like comparing a sonnet sequence with an epic." The mention of epic indicates a larger scale and scope in the new book: not only a larger segment of time (one summer in *Gatsby*, several years in *Tender*), but a more historical perspective as well. Unlike the epic form, however, this work would deal with very contemporary material, a fact which required that he deliberately refrain from "pointing up" dramatic scenes. He was able to get away with that in *Gatsby*, he points out, because the material was essentially exotic. But here, "the material itself was so harrowing and highly charged that I did not want to subject the reader to a series of nervous shocks in a novel that was inevitably close to whoever read it in my generation."[5] The reference to nervous shocks is itself striking in light of the fact that the novel is in part a record of the strained state of nerves in Fitzgerald's marriage, a record whose honesty might indeed shock a reader close to the original events. But the brunt of the sentence is that the novel is decidedly not a case study, that the author wished to avoid exploiting obvious sensational possibilities, and that a certain distance between the reader and the events was a deliberate and necessary feature of the novel's form.

In the same letter Fitzgerald justifies his use of what he calls the "dying fall" as preferable to the "dramatic ending," and his concern for the peculiar nature of the novel's material vis-à-vis the reader is equally evident. Writing to Hemingway a few weeks later, he confesses to have "stolen" this device from him and cites Conrad's Preface to *The Nigger of the Narcissus* as the original source of the theory that "the purpose of a work of fiction is to appeal to the lingering after-effects in the reader's mind as differing from, say, the purpose of oratory or philosophy which respectively leave people in a fighting or thoughtful mood." In the last pages of *Tender*, Fitzgerald explains, he wants to tell the reader that "after all, this is just a casual event," and "to let *him* come to bat for *me* rather than going out to shake his nerves, whoop him up, then leaving him rather in a condition of a frustrated woman in bed."[6]

Aside from the specific technical issues these comments raise, it is clear that Fitzgerald felt that the differences in scope and in materials between *Gatsby* and *Tender* amounted to a different relationship to an imagined reader, that is, a different kind of form. An imagined reader gives to the material a particularity, the possibility of a concrete form. With this in mind, we can return to Sartre, who writes that books serve as "go-betweens," establishing "a historical contact among men who are steeped in the same history and who likewise contribute to its making. Writing and reading are two facets of the same historical fact." By "historical fact" Sartre means the very act of reading, an act to which both writer and reader contribute. The book converts the abstract relation between writer and reader — a relation of separateness — into a concrete one; the book gives the relationship a particularity, an exact form. Moreover, the aesthetic experience which is the product of reading, Sartre argues, is an experience of freedom, of liberation from the oppression and alienation of the "normal" world of history in which both writer and reader are separately "steeped." The freedom won in writing-reading is likewise concrete and particular. It is not, Sartre insists in his existentialist vocabulary, "a pure abstract consciousness of being free," but, "strictly speaking, it *is* not; it wins itself in a historical situation" — which is the concrete situation, or experience, of the book.

But what do we mean by describing a fiction as a "historical situation" in itself? It is obvious that the act of reading can be considered "historical" because it occurs in a specific time and place, because it influences the sense of reality of the reader, and in turn is influenced by the historical limitations of the reader (accounting, for example, for the seriously altered ways Shakespeare is read and performed from age to age). These are, however, contextual versions of "history"; they place the act of reading within a clearly defined setting. But what occurs within that setting has a structure and a coherence of its own, a structure which requires the reader to suspend, to struggle against, his ordinary sense of time. A fictive time structure by itself, of course, is not yet a "history." Carl Becker defined history as "the memory of things said and done." The definition can be usefully applied to fictions. Plots, for example, rely upon a reader's memory as the continuous element in the unfolding of events page by page. Plots require a historical memory, that is, a memory provoked and directed and supplied by the fiction itself. True, fictions often call upon a larger social memory "of things said and done" which the reader can be counted on to bring to the book, but the concrete history within which, in Sartre's terms, the reader's "consciousness of being free" wins itself is created by and contained within the fiction itself. The meaningful "historical situation" of a fiction, then, is that which it creates for itself in collaboration with a reader.

If a fiction is a history, however, it is so in a very specialized and, in a significant sense, unstable way. The ordinary sense of history can be described as consciousness of a sequence of non-repeatable events, related to each other as chronology and, in some minds, as causality. Mere chronology is quite obviously an inadequate structure for a plot, which requires some comprehensible system of causality. A plot will tend to structure events on the basis of congruences, recognitions, reversals, will tend to pattern our perceptions and thus contribute an element of geometry to our awareness of events (including mental events). Temporal awareness begins to bend toward spatial awareness, and history may be in danger of becoming geometry. In "Spatial Form in Modern Literature," Joseph Frank argued that the inherent geometric tendency in plots contributed to a virtual revolution in modern literature, a revolution directed against nineteenth-century historicism and its faith in linear causality. In modern fiction and poetry, he pointed out, myth, in the form of archetypes or prototypes, tends to replace history as the source of significance. The works of Joyce and Eliot, for example, require the reader to perceive resemblances between present and archetypal events not as temporal facts, occurring in linear sequence, but as spatial facts: not as history repeating itself but as history being always fundamentally the same. This procedure in reading modern literature assumes that coherence in our perceptions about ourselves and our world cannot derive from the events themselves but from some atemporal pattern in which the events participate. "The objective historical imagination," writes Frank, has given way to a mythological imagination "for which historical time does not exist."[7]

The "historical situation" of a fiction can, therefore, contain a radically ahistorical experience. This point becomes significant in evaluating the differences once more between *Tender Is the Night* and *The Great Gatsby*. In many ways *Gatsby* is a predominantly spatial form, and *Tender* predominantly temporal. Much of the activity of reading *Gatsby* is taken up with recognitions of symbolic values in the book's geography, in the historical prototypes and mythic archetypes lurking behind Jay Gatsby. Gatsby himself is a character for whom "historical time does not exist." His aspiration toward the past is fully mythic, an aspiration toward a timeless condition, toward a redemption of the unalterable sequence of time, toward a virtually ritualistic "return" to an original incarnation. Of course the novel does not grant him his aspirations, and the terms of his failure are the terms of the book's historical perspective. But that perspective is embodied almost entirely in Nick's point of view, rather than in a process of developing awareness in the reader. The novel concludes at a point which compels us to feel the contours of a historical process behind Gatsby, but the process itself remains off-stage, in a kind of outer darkness. In *Tender Is the Night* Fitzgerald attempted to dramatize the process itself, to bring the on-stage action into a dynamic and intelligible relation to the outer darkness. It remains to examine the technical terms of his attempt and to evaluate its success.

In all cases we submit ourselves to a fiction's pedagogy; we need to learn to become the work's imagined reader. *Tender Is the Night* consists of a great number of episodes connected in seemingly casual and incidental ways. Fitzgerald once commented on his own work: "Whether it's something that happened twenty years ago or only yesterday, I must start out with an emotion — one that's close to me and that I can understand." An emotion is a present experience, a "now," even if it is a reflex or "lingering after-effect" of a past experience. *Tender Is the Night* consists of many "nows" — presents which imply a past. The reader modulates from one to another, experiencing each emotion as an event, and constructing a memory of each separate "now" in developing relations with the others.

The reader's memory is abetted by the narrative's precise chronological structure. The story covers a period from 1917 to 1930, from America's entrance into World War I to the beginning of the Depression. Details from the larger, extra-fictional social memory play at first a relatively inconspicuous role, but in the end they share significantly in the book's historical perspective, linking the career of Dick Diver with the career of American life itself. Most of the action occurs in a four-year period, from 1925 to 1929. The original 1934 version, which I prefer for reasons which will become obvious, is divided into three books. Book One opens in 1925; the predominant though not exclusive point of view of the book is Rosemary's, and we see Dick Diver through her infatuated eyes at his apparent best, his charm most engaging, his control most intact. Chinks in his armor begin to appear, however: increasing loss of self-control with Rosemary, and a mysterious difficulty with his wife. The opening episodes also sketch a setting of pleasurable charm mixed with random violence: the duel, the shooting at the railroad station, the murder of the Negro. The climax of the book occurs in the bathroom of the Divers' suite in Paris where Rosemary finally witnesses Nicole's derangement.

Book Two opens in 1917, eight years earlier, with Dick's arrival in Switzerland. The book takes him through his early affair and then his marriage with Nicole, introduces her sister, Baby Warren, and brings the major cast forward, in Chapter II, to rejoin the present in 1925, immediately following the Paris episode which concluded Book One. Book Two is devoted mainly to Dick's point of view, his sense of himself, and documents the successive stages of his marriage and his decline until the climactic collapse in Rome, where his deterioration and his humiliating attachment to the Warren fortune become most blatantly evident to him and to the reader. The book parallels Book One in several ways. The pastoral isolation of Dick's little clearing on the Riviera beach in the first book is recalled in the isolation of Switzerland from the surrounding violence of the war in the opening paragraphs of Book Two (the allusion to "more intriguing strangers" in the second paragraph of Book Two may be a deliberate echo of "Hôtel des Étrangers" in the first paragraph of Book One); Dick's attachment to Rosemary in Book One brings to mind the early stages of his affair with Nicole in Book Two; and his collapse in Rome virtually parallels Nicole's seizure in Paris after the murder of Peterson. The resemblances, however, serve mainly to reveal important differences between the time periods, differences which point to the unfolding truth of Dick's condition. The resemblances are not geometric repetitions; they serve to indicate a fully temporal process of deterioration in Dick and a corresponding process of illumination in the reader. For example, although the reader is shrewder than Rosemary in Book One and can guess at what expense Dick keeps his charm and his manners apparently intact, the story of his marriage and of the role of Baby Warren traced in the first ten chapters of Book Two begins to clarify those expenses and to prepare the reader to accept knowingly Dick's admission to Mrs. Spears in Chapter II (where, remember, we return to the present), " 'My politeness is a trick of the heart.' " The careful structuring of events in the two books gives such revelations a key role in the developing sense of ambiguity in Dick's character and his condition. The structure prepares the reader to receive such statements and to place their emotional tone in a concrete relation to events that have already taken place.

Book Three, deceptively simple in appearance, is the most difficult section of the novel. To deal with its complexities we need to consider more closely the ambiguities surrounding Dick, to see how they develop and how they relate to the narrative structure. So far the novel's movement has been a progressive unfolding (including a retrogressive filling-in of earlier events) of the truth about Dick, his manners, and his marriage. What Rosemary sees in Book One is steadily exposed as appearance or illusion, a partial view of reality. But appearances are not mere disguises. The illusion is very much a part of the total reality of Dick. Rosemary's point of view is an accurate one with which to begin the novel because what she sees is really there, if seriously incomplete. The full picture proceeds to disclose itself, but not mechanically, the way shadowed areas light up to expose in full clarity what was there all the time. Although the revelation is indeed largely retrospective, it develops progressively; the picture fills out in successive events; relationships and feelings change in the course of time. The truth about Dick is not a secret or a puzzle but a process. The value of Rosemary to the reader is that she demonstrates the dangerous partiality of any point of view which takes an appearance for the entire truth. The whole story is the entire history.

For example, if the opening chapters of Book Two, covering the period from 1917 to 1925, require us to understand the events of Book One as consequences of Dick's choices years ago, they also force us to recognize that the consequences have gotten beyond the original range of his choice to marry Nicole. That choice contained potentialities Dick did not realize at the time, potentialities realized only "in time." The realization is never stated explicitly, but becomes part of the reader's growing awareness. By giving us a seriously partial view of the consequences (Book One, especially the affair with Rosemary) before permitting us a larger view of the original choices, Fitzgerald uses a structural distortion of linear time in order to repeat for the reader something like Dick's own process of illusion and disillusion.

A similar process whereby appearances grow ambiguous in the reader's mind is at work in the descriptive imagery. Gatsby has an unmistakably symbolic landscape in which values inhere in physical forms (the distinctions between West Egg and East Egg, for example, or the stretch of ashes along the road to New York). In Tender, settings contain symbolic suggestions (the "bright tan prayer rug of a beach," for instance), but the suggestions do not comprise a simple moral geography. Instead, landscape is an object of perception; imagery tells how a setting is being perceived, what the perception seizes upon, what it excludes. A dominant feeling in the imagery of a setting may deliberately obscure certain latent possibilities. The opening paragraph of Book One exudes a feeling of quiet and wealthy pleasantness along the Riviera. But contrary muted notes play along the edge of perception: the façade of the hotel is "flushed," the old villas "rotted" — both images unobtrusively injecting suspicions of disease in a scene of apparent good health, decadence at odds with vitality. Similarly, the delicately cultivated space on the beach commanded by Dick's rake and tent and umbrella is defined and conditioned in our awareness by what it excludes. It excludes and rejects the section further up the beach "strewn with pebbles and dead sea-weed," where the equally rejected McKiscos and their crowd sit smoldering in their resentment at Dick's show. " 'We don't know who's in the plot and who isn't,' " complains Violet McKisco. Dick's space also excludes the "brutal sunshine" and the "outer, darker sea." The several exclusions contribute to a scene of virtually theatrical self-sufficiency and consummate social pleasure: "It seemed that there was no life anywhere in all this expanse of coast except under the filtered sunlight of those umbrellas, where something went on amid the color and the murmur." However, what is omitted to create such an illusion does not entirely disappear; the images of the outer world hint at potentialities which five years later, we learn, will be realized. At the end of the book (and of Dick's reign), the beach has become a "club," and "confused shapes and shadows of many umbrellas" now prevail: "new paraphernalia, the trapezes over the water, the swinging rings, the portable bathhouses, the floating towers, the searchlights from last night's fêtes, the modernistic buffet, white with a hackneyed motif of endless handlebars."

This bizarre setting at the end of Book Three recalls in turn an earlier scene in Paris in Book One. Rosemary had accompanied Dick on a visit to a "house hewn from the frame of Cardinal de Retz's palace"; inside the "long hall of blue steel, silver-gilt, and the myriad facets of many oddly bevelled mirrors," the visitors cannot tell "what this room meant because it was evolving into something else, becoming everything a room was not." The image can be taken as a clue to a process operating within the novel itself. The traditional exterior of the house had become a mere "outer shell," expropriated by the new inhabitants to "enclose the future" ("once inside the door there was nothing of the past, nor of any present that Rosemary knew"), and to cross the threshold is to prepare oneself for the evolutions and expropriations of the novel. It is not surprising, then, that what Dick sees on his beach at the end is a fulfillment, even to the "white sun, chivied of outline by a white sky," of potentialities implicit in the opening paragraphs.

Ambiguity is thus a product of the relation between the surface texture of image and event, the manifest meanings, and the underlying potentialities, the latent meanings. The reader needs to exercise a cautious memory as he moves from page to page, allowing feelings and hints to accumulate. Because each episode, each image, and each feeling will have its fullest reality only within the entire process of the book, each taken by itself is ambiguous — as ambiguous as the illusions which led Dick to Nicole.

Book Three and the meanings of the final actions cannot be understood without a clear sense of the role of ambiguity in the novel. The tension between appearance and latency is one form in which we recognize ambiguity; another is the calculated relationships to each other of three groups of images: of theatrical or cinematic illusion, of war, and of time. A simple summary statement about this configuration is that Dick is an actor whose efforts to serve the illusions of others and to live by his own are progressively eroded by realities represented in images of war and time.

The war imagery is especially effective in connecting Dick's inner life with his outer condition, his dreams with his history. A good example is his curious identification with Ulysses S. Grant. Dick in Zurich is like Grant "lolling in his general store in Galena," about "to be called to an intricate destiny." The image suggests, on one hand, a potentially dangerous tendency in Dick toward self-dramatization, toward a conventional hero-complex. On the other hand, certain genuine parallels begin to develop. Grant's public image shifted in his lifetime from hero to goat. The shift, and Grant's entanglements in the financial scandals of the Gilded Age, suggest a precedent for Dick's own career. If nothing else, the identification implies an inner necessity in Dick to find a "destiny" in Nicole. He sees her at first as "this scarcely saved waif of disaster bringing him the essence of a continent." Her trauma typifies a profound civil war, a clash and confusion of values; her incest with her father brings to the surface a disease already lurking in a civilization where "Daddy's Girl" is a sentimental ideal (" 'People used to say what a wonderful father and daughter we were—they used to wipe their eyes,' " says Devereux Warren). The disease represents an infection in ideals which have lost touch with reality and become outer shells to an inner corruption or an inner emptiness. As a clinical psychiatrist, Dick recognizes that professional logic "tended away from the girl." But a more powerful logic drew him toward her, a logic derived from his American background, from "the illusions of eternal strength and health, and of the essential goodness of people; illusions of a nation, the lies of generations of frontier mothers who had to croon falsely, that there were no wolves outside the cabin door." Himself steeped in such illusions, Dick is drawn to Nicole in part as Grant is drawn to the Civil War; both destinies seem to be opportunities for the exercise of a traditional American ideal, a dedication to the healing of moral wounds.

The intricacy of the destiny is based both on the nature of the wound and on the nature of the dedication. Nicole's wealth and its social character complicate the matter of Dick's motives. To some extent he is "bought"; but he also offers himself to be "used." The allusion to Grant once more helps the reader come to an understanding of the complex issues involved. Grant was called to herohood; in practice, as Dick admits to Abe North, it was Grant's destiny to invent the decidedly unheroic "mass butchery" of Petersburg. Invited by circumstances to play one role, he was compelled by history to play another. At the war memorial of Thiepval Dick laments the passing of a world in which Grant's original kind of heroism was possible; here, he tells Rosemary, "all my beautiful lovely safe world blew itself up with a great gust of high explosive love." The significant implication is that traditional heroic impulses lead in the end to "mass butchery." A corollary in his own life is the fact that his "extraordinary virtuosity with people" becomes an instrument of "carnivals of affection," extravagant parties he looks back on "as a general might gaze upon a massacre he had ordered to satisfy an impersonal blood lust." Led by his need for a heroic role to a highly ambiguous destiny (Nicole's wound and her family wealth), Dick suffers a dislocation; love and heroism and the manners of "essential goodness" have gotten entangled with business. Tommy Barban, Dick's successor, is also his exact foil: fighting is his paying job, not a matter of love or heroism. " 'My business is to kill people.' " Later his business will be stocks and bonds. Tommy is also Grant's foil; the general's destiny was finally to become inept and innocent executor of the most scandalous public corruption of the "new" post-Civil War America. Dick, in turn, was "disgusted" to learn that his own wartime assignment was "executive rather than practical." And as Nicole's husband he serves as an executive officer for the Warrens, in charge of producing health for Nicole.

Dick performs his duties much like an actor or director, thus serving the Warrens and realizing his own idealistic character at the same time. Of the Villa Diana he has made an "intensely calculated perfection," a "stage" where "some memorable thing was sure to happen." The perception here is Rosemary's. Herself a product and servant of the illusion-making industry of Hollywood, Rosemary is well qualified to make these observations, especially because she fails to grasp their full meaning. " 'Oh, we're such *actors* — you and I,' " she says to Dick, with more wisdom than she realizes. Dick may wince at the sentimentality of her performance in *Daddy's Girl* and recognize that her "triumph" is well coached. But the performance itself, "her fineness of character, her courage and steadfastness intruded upon by the vulgarity of the world," is a sentimentalized version of his own social "triumph." Rosemary's enactment of the "illusions of a nation" before the cameras is debased by the intrinsic insincerity of Hollywood. But have not his own enactments suffered in the service of a social reality he at bottom cannot accept? For example, his creation, the Villa Diana, disguises the house's true nature: "The villa and its grounds were made out of a row of peasant dwellings that abutted on the cliff — five small houses had to be combined to make the house and four destroyed to make the garden." " 'Nicole's garden,' " Dick says a moment later.

The tensions between Dick's illusion-making talents and his objective social role come to a head in Book Three. The book opens with two observations by the Gregoroviuses, that " 'Nicole's not sick' " but only " 'cherishes her illness as an instrument of power,' " and that " 'Dick is no longer a serious man.' " The rest of the book, presented from Nicole's point of view, seems to extend and qualify these two insights. More and more Nicole seems to free herself of Dick, who more and more withdraws into himself. But the structure of the book is not as simple as it appears. The tantalizing question is precisely what is happening to Dick as he seems to lose hold of himself and his marriage. In a letter to his editor, Maxwell Perkins, while the novel was in proof stage, Fitzgerald insisted on retaining the episode in Book Three set in Cannes, where Dick saves Mary North and Lady Caroline Sibly-Biers in their transvestite escapade with the police. Fitzgerald wanted, he wrote, to show Dick once more as a dignified and responsible person, in order to point up the fact that "his intention dominated all this last part." The comment suggests that Fitzgerald's problem was to strengthen Nicole's point of view while keeping Dick in the leading role, at the center of the reader's attention and respect.

Like Rosemary's and Dick's in the earlier books, Nicole's point of view in Book Three is not the sole perspective. The reader has been creating what might be called a perspective of the story as a whole, a perspective which contains each separate point of view as it does each separate episode. The way Nicole sees the world has a social history and a social content developed within the process of the narrative. As we have seen in the shifting patterns of imagery, a basic feature of that process is the instability of appearances. Apparently dominant facts and impressions contain opposite possibilities, as the book's present contains a thoroughly unlikely future. Thus the pathos of a sick Nicole, a "waif of disaster," had obscured the potentiality of a healthy Nicole. In Book One, in an intrusive but remarkable passage, we learn to anticipate the restoration of Nicole's social history: she was, we learn, "the product of much ingenuity and toil," an expression, even in her trauma, of an entire social system, for whose sake "trains began their run at Chicago . . . chicle factories fumed . . . men mixed toothpaste in vats . . . girls canned tomatoes . . . half-breed Indians toiled on Brazilian coffee plantations. . . ." Thus "she illustrates very simple principles, containing in herself her own doom, but illustrated them so accurately that there was grace in the procedure." Grace and doom coexist in her as historical inheritances, and as we observe her throughout the novel we are preparing to recognize what will happen in the end: the fulfillment of her grace, the accuracy of her restored character as an illustration of the selfish morality of her social class, is identical with her doom. " 'I'm well again,' " she tells Tommy Barban. " 'And being well perhaps I've gone back to my true self — I suppose my grandfather was a crook and I'm a crook by heritage.' " (Earlier we had learned that her rich grandfather had begun his career as a horse thief.) Nicole's surrender to Tommy is given an even wider range of historical connotation in the following passage: "Moment by moment all that Dick taught her fell away and she was ever nearer to what she had been in the beginning, prototype of that obscure yielding up of swords that was going on in the world about her. Tangled with love in the moonlight she welcomed the anarchy of her lover."

Nicole's fulfillment, which is a journey back to her true nature, occurs in time, "moment by moment." It is historical in the personal sense of her individual development in the novel, and also in a larger sense that the novel forces upon us: the transfer of her allegiance, her money, and the power it represents, to a new force typified by a counterrevolutionary mercenary turned stockbroker. Nicole's yielding to Barban becomes an emblem of the yielding of order to disorder, as the crumbling actions of Book Three make clear. The outlaw lovers come together as each other's present opportunity for personal and social survival. In the final scene on the Riviera, Nicole "got to her knees" in a momentary and automatic response to Dick's "papal cross" over the beach that was once his "bright tan prayer rug"; when Tommy pulls "her firmly down," he exercises the discipline she requires to complete her liberation from Dick, and thus certifies the social character of her new self.

Dick's mock blessing of the beach is also a certification of his own freedom from the illusions which have controlled his life. The papal image compels us, moreover, to reconsider the nature of Dick's situation. In his "General Plan" Fitzgerald had described his hero as a "spoiled priest." The term has more than a metaphoric rightness. In the only scene in which we see Dick as a doctor among patients, he tries to comfort an American woman artist whose life had become, incurably, "a living agonizing sore." She reproaches him for his "beautiful words" of comfort, and Dick can only stoop and kiss her forehead and say, as liturgy, " 'we must all try to be good.' " A psychiatrist *manqué*, he performs an essentially religious ritual. We are invited to imagine that in certain circumstances Dick Diver might very well have chosen a priestly vocation like his father's, and that in fact he does perform a priestly role. This is true of his actions not only as a doctor but as a husband and lover as well. To strive to create illusions of invulnerable beauty and goodness is much like presiding over a ritual. Dick's situation is defined by the intersection of two incompatible thrusts: the desire for a permanent "lush midsummer moment outside of time" — for the tender night of Keats's nightingale — and the corrosive action of time and history, "the weariness, the fever, and the fret." Deprived of illusion by time and by new social realities evolving within it, Dick is reduced to sitting in his chair "listening to the buzz of the electric clock, listening to time."

This last image arrives with such powerful effect because it locates the heart of Dick's problem. As a "spoiled priest," as a lover and hero, Dick wants to occupy time entirely, to fill it so completely with his being that it ceases to matter. In his student days, Zurich had been for him "the centre of the great Swiss watch," a sanctuary where time is still. To be at the centre of the watch is to be at Eliot's still point "outside of time." The opposite of this condition is to be totally aware of time, to hear it as a pure substance. Terms like "waste" and "lost" and "spent," applied throughout the book to time, indicate a frame of mind which interprets time as a usable substance, a commodity like money. Both time and money are infinitely calculable to the calculating mind. For Nicole, "the years slipped away by clock and calender and birthday." Time is the reservoir of her power, and as it slips away she learns more and more the need to *use* it:

" 'I've lost so much time,' " But for Dick, "time stood still and then every few years accelerated in a rush, like a quick rewind of a film."

It is clear that Dick feels most alive when "time stood still." He feels increasingly powerless when time accelerates, as it does in Book Three. But it is a mistake to see Dick as entirely passive in this book. Faced with the collapse of his marriage, his career, and his friendships, Dick needs an action through which to extricate himself with some degree of dignity. In an important conversation with Rosemary, shortly before the Cannes episode, Dick provides the reader with a clue to his behavior in Book Three. He lectures Rosemary on the dangers to the success of a dramatic illusion when an actress responds normally to certain extreme events on stage. Her aim should be to get the audience's attention away from the event and back to herself, that is, to the role she is performing. To accomplish this she must sometimes " 'do something unexpected.' " " 'If the audience thinks the character is hard,' " for example, " 'she goes soft on them — if they think she's soft she goes hard.' " " 'The unexpected thing,' " Dick explains, maneuvers " 'the audience back from the objective fact to yourself. *Then* you slide into character again.' "

The comments apply entirely to his own situation. The publicly deteriorating circumstances of his life are the "events" which distract attention from his dramatic "role" or character. He is an actor losing his audience, and his desperate need, for dignity and for a coherent identity, is to recapture enough attention to the self-created illusion of himself to permit an orderly and fairly decent exit. From this point of view — supported by Fitzgerald's comment that Dick's intention dominated the final section of the novel — his departure is a deliberate choice, an acceptance of necessities generated by earlier choices. In effect Dick arranges for his own demise, thus preserving his superiority over the Warrens and Tommy Barban. As he fades deeper into the American provincial landscape in the moving final paragraph, we sense that something of value, self-deceptive and vulnerable as it is, fades with him. His disappearance might be taken as a "plaintive anthem," if the novel's title indeed meant to remind us of the "deceiving" illusions of Keats's nightingale.

In any case it is certain that throughout the novel the reader has witnessed and participated in a struggle between illusion and reality, a struggle contained within the ambiguities of character and episode. The major version of the conflict is the "intensely calculated" life of the Divers, an unstable union of Dick's manners and traditional virtues and Nicole's wealth. There is indeed an "incalculable element," which is how Dick first appears to the book's arch calculator, Baby Warren. His services can be counted up and purchased, but the inner expenses cannot be translated into cash. In the final phases of Dick's decline, as he more and more just sits and listens, unable to imagine a future, we learn that an "incalculable story was telling itself inside him." This is the real story of the novel: the human costs of the bargain with unstable illusions. The unspoken story represents a countermovement to the events, a journey back to beginnings in the American landscape—or, to use another of the cinematic images from the text—a "rewind," consummated in the fade-out of the final paragraph.

Tender Is the Night submits American myths to the test of time. The conflict is enacted by the reader as he experiences the world of the fiction in the process of change. Historical awareness is, as it were, a product of the book. Fitzgerald's understanding of change and of the social structure of feeling had advanced considerably since *The Great Gatsby*. The earlier novel had tried to grasp the world more or less mythically; *Tender Is the Night* creates, with the reader's collaboration, a perspective unrelentingly historical. The reader's work is to assemble the materials of the novel into a fictive history which once attained, is surely one of the most remarkably illuminating experiences in American literature.

Notes

1. *The Man of Letters in the Modern World* (New York, 1955), p. 63.

2. *Tender Is the Night* (New York, 1934). All quotations are from the Scribner Library edition and are used by permission of Charles Scribner's Sons.

3. *What Is Literature?* (New York, 1965), Chapter 3.

4. *The Letters of F. Scott Fitzgerald*, ed. Andrew Turnbull (New York, 1963), p. 182. Quotations are used by permission of Charles Scribner's Sons.

5. *Ibid.*, p. 363.

6. *Ibid.*, pp. 309–10.

7. "Spatial Form in Modern Literature," in *Criticism, The Foundations of Modern Literary Judgment*, eds. Mark Schorer, Josephine Miles, Gordon McKenzie (New York, 1948), pp. 379–92.

The 1970s and 1980s

The Way Home: "But Here There Is No Light"

John F. Callahan*

Throughout *The Illusions of a Nation* I looked at Fitzgerald as a novelist who captured the complexity of the American idealist — the frailty of his psychological and historical self-awareness together with his "willingness of the heart." My chapters on *Tender Is the Night* follow the order of the revised edition in which Malcolm Cowley, respecting Fitzgerald's wishes, rearranged the novel into five chronological books: *Case History*, 1917–19; *Rosemary's Angle*, 1919–25; *Casualties*, 1925 (July to August); *Escape*, 1925–29; and *The Way Home*, 1929–30. Since *Tender Is the Night* powerfully undercuts an idealist view of personality and history, it seems essential to experience the form as well as the substance of Dick Diver's initial great expectations. Likewise, Fitzgerald's voice modulates into different narrative keys in successive parts of the novel; increasingly in *The Way Home*, that of mere recorder, without interpretation, of objects, gestures, and events. This chapter traces the declining trajectory of *Tender Is the Night* as it did when first published almost fifteen years ago, although in some places, thanks to the good offices of the editor, Milton Stern, I have tried to make the pattern of analysis clearer, the illustrations more convincing.

1

"Of all natural forces," Scott Fitzgerald wrote in *The Crack-Up*, "vitality is the incommunicable one," and, he might have added, the quality most essential to survival and to power over history.[1] To explain the transfer of authority from Dick Diver to Tommy Barban at the end of *Tender Is the Night*, I am tempted to propose a male version of Henry Adams's notion of the evolution of historical energy from virgin to dynamo. As the idealist with his ideas, his moral instincts, and, finally, his reading of history, as lost, romantic myth, Diver resembles the decaying

*Reprinted from *The Illusions of a Nation: Myth and History in the Novels of F. Scott Fitzgerald* (Urbana: University of Illinois Press, 1972). © 1972 by the University of Illinois Press. Reprinted with permission from the University of Illinois Press and the author. The essay (chapter eight) has been revised by the author especially for this volume.

187

virgin; whereas Barban, his driving, kinetic energy and magnetism put behind edifice and strategem, behind the material structures of society, often seems more like impersonal dynamo than flesh-and-blood man. Diver's failure, and the failure of the idealist generally, is a failure of tough and sensuous energy, just as Barban's failure, and the failure of plundering, animal-rational man, is the failure of sensibility and tenderness.

The old order that passes away at the end of *Tender Is the Night* is not any order of aristocracy, not the leisure class or its supporting system. What disappears from the stage of history and culture are Dick Diver and the social and psychological sublimations for which he stands. His often illusory and historically vicious " 'good instincts' — honor, courtesy, and courage" black out, as does the conviction that sensibility and aesthetic contemplation can create personalities greater than the sum of their parts. Or, as Fitzgerald later characterized Diver's values and their form of expression, "he is after all a sort of superman, an approximation of the *hero* seen in overcivilized terms — taste is no substitute for vitality but in the book it has to do duty for it."[2]

Because *Tender Is the Night*'s great subject has been personality and the historical, psychological, and perceptual forces which shape it, form in *The Way Home* takes its cue from the changes in these relationships. Of Diver the individual, for example, Fitzgerald wisely decided that aesthetically "from now on he is mystery man, at least to Nicole with her guessing at the mystery."[3.] As his values fade out of his world, Diver's reflective perspective ceases. Increasingly, "his own story" is "spinning out inside him"; no longer can he acknowledge, let alone provide, moral or social guidelines. Nicole, for her part, cannot afford many speculations about Dick's fate. Her leap to a new self requires fracture of her loyalty to both Dick's values and the manners which had enforced them. For her metamorphosis to be complete, complexity must be sacrificed. As Diver dives into his sea chambers and Nicole emerges whole on the shore of the world, the facts become more and more expressive of personality. And I mean facts in the crudest, simplest form. Nicole's new self and her dynastic consolidation through marriage to Barban are reductive states. With power, money, and metallic sensibility for voice, she and he scorn all density, all complexity. And just as facts express Nicole's retuned existence, the facts alone — events, objects, gestures — like stray chords struck on a piano, reverberate the meaning of Diver's end.

At the end of *The Great Gatsby*, Fitzgerald used Nick Carraway's voice to make Gatsby's dream a metaphor for American history. Elements of narrowness and triviality in Gatsby's story and the novel's context turned overstatement into the vehicle for Carraway's universal vision. In *Tender Is the Night* the aesthetic situation is reversed. There, the promise of Diver has been so real, the historical-cultural background so complexly stated and restated, the waste so tragic and evitable, the only way to rouse us further is to pretend that nothing has happened at all. The aesthetic dynamics of the "dying fall" involve, as Fitzgerald explained to Hemingway, "telling the reader in the last pages that, after all, this is just a casual event, and trying to let *him* come to bat for *me* rather than going out to shake his nerves, whoop him up, then leaving him rather in the condition of a frustrated woman in bed."[4.] Climax, then, is a two-way street, a natural process that, with reader or with woman, cannot be imposed by will or by force. Understatement during the coda to *Tender Is the Night* arouses us to protest. We protest and resist both Diver's fate and the possibility that his destiny is our own — inevitably, repetitively.

Tragedy of a noncathartic variety — the cathartic vision seems to me an aesthetic way of upholding the established order, the existing cultural values, with *Oedipus Rex* the prototype — involves a peculiar form of horror. Its horror comes not from the facts of madness, annihilation, and chaos but more from the lack of any voice, any perspective to rearrange reality's fragments in some way, no matter how temporary. Dick Diver's disintegration is horrible because it results from a context and consciousness now incapable of articulation. His values make him a casualty of chaos and lead to a closed circle of perception. What difference does it make where he is, whom he is with, or what he thinks and does? What difference does it make if he is no one? If Fitzgerald, by pretending none of these things makes any difference, stirs our discontent, it may become our imperative to reshape America into a humane society. For the one irreducible given of *Tender Is the Night* is that no individual can develop, creatively or otherwise, in isolation. The chickens of history will come home to roost; no human coop, whether in Europe, or Hollywood, or the Finger Lakes, is free from visitation.

2

In *The Way Home* Fitzgerald changes the dominant way of seeing from *Escape*'s voice of reflective complexity to one where externals undermine the impressions arranged by consciousness over long intervals. Often the question is not so much what is true as whether truth, falsely arrived at, has any meaning. Kathe and Franz Gregorovius, for example, argue mechanically about whether Diver's unhealed scars are the result of a debauch or shipboard boxing. This innocuous argument becomes perceptually sinister because of the relationship between fact and conclusion. If Kathe can persuade Franz that Dick has " 'been on a debauch,' " then Franz will leapfrog to the judgment that " 'Dick is no longer a serious man' " (258–59). The fact that this conclusion does not follow from the mere fact of a debauch does not deter Franz from persuading himself that "he had *never* thought" "that Dick was a serious person" (259, my italics). Thus, facts long-denied become, when acknowledged, instruments of reduction which in turn deny the fluid, complex facts of experience held in common.

More and more, personality becomes unequal to unexpected pressures. In Lausanne, Diver finds his profession inadequate to the likes of Francisco, the young homosexual nobleman, and his personal resources inadequate to the extra tenderness Nicole requires after her ailing father re-enters and, just as abruptly departs from their path. Indeed, life generally has about it an accidental random quality. This sense of life as unpredictable, since it follows Dick's previous capacity to direct coherent dramas out of the ruins of experience, leads the Divers toward immobility. Even to each other they are fast becoming artifacts. "Someone had brought a phonograph into the bar and they sat listening to 'The Wedding of the Painted Doll' " (269). Together and singly, they begin to look to the world to decide their destiny.

At this aptly imprecise point, Diver's meditation about the odd breeding grounds of charm carries him, imperceptibly, into *The Way Home*'s subject: the changes in personality structure emerging in the clash between consciousness and the twentieth century:

> Dick tried to dissect it into pieces small enough to store away, realizing that the totality of a life may be different in quality from its segments, and also that life during one's late thirties seemed capable of being observed only in segments. His love for Nicole and Rosemary, his friendship with Abe North, with Tommy Barban in the broken universe of the war's ending—in such contacts the personalities had seemed to press up so close to him that he became the personality itself; there seemed some necessity of taking all or nothing; it was as if for the remainder of his life he was condemned to carry with him the egos of certain people, early met and early loved, and to be only as complete as they were complete themselves (263).

> "You're not a romantic philosopher—you're a scientist. Memory, force, character—especially good sense. That's going to be your trouble—judgment about yourself" (5).

What Diver meditates on, and what the Rumanian intellectual had warned him about in 1916, is individuation. Neither as scientist nor as romantic philosopher can Dick Diver put all the pieces together again. Not only is personality composed of disjointed segments, but Diver, even though and perhaps because he is still a scientist, no longer conceives even of *observing* it in wholes. Like a romantic philosopher, he is willing to grant totality to a given life; but like a scientist he regards his own life as now incompatible with any synthesis. Indeed, as he refers to "the broken universe of the war's ending," he includes all of his generation in his predicament. Personality structures seemingly integrated by experience, background, and vision flew apart in the war's explosion, and the fragments, assembled again from different directions, did not fit the niches of the old forms. As disintegrations in culture and politics increased—the former leaderless, the latter in search of *Duce* or *Führer*—

historical chaos externalized the collapse, within individuals, of those psychological networks which had formed whatever totalities make a being greater than the sum of its parts. But Diver calls into doubt the notion, central to integration, that the dynamic personality supersedes its segments. For him all that is graspable are the separate segments of reality and self.

What petrifies Diver's broken parts, however, is his inability to shed the egos of those close to him. Not only does he carry, inseparable from his own, "the egos of certain people, early met and early loved," but, in total dependence, he can then "be only as complete as they were complete themselves." In addition, Fitzgerald acknowledges the chaos of contrary egos pulling centrifugally at Diver's weakening core. Ultimately, the flypaper will be captured by the flies. To refer the matter to physics, contrast Diver's refractory relationship with others to Nicole's reflecting habit of being. For intervals she becomes one person or another, but no roots accompany these changes of self. Nicole reflects, mirrors other egos, then sheds them, as a tough and independent actress might her roles. Others are no weight, no resistant, clinging substance to Nicole as they are to Dick. Hers is both a pure and shallow contingency of personality. No doubt this is partly due to the violation and return to normalcy forced on her by her history, just as Dick's confusion about his relationship to the qualities of others suggests the crippling partition in his own past between form and action. Diver cannot separate fact from idealized personal and historical memories; for him, personality knows the world through incorporation. Given his past, his absorption of others is simultaneously an act of terror and over-confidence. History a vanishing memory, Diver is never sure that there is a world open to him, whereas Nicole, sure of her history, fortifies herself through the mirror of others because unconsciously she knows that the ongoing energy of her family's history and fortune pulverizes whatever memories linger of guilt and nonexistence.

Unsure of who and what he is, Dick Diver founds his identity upon others' admiration, an admiration caused and complicated by the fact that he, like Jay Gatsby, reflects back to admirers the same selves they wish to believe in — their best selves. But what does the loved one do with such admiration? There seems little power within him to break down and absorb in different form the egos of those "early met and early loved." Having no living roots, he must rely on others' substance to form his ideals of self. Having long ago chosen ideal heroic uniqueness over historical individuation, Diver seduces others into admiration, for he needs the totalities of other ordinary selves to refract his own epic dimensions. And the most horrifying and crippling characteristic is the "necessity of taking all or nothing," which I would connect to Diver's psychological and historical idealism. After all, the creator does not, he thinks, have to choose between bits of things; the world cannot absorb him; he absorbs the world, his imagination never diminished by other things or beings.

Likewise, Diver's absorption process begins in historical chaos when, as Frederick Henry asserted in *A Farewell to Arms*, facts and fragments were destroying abstractions and calling in doubt the very idea of totality. Perhaps unknown to him, Diver covered his idealist bets with a fearful Cartesian formula: "I am others, therefore I am."

By 1929, when the boom culture in America approached collision with ungrasped realities of the economic system, wealth for the Divers was more and more anonymous and compulsive. "Another element that distinguished this summer and autumn for the Divers was a plenitude of money. Owing to the sale of their interest in the clinic, and to developments in America, there was now so much that the mere spending of it, the care of goods, was an absorption in itself" (276). And by 1930, life, internally, is ceasing to be "simply an awaiting" (275). It is as if this time of immobility parallels the earlier meeting of two funicular cars, one descending, the other ascending the mountain. Dick, having pulled Nicole out of the abyss by his own self-gravity, has begun the sinking process and come equal with her, who is ascending, somewhere between top and bottom.

The repression of healthy desires and of a purposive, achieving manhood has given grotesque, antisocial form to Diver's needs. Greater anonymity leads to self-hatred, fear of annihilation, and, at the same time, greater hostility toward anyone who crosses his path with any comprehension of the tragedy. Nicole—this further shrinks Diver's inner margin—increasingly surfaces and articulates her concerns in a form consistent with her needs. At last she believes enough in her evolving self to accept responsibility for their lives:

> "Some of the time I think it's my fault—I've ruined you."
> "So I'm ruined, am I?" he inquired pleasantly.
> "I didn't mean that. But you used to want to create things—now you seem to want to smash them up" (286).

Nicole's words and actions flow spontaneously from her perceptions and impulses. She reacts instinctively, whereas Dick uses formulas to conceal his true feelings. As his mind creates reasons for their continued marriage, his body jerks away from Nicole's touch. Afraid of this cold withdrawal from a woman he has claimed to love with "a wild submergence of the soul" (235), Diver assumes a new mask, the sinister one of the confidence man:

> He covered her hand with his and said in the old pleasant voice of a conspirator for pleasure, mischief, profit, and delight:
> "See that boat out there."
> It was the motor yacht of T. F. Golding lying placid among the little swells of the Nicean bay, constantly bound upon a romantic voyage that was not dependent upon actual motion. "We'll go out there now and ask the people on board what's the matter with them" (286).

The visitation to Golding's yacht and the aimless evening's cruise illustrate the disappearance of Diver's margin of sanity between his long-denied desires now surfacing as ugly antagonisms — demons without power — and his mask assumed for admiration's sake, his manners, charm, and seductive consideration for others. For Golding's perpetual, lush carnival extends to corrupting excess the romantic social voyages earlier captained by Dick Diver. Unable to escape on his own, unable now to work, unable any longer to anchor his self-indulgence to Nicole's sickness, Diver dallies for dalliance's sake. Unwilling to dive beneath his own facade, he accepts the *Margin* as the real world, antithetical though it is to any "actual motion" still possible in his life. Here then, the Divers' attitudes reverse; Dick seduces Nicole toward luxury, dissonance, a spastic dance; Nicole tries to rally Dick toward discipline, harmony, the tonic chord their life has been striving for through long periods when, often haltingly, they've practiced a regimen of the "simpler virtues." No longer can Diver blame his idleness and disintegration on Nicole. Pathetically, he even invokes Baby Warren's friendship with Golding as a reason for joining the party.

Once aboard, Nicole, the refuser, integrates into the scene; but Diver, the joiner, resists, turns isolate, and comes away humiliated because wit, timing, and grace all fail him. In one sense Diver's garbled, fading actor's drunken performance on the *Margin* pivots on despair; seeing no one and no thing to grasp hold of, he would clear the world's deck until he regains his balance. More directly, his actions fit the framework of tantrum. Increasingly "empty-hearted" toward Nicole, Diver nevertheless had built this socially complex world prop by prop for her sake; now her health, youth, and independence ironically belittle those ten or twelve years in the creator's life. Bereft of clay from which to shape a world, Diver has nothing left but the pretense of creative detachment and impersonality.

To make matters worse, Nicole's seizing of Tommy Barban at the yacht's center stage puts Dick in the position of the missing man who is not missed. Thus his accurate perceptions of the British clinging delusionally to the values and policies of colonialism sound like babble: ". . . It's all right for you English, you're doing a dance of death. . . . Sepoys in the ruined fort, I mean Sepoys at the gate and gaiety in the fort and all that. The green hat, the crushed hat, no future" (290). Fine; natives will overrun British colonies, and the British, with intimidating, clipped manners, will pretend for another twenty years that this is not so. But what of Diver? His historical paradigm of reckless self-deception and vanishing empire, particularly his stumbling expression of it, turns attention to his own "ruined fort" and his dependence on pronouncements to avoid self-perusal. Diver has become one of those whom, like the English, he had always found antipathetic because of their subterfuges.

The unexpected appearance of Tommy Barban counterpoints Diver's self-incriminating prophecy of doom for colonialism. Still a "ruler," still a "hero," Barban opposes Diver, not simply personally, but on the political-historical level. Diver perceives the coming shifts of power in the world, but he lacks the discipline and nerve to break his servitude to an imperial system. Moreover, as a man and as creator, "he lacks that tensile strength — none of the ruggedness of Brancusi, Leger, Picasso"; conversely, Barban, whom Fitzgerald in the same sketch called an "unbourgeoise king or nothing."[5] commits himself to exploits of action which preserve and toughen the status quo. Indeed, Diver and Barban bear some resemblance to the weakening, self-indulgent, self-deceiving Western democracies between the wars on one hand and the emerging fascist coalitions of ruthless, recessive power on the other.

Sexually, the situation's dynamics flow from Nicole's sensibility. From her viewpoint it's as if the submerged male in Diver has struggled free and come to full being in Tommy and his archetypal pursuits: "The foreignness of his depigmentation by unknown suns, his nourishment by strange soils, his tongue awkward with the curl of many dialects, his reactions attuned to odd alarms — these things fascinated and rested Nicole" (288). Wherever established aristocratic orders have been menaced, this soldier of class has kept the clock running on past time. In his very rootlessness, Barban possesses a familiarity with the regions of the earth arousing to Nicole, whose existence goes on in an enervated, artificial garden. Unlike Dick, whose maleness has been bound over to Warren husbandry only, Tommy has defined his course of action and not been tamed by any power or any circumstances. Now, as Nicole "looked among the strangers and found, as usual, the fierce neurotics pretending calm, liking the country only in horror of the city" (289), she understandably allies with this man who has made himself briefly at home in many places and carried away the essence of each different region. Having been reassembled by a marriage that was convalescence and a convalescence that was marriage, she wants to be taken by a man who is just that — a man.

Powerless, and sensing his wife's will to be captured by Barban, Diver threatens to change the game and the stakes. If one compares the contingencies of life to the variables of poker, then Diver's wild card — Nicole's former absolute need to admire him — no longer has special value, but, through the dealer's whim, is simply a deuce. To dominate now, Diver's waning power must choose a final, desperate game of blackjack. Their love dead in life, Diver's will would unite them, momentarily and forever, in the kingdom of death:

> "It would give me so much pleasure to think of a little something I could do for you, Dick."
> He turned away from her and toward the veil of starlight over Africa.
> "I believe that's true, Nicole. And sometimes I believe that the littler it was, the more pleasure it would give you."
> "Don't talk like that."
> His face, wan in the light that the white spray caught and tossed back

to the brilliant sky, had none of the lines of annoyance she had expected. It was even detached; his eyes focused upon her gradually as upon a chessman to be moved; in the same slow manner he caught her wrist and drew her near.

"You ruined me, did you?" he inquired blandly. "Then we're both ruined. So —" (292).

There is a whole new world beyond them — Africa — as dark and unknown, solitary and yet divided as the veiled continent of Diver's own being. For an instant the night's beauty and splendor detach Diver from the trivial and accidental colorations of his personal life. Impersonally for a change, he hearkens back to Nicole's accusation of ruin, its pitying tones, and to his perception of the coming decline of Western imperial nations. And Nicole, magnetized by connection with what is beyond them, even if it be death, yields to his negative force: "Cold in terror she put her other wrist into his grip. All right, she would go with him — again she felt the beauty of the night vividly in one moment of complete response and abnegation — all right, then — but now she was unexpectedly free and Dick turned his back, sighing, 'Tch! Tch!' Tears streamed down Nicole's face. In a moment she heard someone approaching; it was Tommy" (292). Out there the universe — beauty and form. In close humanity — fear and pain, a torture of complexity. Why not sever one's perception of irreconcilables through the simple finality of death?

But, having gone to the end of the line, the stern of the *Margin*, Diver cannot turn over that final ace of spades. As Nicole dares to be his, he turns away with a sigh, as if she had failed some subtle test of moral allegiance:

> Already with thee! tender is the night
>
> . . . .
>
> But here there is no light,
> Save what from heaven is with the breezes blown
> Through verdurous glooms and winding mossy ways.

Finally, this night is not tender; neither from death's gorge nor from life's precipice does any light beckon. Between two worlds Diver stands, paralyzed in each, incapable of contact with either. All right then, Nicole, the woman as well as the "essence of a continent," will be taken — to be honest about it — because of the idealist's failure of discipline and desire, taken by Barban, by the barbarian, by the plunderers, in whatever guise they come.

3

Male fortunes determined, if unfulfilled, Fitzgerald scrutinizes through Nicole and her still evolving resonance as "essence of a continent," the newest forms taken, the latest styles worn, by the body of America.

Once again her private world mirrors her garden where impulses choke off words as signs of life. As before, aesthetic and sexual strains blend in common desire: "In the fine spring morning the inhibitions of the male world disappeared and she reasoned gaily as a flower, while the wind blew her hair until her head moved with it" (295). Again, the generative motion of the living elemental world awakens Nicole's vitality, this time in the daylight on a positive frequency. But back inside with Dick and Tommy she plays Sleeping Beauty still, and expresses her freedom and desire only through symbolic gesture. As if to expropriate Diver's remaining identity — his role as doctor — Nicole confers upon Tommy their last bottle of camphor rub. But, Tommy gone, she lacks the confidence for any verbal showdown; repentant, "aware of the sin she had committed against him" (297), she goes upstairs to minister to the fallen Diver: "She put out her hand as if to rub his head, but he turned away like a suspicious animal. Nicole could stand the situation no longer; in a kitchen maid's panic she ran downstairs, afraid of what the stricken man above would feed on while she must continue her dry suckling at his lean chest" (297). Nicole's process of self-weaning resembles the child's; it's not so much the nourishment as the form of contact which reassures her that the world will be the same after her separation.

Rosemary's return soon substitutes gall for Diver's psychological milk. Now Nicole goes to the beach brittlely resistant and "with a renewal of her apprehension that Dick was contriving at some desperate solution" (298). Unlike five years ago, hysteria is no longer a possible response for her. If her alliance with Tommy on the *Margin* and at the Villa Diana the morning after indicated her simple desire for a stronger man, then the beach episode spurs Nicole to analytical judgment. To choose Tommy, she must see Dick humiliated. For Nicole reality is material and physical, its moral coordinate property; therefore Diver must be a verifiable ruin, physically as well as psychologically, to disappear from her field of reality.

Nicole, herself, awaits not any gradual, organic metamorphosis, but a transformation in speed and composition closer to those rapid elemental changes in chemistry. Fitzgerald associates her leap into new being with an American aesthetic of money and machine: "Nicole had been *designed* for change, for flight, with money as fins and wings. The new state of things would be no more than if a *racing chassis*, concealed for years under the body of a *family limousine*, should be stripped to its original self" (298, my italics). Underneath the hood, the urge toward competition and dominion belittles whatever graceful guise appears to contain such raw power. In Fitzgerald's metaphor for Nicole's metamorphosis, her personality abdicates the creative imperative given by Hart Crane when he wrote that "unless poetry can absorb the machine, i.e., acclimatize it as naturally and casually as trees, cattle, galleons, castles and all other human associations of the past, then poetry has failed of its full contemporary function."[6] But in America the machine captures and absorbs personality. Nicole Warren's leap will not be a flight into more sympathetic and imaginative consciousness. Unlike complex Dedalus, who designed both confining labyrinth and liberating wings, Nicole *has been designed*. An artifact of her inheritance, she will be propelled by the fierce energy of dynastic money, of a civilization's economic system. The limousine and its connotations of class, elegance, and beauty are but concessions to convention, euphemisms which legitimize and strengthen rigidities of class and power.

When he designates money as fuel for the machine, Fitzgerald alludes to the dimension of place and personality. Or, as his middle-class figure in "The Swimmers" said: "Americans should be born with fins, and perhaps they were—perhaps money was a form of fin. In England, property begot a strong place sense, but Americans, restless and with shallow roots, needed fins and wings."[7] Allied to the rootless machine, money will forge such mechanical fins and wings. The automobile, quickly mass-produced, articulated American restlessness and the often random, rootless movement to and from many places, with respect for none. Nicole Warren's technologically created self should be compared to a "racing chassis," for as a wanderer, an exile, a lady of many places, not one of them known by her, she will race from place to beautiful place seeking proprietary rights, while true destination eludes her and her new chauffeur, Barban, the dare-devil driver.

As always, Fitzgerald does not permit metaphor to drown out the voice of Nicole's personality: "Nicole could feel the fresh breeze already— it was the wrench she feared, and the dark manner of its coming" (298). Her birth will be neither so simple nor so clean as a chassis rolling off one of Henry Ford's assembly lines. For the purpose of Nicole's metamorphosis, the Adam and Eve birth myth seems to reverse its male-female values of independence and dependence. In the beginning as *Genesis* told it and as it operated within Dick Diver, the male dreamed his Eve and woke to find the form of his image embodied in the substance of his own flesh. Psychologically, Nicole came of Diver; a part of her existed for him in fantasy before she ever appeared in his world. Now, however, Nicole seems unable to come to new and separate birth until Diver goes to sleep again, but a sleep of nightmare, not of dream. "The wrench she feared" is the act of psychologically breaking from his side, and "the dark manner of its coming" means dissolution of the parent self, of Dick's self, intact yet incomplete without her, and cut off from contact with woman and with everything else in the world. It's as if to stay in Eden means death and that, in the modern America of this novel, only the woman takes her chances in the fallen world of history and society. The man Diver will sleep until death parts him from his dreams. The dream and its idealizing framework of perception, rather than Eve, destroys this American Adam. Or, as Fitzgerald described the transfer of vitality from Dick to Nicole: "It seems as if the completion of his ruination will be the fact that cures her—

almost mystically."[8] Dick may have mastered the paternal role, but Nicole has had too many fathers; to be whole, she must break the pattern.

Just as Fitzgerald renders Nicole as an industrial object which pulls its weight in the total system, Nicole begins to see Diver less as man and more as thing. Her choice of object too relegates Diver to an undynamic, past context very different from her own. "His old expertness with people," she compares to a "tarnished object of art" (300). Sensing this and down to the nub of himself, Diver turns to physical accomplishment, a "lifting trick" expressive of stamina and timing. Performed for Rosemary, a stranger to his actual condition, Diver's exhibition becomes a psychological artifice as well. But, these acrobatics having failed humiliatingly, what seems to separate Nicole most utterly from Diver is his own mere detachment. "Expressionless, alone with the water and the sky" (303), his mask belittles Nicole's pity and, worse than that, her straining with him as he had tried to lift the man on his shoulders. His silent, arrogant disclaimer of actions, which, moments before, he had put body and soul into accomplishing, drives off any love or sympathy. As the idealist gathered others around him in success, the skeptic bears the conditions of human failure alone. His seems a stance of false dignity. Unable to love, Diver cannot come out of himself to allow anyone else to even touch him.

Back on the beach, with Rosemary for catalyst, Diver tries to codify the relationship between roles and personality. " 'The danger to an actress is in responding' " (306); and responding, it develops, consists of external-izing one's genuine emotions in a trying situation. The difficulty, given the egocentric necessity of an actress, is that spontaneity focuses the audience's attention on whatever is objective in the situation, instead of on the actress. According to Diver, Rosemary as an actress should " 'do the unexpected thing until you've maneuvered the audience back from the objective fact to yourself' " (306). On stage and — since the dramatic metaphor has tutored personality in this novel — in life your best self is expendable. Individuality depends upon a capacity to deny contingency and to substitute an unexpected, unfelt gesture for the " 'correct emotional responses — fear and love and sympathy' " (306). This theory accepted, any spontaneity would come from faculties of calculation rather than the heart's sources of sympathy. Addressed to Rosemary, Diver's advice has some pertinence, for she lacks both an emotional and a perceptual life. Only tricks of the trade rescue her from mediocrity. Diver, however, to ease his malaise, follows T. S. Eliot's advice and calls on form as a means of escape from passion and personality.[9]

To preserve an identity worthy of center stage, Diver has molded his role and gestures out of a self less and less capable of responding with anything but bitterness. Time and time again, he blunts Nicole's critical perception of one or another of his failings by substituting detachment for spontaneous emotional response. Nicole thus wonders about his once uncharacteristic lapses and forgets the annoying "objective fact." The

dramatic situation enclosing Diver while he speaks illustrates the limitation of his paradigm. With his "unexpected" lecture, he has stolen center
stage from gullible Rosemary, but there is no longer enough there to hold
Nicole's attention. For her, the elaborateness of the ploy signifies his
desperation. But perhaps Nicole's abrupt departure is what Dick desires;
you no longer know his motives, nor do you have faith in their consequences. As actor-director, he is no longer interesting; his technique has
become more abstract than dramatic.

Her ego stymied in the labyrinth, Nicole retraces her steps back
toward the starting point of the Warren past. Lost in Diver's world of
euphemism and, now, annihilation, she'll reject sensibility and tenderness
and do what a healthy, intact Warren would have done in the beginning:
marry a man of power, Tommy Barban, a twentieth-century barbarian of
the old order. Fed up with those places "where she had played planet to
Dick's sun" (307), Nicole does not rebel against male authority; what
seems intolerable is that Dick's "sun" shines with gaslight upon the
twentieth century. Long ago her broken self gave over the thinking to him,
but Diver's mind denied reality through genteel affectations: "It had been
a long lesson but she had learned it. Either you think—or else others have
to think for you and take power from you, pervert and discipline your
natural tastes, civilize and sterilize you" (308). Her defensive, either-or
rhetoric, ironically strikingly close to that of dispossessed minorities,
tenaciously reinforces the Warrens' opposition to any diminution of their
power. Diver's values were blown to bits in the trenches—"All my
beautiful lovely safe world blew itself up here, with a great gust of high
explosive love" (118)—and the rubble no longer camouflages Nicole's
unsatisfied female needs.

Through all of Nicole's changes, Diver continues to act like a man
condemned to replay forever one of the games in *Alice in Wonderland.*

> "Thank y' father-r
> Thank y' mother-r
> Thanks for meeting up with one another—"

"I don't like that one," Dick said, starting to turn the page (308).
Forced to deal with submerged reality, Diver's instincts go back to the
nineteenth century; his reflex belongs not so much to the psychiatrist and
husband who recognize and encourage a woman's strength and possibilities as it does to the Victorian gentleman, perhaps to his clergyman father
who thought that, if ignored long enough, nasty facts would go away. Dick
too retreats, but not to those spare-bodied ancestors of early Virginia or to
that vitality represented by Mad Anthony Wayne and the great-
grandfather who was governor of North Carolina. For form's sake Diver
returns to the highly conscious good manners learned early from his father
and manners which served that clergyman well in Gilded Age drawing
rooms and ladies' teas. Such affected social graces may have determined

the young Southerner's survival in the North during that period, but they are, in the twentieth century, a substitute for life and vitality. Whatever their effect upon women initially, these manners emasculate the men who wear them, make them first overrefined men, and then boys. Nicole, partly because of Dick's failure, looks to the past for a tradition of mere strength and ruthlessness, while Diver seeks to rationalize weakness and incapacity. Both find what they seek—parallel histories that cannot meet without conquest and absorption.

Like Pallas Athene with whom she earlier allied herself, Nicole Warren leaves little to chance. As she prepares for Tommy Barban, whom she has summoned, she sees herself as capital property—in all its changing guises—as well as woman: "She bathed and anointed herself and covered her body with a layer of powder, while her toes crunched another pile on a bath towel. She looked microscopically at the lines of her flanks, wondering how soon the fine, slim edifice would begin to sink squat and earthward" (309). Simultaneously, she is filly and horse-trader, herself with female desires and Sid Warren, Robber-Baron. How much am I worth? she inquires, while bathing and anointing abdicate their religious and sexual purpose for a fertility of capital value. Subtly, the metaphorical object evolves from horse to edifice with its suggestion of the great American skyscrapers, those houses of monopoly power for the expanding American financial empire. Clearly, Fitzgerald transforms Nicole as "essence of a continent" into twentieth-century America, for in the nineteenth century the country's resources were natural things. Then, the land and its inhabitants—tribal grounds, horses and humans—were traded. Now, in 1930, the character of the nation shows in its architectural face. Skyscrapers shelter an increasingly bureaucratic remote system, so that Fitzgerald's choice of edifice contrasts with Hart Crane's vision of modern technology (the Brooklyn Bridge) as a span between body and consciousness, between the spaces of a yet to be unified continent. Because he compares woman, not man, to edifice, Fitzgerald recalls Paul Rosenfeld's description of the American leisure woman as a "magnificently shining edifice." "Flowing of line and rich in material, it has also made of her a dwelling uninhabited, gray, chill like the houses where the furniture stands year-long in twilight under its shrouds. For, in keeping the male undeveloped and infantile, American culture has attributed the masculine principle to the female, and divided the female against her proper intuitions."[10]

As Nicole derives her historical image first from natural and then from architectural phenomena, so her psychological self-impression is inculcated by Hollywood, that funneler of dreams to every citizen, rich and poor. In *Tender Is the Night* the women become Daddy's Girls one way or another: Baby Warren, the unattached, androgynous object who has superimposed a Robber Baron consciousness upon her wooden body; Rosemary Hoyt, who, on the screen, lures the world away from realities of time and history, and, in life, lures men away from maturity. Finally, Nicole too surrenders what is of value in herself—"the essential structure and economy," the "promise" of a "true growing" (33)— for Rosemary's notion of youth as power. It's as if loss of innocence means the end rather than the beginning of human fulfillment. For maturity involves personality with dissipation and death. Adult perception carries with it painful conviction of life's unalterable necessities; whereas innocence cultivates a sense of invulnerability, imperviousness, and imperishability. Perhaps one reason women do not grow up is that the men who determine mass culture in America are psychological boys who require younger sisters for mates. In any case, Nicole Warren's particular desire "to be worshipped again, to pretend to have a *mystery*," follows from her consciousness of loss, because of her illness, of "two of the great arrogant years in the life of a pretty girl" (309, my italics). Thus, for Nicole and perhaps for America, the lust for false youth is a fearful, immature response to the ravishing of girl and of continent when each was genuinely young and uncontaminated.

In Nicole's encounter with Barban, an opposition between natural and civilized states occurs once more. But when he asks her, " 'Why didn't they leave you in your natural state?' " he's talking about a condition of personality where action is beyond morality, not about any Edenic state where innocence and spontaneity are values and ways of being. He is referring to Nicole's power to pick and choose among the world's best: " 'I'm just a whole lot of simple people,' " she tells him. Clearly, this collection of persons depends more upon her imperial, dynastic context than it does upon any condition of innocence. For her, freedom from the usual psychic bankruptcy, after the losses inflicted by violation, flows from her money. No matter what tremors may shake exposed buildings, this American edifice, girded by money, property, and connections, remains an intact skeleton. Whatever quivers get through affect only the surfaces of self and society.

Assessing her "white crook's eyes" as she and Barban ride to Nice, Nicole concludes decisively: "Very well then, better a sane crook than a mad puritan' " (312). This utter paucity of alternatives terribly indicts the American condition. We have watched a strain of puritan neurosis paralyze Dick Diver because, in his idealist self-worship, he first identified himself as elite and elect and then believed in his power to determine the election of others. Then, implicated in complexities of desire and guilt, he could not face the world but clung, in his mind, to images of innocence and beauty. At last he hates himself and the world because of realities he did not acknowledge before his ideal vision bound him to a wheel of unfulfilled desire. In the face of reality's contingencies and necessities, ideal and moral absolutes turn Diver away from life and history toward an isolate, martyr's existence—an asceticism from compulsion, in a body still yearning for satisfaction. "He was in love with every pretty woman he saw now, their forms at a distance, their shadows on a wall" (219). Rightly perhaps, Nicole rejects this deathbound way of seeing and living. But what of "sane crook"? Why are "sane" and "crook" linked? What conception of personality emerges? Clearly, this paradigm confirms the social Darwinist conception of society and the individual. For sanity consists of, and is verified by, survival. And one survives through seizure and mastery, by a violent predatory cycle of strong and weak which governs the life process and metes out death and extinction to creatures and species unable to cope with and adapt to the changing conditions of this perpetual struggle. In America, the "material interests" of Conrad's prescient *Nostromo* were able better than the idealists to build an empire on the rock of elect doctrine. Always concerned with evidence, demonstration, and proof, materialists demand earthly evidence of any individual's privilege. For them election meant wealth, and wealth requires power.

The limitation of Nicole's "sane crook" prescription is that it denies a certain rich part of her nature and of human personality in general. Neither does it deal with the demonic turn often taken when sensibility and tenderness are trampled within a person. If her paradigm is accepted by a society and among societies, then Spengler's prophecy of "gang rule," of "the world as spoil" to be taken by the most brutal and cunning plunderers will come true — as, in fact, it was realized by the Fascist coalitions.[11] Since sanity depends upon theft and force, what happens when America, or that new world of Africa, is stolen and ravished entirely? Ultimately, the prey disappear, and the sane crooks must fight each other. If the integrity of others is not perceived and respected in action, on what psychological foundation will identity rest except that of dominion? What Jonathan Edwards, that idealist of humane method and sensibility, two hundred years ago called "benevolence" (disinterested affection) toward other beings seems in Fitzgerald's and our own twentieth-century America a first principle of sanity and survival.

So much for the hope of a new world, a reconstructed social and economic order in America. What the Warren-Barban alliance prophesies is the reformation and revitalization of America's imperial power. In this connection D. H. Lawrence's analysis of the emerging historical situation offers a vision even more terrible than Spengler's prophecy of a worsening cycle of dynamic, barbaric, anarchic civilization:

> For there are not now, as in the Roman times, any great reservoirs of energetic barbaric life. Goths, Gauls, Germans, Slavs, Tartars. The world is very full of people, but all fixed in civilizations of their own, and they have all our vices, all our mechanisms, and all our means of destruction. This time, the leading civilization cannot die out as Greece, Rome, Persia died. It must suffer a great collapse, maybe. But it must carry through all the collapse the living clue to the next civilization.[12]

Unlike Spengler's notion of the earth ruled and patrolled by its dregs, Lawrence's categorical prophecy assumes that no matter how ragged the coat of civilization, certain threads are woven in continuity. If we try out Lawrence's imperative on the metallic evolutions strengthened by the merger of Barban and Warren, we must conclude that Fitzgerald does not look for the collapse, cyclic or linear, of America's capitalist industrial system. Rather, he proposes an additional consolidation of power and wealth through Tommy Barban's authority and courage, with Barban the representative of a new elite—cultured, reactionary, nihilist leaders.

To set in motion this latest strain of American aristocratic-barbaric civilization, Fitzgerald brings Tommy and Nicole to Beaulieu, easternmost spot on the French Riviera. "Symbolically she lay across his saddle-bow as surely as if he had wolfed her away from Damascus and they had come out upon the Mongolian plain" (316). The echo of hoof-beats conjures up North African slave markets and girls bought and stolen away to tribal destinations across the steppes to Mongolia, with evocations of Genghis Khan, who terrorized and exploited Europe as its later civilized-barbaric conquerors would America, Africa, and Asia. Here Nicole gladly surrenders herself—woman, property, and continent—to Barban's displaced, impersonal male authority.

Imperceptibly, she rejects Diver's values and their genteel codification as a system of interlocked manners and morals: "Moment by moment all that Dick had taught her fell away and she was ever nearer to what she had been in the beginning, prototype of that obscure yielding up of swords that was going on in the world about her. Tangled with love in the moonlight she welcomed the anarchy of her lover" (316). Whose swords? What surrender? Prototype Nicole certainly is, but her new union opposes the genuine sensibility of some eighteenth- and early nineteenth-century European and American families who, often because of roots in what Yeats romantically called "one dear perpetual place," brought to their exercise of power and authority a degree of loveliness, custom, ceremony, and aesthetic grace.[13] The Warrens, now the Barbans, represent an aristocracy reconstructed along quasi-feudal principles, whose muscle does not derive from continuity, originality, or sensibility, but from simple money, complex property, and the centrifugal power these things confer in a modern imperial system. One should not be misled by the allusion to anarchy. For anarchy, as fascism so well showed, can be both catalyst and instrument for the totalitarian exercise of political power. Likewise, at this time, fascism signaled an abandonment of the attempt to evolve genuine democracies from republics whose original base and intent were elitist in nature. Now Barban may be anarchic to fulfill his desires and to become one of the new rulers, but he is not anarchic in any political, economic, or philosophic sense. Rather, he would impose ruthless punishment upon any who oppose consolidation of personal fortunes within national and supranational concentrations of wealth and power. Moreover his merger with Nicole symbolically parallels the gut alliances of fascism. The industrial

Warrens in coalition with the militarist Barban form a cartel eager for spoils, with all the world their prey.

4

Back at the Villa Diana, now stripped of mystery and spontaneity, Nicole pauses to consider the unspoken depths of her tie to Dick. Here, at the last, Diver's body directs and acts for his being. There exists no more stage, no props; in their absence, gestures flow unconsidered, unimpeded, unexpurgated from deepest consciousness. When Dick does not answer her accusations of cowardice and failure, Nicole shakily begins "to feel the old hypnotism of his intelligence, sometimes exercised without power but always with substrata of truth under truth which she could not break or even crack" (310). In its silent intimidation, Diver's intelligence conceals a confused and paralyzed self which now chooses to be mired in complexities in order to rationalize away realities of desire and history. Neither personality nor history stands still; whether motion be forward or backward, dynamic or entropic, there is motion and change. Unfortunately, when Nicole rejects Diver's euphemism and gentility, she scorns as well genuine values of personality — benevolence, consideration, and tolerance. Although Diver's nostalgic humanism comes to mask viciousness, at his best he did recognize aesthetic form and humane sensibility as essentials in a richly developed nature. Before his own self split apart, there was in Diver, as there seems always to be in Fitzgerald's sympathetic complexity, a commitment to warmth and tenderness as qualities upon which civilized men and women and societies should stand. Nicole's transferral to Barban ends the search for personality on the basis of a true and complex relatedness. The elegant flowing lines of the limousine have been scrapped and melted back to ore; all that remains is the chassis, the essential machine.

At liberty now from Nicole, Dr. Diver is not liberated from the motivations, the vision, and the inner weakness which patterned his life. To make this absolutely clear, Fitzgerald invents an episode in which Diver, against his own common sense, goes into verbal combat as a knight in service of the leisure class. This time far from being at its "truly most brilliant and glamorous," the leisure class exhibits only perversity and squalor.[14] In any case the knight's ordeal consists of freeing from prison Mary North Minghetti and Lady Caroline Sibley-Biers who have been jailed as a result of their sexual duplicity. Diver, the rescuer, possesses no magic with which to lift the curse of sterility. All he does, in mythic terms, is release the sick women into the world to further pollute the wasteland: "He would have to go fix this thing that he didn't care a damn about, because it had early become a habit to be loved, perhaps from the moment when he had realized that he was the last hope of a dying clan" (321). Now the "last hope" of this or any other "dying clan" has choices. He can forget the clan or pick and choose among its values; he can extend the best of past traditions to persons whose different vitality and history might create richer, more integrated kinships suitable for the changed conditions of the present. Or, lacking confidence and fearful of failure, he can serve the establishment which has put out of business his and many another clan. Finally, his servant's cry of "Use me!" translates self-doubt and uncertainty about his place in the scheme of things into a plea for approval by those who own the mansion.

Ben Franklin, Booker T. Washington, S. I. Hayakawa — success for those who start as outsiders in America ultimately depends upon whether their rise involves incorporation into the American establishment. This need to belong, to be legitimate, to be approved and admired, has its origins in the failure of roots in America, a failure of lineage. In a passage from "The Swimmers," later distilled into the *Notebooks*, Fitzgerald talks about the process through which abstract illusion and material power distort and betray the impulse to serve America democratically: "France was a land, England was a people, but America, having about it still that quality of the idea, was harder to utter — it was the graves at Shiloh and the tired, drawn, nervous faces of its great men, and the country boys dying in the Argonne for a phrase that was empty before their bodies withered. It was a willingness of the heart."[15] Clearly, Fitzgerald distinguishes between the poor "country boys dying in the Argonne" and Richard Diver, lured by his middle-class educational draft deferment to delusions of privilege in Vienna. Both respond to the bait of empty phrases, but there is a pathos about the dead boys' innocence of American power — an excuse, whereas Diver's idealist complicity is less "a willingness of the heart" than a willingness to risk identity, integrity, and independence on behalf of his own American future.

Given the facts of American history — its great building blocks of genocide, slavery, plunder of a continent — alongside the eloquent affirmations of the Declaration of Independence — innocence as a point of view is by now a national crime. About those lost American dead, Fitzgerald shows considerate respect. Moved by their "willingness of the heart," their intuitive commitment to their nation he elegizes them because in American history there seems little opportunity to tie that moral willingness to national policies. His heart "determined to make them otherwise," Fitzgerald's intelligence sees and records the possibility that, in America, "things are hopeless."[16]

Rescuing the two decadent women, Diver uses wit and parody to spare himself humiliation as well as to serve his masters well. Yet his parody of American and British fortune and nobility reinforces the very realities he seems to undermine. Still present in Diver beneath the irony is a hint of the pride defined by David Halberstam in his trenchant essay on McGeorge Bundy: "He believed if *he* set *his mind* to it there was nothing *American power* couldn't do."[17] The fact is that Diver's garbled, highly

ironic allusions to John D. Rockefeller, Mellon, and Lord Henry Ford free
the women, exactly because these are not fictitious names in a vacuum but
actual men behind American power. In *Tender Is the Night*'s vision of
America, there is no vessel for that "willingness of the heart" so essential to
the creation of a history that will dignify individual personality.

It remains, through confrontation with Barban, with Nicole as booty
and witness, for Fitzgerald to finish off Diver even as a will. In an
important way neither Dick nor Tommy is central here; the exchange
relies upon Nicole as conductor of energy, "so that their emotions pass
through her divided self as through a bad telephone connection" (327).
Once more Fitzgerald locates Nicole's reference point in a metallic object,
an instrument which scientifically, mechanically, automatically, registers
and also distorts the complexities of human voices, desires, and personalities. In the conversation Diver parries into absurdity Tommy's rational,
logical case for divorce. At last, when Tommy impatiently switches to
impulse, Diver withdraws matter of factly, as if his abdication depended
not upon any involvement or any passion but simply upon the appropriate
mode of perception:

> "That is so useless. Nicole and I love each other, that's all there is to
> it."
> "Well then," said the Doctor, "since it's all settled, suppose we go back
> to the barber shop" (329).

Fitzgerald's rare use of "the Doctor" suggests an impersonal case. No
longer lover or husband, Diver thinks to preserve his dignity by washing
his hands in the most careful fashion. Such meticulousness has nothing to
do with the patient, the wife, the woman, the person, Nicole, but signifies
all that is left of Diver — a mere persona of professional form.

But suddenly, in the midst of their conversation, another world comes
into being. Circles of reality widen from the Tour de France or from
Diver's table, whichever one chooses as the arbitrary starting point:

> First was a lone cyclist in a red jersey, toiling intent and confident out of
> the westering sun, passing to the melody of a high chattering cheer.
> Then three together in a harlequinade of faded color, legs caked yellow
> with dust and sweat, faces expressionless, eyes heavy and endlessly tired.
> Tommy faced Dick, saying: "I think Nicole wants a divorce — I
> suppose you'll make no obstacles?"
> A troupe of fifty more swarmed after the first bicycle racers, strung
> out over two hundred yards; a few were smiling and self-conscious, a
> few obviously exhausted, most of them indifferent and weary. A retinue
> of small boys passed, a few defiant stragglers, a light truck carried the
> victims of accident and defeat (328–29).

This impersonal trail of life sobers even Barban into a qualified courtesy.
From the race there is no exile; even its victims are borne along the course
in a truck, a mockery of past effort, past vitality. Aesthetically, the bicycle

race is exactly that—a bicycle race; no symbol, no allusion, no moralism arrives to assign it an ordered place. Its sheerly perceptual modality corresponds to that anonymous relationship experienced by Tommy and Nicole in their order of personality. Although there may be associations between Diver's passage out of life and the decrepitude of the cyclers, the connection does not reach us in any simply equivalent way. Achieved here is the aesthetic of "magic suggestiveness"[18] which Joseph Conrad and Edmund Wilson, in essays mulled over by Fitzgerald, both related to music, "the art of arts." "One of the principal aims of symbolism," Wilson wrote, "was to approximate the indefiniteness of music."[19] Indeed, the scene ends with the music of film. As Diver fades out through widening circles of reality, Nicole's eyes simulate a camera until with a vanishing poof his existence ceases to be verified. At this point, Nicole's perception has less freedom and range than a camera's. Her mobility riveted by other circumstances, her eyes, at least in relation to Diver's movements, are not moving but stationary.

Fittingly, Fitzgerald renders the last scenario from the beach (the beach that Diver built) in a triple perspective which fulfills the form and prophecy of *Rosemary's Angle*: Nicole's and her companions'; Dick's; and the event's—impersonal and without moral or historical interpretative structure. Allusion and reflection recede before fact and event. Tempted to direct a last drama, Diver creates, with intellect and no emotion or imagination, a world empty save for him and Mary Minghetti. His manufactured desire desperately asserts mind over matter in order to stave off the unalterable circumstances of his context. His synthetic drama seems an act geared to nothing but himself and, even there, geared only to the masturbation of his ego. Now an idealist confidence man, Diver does not for a moment entertain the illusion he would make real to Mary. But, with a sudden lens change, Fitzgerald clarifies Diver's motive: "His eyes, for the moment clear as a child's asked her sympathy and stealing over him he felt the old necessity of convincing her that he was the last man in the world and she was the last woman. . . . Then he would not have to look at those other figures, a man and a woman, black and white and metallic against the sky . . ." (332). In this inorganic, artificial garden, Tommy and Nicole are Adam and Eve. Leisured, self-sufficient, metallic creations, they are sustained in their garden by the system which exploits and dehumanizes the world. Fiercely brittle, they lack all hope of fluidity, depth, and richness of being. For these twentieth-century historical archetypes, creation consists of metamorphosis not from the earth's slime but from the inorganic matter of the machine. Like computers, what is most formidable about them is the fact of their stark, programmatic existence.

Against this reality, the plastic world Diver conjures up silently with Mary, and which she grasps at, disappears first in his mind and then from their movable stage: "His glance fell soft and kind upon hers, suggesting an emotion underneath; their glances married suddenly, bedded, strained together. Then, as the laughter inside him became so loud that it seemed as if Mary must hear it, Dick switched off the light and they were back in the Riviera sun" (333). Here drama and gesture do not extend consciousness but create a facade for unrevealed perceptions. Diver's interior laughter — in the neurotic, laughter serves isolation instead of communication — recalls his faculty of detachment, yet in the past that quality worked on behalf of engagement rather than abdication. Diver's fantasies of sexuality utterly protect and prevent him from any sensuous contact. His intelligence feeds only on its own shrinking carcass.

Whatever actions Diver performs open up alternatives to others only. Even his last gesture, a papal cross of renunciation, seems calculated to inspire motion toward him by Nicole, but she has surrendered her remaining freedom to Barban: " 'I'm going to him,' Nicole got to her knees. 'No, you're not,' said Tommy, pulling her down firmly. 'Let well enough alone' " (333). This moment signifies the final conquest. Her simple autonomous impulse he repels by virtue of physical force. Tommy lives and has prospered in a monolithic world, and he will permit no complexity or diversity of response, even if such an action involves no division of allegiance. "Let well enough alone" means Barban intends to shut the gates of his garden against the world until all antithetical creatures are exiled or extinct.

5

The brief coda to *Tender Is the Night* reverberates themes, pans time and space, and blacks out those perspectives through which Fitzgerald had been rendering Diver's loss of self and history. We cease to see Diver, either directly or through anyone else's eyes, whether character or novelist; all we have about him is second-hand information — letters from him to Nicole and, finally, bits of gossip that filter back to her. Facts, what few facts there are, grow less and less graspable; suppositions replace facts, and assumption becomes commensurate with truth.

Like America's original natives, Diver wanders from place to place until he loses name, identity, and connection with other persons, other things, other times and places. From postmarks Nicole traces him to Geneva, New York, a long journey from that other Geneva whose cultural vision has so haunted Diver. Now there is no cultural center and no anarchy either, for the Warren-Barban cartel prospers greatly even in the face of world depression. But history must be satisfied with Nicole's vague memory. All flesh scraped away, Fitzgerald's ending appears with taut aesthetic perfection: "She looked up Geneva in an atlas and found it was in the heart of the Finger Lakes section and considered a pleasant place. Perhaps, so she liked to think, his career was biding its time, again like Grant's in Galena; his latest note was post-marked from Hornell, New

York, which is some distance from Geneva and a very small town; in any case he is almost certainly in that section of the country, in one town or another" (334). Nicole Warren, contemporary national goddess, discovers America through an atlas. Could it be there is a place untouched, a "section of the country" unsectioned by the centuries of exploration and exploitation? From Nicole we'll never know. Letter gives way to note, and note to guess; Buffalo—for red man and for beast American names commemorate annihilation—yields to a succession of small towns which fade to "a very small town." Diver's journey, its purpose, duration, and destination, all are distilled by the indefinite, uncaring "some."

About history Nicole is as ignorant as she is of geography. For after President Grant presided over a Reconstruction which gradually abandoned the pursuit of democratic equality in favor of the Republican Party's allegiance to big business and tolerance for the Jim Crow rule of the New South, he returned to Galena. There, in the 1880s, biding his time until death, he wrote his *Personal Memoirs*, absolved in his own mind from complicity in the nation's degradation. Euphemistically he refers in the final pages to the Civil War, almost oblivious to the tragic course of American history during the intervening twenty years. "The war has made us a nation of great power and intelligence. We have but little to do to preserve peace, happiness, and prosperity at home, and the respect of other nations. Our experience ought to teach us the necessity of the first; our power secures the latter. I feel that we are on the eve of a new era, when there is to be great harmony between the Federal and Confederate. I cannot stay to be a living witness to the correctness of this prophecy; but I feel it within me that it is to be so."[20] At whose cost this hypothetical harmony will come Grant does not say; he merely substitutes prophecy for analysis and judgment. With Grant's fading life as backdrop for Diver's decline, it is fitting and proper for Fitzgerald now to invoke history only elliptically. Unlike Grant, Diver has no last words of encouragement or bitterness; he has no voice at all. But his talents have been destroyed by the same forces of innocence and idealism within, and aggrandizement without, which rendered Grant historically ineffectual after an auspicious beginning. As Diver's chronicler, Nicole too resembles Grant. How American it is to remember with sentimental conviction whatever it is we have degraded.

Although, because vague, Nicole's casual tones would make everything well, the unassuming camera through lingering, dissolving wide angle shots follows Diver farther and farther from any center of human consciousness. Diver and the America he could not discover because he would not accept its reality are too blurred to be observed in a closeup. By contrast, at the end of *The Waste Land*, T. S. Eliot offers his personae and his audience fragments to "shore up against [their] ruins," but in *Tender Is the Night* form provides no such alternative. On the contrary, here form has extinguished its own light for the journey into darkness. For Diver and perhaps for America the night will not be tender — not in any case or any aspect:

> We were the last romantics — chose for theme
> Traditional sanctity and loveliness;
> Whatever's written in what poets name
> The book of the people; whatever most can bless
> The mind of man or elevate a rhyme;
> But all is changed, that high horse riderless,
> Though mounted in that saddle Homer rode
> Where the swan drifts upon a darkening flood.[21]

To even survive, Fitzgerald's form implies, we leave Dick Diver in some forgotten place, leave him there like that other lost dreamer, that first "fabulous voyager" of our literature, Rip Van Winkle, sleeping the sleep of oblivion. Worse off than Rip at the end, Dick Diver has no home to return to, no emerging generation to hear his voice and absorb his story.

"The way home we seek," Ralph Waldo Ellison has written, "is that condition of man's being at home in the world, which is called love, and which we term democracy."[22] At his best this was Diver's quest, and certainly it is the quest pursued by F. Scott Fitzgerald. At the close of *Tender Is the Night* he dared to advance it by his compassionate, burning, purging, terrifically honest account of the end of illusion — for Dick Diver if not yet for the nation.

Notes

1. F. Scott Fitzgerald, *The Crack-Up*, ed. Edmund Wilson (New York: New Directions, 1945), p. 74.

2. Andrew Turnbull, ed., *The Letters of F. Scott Fitzgerald* (New York: Charles Scribner's Sons, 1963), p. 567.

3. Fitzgerald's sketch for *Tender Is the Night*, Appendix 3, Arthur Mizener, *The Far Side of Paradise* (Boston: Houghton Mifflin, 1965), p. 352.

4. Turnbull, ed., *Letters of F. Scott Fitzgerald*, p. 310.

5. Fitzgerald sketch in Mizener, *The Far Side of Paradise*, p. 348.

6. Hart Crane, *The Collected Poems*, ed. and intro. by Waldo Frank (New York: Liveright, 1946), p. 177.

7. F. Scott Fitzgerald, in notes to *Tender Is the Night* in *Three Novels* (New York: Charles Scribner's Sons, 1953), p. 355.

8. Fitzgerald sketch in Mizener, *The Far Side of Paradise*, p. 352.

9. T. S. Eliot, "Tradition and the Individual Talent," *Selected Essays: New Edition* (New York: Harcourt, Brace, 1950), p. 11.

10. Paul Rosenfeld, *Port of New York* (Urbana: University of Illinois Press, 1961), pp. 209–10.

11. This cultural prophecy of Spengler's made a powerful impression on Fitzgerald's sense of history. See Turnbull, ed., *Letters of F. Scott Fitzgerald*, p. 290.

12. D. H. Lawrence, *Psychoanalysis and the Unconscious and Fantasia of the Unconscious* (New York: Viking Press, 1960), p. 208.

13. W. B. Yeats, "A Prayer for My Daughter," *The Collected Poems of W. B. Yeats* (New York: Macmillan, 1956), p. 186.

14. Fitzgerald sketch in Mizener, *The Far Side of Paradise*, p. 346.

15. Fitzgerald, *The Crack-Up*, p. 197.

16. *Ibid.*, p. 69.

17. David Halberstam, "The Very Expensive Education of McGeorge Bundy," *Harper's*, vol. 239 (July, 1969), p. 32. My italics.

18. Joseph Conrad, "Preface," *The Nigger of the Narcissus* (New York: Doubleday, Page, 1924), p. xiii.

19. Edmund Wilson, as quoted by Sheilah Graham in *College of One* (New York: Bantam Books, 1968), p. 110.

20. *Personal Memoirs of U. S. Grant* (New York: Charles L. Webster, 1886), vol. 2, p. 553.

21. Yeats, "Coole Park and Ballylee, 1931," *Collected Poems*, p. 240.

22. Ralph Ellison, *Shadow and Act* (New York: Random House, 1964), pp. 105–06.

Fitzgerald's "Figured Curtain": Personality and History in *Tender Is the Night*

Bruce L. Grenberg*

From "May Day" (1920) to "Early Success" (1937), F. Scott Fitzgerald characteristically interweaves personal and historical perspectives within his fiction to present a singularly intense and immediate commentary on the era. For him history is never abstract — something that happens *to* people; it is live and compelling, springing from the hearts and minds of individuals. It is, as it were, the enactment of man's personality, the outward show of his inner being.[1] In "The Rich Boy" (1926) Fitzgerald states his position quite openly and explicitly: "Begin with an individual, and before you know it you find that you have created a type; begin with a type, and you find that you have created — nothing."[2] Most evident in stories like "The Diamond as Big as the Ritz," "May Day," and "Babylon Revisited," Fitzgerald's continuing preoccupation with personality and history culminates in *Tender Is the Night*, his most complex and comprehensive statement on his generation and, hence, the most ambitious of his works.

The early titles Fitzgerald gave his novel manuscript, "Our Type" and "The World's Fair," imply generally the breadth and depth of his concern. And when to his friend John Peale Bishop Fitzgerald characterized *Tender Is the Night* as something like a "philosophical, now called psychological

*Selected from the *Fitzgerald / Hemingway Annual 1978*, edited by Matthew J. Bruccoli and Richard Layman (© by Gale Research Company, Detroit, Michigan, United States of America; reprinted by permission of the publisher), Gale Research, 1979, pp. 105–36.

novel,"[3] he was clearly suggesting by that apposition of terms his intention to project a universalized historical drama through the personal drama of his limited *personae*. Among recent critics, Matthew J. Bruccoli has commented on Fitzgerald's fascination with World War I records during the years he worked on the novel, and Robert Sklar argues persuasively that Fitzgerald's reading of Shane Leslie and of Spengler's *Decline of the West* in 1927 left a lasting impression on the work.[4] Indeed a number of critics have made general observations on Fitzgerald's fascination with history throughout the composition of the novel.[5] What has been lacking heretofore in criticism of the novel, and what I attempt to provide in this paper, is an explication of Fitzgerald's detailed conception of history as it relates specifically to his conception of character, theme, and structure.

At the outset I would like to disclaim wholly the all too prevalent view that in Fitzgerald's works historicity functions merely as glossy topicality, serves merely as an enhancing background to "popular" fiction. Rather, Fitzgerald is a "critical," a "philosophical," and, if you will, a "moral" historical novelist, intent on comprehending and explaining in rational terms the motives and implications of human events, viewed simultaneously as personal experience and public phenomena. Indeed, Fitzgerald has little sympathy for those who conceive of history as a simple sequence of recorded events; for him history holds the most profound meaning. In a passage once intended for *Tender Is the Night*, he defined history as "a figured curtain hiding that terrible door into the past through which we all must go."[6] Thus conceived, history in fact conceals its truth from those who passively view the "figured curtain" of human events as some sort of fascinating, but uninterpreted hieroglyph. But for those who penetrate the hieroglyph and draw aside the curtain, history reveals the deepest, if the darkest, truths.

Fitzgerald's historical concerns in *Tender Is the Night* are, indeed, both deep and dark. The ten-year period which the book illuminates is summarily and explicitly defined by him in "Echoes of the Jazz Age": "The ten-year period that, as if reluctant to die outmoded in its bed, leaped to a spectacular death in October 1929, began about the time of the May Day riots in 1919."[7] And this metaphorical personification of historical events is persistent in Fitzgerald's mind. He characterizes the 1919 riots themselves as springing from the universal feeling that "something had to be done with all the nervous energy stored up and unexpended in the War";[8] he characterizes the "golden boom" of the 1920s as the release of that unexpended human energy in "the greatest, gaudiest spree in history."[9] This precise historical period, with "its splendid generosities, its outrageous corruptions and the tortuous death struggle of the old America,"[10] is the informing essence rather than the topical background of *Tender Is the Night*. Throughout the novel Fitzgerald interprets history's curtain and takes us through that door to our past — gently, with the artist's "trick of the heart" — as he charts his generation's strangely hopeful passage from World War I to the Great Depression.

To appreciate Fitzgerald's consummate skill in fusing personality and history we must first recognize that when he centered the novel's motivation and action in Nicole's schizophrenia, he was thinking in metaphorical as well as in clinical terms. Explicitly, his notes on Nicole reveal his conception of her character in specific historical terms, for in trying to define her role in the novel, he concentrated not upon her psychiatric development *per se*, but upon the sequence of significant dates in her life. She is born in 1901; in 1914 her courting begins; in June 1917, the "catastrophe" occurs; and in February 1918, she takes up residence in the Clinic. Then,

> To middle October bad period
> After armistice good period
> He returns in April or May 1919
> She discharged June 1, 1919. Almost 18
> Married September 1919. Aged 18[11]

These particular dates cannot be viewed merely as an author's memory log to aid in keeping the narrative straight. Their most salient feature is their uncanny correspondence with the most significant dates of the first two decades of the twentieth century. Even more explicitly, the significant dates in Nicole's personal history correspond to those marking America's involvement in *the* great event of the early century — World War I. Nicole is born precisely with the twentieth century (1901), and her sexuality, which proves so disturbing and rife with conflict, emerges in 1914, coincident with the beginnings of the war. Nicole is raped by her father in June 1917, the exact month in which American troops first landed in France, perhaps the first historical event discomfiting America's traditional posture of splendid isolation from European affairs. Yet Nicole doesn't seem to realize the full horror of her experience and doesn't enter the Clinic until February 1918, just as America didn't realize the implications of her commitment to the war until American soldiers made their delayed entry into the fighting on the Western Front on 31 January 1918.

The analogy between Nicole's sickness and America's participation in the war is extended and quite precise. Nicole suffers a "bad period" from February until October 1918: the Germans launched their last great offensive in March 1918, and American troops, who first appeared in the front lines 31 January 1918, fought intensely, impressively, but indecisively until October, when Germany began the general retreat which was to end with her surrender. The Armistice, of course, came in November, at which time Nicole inexplicably recovers from her illness and begins a "good period." To be sure, the twentieth century is "Nicole's Age," Fitzgerald's title for the note on her character; her experience and her suffering typify rather than merely illustrate the experience and suffering of an immature America in the opening decades of the twentieth century.

For Devereux Warren, in his role as Nicole's father, virtue is but a mask to his true self-interest just as for France, Germany, England, and Russia alike the patriotic virtues of courage, honor, duty, and loyalty cloaked the naked truth of *Realpolitik* and imperialism. As Devereux Warren's confession to Dr. Dohmler reveals, he was attempting to act out with Nicole the sentimental ideals of a self-satisfied social norm: "People used to say what a wonderful father and daughter we were—they used to wipe their eyes."[12] And he tries to rationalize his behavior as being motivated solely by loyalty to domestic ideals and, particularly, by "selfless" love for Nicole: "After her mother died when she was little she used to come into my bed every morning, sometimes she'd sleep in my bed. I was sorry for the little thing" (p. 170). But ultimately he cannot hide the possessiveness within him: "We used to say, 'Now let's not pay any attention to anybody else this afternoon—let's just have each other—for this morning you're mine' " (p. 171). Nor can he prevent the violence generated by this aggressive self-interest: "We were just like lovers—and then all at once we were lovers—and ten minutes after it happened I could have shot myself—except I guess I'm such a Goddamned degenerate I didn't have the nerve to do it" (p. 171). Devereux Warren's rape of Nicole has the immediacy and shock of personal experience, to be sure, but at the same time it dramatizes and specifies the emotional reality behind the larger trauma of the war. Incestuous rape is an apt metaphor for the intra-familial, self-destructive conflict of World War I, a war in which two opposing nations were led by grandchildren of Queen Victoria, a war in which no nation was really victorious.

The effect of the rape upon Nicole is most clearly and directly expressed in her letters (1918–1919) to Captain Dick Diver, written while she is a patient at Dohmler's Clinic and while Dick serves his military duty in a psychiatric unit at Bar-sur-Aube. And though these letters are of considerable psychiatric interest, their more comprehensive purpose lies in their identification of Nicole's personal trauma with the broader cultural trauma of the war. Again Fitzgerald is explicit: he divides the letters "into two classes, of which the first class, *up to about the time of the armistice*, was of marked pathological turn, and of which the second class, *running from thence up to the present* [i.e. 1919], was entirely normal, and displayed a richly maturing nature" (pp. 159–60, my emphasis). From their inception then, these letters are not intended as expressions of a literal lunatic, rather, they are Ophelian utterances, burying sense within nonsense, essense within evanescence. They define not merely the pained and frightened soul of an eighteen-year-old girl in a Swiss asylum; they define all the pain and fright of a century only eighteen years old but already at the edge of despair.

Unlike the merely suggestive ravings of Ophelia, Nicole's letters do yield a consistent theme: her pain and disorientation originate not so much with the rape itself as with her awareness that her father had bred her a victim to his lies. Her trust in him and in his self-proclaimed, selfless love had made her vulnerable to unexpected attack. Thus Nicole, like so many of the participants in the war, sees herself as having been betrayed by her own inherited ideals—"what I had been taught to associate with the role of gentlemen" (p. 160). She finds herself in "what appears to be a semi-insane-asylum, all because nobody saw fit to tell me the truth about anything. If I had only known what was going on like I know now I could have stood it I guess for I am pretty strong, but those who should have, did not see fit to enlighten me" (p. 162).

Appropriately enough, the letters begin with a reference not to madness, but to the military and the war: "I thought when I saw you in your uniform you were so handsome. Then I thought Je m'en fiche French too and German" (p. 160). And though Nicole knows Dick is a doctor, she continues throughout her correspondence to address him as "Mon Capitaine," "Captain Diver," "Dear Captain Diver," and finally as "Dear Capitaine"—a polyglot salutation fitting to an American in France in 1918.

Such pointed, cumulative details virtually demand that we read Nicole's letters as a personal paradigm for the larger madness of the Western world. Indeed, in mid-1918 Nicole's words to Diver might well have served as the A. E. F.'s motto: "I am lonesome all the time far away from friends and family across the Atlantic I roam all over the place in a half daze" (p. 163). And the fluctuations in Nicole's health during her last weeks at the clinic correspond to the vicissitudes of the last stages of the war. Shortly before getting better Nicole relapses into the uncertainty and frustration of one who has been cut off from her cultural roots: "I think one thing today and another tomorrow. That is really all that's the matter with me, except a crazy defiance and a lack of proportion. I would gladly welcome any alienist you might suggest. Here they lie in their bath tubs and sing Play in Your Own Backyard as if I had my backyard to play in or any hope . . . which I can find by looking either backward or forward" (p. 163). (In the summer of 1918 the Germans again drove to the Marne in a frantic last effort to break through to Paris, and the A. E. F. found itself at Chateau Thierry and the Meuse-Argonne, far removed from the safe "backyards" of nineteenth-century American idealism.) After this uncertainty there is a month with no word from Nicole, and then "suddenly the change"—that is, to the "entirely normal, richly maturing nature." Her "acute and down-hill" schizophrenia comes to a clinically improbable, but metaphorically poignant end; Nicole "recovers" as the war ends:

—I am slowly coming back to life . . .
—Today the flowers and the clouds . . .
—The war is over and I scarcely knew there was a war . . . (p. 164)

Neither the war's end nor Nicole's "recovery" can be intended as a complete resolution of conflict. Rather, each represents a subtle remission of continuing trauma and disorientation, and a bewildered longing for a security that once existed, or at least had been thought to exist. For inherent in Nicole's situation is the question that haunted the Western world after 1918: if the old ideals of order, love, propriety and property, honor, and social responsibility were irrevocably lost in the war, and the "true" nature of society was revealed to be irrational chaos springing from man's aggressive self-interest and amoral will to survive, could the war's survivors find or invent *any* principles to govern individual and social behavior?

Fitzgerald's fictional portrayal of this paradoxical desire within denial is characteristically original, and, it seems to me, psychologically as well as artistically convincing. True to the metaphor of schizophrenia in the novel, Nicole and the war generation she represents can neither assent to the nineteenth-century values which had deceitfully concealed their own hollowness nor accommodate the destructive chaos that had been born out of that hollowness. But such a suspension of belief can lead only to a complete paralysis of being, and Nicole and her generation find themselves forced into a pragmatic choice of the lesser evil. In terms of the novel's psychiatric metaphor, Nicole can "transfer" to Dr. Dick Diver her remembered affection for her father and the ideals he represented prior to the catastrophe; in terms of the novel's historical analogue, the survivors of the war find themselves reverting to an uneasy faith in nineteenth-century idealism simply because in 1919 there is no other faith possible.

As the character embodying these contradictory nineteenth-century ideals in a world which at best can grant them only conditional assent and ultimately must abandon them altogether, Dick Diver is, understandably, resistant to easy explanation. He has been termed a "spoiled priest" who "lost his idealism and was finally corrupted by his flock," who at the end of the novel is "both ruined and spent, an emotional bankrupt . . . lacking the energy to be a charlatan."[13] He has been seen as pandering his vitality to rich expatriates, only to fall victim "to the comfort that corrupts the will and destroys ambition."[14] He is viewed as a poor boy "struggling to make good" by playing "the priestly role of father-confessor to a crowd of rich, spoiled Americans."[15] Or he is an "American Everyman" journeying through "a multitude of temptations — and succumbing to all of them: Money, Liquor, Anarchy, Self-Betrayal, Sex."[16] For Robert Sklar, Diver is the "genteel romantic hero" of nineteenth-century America, who serves "as a smoke screen to cover up the truth Nicole so tragically discovered, to divert energies and desires into harmless pursuits through the power of his romantic imagination."[17] Even those critics who argue that Dick's admirable qualities of goodness and integrity persist to the end of the novel suggest that his virtue is wastefully expended by his dedication to the leisure classes.[18]

Whether defining Dick as a ruined idealist or a fraudulent psychiatrist,[19] all the interpretations of his character, and consequently of the whole novel, rest on the assumption that Nicole typifies and represents the American leisure class exclusively, that she is, in brief, merely rich and merely neurotic. But insofar as Nicole represents young, naive America in the twentieth century, disillusioned in her ideals and shattered by the unforeseen violence of World War I, Dick's efforts to bring her back to wholeness must be interpreted in a very different light. Dick in this context does become a truly believable culture "hero" like Grant, embodying his society's highest aspirations in spite of his own human shortcomings: "It was themselves he gave back to them, blurred by the compromises of how many years" (p. 69). And his ultimate failure to "cure" Nicole in this larger context is nothing less than the tragic failure of American idealism in the twentieth century. As in *The Great Gatsby*, "May Day," "The Diamond as Big as the Ritz," and so many of his stories from the Twenties, Fitzgerald in *Tender Is the Night* depicts an America whose ideals, noble in themselves, are becoming untenable, whose idealists, by the very virtue of their ideals, are being corrupted, or crushed and cast out by a new culture progressively giving itself over to material, amoral pleasure.

Dick's nineteenth-century ideals and sensibilities survive well into the twentieth century simply because they are not exposed directly to the shock of World War I. Young and inexperienced in 1917, Dick is buoyed up by "illusions of eternal strength and health, and of the essential goodness of people; illusions of a nation, the lies of generations of frontier mothers who had to croon falsely, that there were no wolves outside the cabin door" (p. 154). And though Switzerland is "washed on one side by the waves of thunder around Gorizia and on another by the cataracts along the Somme and the Aisne" (p. 151), Dick remains safe in his insular innocence: "the war didn't touch him at all" (p. 151). Even when Dick returns to Zurich in 1919, supposedly having "been to war" for two years, he reaffirms his innocence by telling Franz, "I didn't see any of the war" (p. 157).

Thus, Fitzgerald characterizes in Dick's "innocence" the residual force of nineteenth-century idealism which survived the war. (As well as the punitive Versailles Treaty, the war's end did give birth to the idealized League of Nations.) Such innocence and such idealism of course *are* impossible illusions to those who have felt and seen the "Batter of guns and shatter of flying muscles" Wilfred Owen describes in his poem "Mental Cases." "These are men whose minds the Dead have ravished," says Owen; theirs is the world in which Nicole, agonizingly, amazingly, lives. But in Dick, Fitzgerald creates the psychiatrist-healer of such torment.

When Dick returns in 1919 to Zurich, to Nicole, and to his "intricate destiny," his hubristic determination "to be a good psychologist — maybe to be the greatest one that ever lived" (p. 174) defines the greatness of his vision and at the same time foreshadows the inevitability of his failure. For

Dick demands too much of his "psychiatry." Unlike Dr. Dohmler and Franz Gregorovious, whose clinical method offers only a sanitized "refuge for the broken, the incomplete, the menacing, of this world" (p. 159), Dick through his psychiatry attempts to regenerate the survivors of nightmare and recreate a world of purpose and order in which meaning, not mere existence, is possible. Thus, Dohmler and Franz ultimately can only treat Nicole. Dick marries her.

Dick's commitment to Nicole, therefore, is whole and personal — metaphorically rather than narrowly therapeutic. With his nineteenth-century ideals of courage, honor, courtesy, loyalty, and love, Dick attempts to lead Nicole out of Switzerland's unreal sanity, first to the half-safe, half-controlled, half-real world of the Villa Diana, then back through the remembered horrors of Beaumont Hamel and Thiepval to the naked reality of Paris, Rome, and Naples, reality fraught with endless danger, endless possibility.

Nowhere else in his fiction does Fitzgerald depict so clearly or so forcefully the antinomies of mind and character that for him define the modern man, paradoxically driven by the "sense of the futility of effort and the sense of the necessity to struggle; the conviction of the inevitability of failure and still the determination to 'succeed' — and, more than these, the contradiction between the dead hand of the past and the high intentions of the future."[20] Further, in Dick's tortured efforts to rekindle light and purpose in Nicole's world Fitzgerald dramatizes what he defines elsewhere as the mark of a "first-rate intelligence": "the ability to hold two opposed ideas in the mind at the same time, and still retain the ability to function"; Dick *is* "able to see that things are hopeless and yet be determined to make them otherwise."[21] And if Dick's nineteenth-century will to believe that life can be made coherent and rational appears as historical fiction to the twentieth century, Fitzgerald dramatizes it as a noble, a tragic, perhaps even a necessary and "supreme" fiction.

From beginning to end, Dick and Nicole's marriage is a contest, compressing within itself all the uncertainties and paradoxes of the 1920s. Although the sobriquet "Dicole" suggests the inseparability of Dick and Nicole "in the first days of love," it soon becomes clear that their union is one of uneasy confluence and embattled wills. To prevail over Nicole's madness, Dick must perpetually attract, woo, and win her to his idealizing vision. She, to be sure, is momentarily charmed by the correspondence between Dick's promise of love and peace and her own recollections of childhood's innocent dreams: "When I get well I want to be a fine person like you, Dick" (p. 211). But she is also persistently seduced by the power of the Warren family and its money: "They were an American ducal family without a title — the very name written in a hotel register, signed to an introduction, used in a difficult situation, caused a psychological metamorphosis in people" (p. 208). And under the influence of this amoral vision, which sees power as antecedent to value, Nicole (like her sister,

Baby) can only view Dick's idealism, no matter how qualified, as an inversion of reality: "You used to say a man knows things and when he stops knowing things he's like anybody else, and the thing is to get power before he stops knowing things. If you want to turn things topsy-turvy, all right, but must your Nicole follow you walking on her hands, darling?" (p. 212).

Furthermore, Dick's relationship to Nicole is essentially flawed by the contradictions inherent in his attempt to be both husband and doctor to her. In both roles, of course, Dick is trying to reaffirm the ideal of selfless love which Devereux Warren had virtually destroyed, marriage serving as an apt metaphor for the elevation of self-interest (sexual desire) into a social ideal (the family). But Dick knows, and we know, that the desires of a husband and the responsibilities of a physician are scarcely more compatible than the desires of a lover and the responsibilities of a father. And Dick is aware, further, that his commitment to curing Nicole prevents him to a considerable degree from living with her. In fact, the ideal of selfless love which Dick prescribes for Nicole's cure is in the very act of prescription self-defeating, for he can win Nicole over to himself only at the cost of her independent selfhood. And, as we shall of course see, if he allows her complete self-determination, he loses her absolutely.

From 1919 to 1925, "from Woolloomooloo Bay to Biskra," Nicole reveals her "schizophrenic" inability to live with reality or to escape from it, to trust in ideals or to disbelieve them. Her interior monologue which recounts the period reveals an essential confusion of identity, polarized significantly (in terms of subsequent events) between Dick and Tommy Barban: "When I talk I say to myself that I am probably Dick. Already I have even been my son, remembering how wise and slow he is. Sometimes I am Doctor Dohmler and one time I may even be an aspect of you, Tommy Barban" (p. 212). And her desire to flee to an inner sanctum of unknowing innocence — "Life is fun with Dick" (p. 210); "We'll live near a warm beach where we can be brown and young together" (p. 211) — is opposed with equal force by a desire to grasp her experience, however horrible — "I am tired of knowing nothing and being reminded of it all the time" (p. 211). It is at this point of perfect but unstable balance between contrary and warring values that Dick and Nicole move to the Riviera. It is at a critical point of no return for western civilization that the novel begins — truly in medias res. It is June 1925; the crucial decade of the 1920s is half past, half future.

The novel begins on the beach lying below Gausse's Hotel des Etrangers, the beach which Dick has "made out of a pebble pile" and which now appears as a "tan prayer rug" set down before "the distant image of Cannes, the pink and cream of old fortifications" (p. 3). As he suggests in a later reflection, Dick sees himself in 1925 as "the last hope of a decaying clan" (p. 391), and gathering together the detritus of souls cast up on his beach, he tries to make them whole — by giving them a party, "furnishing the background, the experience, the patience" against which the others will be able "to enjoy again the spells of pastoral tranquility recollected from childhood."[22]

By 1925, however, Dick's view of Nicole and the generation for which she is the synecdoche has undergone a "qualitative change"; his assured confidence of 1919 has been replaced by a more mature, but also a more ambivalent vision—less sure in its definition. Including old generation and new, sun-browned and moon pale, experienced, naive, and those drones "preserved by an imperviousness to experience and a good digestion into another generation" (p. 8), Dick's party is seen to be a "desperate bargain with the gods" (p. 27), one of his "performances" to insure that each day be "spaced like the day of the older civilizations to yield the utmost from the materials at hand, and to give all the transitions their full value" (p. 26). As such, the party is a monument to Dick's nineteenth-century ideals of rational order and purpose. But his ideals include a commitment to truth as well, and since he cannot deny the existence of violence and chaos, Dick wishes his party to be "really *bad*," to include "a brawl and seductions and people going home with their feelings hurt and women passed out in the cabinet de toilette" (p. 35). Dick's "bad party," as its rubric suggests, is a reflection of his ambivalence, for through it he is not trying to eliminate chaos so much as he is trying to give it manageable form; he is trying to subdue man's worse nature by a simple, direct appeal to his better self.

The party begins very well indeed. The markedly heterogeneous group of Abe and Mary North, Tommy Barban, the McKiscos, Campion, Dumphry and Abrams, Rosemary Hoyt, and the Divers had been at table but half an hour when "a perceptible change had set in—person by person had given up something, a preoccupation, an anxiety, a suspicion, and now *they were only their best selves and the Diver's guests*" (p. 42, my emphasis). For the moment, at least, Dick makes the world "safe" for this lost generation, gives the party a seeming wholeness and security which the real world lacks. In the most memorable image of the party, "The table seemed to have risen a little toward the sky like a mechanical dancing platform, giving the people around it a sense of being alone with each other in the dark universe, nourished by its only food, warmed by its only lights" (p. 44).

Dick creates this moment of touching beauty by an impressive act of individual will, "his arms full of the slack he had taken up from others, deeply merged in his own party" (p. 43). In this *tableau vivant* comparable to any in Faulkner, Hemingway, or James Joyce, Fitzgerald creates a mystical moment in which Dick arrests all motion, suspends all distinctions, and elevates his guests to a plane removed from the confines of space and time. Yet "things fall apart; the centre cannot hold": Dick's nineteenth-century will to believe cannot be "transferred" permanently to these children of the twentieth century, and the party ends badly. Nicole breaks down; Violet McKisco panics; and there is an absurd duel on the golf course in which no one is injured, and Rosemary Hoyt can only laugh — hysterically.

For Dick the two most important people at the party are Nicole and Rosemary, for together they embody the complex object of his passionate idealism. Enough has been said about Nicole seen as the synecdoche of the war generation; by analogy, Rosemary compresses within her character all the salient features of the postwar generation. In one sense she is a mid-decade reincarnation of Nicole, a "Daddy's Girl" anachronistically possessing a prewar innocence: "Her body hovered delicately on the last edge of childhood — she was almost eighteen, nearly complete, but the dew was still on her" (p. 4). But the "raw whiteness" of her body identifies her with the McKiscos, Campions, *et al*, whose imperviousness to experience she shares; in the entire novel she does not comprehend, properly speaking, any one or any thing. And if from the mid-decade perspective of 1925 Nicole has become the dark past within whom Dick tries to rekindle light, Rosemary (now eighteen, notably the same age as Nicole when Dick first met her) stands as the pale future seeking her color and definition in the uncertain origins which only Dick can explain.

Within this metaphorical context, Nicole's relapse and Rosemary's hysteria at the end of the party define Dick's failure to provide new hope for the war generation and understanding for the generations that follow. Structurally and thematically this initial failure of the party prefigures Dick's repeated failures; throughout the novel violence does erupt, irrationally yet persistently, out of good feelings and the best of intentions — in the train station, in the hotel, in the police station and clinic, in kitchen and bathroom. And Dick more and more clearly becomes the man who can explain, but not explain away, the world's ugliness.

Immediately after the Riviera party with its absurd duel, Dick takes Nicole, Rosemary, and Abe and Mary North to Paris, the image and substance of modern, postwar life-in-death, as we shall see. But to define this world most precisely, Fitzgerald takes us back, with Dick, Abe, and Rosemary, to the world of Beaumont Hamel and Thiepval, the world of 1916 and the Battle of the Somme.[23] And here at the *locus classicus* of the war's mindless futility, as we listen to Dick's poignant interpretation of the century's greatest trauma, we recognize just how profound, yet how helpless, he truly is.

Dick's interpretation of the war is intensely symbolic rather than military or narrowly political; it is philosophical rather than nationalistic. Indeed, looking out upon Beaumont Hamel and Thiepval, Dick is stricken by the likeness of the opponents, the similarity of their motivations, the identity of their fates. Throughout his resume he refuses to distinguish between French, English, and German, seeing them all simply as mutual participants in the battle. To fight at the Somme on whatever side, he says, "You had to have a whole-souled sentimental equipment going back further than you could remember. You had to remember Christmas, and postcards of the Crown Prince and his fiancee, and little cafes in Valence and beer gardens in Unter den Linden and weddings at the mairie, and going to the Derby, and your grandfather's whiskers" (p. 75).

Ultimately, the Somme is "the last love battle" in Dick's historical view; in it the virtues of "religion and years of plenty and tremendous sureties," wedded to the unrestrained imaginative force of "Lewis Carroll and Jules Verne and whoever wrote Undine" (p. 75), paradoxically gave birth to grotesque horror. In short, Dick's interpretation of the Somme conflict stands as a definition of the European tragedy which America willingly, if mistakenly, accepted for her own. And this battle, standing as archetype to the war's horrifying consumption of life and sanity, makes Dick's sense of *complete* loss rhetorically and emotionally true: "*All* my beautiful lovely safe world blew itself up here with a great gust of high explosive love" (p. 75, my emphasis).

This sense of universal loss is so powerfully evoked that we never question the historical propriety of the "red-haired girl from Tennessee whom they had met on the train this morning, come from Knoxville to lay a memorial on her brother's grave" (pp. 76–77). Though America did not fight at the Somme, for Fitzgerald it is no less than a certainty that amid the "infinitesimal sections of Wurtemburgers, Prussian Guards, Chasseurs Alpins, Manchester mill hands and old Etonians," pursuing their "eternal dissolution under the warm rain" (p. 78), there lies an American who cannot be found.

Thus, western idealism carried the seeds of its own destruction. But for Fitzgerald the war didn't happen "over there" or "back then"; his concern in the novel is not with those who died at the Somme but with those who lived beyond that moral point of no return. And Dick's interpretation of the war is immediately and equally valid as a diagnosis of Nicole's traumatic experience, in which "love," "tremendous sureties," and "years of plenty" also gave way to eruptive violence. Thus, in the disheartened and cynical Abe, once a composer now just a drinker, we see all the creative energy irrevocably destroyed in the war, and in the feckless Rosemary we find all the pointless energy of the generation born too late for disillusionment, whose members in their self-concentration can conceive of no loss greater than a personal desire unfulfilled.

For Abe, who "had seen battle service" (p. 74), Beaumont Hamel and Thiepval hold no dreamy, philosophical reminiscences; he responds to complex, ineluctable reality with simplistic, self-destroying pessimism: "There are lots of people dead since and we'll all be dead soon" (p. 74). Even more disappointing is the response of Rosemary, for whom Dick recreates history in order to make a bridge between their ages. She is carried momentarily by the intensity of Dick's concern — if he had said "they were now being shelled she would have believed him that afternoon" (p. 74). But "I don't know" is her persistent refrain, and she doesn't. She doesn't know whether Dick's lovely safe world blew itself up in 1916, 1919, or any other time. For her the battle is not a trauma, but a "thrilling dream" arousing not anguish, but warm, uninformed sentimentality: "altogether it had been a watery day, but she felt that she had learned something, though exactly what it was she did not know" (p. 77).

Within this context of Abe's conscious withdrawal and Rosemary's blissful ignorance, Dick's ambivalence is delicately yet firmly defined. Dick has seen too much of Abe's world to succumb to Rosemary's naive sentimentalities ("Later she remembered all the hours of the afternoon as happy" [p. 77]). But born with the end of the 19th century (1891 according to Fitzgerald's notes),[24] Dick is the last surviving devotee of that era's ideals. And he must live by his faith, however futile it might prove, for he has no other: "The silver cord is cut and the golden bowl is broken and all that, but an old romantic like me can't do anything about it" (p. 76). The proper image of Dick is that of Icarus flying to the sun though he knows the wings made by his father are fatally waxen. Or, he is the "old romantic" of Shakespeare's sonnet, in whom "thou see'st the glowing of such fire, / That on the ashes of his youth doth lie, / As the deathbed whereon it must expire, / Consumed with that which it was nourished by." To be sure, Dick cannot splice the silver cord nor mend the golden bowl of the world's fact. But tragically determined to nurse his own vision to the last, he can render the meaning of history into a "whole affair" in the alembic of his ordering mind, thus creating from horror "a faint resemblance to one of his own parties" (p. 78). He can charm Rosemary, and he can support Abe. He can even sustain—for the moment—Nicole, abstracted and restless, moving closer and closer to reality's true heart of darkness.

When the action returns to Paris from the Somme battlefield, we see just what the modern world can be, and is, without Dick's controlling moral energy. The pattern of this new world is set by the Parisian house "hewn from the frame of Cardinal de Retz's palace in the Rue Monsieur" (p. 94). Explicitly the house is said to "enclose the future," and its inmates are perfect types of the species, postwar man: "They were very quiet and lethargic at certain hours and then they exploded into sudden quarrels and breakdowns and seductions" (p. 95). Indeed, throughout the remainder of the novel aimless violence will continue to explode out of just such dazed preoccupation and lethargy.

It is thoroughly appropriate that Abe, not Dick, dominates the Parisian scene. Possessed merely of a "survivant will, once a will to live, now become a will to die" (p. 108), Abe has "given up about everything" and is tired—even of friends—to the point of death. Hence, his departure from Paris clearly signals the end of life, not a new start: for him, "it was such a long way to go back in order to get anywhere" (p. 106).

Fitzgerald is emphatic. Just as the train whistles and moves, just as Abe waves and Dick responds, "the sound of two revolver shots cracked the narrow air of the platform" (p. 109). And these shots fired by Maria Wallis, "the young woman with the helmet-like hair" (p. 109), effectively mark the turning point in the novel's thematic development.[25] As "echoes of violence," the shots serve as a remembrance of things past, of the war and the original "concussions that had finished God knew what dark matter" (p. 112) — as one observer notes, there is "assez de sang pour se croire a la guerre" (p. 112). But the shots also foreshadow the events of 1928, the year in which Dick must say good-by to Abe for the last time, must say good-by to his father forever, must say good-by, finally, to *all* his fathers. Most subtly and perhaps most significantly, the shots and their aftermath foreshadow the only world that will remain to Dick after 1928 — the world of Rosemary, Baby, and Nicole, a world in which Dick learns painfully what it means to live long after he has been shot "through his identification card."

As the last remnant of an older America in a changed world, Dick does not cope well with modern, senseless violence — even in 1925. He sees no causes, no goals, no meaning at all in Maria Wallis's action, and for the first time in the novel he can think of nothing to do or say. Nicole, of course, is already more acclimatized to a valueless world, and, as Milton Stern points out, she for the first time "takes over and firmly prevents Dick from acting as savior, party-director, doctor."[26] From this point on, in fact, Nicole will always adjust more readily than Dick to the world. Yet Fitzgerald makes clear that with the waning of Dick's energy and vision, something of value is being lost. At the end of the Wallis affair both Nicole and Rosemary ("who was accustomed to having shell fragments of such events shriek past her head") want Dick "to make a moral comment on the matter and not leave it to them." And when he is unable to "resolve things into the pattern of the holiday," they are aware of the missing element: "so the women, missing something, lapsed into a vague unhappiness" (pp. 111–12). In that simple understatement whereby the complex inheritance of Dick's moral force becomes merely "something" missing, Fitzgerald captures the paradox of that force seen as essential, yet forever lost.

The scene in the Gare St. Lazare points ahead to a world in which expressive force must and will operate devoid of any moral purpose; the nineteenth-century American ideal of power and moral purpose indissolu-bly joined has been shattered. Dick himself is clearly aware of the "turning point in his life" (p. 119). He knows that his survival and dignity can come "only with an overthrowing of his past, of the effort of the last six years," knows that after 1914–1918 neither Nicole nor America can ever be truly innocent again. It is perhaps worth noting here, even as a supposition, that had Dick been able to accept a world without innocence he might have been able to come to terms with Nicole's and his own imperfections; beyond supposition, it is Dick's essential tragedy that his ideals allow for no re-vision. Like his predecessor, Jay Gatsby, Dick is trapped by the irresistible beauty of his own remembered dreams. From the memorable scene in Voisins to the end of the novel, whatever "repose" Dick has serves wholly as self-insulation from a world inimical to his dreams; whatever happiness he has must take the dubious form of fading memories. Thus Dick fondly recalls himself "on his father's knee, riding with Moseby [sic] while the old loyalties and devotions fought on around him" (p. 131); yet by this whole-hearted loyalty to "the maturity of an older America," Dick must share the fate of its gold star mothers—"who had come to mourn for their dead, for something they could not repair" (pp. 130–131).

Dick's love affair with modernity, his infatuation with Rosemary, can be but a momentary fling. Naturally enough, he loves Rosemary's newness: " 'You're the only girl I've seen for a long time that actually did look like something blooming' " (p. 27) he tells her at the Cote d'Azur. But he can only wince at the "vicious sentimentality" of her parodic innocence in the role of *Daddy's Girl*. And though on the one hand he wishes to "remove the whole affair from the nursery footing upon which Rosemary persistently established it" (p. 111), he also realizes that the affair is founded on precisely those "brave illusions" of the "nursery"— "tremendous illusions . . . that the communion of self with self seemed to be on a plane where no other human relations mattered" (p. 98). In love with Rosemary's promise, Dick tells her so, but he tells her in the same breath: "Nicole and I have got to go on together. In a way that's more important than just wanting to go on" (pp. 98–99). For ultimately Dick is committed to continuity of purpose and action in his own life and in the lives of others, even though he knows that continuity, philosophically and historically, is not possible.

Committed to the unyielding past and attracted to the implacable future, Dick at the end of Book I is the living persona of anxiety, fully occupied in controlling himself—his chin dominating "the lines of pain around his mouth, forcing them up into his forehead and the corner of his eyes, like fear that cannot be shown in public" (p. 137). As a moral idealist in 1925, Dick is a charming, admirable, but archaic remnant of an older civilization, struggling to maintain himself in a thoroughly alien world.

This mid-decade America introduced by the war-echoing shots in the Gare St. Lazare is defined conclusively in the events at the Hotel Roi George which end Book I. Abe, avatar of all that is lost, desperate, and failing, reappears, bringing with him the incredible figure of Jules Peterson, Afro-Scandinavian inventor of shoe-polish. In this comedy of errors, Fitzgerald avoids the ludicrous only by translating it into the grotesque; bad burlesque and mock melodrama became bloody murder. And Nicole relapses again. But her demands of 1925 are no longer susceptible to Dick's assurances of 1919. Dick has been weakened by the expenditure of his own moral energy and must appeal to Nicole's strength: "Control yourself!" he repeats three times as Book I closes on 1925.

Of course Nicole cannot control herself completely—yet. In Fitzgerald's concept of historical dialectic, the old nineteenth-century idealism, which in 1925 was strangling itself with uncertainties and inherent weaknesses, had yet another four years before its course was to be fully run. And in Dick's career and life from 1925 to 1929 Fitzgerald depicts the final, tragic act of this idealism, fighting an heroic but futile rearguard action against modernity. The shallowness of Rosemary's vanity, the hardness of Tommy's self-gratification, and the all-consuming selfishness of Nicole's lust for things and for power ultimately triumph over Dick's vision of what *ought* to be, for his moral idealism no longer answers the needs of an age intent merely on survival. Yet, in spite of its inherent flaws and its ultimate failure, it is Dick's vision which haunts our memory of the novel as surely as the remembered ideals of our "naive" fathers haunt us, as surely as the nightingale's song haunted Keats: "Was it a vision, or a waking dream? / Fled is that music:—Do I wake or sleep?" History to Fitzgerald is, indeed, a highly "figured curtain," no more simple than the complex, ambivalent persons who create it.

In the perverse way of such matters, as Dick's vital moral energy lessens, he finds himself harder and harder pressed to "keep up a perfect front" for Nicole, "now and to-morrow, next week and next year" (p. 217).[27] In the interest of emotional economy, the morning after Nicole's breakdown in Paris, Dick takes her back to the more restricted, hence safer, reality of the Riviera. But even at the time he realizes the return to the Cote d'Azur is a "going away rather than a going toward" (p. 218), a retrenchment rather than a liberation. The beach which Dick built as an oasis of sanity amid a Sahara of madness is now besieged by Bartholomew Tailor, Mrs. Abrams, and the rest of "Ciro's Menagerie." A heterogeneous mob, "members of orchestras, restaurateurs, horticultural enthusiasts, shipbuilders . . . and members of the Syndicat d'Initiative" (pp. 223–224), has replaced Dick's select and carefully chosen coterie at Gausse's Hotel and the summer Casino at Juan les Pins. Significantly, it is Nicole who adapts best to this shapeless activity; by the end of the year she becomes "well-knit again." In a kind of perverse transference of physical energy, the "lines of pain" forming around Dick's mouth allow Nicole to live "without tension, without the tight mouth, the unmotivated smile, the unfathomable remark" (p. 224).

As Nicole expands her activities, Dick's sphere of influence narrows, leaving him in command only of "his work house and the ground on which it stood" (p. 222). And even within the work house, "the bars of gilded metal that he used as paperweights along the sheaves of notes" (p. 217) remind him that Nicole's "income had increased so fast of late that it seemed to belittle his work." "Inundated by a trickling of goods and money," Dick slowly drowns in Nicole's desire "to own him, wanting him to stand still forever" (p. 223). The year 1925 ends on a point of perfect balance between Nicole's growing strength and Dick's waning energy.

Prophetically, in mid-decade Dick stands immobilized, "listening to the buzz of the electric clock, listening to time" (p. 223).

From this point Dick begins to fall back in his battle against the all-consuming self-interest by which Fitzgerald characterizes the modern attitude. The barren and onanistic Baby Warren, who concentrates in herself the Warrens' mindless lust for power and possessions, serves as the dramatized persona of Nicole's increasingly amoral nature; consequently, she also stands as antagonist and inverse barometer to Dick's rapidly failing moral vision. Dick knows "Baby is a trivial, selfish woman" (p. 235) and sees, beneath her lies, her true opinion of him: " 'We own you, and you'll admit it sooner or later. It is absurd to keep up the pretense of independence' " (p. 232). But simply being aware of Baby's corruption does not give Dick the power to cope with her; his acceptance of Warren money to finance his clinic has involved him inextricably with all that he despises.

No longer the last hope of a decaying clan, Dick is now reduced to the futile task of "sorting the broken shells" of the "Humpty-Dumpty" Western world. And in another kind of reverse transference of energy, Baby's harsh antipathy brings out something of the same in Dick. His uncharacteristic statement " 'There's too much good manners' " and his perverse, untoward baiting of the young Englishman (cf. pp. 233–234) reveal his strain and the self-defeating result of his trying to keep up a "perfect" front. The devil's bargain Dick makes with Baby in financing the clinic is in fact the greatest compromise he ever makes with his own beliefs. What he gains is a brief period in which to comfort those he can no longer help. What he gives up becomes clear in Rome, in 1928: "whatever Dick's previous record was, they now possessed a moral superiority over him for as long as he proved of any use" (p. 306).

With emphatic suddenness Fitzgerald leaps from the decisions and indecisions of 1925 to the events of 1927, which in turn serve as general commentary and prelude to the novel's climax and conclusion in 1928–1929. The drama of 1927 begins as Dick awakes "after a long dream of war" and goes to the bedside of the pathetic woman suffering from neuro-syphilis, diagnosed as "nervous eczema." Ravaged and rapidly decomposing through the inheritance of a corrupt love, this sensitive soul is indeed correct in seeing herself "as a symbol of something." Consistent with the book's imagery, her illness is described as a lost battle; truly her innocent beauty, imagination, youth and charm are fled. But as she is thus being compared implicitly with Nicole and Abe North, we also see that her failure is Dick's. For like her, Dick is "fine-spun, inbred," and lacks that "measure of peasant blood" necessary to those explorers who perforce must "take punishment as they took bread and salt, on every inch of flesh and spirit" (p. 242). The suffering, unnamed woman is quite clearly a symbol of both aspects of the modern trauma, of all Nicole's innocence capriciously destroyed, and of all Dick's idealism, terribly futile. How touching, yet how futile, and how tragic a picture it is as Dick stoops to kiss the dying artist; how poignant his farewell: "We must all try to be good" (p. 243).

In 1927 Dick does not try to save his broken patients. He "makes his rounds." He now admits there is "nothing much to be done" for the fifteen-year-old girl whom we readily identify with the young Nicole, this mad girl "brought up on the basis that childhood was intended to be all fun" (p. 243). Like the wasted parent of a mad child once docile, now grown to be overpowering, Dick finds it harder and harder to muster his tired, paralyzed faculties. He also realizes now that in the six years with Nicole "she had several times carried him over the line with her . . . had succeeded in getting a point against his better judgment" (p. 246). And haunting Dick ultimately is his self-reflection in the "collapsed psychiatrist," to whom Dick croons falsely "that he was better, always better." As an experienced explorer into the wilderness of the human heart, Dick in 1927 knows that the wolves not only are at the door, they are inside the house itself. In 1927, in Switzerland *deja vu*, the question is no longer one of "curing" Nicole; the question now is whether Dick can save himself.

Nicole's increasing power and consequent control over Dick reveal themselves at the Agiri Fair. When Nicole becomes pointlessly hysterical on the ferris wheel, she overwhelms Dick's reasonable admonitions with simple, point-blank hostility. Immediately, Dick prepares once more "to sit a long time, restating the universe for her," but he quickly recognizes his acutely limited control over her now: "He felt it necessary that this time Nicole cure herself; he wanted to wait until she remembered the other times, and revolted from them" (p. 250).

In 1927 Dick's commitment to reason and his hope for its supremacy are equally futile. Nicole, indeed, does remember the "other times" of violence and disorder, but far from rebelling against them, she embraces them as reality itself. What she rebels against is Dick and his rule. And her declaration of independence from his ordered world is immediate and categorical: on the way home from the fair she tries to kill Dick, herself, and their children. Completely aware of her action, Nicole can only laugh "hilariously, unashamed, unafraid, unconcerned . . . as after some mild escape of childhood" (p. 251). " 'You were scared, weren't you?' " she taunts Dick: " 'You wanted to live!' " (p. 251). For Nicole there is no essential difference between life and death; both are abstractions without significance. Dick's values, Dick's dreams, Dick's life have not prevailed, and power has become the world's only reality, exertion of power man's only grip upon existence.

Avatar of the new order is Tommy Barban, who reenters the novel in the singularly fitting setting of "the Marienplatz in Munich" where "The air was full of politics, and the slap of cards." In this cynical, aggressive world of *Realpolitik* Tommy is a "ruler" and a "hero," characterized essentially by his "martial laugh." He is, most of all, Dick's antagonist, the antithesis to all his ideals.

Tommy's narration of Prince Chillicheff's escape from Russia and his bringing to light Abe North's death in a New York speakeasy reflect at once the decline of the old order and the birth of the new. Both the Prince and Abe are "parched papier mache relic[s] of the past" (p. 258); both have necessarily yielded to overpowering force—whether it be that of the Red Guard or of New York thugs is of little consequence. By contrast, Tommy *is* the man of force, perpetually "relaxed for combat," without cause, faith, or loyalty. He specifically doesn't wish to be "heroic" in Mr. McKisco's sentimental sense—"to fight on the just side." " 'How do you find out which it is?' asked Barban dryly." His attitude is as simple and uncluttered as it is inhuman: "Well, I'm a soldier. . . . My business is to kill people" (p. 45). Amoral and self-indulgent, Tommy worships the power of money, which can bring him his dreams of good food, good clothes, and "good" women, and his only church is the stock market, where "everybody . . . is making millions." Caring no more for Abe lying dead in New York than for the "three Red Guards dead at the border" (p. 258), Tommy is ultimately committed only to himself—to his own survival and self-indulgence.

In direct contrast, Dick is stricken by Abe's death and mourns the irrecoverable past. He walks in step with the "slow mournful march" that wakens him the morning after talking with Tommy. The column of war veterans marches "slowly with a sort of swagger for a lost magnificence, a past effort, a forgotten sorrow," and "Dick's lungs burst for a moment with regret for Abe's death, and his own youth of ten years ago" (p. 261). Dick's intricate destiny is entering its final phase—of precipitous decline. It is 1928.[28]

For Fitzgerald the years 1928–1929 are the years of crisis defining the modern phase of America's history. The period is signally defined by the death of Abe and the death of Dick's father. It is then marked by the sudden death of the long lingering neuro-syphilitic artist and by the contrasting, miraculous deathbed "recovery" of Devereux Warren, by Dick's unfeeling, sterile seduction of a careless Rosemary and by his irrevocable loss of Nicole to Tommy. It is marked by Dick's descent into the Roman city of dreadful night, where he is saved only by his persistently dark angel, Baby, and marked by Nicole's ascent to power. Ultimately, the period is defined by Dick's recognition of his own inability to make people happy.

The death of Dick's father informs the last half the novel. In a serious, reflective sense, Dick sees all of an earlier, simpler America in his father; as he travels southward to Virginia he can almost hear "the rasping wheels of buckboards turning, the lovely fatuous voices, the sound of sluggish primeval rivers flowing softly under soft Indian names" (p. 267). And in his father's death, Dick sees the passing of all those who once believed that "nothing could be superior to 'good instincts,' honor, courtesy, and courage" (p. 266). His stunning, brief eulogy, "Good-by, my father—good-by, all my fathers," signals the end of an era; Dick truly is the last mourning survivor of all those dead, with "their weather-beaten faces with blue flashing eyes, the spare violent bodies, the souls made of new earth in the forest-heavy darkness of the seventeenth century" (p. 267). The "good instincts" and "spare violence" which for one historical moment had lived the illusion of a common purpose have, in another historical moment, revealed their true incompatibility. Thus Dick leaves Virginia and its dead dreams forever; he returns to an alien, unyielding Europe, to Rome and to Rosemary—as it were, to his dying future.

Leaving the honor, courtesy, and courage of his fathers behind, Dick finds himself on the same Atlantic steamer as the McKiscos. Caricatures of the banal world of false art and false thought, the McKiscos prepare us for Rosemary—appropriately engaged in filming *The Grandeur that was Rome*. Rosemary, amid the poses, the props, the mascara and the petty jealousies of the Roman movie set, is still "young and magnetic," but she is morally a Topsy, who just "growed." (Dick's explicit comparison of Rosemary to his daughter, Topsy, effectively and immediately rekindles the book's whole complex of psychological and historical themes.) She is older in 1928 than she was in 1925, and she has had more "experience." But she has not learned a thing.

Rosemary, in short, is one of those "risen to a position of prominence in a nation that for a decade [since 1918] had wanted only to be entertained" (p. 278).[29] In a broadly metaphorical sense, she is one of a large company of self-deluded "actors" who think themselves "people of bravery and industry" but who are merely "on the hop" (p. 278). Emotionally she is still "Daddy's Little Girl," but with a perverse sex appeal; she wears black pajamas, reads Albert McKisco, and coyly "necks" with a thirty-eight-year-old man. Almost needless to say, for both Dick and Rosemary it is a futile *recherche du temps perdu*. The sterility of her world and the pathos of his now strain together to reach the anticlimax so clearly reflected in Fitzgerald's syntax and diction: "She wanted to be taken and she was, and what had begun with a childish infatuation on a beach was accomplished at last" (p. 278).

The remainder of Book II charts Dick's tortured wanderings in Rome, his city of dreadful night. No sooner has Dick "accomplished" his seduction of Rosemary than Baby Warren reappears, signalling, as she always does, bad times for Dick. And these times are Dick's worst. For he is old in a world of youth; he can do nothing to win Rosemary against the blandishments of Nicotera. Dick is weak in a world where only strength matters; he can make no headway against the countinghouse mentality of Baby, who answers moral questions with financial statements: "there's so *much* money now. Plenty for everything, and it ought to be used to get Nicole well" (p. 280).

Dick's response to this alienating world is less heroic perhaps, but certainly more human than that of Hemingway's Jake Barnes, Frederic Henry, or Robert Jordan, for Dick cannot indefinitely maintain his "purity of line through the maximum of exposure."[30] Dick is a man subject to history and human change like the rest of us, and when history's stream changes course, leaving him to flounder in a drying channel, he, like the rest of us, strikes out blindly in panic and frustration. In this light Dick's bigotry toward the French and the Italians, his drunkenness, his violence with the cabmen, and his pointless baiting of the police do not mark his acquiescence to the calculated violence of Baby's world; they mark his violent, but futile protest against her world's recalcitrance to moral order. But violence in the service of virtue is nevertheless violence, and Dick's personal vision of a lovely safe world blows itself up in 1928 as surely as his larger Victorian world blew itself up in 1914–1918.

Though Dick is an extraordinarily complex character, as we have seen, Fitzgerald makes clear that his conception of Dick is essentially tragic. Amid the defeat and hopelessness of his experience in Rome, Dick is identified with Keats, the genius prematurely withered in a world of crass materialism and cheap pleasure. The picture that Rome lastingly imprints on Dick's mind is "the walk toward the American Express past the odorous confectioneries of the Via Nationale, through the foul tunnel up to the Spanish Steps, where his spirit soared before the flower stalls and the house where Keats had died" (p. 288).

Book III of *Tender Is the Night* is the story of sane crooks and one mad puritan. Set in 1929, it chronicles the end of the decade in which heartless money and amoral force carry the day at the expense of moral values and purposive behavior. Like a final fade out in a spurious Hollywood epic, rude self-interest joins with the glamour of wealth to seduce America's taste and desires with a travesty of her original dreams of endless moral expansion, making the nation of Jefferson and Lincoln and Wilson merely the most powerful nation in the world. Dick's waning energy is viewed against the background of the general social chaos generated by Mary Minghetti, Lady Caroline Sibley-Biers, T. F. Golding, and the rest of the "new crowd" on the Riviera; his defeat is assured when Nicole deserts him in favor of Tommy Barban.

The Divers' return to the Villa Diana in the summer of 1929 signals the final retrenchment of Dick's original vision. As ideally he might have governed nations, by a "long, careful watchfulness, the checking and balancing and reckoning of accounts, to the end that there should be no slip below a certain level of duty" (p. 331), Dick now governs—his children. In the large arena of his life, his old "good instincts" are no match for Nicole's growing selfishness and capricious will. When she begins to reason "as gaily as a flower, while the wind blew her hair until her head moved with it," when she becomes "content and happy with the logic of, Why shouldn't I?" (pp. 356–357), the days of Dick Diver, the old man of an older America, are indeed numbered.

For Fitzgerald the historical issue of 1929 could be stated summarily as the conflict between the pursuit of self-gratification and the maintenance of moral principles and propriety; dramatically, the crisis centers upon a small bottle of camphor rub. This small bottle of balm is provocatively and irresistibly symbolic. "It's American," and Dick "believes in it;" yet it is also "extremely rare" and Dick has only one bottle left (pp. 358–359). In so few remarks the bottle of rub is invested with all the values Dick has stood for throughout the novel—healing love, care, and what Fitzgerald once called the definitive American characteristic—"a willingness of the heart."[31] Tossing the bottle to Tommy with a cautionary "Now catch it," Nicole is fully aware that she is betraying Dick, his principles, his love, his work, and his devotion. Her final remark to him is worthy of Baby: "We can always get another jar—" (p. 359).

Fitzgerald describes Nicole in 1929 as "delicately balanced . . . between an old foothold that had always guaranteed her security, and the imminence of a leap from which she must alight changed in the very chemistry of blood and muscle" (p. 361). But in this crisis of 1929 it is Nicole who will survive, she who will feel "the lifting of a burden, an unblinding of eyes" (p. 362). Now hating Dick's world, "with its delicate jokes and politenesses, forgetting that for many years it was the only world open to her," Nicole welcomes her original self, "designed for change, for flight, with money as fins and wings" (p. 362).

Nicole simply has outlived Dick's dreams, which now lie "buried deeper than the sand under the span of so few years" (p. 363). Her inheritance of moneyed power no longer needs or seeks the approval of moral idealism. Or, to put it another way, Dick's inheritance of moral idealism has been spent maintaining the illusion of its own necessity. Dick's once wonderful beach is "perverted now to the tastes of the tasteless" (p. 362), and Dick, once the mandarin of culture, is now merely "a deposed ruler secretly visiting an old court" where he could "search . . . for a day and find no stone of the Chinese Wall he had once erected around it, no footprint of an old friend" (p. 362). His old strengths drained and then scorned, Dick can no longer resurrect his old world.

The precise nature of Dick's diminished position in the changed world of 1929 is dramatically compressed in the aquaplaning scene. Unlike Nicole, who "refused her turn" on the board, and unlike Rosemary, who "rode the board neatly and conservatively, with facetious cheers from her admirers" (p. 365), Dick can still muster the energy "to try his lifting trick" (p. 366). Desperately he tries three times to lift a man upon his shoulders, "then he was simply holding his ground, then he collapsed . . . and they went over, Dick's head barely missing a kick of the board" (p. 367).

Though Nicole considers Dick to be showing off for Rosemary, we clearly view the scene as a synecdoche of Dick's longtime efforts to lift everyone — especially Nicole. In the larger context Dick has indeed "put his heart into the strain, and lifted," but what "he had done . . . with ease only two years ago" (p. 366) leaves him now "floating exhausted and expressionless, alone with the water and the sky" (p. 367).

Dick *is* beaten. In fact, as he tells Rosemary after the aquaplane fiasco: "The change came a long way back — but at first it didn't show. The manner remains intact for some time after the morale cracks" (p. 368). Dick has been slowly but irresistibly crushed by the same force giving ascendance to Nicole — by the "billions" and "trillions" of the booming stock market, by the "plenitude of money" which became "an absorption in itself" (p. 332). How appropriate it is that Nicole's new transference — from Dick to Tommy — should be initiated on the "Margin," the yacht of T. F. Golding. This scene of reunion between Nicole and Tommy is redolent of wealth tentatively gained and tenuously held, of lives bordering upon each other, but not bonding: "Golding's cyclonic arms blew them [Dick and Nicole] aft without touching them" (p. 346). From this point of transference, all Dick has left of himself is his poise, stretched taut over the hollow laughter and despair within. What Tommy offers Nicole is hard confidence, "good stocks in the hands of friends" and "all the old Languedoc peasant remedies." Truly the day of the barbarian has come.

The new barbarism is revealed clearly and emphatically when Tommy and Nicole seduce each other in the small room of a hotel on a beach outside Nice. There is no love or warmth of any kind in what merely amounts to coincidental self-gratifications. "Thinking with Dick's thoughts," Nicole realizes the affair is a "vulgar business . . . without emotion"; on the other hand, she is compelled by her desire to do what she is "tempted to do and pay no penalty for it" (p. 376). Tommy is equally amoral, equally aggressive. He feels no need to understand Nicole or to explain his actions: "Symbolically she lay across his saddle-bow as surely as if he had wolfed her away from Damascus and they had come out upon the Mongolian plain" (p. 384). Together they perform a travesty of love making, each forgetting the other in a perversely inverted sexuality. While Tommy plays the role of a "fighting Puck, an earnest Satan," Nicole becomes, in a most telling image, a "decapitated animal" (p. 380).

The world immediately outside Tommy and Nicole's hotel room offers a graphic commentary on the new alliance. Within the hotel itself, only two floors below, the brawling American sailors and the French poules who "follow them from place to place wherever the ship goes" suggest on a level only slightly more sordid the vulgarity and anarchy of unrestrained self-indulgence. In a complex crossover of values, the half-French, half-American Tommy is comparable both to the whores, who mindlessly perform for American wealth and power, and to the sailors, who mechanically indulge themselves in pleasure. In like manner, Nicole, the

European-American, seeks simple stimulation like a whore and, like the sailors, looks to more promising shores, secure in her sense of power.

But finally it is the American battleship anchored in the bay outside the hotel that perfectly exemplifies the union in Nicole and Tommy of money's power and selfish, aggressive purpose. In fact, in his eagerness to make the parallel between ship and lovers exact, Fitzgerald almost overwrites the scene. Precisely as Tommy and Nicole prepare to leave, as he is "pulling the shoulder strap of her slip into place with his teeth . . . a sound split the air outside: CRACK — BOOM-M-m-m! It was the battle-ship sounding a recall" (p. 382). Precisely as Tommy and Nicole leave the room, the poules break in to wave good-by to the sailors with a flag made from step-ins — "Oh, say can you see the tender color of remembered flesh? — while at the stern of the battleship arose in rivalry the Star-Spangled Banner" (p. 383).

Nicole thus returns "to what she had been in the beginning, prototype of that obscure yielding up of swords that was going on in the world about her" (p. 384). Corollary to Nicole's regeneration is Dick's return to his origins — to the obscurity of the Finger Lake region in New York state, to the withering green breast of the once New World. But Nicole's ascend-ance over Dick is itself founded upon a fateful illusion and fraught with a controlling irony that would have been painfully obvious to readers of 1934, had any recognized Fitzgerald's historical purposes. For if only with the accuracy of hindsight, the reader of that year could have seen the imminent disaster awaiting those who in July 1929 followed the creed of "Why shouldn't I?" The reader of 1934 could have seen that the arrogant dreams of a sunny July beach — dreams of permanent wealth, endless power, and the right to do what one was tempted to do and pay no penalty for it — had led to the nightmare of October's Black Friday and to the grim years of the Great Depression.

For Fitzgerald the issuing events of history are thus as complex as their origins, both springing from the incalculably wrought human heart. The human passion for self-determination which made "idealism" the dominant force in nineteenth-century philosophy and politics inevitably had overextended itself and in World War I could scarcely bear the horror of its own creations. Dick's "beautiful lovely safe world" did blow itself up, and in 1929, with no one to love and no one left to love him, Dick retreats deeper and deeper into upper New York State, a Keatsian wood of indefinite place and uncertain time. But Nicole's acceptance of aggression and self-indulgence as the basic principles of her behavior doesn't rectify the excessive errors of the earlier idealism so much as to ratify their failure. And her future, as Fitzgerald clearly implies, will be written in a hard, but cramped hand, and will tell the story of hollow men: "New vistas appeared ahead, peopled with the faces of many men, none of whom she need obey or even love" (p. 379). Her world, unlike Dick's, will not blow itself up with a "great gust of high explosive love"; it will linger on in the discontent of those whose wants are insatiable—it will end, we are assured, with a whimper.

In every sense *Tender Is the Night* marks the culmination of Fitzgerald's art. It is nurtured by the same vision and techniques we find in "May Day," "The Diamond as Big as the Ritz," *The Great Gatsby, The Beautiful and Damned*, "Babylon Revisited," but it is a riper, more mature work, founded upon a maturity and historical perspective that could come to Fitzgerald only with the passage of time. His long struggle with the writing of the book, the many changes and alterations he incorporated into it as his imagination feasted upon the decade-long struggle between Old and New America, all testify to his patient determination to capture honestly the complex essence of an era. To finish *this* novel, he had to wait, as it were, for history to declare itself definitively. And it did—in October 1929.

More than any other work, *Tender Is the Night* makes it clear that Fitzgerald's creative vision and expression required the presence of moral questions—if not necessarily answers, required a conception of history founded upon purposive human activity—if not necessarily "manifest destiny." And, finally, *Tender Is the Night* presents with the clearest intensity Fitzgerald's profoundly paradoxical conception that man's nobility lies in his unyielding efforts to be his *best* self—even when faced with certain defeat, that man's tragedy lies in his failure to recognize his own limitations and live with them.

Notes

1. See Malcolm Cowley, "Introduction," *The Bodley Head Scott Fitzgerald* (London: Bodley Head, 1963), V, 17–18: "In victory and defeat Fitzgerald retained a quality that very few writers are able to acquire: a sense of living in history. Manners and Morals were changing all through his life and he set himself the task of recording the changes. They were revealed to him, not by statistics or news reports, but in terms of living characters, and the characters were revealed by gestures, each appropriate to a certain year."

2. *All the Sad Young Men* (New York: Scribners, 1926), p. 1.

3. Arthur Mizener, *The Far Side of Paradise: A Biography of F. Scott Fitzgerald*, 2nd ed. (Boston: Houghton Mifflin, 1965), p. 265.

4. Matthew J. Bruccoli, *The Composition of "Tender Is the Night"* (Pittsburgh: University of Pittsburgh Press, 1963), p. 102; Robert Sklar, *F. Scott Fitzgerald: The Last Laocoon* (New York: Oxford University Press, 1967), p. 257. See also Kermit W. Moyer II, "The Historical Perspective of F. Scott Fitzgerald," Diss. Northwestern University 1972.

5. See Alan Trachtenberg, "The Journey Back: Myth and History in *Tender Is the Night*," in *Experience in the Novel*, ed. Roy Harvey Pearce (New York: Columbia University Press, 1968), pp. 133–63; Milton R. Stern, *The Golden Moment: The Novels of F. Scott Fitzgerald* (Urbana: University of Illinois Press, 1970); John F. Callahan, *The Illusions of a Nation: Myth and History in the Novels of F. Scott Fitzgerald* (Urbana: University of Illinois Press, 1972); Richard D. Lehan, *F. Scott Fitzgerald and the Craft of Fiction* (Carbondale & Edwardsville: Southern Illinois University Press, 1966); William A. Fahey, *F. Scott Fitzgerald and the American Dream* (New York: Cromwell, 1973); and Tom C. Coleman III, "The Rise of Dr. Diver," *Discourse*, 13 (Spring 1970), 226–38. Almost all these writers would agree with

Stern's general proposition that "an entire civilization can be tested and evaluated in the values that surround the fate of the hero of the novel" (p. 291). Most tantalizing of the arguments is Alan Trachtenberg's view that "temporal process" itself is the primary motivation to the narrative. Callahan makes the most ambitious effort to read the novel historically, but his reading is disappointingly less than helpful, for he errs in viewing Dick's story as one in which "personality had not yet fathomed history or clashed with circumstances" (p. 73). I argue, in fact, that it is precisely the interpenetration of personality and history that constitutes Dick's story. Fahey in effect undermines his own argument by erroneously identifying the battlefield of Book I, Chapter XIII as that of the Second Marne.

6. "The Note-Books," *The Crack-Up*, ed. Edmund Wilson (New York: New Directions, 1945), p. 173; a Mr. Brugerol (who later developed into Tommy Barban) is speaking to McKisco.

7. "Echoes of the Jazz Age," *The Crack-Up*, p. 13.

8. "Echoes of the Jazz Age," *The Crack-Up*, p. 13.

9. "Early Success," *The Crack-Up*, p. 87.

10. "Early Success," *The Crack-Up*, p. 87.

11. *The Far Side of Paradise*, "Appendix B," p. 350.

12. *Tender Is the Night* (New York: Scribners, 1934), p. 171. Further references are to this edition, and page citations will be included in my text.

13. Bruccoli, pp. 83–84.

14. William Goldhurst, *F. Scott Fitzgerald and his Contemporaries* (Cleveland & New York: World, 1963), p. 206.

15. Henry Dan Piper, *F. Scott Fitzgerald: A Critical Portrait* (New York: Holt, Rinehart & Winston, 1965), pp. 158–216.

16. James E. Miller, Jr., *F. Scott Fitzgerald: His Art and His Technique* (New York: New York University Press, 1964), p. 142.

17. Sklar, pp. 283–284. See also Edwin T. Fussell, "Fitzgerald's Brave New World," in *F. Scott Fitzgerald: A Collection of Critical Essays*, ed. Arthur Mizener (Englewood Cliffs, N.J.: Prentice-Hall, 1963), p. 50.

18. John Kuehl, "Scott Fitzgerald: Romantic and Realist," *University of Texas Studies in Literature and Language*, 1 (Autumn 1959), 423, sees Dick as a tragic hero with "one serious flaw — social climbing — in a situation where the flaw destroys him." Eugene White, "The 'Intricate Destiny' of Dick Diver," *Modern Fiction Studies*, 7 (Spring 1961), 55, is one of the few "psychological" critics who object to those who interpret Dick as "something less than heroic and considerably less than a tragic figure": "Dick Diver is a man who because of his deep love for Nicole Warren makes a deliberate choice with full realization of the dilemma which it will eventually force upon him."

19. For the best single example I know of a thorough, logical, but for me misdirected, reading of the implications of Dick's profession and his psychological condition, see Mary E. Burton, "The Counter-Transference of Dr. Diver," *Journal of English Literary History*, 38 (September 1971), 459–71. Henry Dan Piper, pp. 222–23, exemplifies the kinds of problems generated by reading the psychiatric element of the novel too literally: "Another mistake was his decision to make Dick Diver a psychiatrist. . . . Despite Fitzgerald's interest in the technical aspects of Zelda's condition, and his many conversations with her physicians, he really did not know enough about psychiatry to treat it authoritatively. Most important of all, he did not understand how a psychiatrist's mind works." Only F. J. Hoffman, "The 'Irresistible Lothario': F. Scott Fitzgerald's Romantic Hero," in *The Twenties: Poetry and Prose*, ed. Richard E. Langford and William E. Taylor (DeLand, Florida: Everett Edwards Press, 1966), p. 61, seems to see Fitzgerald's intent clearly: "It is foolish to test Fitzgerald on the grounds of his use of the psychiatric condition. This is, after all, a major metaphor, as useful as any other within the limits of Fitzgerald's skill in using it."

20. "The Crack-Up," p. 70.

21. "The Crack-Up," p. 69.

22. This definition of what it means to give a party is taken from Fitzgerald's short story, "One Trip Abroad" (1930), *Afternoon of an Author* (Princeton: Princeton University Library, 1957), p. 148.

23. Most military historians view the five month Battle of the Somme as having turned the tide of the war, though at frightful cost (see A. H. Farrar-Hockley, *The Somme* [London: Pan Books, 1966]). Thus Fitzgerald's choice of this particular battle as his synecdoche for the war has considerable historical justification.

24. Mizener, p. 349.

25. Stern, pp. 360–61, the only reader to give this scene full weight, though his analysis is somewhat different from mine.

26. Stern, p. 361.

27. Fitzgerald picks up the narrative thread from Book I in Chapter XI, Book II.

28. Although there is considerable confusion in the chronological references in the last third of the novel, I see little reason to doubt Fitzgerald's specific reference to 1928 (on p. 211) when Dick returns to Rome from his father's funeral in America. Malcolm Cowley's revision of the chronology in his edition of the novel (New York: Scribners, 1951) seems to be based more on Cowley's sense that "the author needed more elapsed time to accomplish Dick's ruin — five years instead of four — and actually 1930 was better for the historical background than 1929" (Cowley, p. 355) than on Fitzgerald's sense of narrative direction. Cowley silently alters Fitzgerald's explicit reference mentioned above from 1928 to 1929 and then interpolates the dating in the final portion of the book as "The Way Home: 1929–1930." Yet, as Matthew Bruccoli persuasively argues (pp. 214–15), this manipulation of dating creates as many problems as it solves, for the new chronology certainly doesn't accommodate "Tommy's remark to Nicole on the *Margin* that his stocks are doing well" — a remark which "surely . . . belongs to 1929, not 1930" (Bruccoli, p. 215). Nor can Cowley's revised dating accommodate the observation made by Nicole during Dick's aquaplane attempts, that "last summer on the Zugersee they had played at that pleasant water game . . ." (p. 282), for even within Cowley's dating, the last summer Dick and Nicole spend on the Zugersee is that of 1928 (see Cowley, p. 352, note to p. 196). To be sure, Fitzgerald seems to have bungled in referring to Rosemary's return to the Riviera after five years, but this error can be accounted for easily and persuasively by Bruccoli's suggestion that Fitzgerald "seems to have been confused by counting 1925 as a full year" (p. 214). And the preponderance of evidence favors the view that Fitzgerald adhered to his original plan of ending the novel in July 1929, a plan by which "the unexpressed idea that the new breed of new-rich Riviera people have less than four months of paper profits left gives the conclusion a special feeling" (Bruccoli, p. 214).

29. Cf. "Echoes of the Jazz Age," *The Crack-Up*, p. 15.

30. Ernest Hemingway, *The Sun Also Rises* (New York: Scribners, 1926), p. 174.

31. "Note-Books," *The Crack-Up*, p. 197. In this Note-Book entry (which appeared in his 1929 story "The Swimmers") Fitzgerald defines America in terms of her idealism and the trauma of war: "France was a land, England was a people, but America, having about it still that quality of the idea, was harder to utter — it was the graves at Shiloh and the tired, drawn, nervous faces of its great men, and the country boys dying in the Argonne for a phrase that was empty before their bodies withered. It was a willingness of the heart."

Vitality and Vampirism in *Tender Is the Night*

James W. Tuttleton*

> I am not nor mean to be
> The Daemon they made of me.
>
> —H.D., *Helen in Egypt*

The gist of this paper is a simple but lurid thesis: first, that there is a motif of female vampirism latent in *Tender Is the Night*; second, that this theme is a constant in Fitzgerald's fiction from *This Side of Paradise* onward; and third, that while this motif expresses one of Fitzgerald's recurrent anxieties about woman's consuming power, it takes its form from a literary source—the poetry of John Keats.

We are all familiar with the image of the golden girl, the lovely woman of the romantic dreamer's illusion, the lost Ginevra King, the young, elusive Zelda Sayre—women who created "those illusions that give such color to the world," Fitzgerald wrote, "that you don't care whether things are true or false as long as they partake of the magical glory."[1] I cannot deal here with the many positive images of Fitzgerald's lovely and appealing women. I want rather to deal with another aspect of woman—also a constant in Fitzgerald's fiction—and often involving the same girl: the beautiful enchantress, the alluring and seductive but ultimately daemonic and destructive woman—figured frequently and openly as a vampire who drains the hero of his vitality. Keats is the source of this image, and the psychic dynamic of ambivalence that made Keats recur to the image was virtually identical in Fitzgerald.

I

The evidence for Fitzgerald's knowledge of Keats is extensive and cannot even be summarized here.[2] *Tender Is the Night* takes its title from Keats's "Ode to a Nightingale." And a number of books and articles have usefully linked the two works—the setting of the Riviera with Keats's Provençal sunburnt mirth, the seductive death wish in both texts, the "nights perfumed and promising, the dark gardens of an illusory world,"[3] and the personae who, as Abe North puts it, are "plagued by the nightingale."[4]

These and many incidental references in the novel to Keats's "Ode" are helpful. But *Tender Is the Night* was a very late title choice. The novel was not written and revised with the "Ode" principally in mind. It is my contention here that a significant Keatsian source is to be found in three of Keats's narrative poems which deal with the man-woman relationship in a

*This essay was written for this volume and is published here for the first time by permission of the author.

strikingly similar way: "Endymion," "La Belle Dame sans Merci," and "Lamia."

In all of these poems an idealistic youth, a romantic dreamer, falls in love with a beautiful creature. She may be Cynthia, the Moon-Goddess, or one of her lovely female incarnations. In only one poem, "Endymion," does the protagonist — after suffering great anguish of love sickness — attain his aetherial love with the Goddess. In "Endymion" the Moon-Goddess, in her aspect as Cynthia, is a positive divine energy. But in her aspect as Diana or Hecate — goddess of the moon, earth, and underground realm of the dead and regarded as the goddess of sorcery and witchcraft — her allurements are sinister and work to the destruction of the male protagonist in Keats's poems. In *The White Goddess* Robert Graves has devoted an odd but learned book to the positive and negative images of this anima of the unconscious, in its lunar, literary, and folkloric manifestations.

In "La Belle Dame sans Merci," we remember, a Knight is found alone and wandering on a cold hillside. He tells the narrator of the poem that he has encountered a Lady in that wild landscape — "Full beautiful, a faery's child" — who took him to an "elfin grot" where, after their sweet moans of love, she lulled him to sleep. In this sleep he had a dream of pale kings, princes and warriors who cried out to him "La belle dame sans merci / Thee hath in thrall." Upon awakening, he is found alone, languid, épuisé, wandering purposelessly in the withered landscape.

This beautiful faery's child has taken the Knight to her elfin grot, where an act of erotic fulfillment has occurred; she has devitalized him — sexually and psychically, leaving him, like his predecessors, pale and bloodless, enchanted and enthralled in a living death. Nothing in the poem suggests that the woman has a serpentine form; but in the folkloric and literary sources of "La Belle Dame," it is clear that the figure metamorphoses into her enchanting form out of the form of a serpent, hag, or witch. And her lethal intent is to vivify herself by sucking out of the young man his life's blood. In Keats's "Lamia," this metamorphosis is explicitly described: the vampire witch transforms herself from a hissing and coiling serpent into the form of a beautiful woman who offers fair young Lycius the dream of love, to which he capitulates, until the serpent is unmasked by the sage philosopher Apollonius — whereupon she vanishes in a scream, Lycius dying just thereafter, a victim of her debilitating enchantment and the shock of the revelation of her poisonous betrayal of innocent love.

II

What is the relation of these poems to *Tender Is the Night?* We must take note, first, of Fitzgerald's lifelong fascination with the lamia figure. In *This Side of Paradise*, amongst his other readings, Amory Blaine reads " 'Belle Dame sans Merci'; for a month was keen on naught else."[5] He becomes enchanted with Rosaline Connage (modelled on Zelda), whom the used-up and rejected Howard Gillespie calls " 'a vampire, that's all' " (193). Amory's next girl, Eleanor Savage, is truly moon-mad: "a witch, of perhaps nineteen" (243), she puts Amory "in a trance" (245). Afterward, she represented "the last time that evil crept close to Amory under the mask of beauty, the last weird mystery that held him with wild fascination and pounded his soul to flakes" (238). Somehow he knows that she is complicit in a dark evil. The following passage is of paramount importance in understanding the inner dynamics of Fitzgerald's ambivalence about women: "The problem of evil had solidified for Amory into the problem of sex. . . . Inseparably linked with evil was beauty. . . . Amory knew that every time he had reached toward it longingly it had leered out at him with the grotesque face of evil. Beauty of great art, beauty of all joy, most of all the beauty of women" (302).

The manuscript of *The Beautiful and Damned* indicates that Fitzgerald originally intended to call it "The Beautiful Lady Without Mercy," but he cancelled the title; and the manuscript also has a cancelled epigraph from this Keats poem. In the novel, the character Richard Caramel publishes a book called *The Demon Lover*. The aetherial beauty of the Moon-Goddess in *The Beautiful and Damned* incarnates itself in the form of the 1920s: of a "susciety gurl," "a ragtime kid, a flapper, a jazz-baby and a baby vamp."[6] While "vamp" was a common slang term in the 1920s for a flirt, its deeper resonance should not be underestimated. A section of Book I is called "Portrait of a Siren" (and features an erotic Geraldine, the name of Coleridge's lamia in "Christobel"), as well as a section called "The Beautiful Lady," concerning Gloria Gilbert, of whom Fitzgerald remarks, she was "beautiful — but especially she was without mercy" (116). Mrs. Granby thinks she may be a vampire (186), as indeed she is. And at the end, Anthony is reduced to childish impotence, playing with his stamp book, fully in Gloria's control, then dreaming of an escape to Italy, specifically to the Piazza de Spagna, where, not incidentally, Keats lived and died.

This vampire role is also played by Daisy Fay in *Gatsby*. Gatsby, according to William Bysshe Stein, succumbs "to the enchantments of the reincarnation of Morgan le Fay."[7] And the figure is right in Milton R. Stern's *The Golden Moment: The Novels of F. Scott Fitzgerald*, where he writes of the desexualizing power of rich women: "As moneyed 'female' destroys energy (Daisy's killing Myrtle, her indirect destruction of Gatsby), sucking it up like a vampire and leaving corpses strewn after her, the hardening, using female becomes indistinguishable from the predatory male."[8]

The *Esquire* articles that describe Fitzgerald's complete collapse in the mid-1930s, just after the completion of *Tender Is the Night*, dwell obsessively with the theme he had developed in the novel, the loss of vitality. He remarks that of all natural forces "vitality is the incommunicable one. In the days when juice came into one as an article without duty, one tried to distribute it — but always without success; . . . vitality never 'takes.' You have it or you haven't, like health or brown eyes or honor or a baritone voice." Later, he posed the question "of finding why and where I changed, where was the leak through which, unknown to myself, my enthusiasm and my vitality had been steadily and prematurely trickling away."[9] The issue was obsessive with him, though the answer was never fully grasped. Partial explanations must include Zelda's consuming need, her madness, paternal anxieties, his own alcoholism, his Depression-era poverty, self-contempt at the overproduction of second-rate magazine stories, the loss of an audience for his novels in the nine years after *Gatsby*, and the marginal reception of *Tender Is the Night*. An equally compelling reason for this loss of vitality was his tendency, arising out of his fragile sense of self and intensified by the novelist's task of entering into other identities, to merge with more attractive Others, resulting in the destabilization of ego boundaries and the loss of identity.

The diminution of Fitzgerald's sexual, emotional, psychic, professional, in short his creative vitality is central in *Tender Is the Night* and is dramatized as an affect that gradually overcomes Dick Diver in the process of courting, marrying, and curing Nicole Warren through psychoanalytic processes involving transference and counter-transference. So central is it in Fitzgerald's imagination that every major character in the book is assessed in relation to his or her vitality, or the lack of it. The scenario of the novel notes that the actress is "simply reeking of vitality, health, sensuality."[10] And Dick tells Rosemary: "That vitality, we were sure it was professional — especially Nicole was. It'd never use itself up on any one person or group" (49). Throughout her illness, Nicole does not have it: ". . . she sought in [other people] the vitality that had made them independent or creative or rugged, sought in vain — for their secrets were buried deep in childhood struggles they had forgotten" (236–37). Abe North lacks it; in fact, all the sanitarium patients lack vitality to Lanier, Dick's son: ". . . the patients appeared to him either in their odd aspects, or else as devitalized, over-correct creatures without personality" (237).

But Fitzgerald focussed his theme of waning vitality principally in Dick's disintegration. As the novel proceeds we become acutely conscious of his waning powers. Half way through the action, Tommy Barban tells Dick that he doesn't look "so jaunty as you used to, so spruce, you know what I mean." Fitzgerald observes that "the remark sounded too much like one of those irritating accusations of waning vitality" (257). As Dick's descent continues, he comes to recognize that "He had lost himself — he could not tell the hour when, or the day or the week, the month or the year" (262). He reflects that at an earlier meeting with Rosemary he had "been at an emotional peak," but "since then there had been a lesion of enthusiasm" (271). In a later scene, after half an hour of Collis, who is pursuing Rosemary, "he felt a distinct lesion of his own vitality" (290).

Toward the end, he confesses to Rosemary that he had "gone into a process of deterioration" (368). And afterwards, "though Nicole often paid lip service to the fact that he had led her back to the world she had forfeited, she had thought of him really as an inexhaustible energy, incapable of fatigue — she forgot the troubles she caused him at the moment when she forgot the troubles of her own that had prompted her" (388). Even the hack novelist McKisco "realized that he possessed more vitality than many men of superior talent," like Dick, "and he was resolved to enjoy the success he had earned" (268).

III

How does this motif of loss of vitality connect with the vampire motif? Is Nicole a lamia who devitalizes Dick in ways reminiscent of the Keats poems? Let me observe at first that Fitzgerald does not directly characterize Nicole in images of the serpentine woman, the lamia, or vampire. To have done so would undercut reader sympathy for Nicole too much. The serpent woman figure is displaced onto others and, later, generalized in wider images of the battle between the sexes. Even so, the Keatsian analogues resonate powerfully. The language of faery enchantment permeates the early part of the novel, where Dick falls under Nicole's spell. In this novel, though, the psychoanalytic process of transference substitutes for the older folkloric vampire imagery. Fitzgerald's understanding of transference, a complex psychoanalytic concept, is limited and rudimentary. What it comes down to is the transference of Dick's health to Nicole, his vitality to her. This analytic concept, which he had discovered in talking to Zelda's doctors and in reading about mental illness, replaces in substantial measure the older folkloric images of the vampiric woman.

Nevertheless, several significant associations in the novel make plain the continuing undercurrent of Keatsian vampirism in *Tender Is the Night*. The Murphys' Villa America is renamed the Villa Diana, the name of the Moon-Goddess, and Nicole is her incarnation. Fitzgerald deletes from the title-page epigraph from the "Ode" two lines that, by their sheer absence, call attention to the power of the Lunar Goddess: "And haply the Queen-Moon is on her throne, / Cluster'd around by all her starry Fays." Nicole's garden is the site of the first magical enchantment, the feast where the fireflies dance, the table appears to levitate, and the people are strangely made to feel "a sense of being alone with each other in the dark universe, nourished by its only food, warmed by its only lights" (44). This feast is not accidentally reminiscent of the feasting scene in "Lamia" and the "honey wild and manna dew" of "La Belle Dame." Yet of her garden, or elfin grot, Dick says that it is diseased: Nicole "won't let it alone — she nags it all the time, worries about its diseases. Any day now I expect to have her come down with Powdery Mildew or Fly Speck, or Late Blight" (36). Corruptions infest it. Yet in that enchanted darkness Nicole is transfigured, for Rosemary, into "one of the most beautiful people she had ever known. Her face, the face of a saint, a viking Madonna, shone through the faint motes that snowed across the candlelight, drew down its flush from the wine-colored lanterns in the pine" (43). Because these motes blur Rosemary's vision, seduce her through Nicole's magic, we need not be surprised that soon enough even Rosemary herself will become a starry Fay, will come to possess "all the world's dark magic; the blinding belladonna, the caffein converting physical into nervous energy, the mandragora that imposes harmony" (215). In this scene, as Rosemary watches Nicole, Abe North is talking to Rosemary about his "moral code": " 'Of course I've got one,' he insisted, ' — a man can't live without a moral code. Mine is that I'm against the burning of witches. Whenever they burn a witch I get all hot under the collar' " (43) This juxtaposition of feminine images — Madonna and Witch — coalesces the sexual attraction-repulsion affect underlying Fitzgerald's best, or at least most complex, characterizations of women. Abe can observe this because he has for years been enchanted with Nicole, is in fact "heavy, belly-frightened, with love for her . . ." (107).

There are, in fact, three serpent women in the novel — displacements of the lamia aspect of Nicole: ". . . a trio of young women sitting on the bench. They were all tall and slender with small heads groomed like manikins' heads, and as they talked [about the Divers and their entourage] the heads waved gracefully about above their dark tailored suits, rather like long-stemmed flowers and rather like cobras' hoods." In fact, Fitzgerald calls them "the three cobra women" (95–96). Another incarnation of the destructive power of the Moon-Goddess occurs in Maria Wallace, with the (Viking?) "helmet-like hair" (109), who shoots an unnamed man right through his identification card, leaving him sprawled on the train station platform without a self.

In the sanatarium garden scene where Nicole seduces Dick, Fitzgerald describes Nicole's face as emerging from its surrounding hair "as if this were the exact moment when she was coming from a wood into clear moonlight. The unknown yielded her up; Dick wished she had no background, that she was just a girl lost with no address save the night from which she had come" (179). Indeed it is the night — ruled by Diana — from which Nicole has emerged, more so than from Chicago. Of her singing, Fitzgerald remarks: "On the pure parting of her lips no breath hovered" (180), an inescapable spondaic verbal echo of the lines in "La Belle Dame": ". . . the sedge is wither'd from the lake, / And no birds sing." But Dick can hear nothing of her real song: what song the siren sang, a ditty of no tone, enchants him utterly.

In this seduction, the process of vampiric draining begins. After they kiss and she says to herself "I've got him, he's mine," Dick "was thankful to have an existence at all, if only as a reflection in her wet eyes" (203). As in "La Belle Dame," Nature too is transformed at this appropriation of Dick's selfhood. A storm erupts, fierce torrents of rain fall: "Mountains and lake disappeared — the hotel crouched amid tumult, chaos and darkness" (204). Although Dick feebly resists being bought, afterward, that night, "Her beauty climbed the rolling slope, it came into the room, rustling ghost-like through the curtains" (205). Soon enough, he is signing their letters "Dicole" (136), as his identity drains into her; later, "somehow Dick and Nicole had become one and equal, not apposite and complementary; she was Dick too, the drought in the marrow of his bones. He could not watch her disintegrations without participating in them" (249). He even becomes more feminized, appearing at one point, on the beach, in a pair of black lace panties Nicole has given him. "Well, if that isn't a pansy's trick" (26), remarks Mrs. McKisco contemptuously, reminding us of how homosexuality and lesbianism, perversions of rightly directed human sexuality, give the novel an ominous undertone.

Kathe Gregorovius claims that Nicole "only cherishes her illness as an instrument of power" (310). And in her transference to Dick, she drains him of his vitality, his inexhaustible energy, his very self. Her cure complete, she consummates an affair with Tommy Barban with calculated intention. The change is evident in her white crook's eyes, suggesting her complicity in the social and personal evil of her family and class. And Dick, swallowed up like a gigolo, is bereft of an ego, his self transformed into a vacuum, now filled up only by the egos of others, with all of their broken imperfections. At the end, he has the bitter knowledge that, with Nicole, "he had made his choice, chosen Ophelia, chosen the sweet poison and drunk it" (391).

Hamlet, of course, does not drink poison, but this image interestingly conflates the madness of Zelda-Nicole with the love of Keats for Fanny Brawne. "Ask yourself my love whether you are not very cruel to have so entrammeled me, so destroyed my freedom," Keats wrote to her. Keats even avoided seeing her at the end, because a visit was not so much a visit as "venturing into a fire." The phrase "sweet poison" in Tender comes from one of Keats's letters to her: "I have two luxuries to brood over in my walks, your Loveliness and the hour of my death. O that I could have possession of them both in the same minute. I hate the world: it batters too much the wings of my self-will, and I could take a sweet poison from your lips to send me out of it."[11] If Keats was half in love with easeful death, as he declined so poignantly from tuberculosis (an illness from which, incidentally, Fitzgerald suffered), Dick wanted "to die violently instead of fading out sentimentally" (49). But it is his fate to have emerged from Nicole's elfin grot depleted, to wander purposelessly throughout upstate New York.

IV

This view of woman — as an enchanting but sinister destroyer who drains a man of his vital energies, leaving him spent and empty of a self —

is of course insulting to women. But during his darkest hours, Fitzgerald felt, however wrongly, the terrors of what I can only call Zelda's oral cannibalism. He wrote to Dr. Squires, apropos of the unfairness of *her* writing fiction about *his* themes, *his* subjects, that he could not "stand always between Zelda and the world and see her build this dubitable career of hers with morsels of living matter chipped out of my mind, my belly, my nervous system and my loins."[12] There is no doubt that Fitzgerald, like Dick, felt that he had exchanged his vitality for his wife's sanity. After quarreling with Zelda about her using *Tender* material for her own fiction, he composed this note: "As I got feeling worse Zelda got mentally better, but it seemed to me that as she did she was also coming to the conclusion that she had it on me, if I broke down it justified her whole life—not a very healthy thought to live with about your own wife. . . . Finally four days ago told her frankly and furiously that had got & was getting rotten deal trading my health for her sanity and from now on I was going to look out for myself & Scottie exclusively and let her go to Bedlam for all I cared."[13]

If the critic's task is to understand these feelings and their transformation into fiction, however denigrating they may have been to Zelda or may be to other women, some sympathy must arise in our conclusion that the daemonic image of woman arose out of Fitzgerald's deep feelings of insecurity as a person, out of the destabilization of ego boundaries as he headed for his breakdown, out of his ambivalence over female sexuality in a newly liberated age, and out of a profound anxiety over his own manliness—castration fears, frankly, as Zelda questioned his virility and accused him of homosexuality. At the root of this fragile sense of self is of course the looming figure of Mollie McQuillan Fitzgerald, the powerful mother to whom ultimately these engulfing images refer. It is no malarkey to say that he spent his whole lifetime running away from her, even as a child fantasizing that he was not her son but rather a foundling, descended from the royal house of Stuart, a displaced prince. But his "possession" by her, and what that did to his relationship with Zelda, is the subject of another paper.

To his credit, Fitzgerald did not abandon Zelda. "Vitality shows in not only the ability to persist but in the ability to start over,"[14] he recorded in his notebook. If, as he remarked in "The Crack-Up," "It was strange to have no self," if "there was not an 'I' any more—not a basis on which I could organize my self-respect," not even that "limitless capacity for toil that it seemed I possessed no more,"[15] still, Fitzgerald did pull himself together; he went on working, supported Scottie and Zelda, whom he deeply if ambivalently loved, pasted it together, and attained some kind of stability, thanks paradoxically to Sheilah Graham. Had he lived to complete it, *The Last Tycoon* might have reflected the kind of artistic purity he had first achieved in *The Great Gatsby*. But so deeply implanted was his insecurity and his ambivalence about women that no doubt this spoiled priest of a novelist would have recreated, again and again, The Beautiful Lady Without Mercy.

Notes

1. *Correspondence of F. Scott Fitzgerald*, ed. Matthrew J. Bruccoli and Margaret M. Duggan with the assistance of Susan Walker (New York: Random House, 1980), p. 145.

2. John Kuehl has rightly remarked that "John Keats was Fitzgerald's favorite author." Kuehl's account of Keats's influence is to be found in "Scott Fitzgerald's Reading," *The Princeton University Library Chronicle*, 22 (Winter 1961):61–62; cf. also Kuehl's "Scott Fitzgerald: Romantic and Realist," *Texas Studies in Literature and Languages* 1 (1959):412–26. Sheilah Graham's *Beloved Infidel* (New York: Bantam, 1959) and *College of One* (New York: Viking, 1966) are indispensable in defining the Keats relation. For more specialized studies see also William Bysshe Stein, "Gatsby's Morgan Le Fay," *Fitzgerald Newsletter* No. 15 (Fall 1961):67; Dan McCall, " 'The Self-Same Song that Found a Path': Keats and *The Great Gatsby*," *American Literature* 42 (1971):521–30; Tristram P. Coffin, "Gatsby's Fairy Lover," *Midwest Folklore* 10 (Summer 1960):79–85; Richard L. Schoenwald, "F. Scott Fitzgerald As John Keats," *Boston University Studies in English* 3 (Spring 1957):12–21; John Grube, "*Tender Is the Night*: Keats and Fitzgerald," *Dalhousie Review* 44 (1964–65):433–41; and William E. Doherty, "*Tender Is the Night* and the 'Ode to a Nightingale,' " in *Explorations of Literature*, ed. Rima Drell Reck (Baton Rouge, La.: Louisiana State University Press, 1966), pp. 100–114.

3. Doherty, "*Tender Is the Night* and the 'Ode to a Nightingale,' " 101.

4. F. Scott Fitzgerald, *Tender Is the Night* (New York: Scribner's, 1934), p. 55. Subsequent references to this work will be given in parenthesis in the text.

5. F. Scott Fitzgerald, *This Side of Paradise* (New York: Scribner's 1920), p. 57. Subsequent references to this work will be given in parenthesis in the text.

6. F. Scott Fitzgerald, *The Beautiful and Damned* (New York: Scribner's, 1922), p. 29. Subsequent references will be given in parenthesis in the text.

7. Stein, "Gatsby's Morgan Le Fay," 67.

8. Milton R. Stern, *The Golden Moment: The Novels of F. Scott Fitzgerald* (Urbana, Ill.: University of Illinois Press, 1970), p. 326.

9. F. Scott Fitzgerald, *The Crack-Up*, ed. Edmund Wilson (New York: New Directions, 1945), pp. 74. 80.

10. Arthur Mizener, *The Far Side of Paradise* (New York: Vintage Books, 1959), p. 334.

11. John Keats, *Complete Poems and Selected Letters*, ed. Clarence DeWitt Thorpe (New York: Odyssey Press, 1935), pp. 616, 627, 621.

12. Quoted in Nancy Milford, *Zelda: A Biography* (New York: Harper & Row, 1970), p. 222.

13. Scott Donaldson, *Fool for Love: F. Scott Fitzgerald* (New York: Congdon and Weed, 1983), p. 86.

14. *The Notebooks of F. Scott Fitzgerald*, ed. Matthew J. Bruccoli (New York: Harcourt Brace Jovanovich, 1978), p. 57.

15. Fitzgerald, *The Crack-Up*, p. 79.

Tender Is the Night: A Cross-Referenced Bibliography of Criticism
Joseph Wenke*

The purpose of this bibliography is to provide an accurate list of all the English language materials that have contributed to the critical reputation of *Tender Is the Night*. In compiling this list, I have generally included articles and books that contain mere mentions of *Tender Is the Night* only if the references are of scholarly interest. Otherwise I have required that items include at least a briefly sustained discussion or several interpretive references to the novel. I have listed bibliographies only if they contain descriptive annotations. I have included bibliographical essays only if they discuss more than a particular year's scholarship on *Tender Is the Night*. I should also state that because of the obvious limitations imposed by publishing schedules, I have not attempted to make the bibliography comprehensive beyond 1980.

I have not attempted to compile a fully annotated bibliography. The notes are intended to guide the reader to reprintings. Page numbers appearing within brackets indicate specific page numbers of references to *Tender Is the Night* within articles or sections of books.

I have divided the bibliography, which is organized chronologically by year, into two separately numbered sections, periodicals and books (which includes book sections and pamphlets). In referring to items in the bibliography, I have used the prefix "P" for periodical and "B" for book together with the number of the item being cross-referenced.

Periodicals

The 1930s

1. "F. Scott Fitzgerald Is Visitor In City; New Book Appears Soon." *Charlottes-ville (Va.) Daily Progress*, 25 May 1933, p. 1.
2. Gray, James. "Scott Fitzgerald Writes New Novel to Run in Magazine." *St. Paul Dispatch*, 28 November 1933, p. 12.
3. — — —. "First Installment of Fitzgerald Novel Is Disappointment." *St. Paul Dispatch*, 25 December 1933, p. 8.
4. "Decadence: Fitzgerald Again Tells a Sinful, Ginful Tale." *News-Week* 3 (14 April 1934):39–40.
5. "A New Fitzgerald." *Princeton Alumni Weekly* 34 (4 May 1934):665. Reprinted in B89, p. 382 and B125, p. 315.
6. "New Novels: Dream-Worlds and Reality." *Herald* (Glasgow), 20 October 1934, p. 2.

*This bibliography was prepared for this volume and is published here for the first time by permission of the author.

7. "The Psychological Novel." *Spectator* (London) 153 (21 September 1934):410.
8. "Scott Fitzgerald Essays Return to Novel Writing." *Milwaukee Journal*, 22 April 1934, Sec. 5, p. 3. Reprinted in B125, pp. 313–14.
9. "Sophisticates Abroad." *Time* 23 (16 April 1934):77. Reprinted in B125, pp. 312–13.
10. "A Study in Disillusion." *Saturday Review* (London) 158 (8 December 1934):501.
11. "Tender Is the Night." *Springfield (Mass.) Sunday Union and Republican*, 29 April 1934, p 7E.
12. "*Tender Is the Night.*" *Times Literary Supplement* (London), 27 September 1934, p. 652.
13. A., D. F. "A Modern Tragedy." *Guardian* (Manchester), 19 October 1934, p. 7.
14. A[dams], J. D[onald]. "Scott Fitzgerald's Return to the Novel." *New York Times Book Review*, 15 April 1934, p. 7. Reprinted in B89, pp. 379–80 and B125, pp. 304–06.
15. Anderson, Katherine McClure. "Today's Book." *Macon Telegraph*, 11 April 1934, p. 4. Reprinted in B125, pp. 287–88.
16. Beck, Clyde. "The Doctor and the Movie Star." *Detroit News*, 14 April 1934, p. 20. Reprinted in B125, p. 298.
17. Borland, Hal. " 'Of Making Many Books—.' " *Philadelphia Public Ledger*, 13 April 1934, p. 9. Reprinted in B125, pp. 293–94.
18. Brickell, Herschel. "Americans Abroad." *North American Review* 237 (June 1934):569–70. Reprinted in B125, p. 322.
19. – – –. "Books on Our Table." *New York Post*, 14 April 1934, p. 13.
20. Butcher, Fanny. "New Fitzgerald Book Brilliant; Fails as Novel." *Chicago Tribune*, 14 April 1934, p. 10. Reprinted in B125, pp. 298–99.
21. Canby, Henry Seidel. "In the Second Era of Demoralization." *Saturday Review of Literature* 10 (14 April 1934):630–31. Reprinted in B89, pp. 370–72 and B125, pp. 300–01.
22. Chamberlain, John. "Books of The Times." *New York Times*, 13 April 1934, p. 17. Reprinted in B18, pp. 95–98; B89, pp. 372–74; and B125, pp. 294–96.
23. – – –. "Books of The Times." *New York Times*, 16 April 1934, p. 15. Reprinted in B18, pp. 98–99; B89, pp. 374–75; and B125, pp. 311–12.
24. – – –. "Books of The Times." *New York Times*, 20 September 1934, p. 21.
25. Clarage, Eleanor. *Cleveland Plain Dealer*, 13 April 1934, p. 7.
26. Coleman, Arthur. "Fitzgerald's Stature Is Increased by His Novel About Americans in France." *Dallas Morning News*, 15 April 1934, Sec. 3, p. 10. Reprinted in B125, p. 306.
27. Colum, Mary M. "The Psychopathic Novel." *Forum and Century* 91 (April 1934):219–23. Reprinted in B125, pp. 283–86.
28. Cowley, Malcolm. "Breakdown." *New Republic* 79 (6 June 1934):105–06. Reprinted in B71; B89, pp. 387–90; B102, and B125, pp. 323–25.
29. Daniel, Frank. " 'Tender Is the Night.' " *Atlanta Journal*, 20 May 1934, Magazine Sec., p. 14. Reprinted in B125, pp. 320–21.
30. Diamant, Gertrude. "Child Prodigy." *American Mercury*, 33 (October 1934):249–51. Reprinted in B125, pp. 328–31.
31. Fadiman, Clifton. "F. Scott Fitzgerald." *New Yorker* 10 (14 April

1934):112–15. Reprinted in B89, pp. 376–78 and B125, pp. 301–03.

32. G., C. M. "F. Scott Fitzgerald Follows the Times in Complicated Tale." *Albany Knickerbocker Press*, 13 May 1934, Sec. 4, p. 7.

33. Gannett, Lewis. "Books and Things." *New York Herald Tribune*, 13 April 1934, p. 15. Reprinted in B125, pp. 296–97.

34. Gould, Gerald. "New Novels." *Observer* (London), 14 October 1934, p. 6.

35. Grattan, C. Hartley. *Modern Monthly* 8 (July 1934):375–77. Reprinted in B18, pp. 104–07 and B125, pp. 326–28.

36. Gray James. "Fitzgerald Serial Improves Greatly As Story Advances." *St. Paul Dispatch*, 18 January 1934, p. 6.

37. – – –. "Scott Fitzgerald Re-Enters, Leading Bewildered Giant." *St. Paul Dispatch*, 12 April 1934, Sec. 1, p. 8. Reprinted in B9 and B125, pp. 288–90.

38. Gregory, Horace. "A Generation Riding to Romantic Death." *New York Herald Tribune Book Review*, 15 April 1934, p. 5. Reprinted in B125, pp. 306–08.

39. Hansen, Harry. "The First Reader." *New York World-Telegram*, 12 April 1934, p. 25. Reprinted in B125, pp. 291–92.

40. Harding. D. W. "Mechanisms of Misery." *Scrutiny* 3 (December 1934):316–19. Reprinted in B18, pp. 100–03 and B49, pp. 143–45.

41. Hart, Philomena. "Among the Lost People of Three Notable Volumes." *Providence Sunday Journal*, 22 April 1934, Sec. E, p. 4.

42. Jones, E. B. C. "New Novels." *New Statesman and Nation*, NS 8 (22 September 1934):364–66 [366].

43. Lewis, Gordon. "Scott Fitzgerald Is Author of New Novel." *Charlotte News*, 6 May 1934, Sec. 2, p. 9. Reprinted in B125, pp. 317–18.

44. Loveman, Amy. "Books of the Spring." *Saturday Review of Literature* 10 (7 April 1934):610.

45. Luhan, Mabel Dodge. "Scott Fitzgerald a Modern Orpheus." *New York Herald Tribune Books*, 6 May 1934, p. 21.

46. M., M. "Moved by Futility." *Los Angeles Times*, 6 May 1934, Part 2, p. 7.

47. MacMillan, H. A. "Mr. Fitzgerald Displays His Little White Mice." *St. Paul Daily News*, 22 April 1934, Magazine Sec., p. 4. Reprinted in B125, p. 313.

48. March, Michael. "Page After Page." *Brooklyn Citizen*, 11 April 1934, p. 11.

49. Marsh, D'Arcy. "Ebb Tide." *Canadian Forum* 14 (July 1934):404.

50. Murphy, Spencer. "Scott Fitzgerald Develops Novel Idea in His Latest Book." *Charlotte Observer*, 20 May 1934, sec. 3, p. 8. Reprinted in B125, pp. 321–22.

51. O., H. "Psychiatrist and Patient." *Baltimore Evening Sun*, 21 April 1934, p. 6.

52. P., E. R. "New Fitzgerald Novel Is Parade of Neurotic Case." *Cleveland Plain Dealer*, 29 April 1934, Women's Magazine & Amusement Sec., p. 17.

53. P., S. "Psychiatrist." *Cincinnati Enquirer*, 28 April 1934, p. 7.

54. Patterson, Curtis. "Pathology Rears Its Ugly Head." *Town & Country* 89 (15 April 1934): 42, 70 [42].

55. Peterson, G. L. "The Booking Office." *Minneapolis Tribune*, 6 May 1934, Sec. [3], p. 11.

56. Potter, Merle. "Americans In Other Lands." *Minneapolis Journal*, 15 April 1934, Editorial Sec., p. 7.

57. Quennell, Peter. "New Novels." *New Statesman and Nation* NS 7 (28 April

1934):642. Reprinted in B89, p. 381.

58. Rahv, Philip. "You Can't Duck Hurricane Under a Beach Umbrella." *Daily Worker*, 5 May 1934, p. 7. Reprinted in B89, pp. 383–84 and B125, pp. 315–17.

59. Rascoe, Burton. "Esquire's Five-Minute Shelf." *Esquire*, 1 (April 1934), 133, 159, 161, 162–63 [133, 159]. Reprinted in B125, pp. 286–87.

60. Riley, Edith Carl. "*Tender Is the Night.*" *Houston Post*, 15 April 1934, sec. [2], p. 9.

61. Rogers, Cameron. "Fitzgerald's Novel a Masterpiece." *San Francisco Chronicle*, 15 April 1934, p. 4D. Reprinted in B125, pp. 309–10.

62. Seldes, Gilbert. "True to Type — Scott Fitzgerald Writes Superb Tragic Novel." *New York Evening Journal*, 12 April 1934, p. 23. Reprinted in B125, pp. 292–93.

63. Soskin, William. Untitled. 12 April 1934. Reprinted in B125, pp. 332–34.

64. Stern, G. B. " 'Daring' in Novels — Old Style and New." *Daily Telegraph* (London), 19 October 1934, p. 6.

65. Troy, William. "The Worm i' the Bud." *Nation* 138 (9 May 1934):539–40. Reprinted in B89, pp. 385–87 and B125, pp. 318–20.

66. Wagner, Charles A. "Books." *New York Sunday Mirror.* 15 April 1934, p. 24.

67. Walley, Harold R. "The Book Worm's Turn." *Ohio State Journal*, 6 June 1934, p. 5. Reprinted in B125, pp. 325–26.

68. Walton, Edith H. *Forum and Century* 91 (June 1934):iv–v. Reprinted in B125, pp. 322–23.

69. – – –. "Stale; Unprofitable." *New York Sun*, 14 April 1934, p. 30. Reprinted in B125, pp. 303–04.

70. Weeks, Edward. *Atlantic Monthly* 153 (April 1934):17. Reprinted in B125, p. 287.

71. Wilson, Rowena. "Scott Fitzgerald Leads Through Winding Ways." *Savannah Morning News*, 15 April 1934, Sec. 2, p. 10. Reprinted in B125, pp. 310–11.

72. *Journal of Nervous and Mental Disease* 82 (July 1935):115–17. Reprinted in B89, pp. 390–92 and B125, pp. 331–32.

73. Buttita, Anthony. "Fitzgerald's Six Generations." *Raleigh (N.C.) News and Observer*, 1 September 1935. p. 3.

74. Moore, Harry Thornton. "The American Novel Today." *Mercury* (London) 31 (March 1935):461–67 [467].

75. Bishop, John Peale. "The Missing All." *Virginia Quarterly Review* 13 (Winter 1937):107–21 [115–16]. Reprinted in B11.

The 1940s

76. "Notes and Comment." *New Yorker* 16 (4 January 1941):9. Reprinted in B89, p. 474.

77. Gingrich, Arnold. "Editorial: Salute and Farewell to F. Scott Fitzgerald." *Esquire* 15 (March 1941):6. Reprinted in B89, pp. 477–81.

78. O'Hara, John. "Certain Aspects." *New Republic* 104 (3 March 1941):311. Reprinted in B61.

79. Schulberg, Budd, Jr. "Fitzgerald in Hollywood." *New Republic* 104 (3 March 1941):311–12. Reprinted in B18, pp. 109–12.

80. Wescott, Glenway. "The Moral of Scott Fitzgerald." *New Republic* 104 (17 February 1941):213–17. Reprinted in B8; B18, pp. 116–29; B40, pp. 209–23; and B45.

81. Gurko, Leo and Miriam. "The Essence of F. Scott Fitzgerald." *College English* 5 (April 1944):372–76.

82. Weir, Charles, Jr. " 'An Invite with Gilded Edges': A Study of F. Scott Fitzgerald." *Virginia Quarterly Review* 20 (Winter 1944):100–13. Reprinted in B18, pp. 133–45.

83. Brady, Charles A. "The Portable F. Scott Fitzgerald." *Best Sellers* 5 (15 October 1945):129–31.

84. Embler, Weller. "F. Scott Fitzgerald and the Future." *Chimera* 4 (Autumn 1945):48–55. Reprinted in B18, pp. 212–19.

85. Flandrau, Grace. "Fitzgerald Panegyric Inspires Some Queries." *St. Paul Pioneer Press*, 9 September 1945, Mag. p. 6.

86. Kazin, Alfred. "Fitzgerald: An American Confession." *Quarterly Review of Literature* 2, no. 4 (1945):341–46. Reprinted in B18, pp. 172–81 and B25.

87. Piper, H. D. "The Last Decade." *Interim*, 2, No. 1 (1945), 39–43 [40].

88. Schneider, Isidor. "A Pattern of Failure." *New Masses* 57 (4 December 1945):23–24.

89. Trilling, Lionel. "F. Scott Fitzgerald." *Nation* 159 (25 August 1945):182–84. Reprinted in B13; B18, pp. 194–204; B29; B40, pp. 232–43; and B49, pp. 11–19.

90. Troy, William. "Scott Fitzgerald – the Authority of Failure." *Accent* 6 (Autumn 1945):56–60. Reprinted in B12; B18, pp. 187–93; B40, pp. 224–31; B49, pp. 20–24; and B53.

91. Wanning, Andrews. "Fitzgerald and His Brethren." *Partisan Review* 12 (Fall 1945):545–51 [549]. Reprinted in B18, pp. 160–68 and B49, pp. 57–63.

92. "Fitzgerald Novel Sold to Screen." *New York Times*, 23 November 1946, p. 10.

93. Berryman, John. "F. Scott Fitzgerald." *Kenyon Review* 8 (Winter 1946):103–12 [107–08].

94. Grobman, Feb. "Scott Fitzgerald: Athenian Among Greeks." *Foreground* 1 (Winter 1946):60–69 [passim].

95. M[izener], A[rthur]. "The Portable F. Scott Fitzgerald." *Kenyon Review* 8 (Spring 1946):342–43.

96. Mizener, Arthur. "Scott Fitzgerald and the Imaginative Possession of American Life." *Sewanee Review* 54 (Winter 1946): 66–86 [80–83]. Reprinted in slightly revised form in B10; B18, pp. 23–45; and B20.

97. – – –. "A Note on 'The World's Fair.' " *Kenyon Review* 10 (Autumn 1948):701–04.

98. Ross, Alan. "Rumble Among the Drums – F. Scott Fitzgerald (1896–1940) and the Jazz Age." *Horizon* 18 (December 1948):420–35 [423, 429, 431–33].

99. Adams, Theodore S. "A Noble Issue." *Gifthorse* (1949), pp. 35–43.

100. Hersey, John. "Three Memorable Books of the Past 25 Years – 'My Candidates.' " *New York Herald Tribune Weekly Book Review*, 25 September 1949, p. 10.

101. Kallich, Martin. "F. Scott Fitzgerald: Money or Morals." *University of Kansas City Review* 15 (Summer 1949):271–80 [275–77].

102. Mizener, Arthur. "Scott Fitzgerald: Moralist of the Jazz Age." *Harper's*

Bazaar 83 (September 1949):174–75, 247–49, 252, 254 [passim].
103. Savage, D. S. "Scott Fitzgerald, the Man and His Work," *World Review* NS No. 6 (August 1949):65–67, 80 [67].

The 1950s

104. "Power without Glory." *Times Literary Supplement* (London), 20 January 1950, p. 40. Reprinted in B18, pp. 205–11.
105. Wilkinson, Burke. "Scott Fitzgerald: Ten Years After." *New York Times Book Review*, 24 December 1950, pp. 7. 10.
106. "Tips for the Bookseller." *Publisher's Weekly* 159 (10 February 1951): 879–80.
107. Brégy, Katherine. "F. Scott Fitzgerald – Tragic Comedian." *Catholic World* 173 (May 1951):86–91 [90].
108. Chamberlain, John. "A Reviewer's Notebook." *The Freeman* 2 (19 November 1951):121–22 [122].
109. Cowley, Malcolm. "Fitzgerald: The Double Man." *Saturday Review of Literature* 34 (24 February 1951): 9–10, 42–44 [passim].
110. – – –. "Fitzgerald's 'Tender' – The Story of a Novel." *New Republic* 125 (20 August 1951):18–20. Reprinted in B15 and B22.
111. Fiedler, Leslie A. "Notes on F. Scott Fitzgerald." *New Leader* 34 (16 April 1951):23–24. Reprinted in B23 and B49, pp. 70–76.
112. Harding, D. W. "Scott Fitzgerald." *Scrutiny*, 18 (Winter 1951–52), 166–74 [passim].
113. Hughes, Riley. "The American Novel Through Fifty Years." *America* 85 (12 May 1951): 164–66. Reprinted in B17.
114. Lewis, R. W. B. "Fitzgerald's Way." *Hudson Review* 4 (Summer 1951): 304–309 [passim].
115. Mizener, Arthur. "An Author's Final Version." *Saturday Review of Literature* 34 (8 December 1951): 19.
116. – – –. "F. Scott Fitzgerald: A Biography." *Atlantic Monthly* 187 (February 1951): 72–80 [78–79]. Excerpted from B19.
117. Piper, Henry Dan. "F. Scott Fitzgerald and the Image of His Father." *Princeton University Library Chronicle* 12 (Summer 1951): 181–86.
118. Poore, Charles. "Books of The Times." *New York Times*, 15 November 1951, p. 27.
119. Savage, D. S. "The Significance of F. Scott Fitzgerald." *Envoy* 5 (June 1951): 8–21. Reprinted in P128 and B49, pp. 146–56.
120. Schulberg, Budd. "Prodded by Pride and Desperation." *New York Times Book Review*, 18 November 1951, pp. 5, 38.
121. Thurber, James. " 'Scott in Thorns.' " *Reporter* 4 (17 April 1951): 35–38 [passim]. Reprinted in B34 and B43.
122. Trilling, Lionel. "Fitzgerald Plain." *New Yorker* 26 (3 February 1951): 79–81.
123. Farrelly, John. "Scott Fitzgerald: Another View." *Scrutiny* 18 (June 1952):266–72.
124. Fussell, Edwin S. "Fitzgerald's Brave New World." *ELH* 19 (December 1952): 291–306 [299–304]. Reprinted in revised form in B40, pp. 244–62 and B49, pp. 43–56.
125. Greenleaf, Richard. "The Social Thinking of F. Scott Fitzgerald." *Science and Society* 16 (Spring 1952):97–114 [110–11 et passim].

126. Houston, Penelope. "Visits to Babylon." *Sight and Sound* 21 (April–June 1952):153–56.
127. Reece, David C. "The Novels of F. Scott Fitzgerald." *Cambridge Journal* 5 (July 1952):613–25.
128. Savage, D. S. "The Significance of F. Scott Fitzgerald." *Arizona Quarterly* 8 (Autumn 1952):197–210. Reprint of P119; reprinted in B49, pp. 146–56.
129. Wechsler, Henry. "The Theme of Failure in F. Scott Fitzgerald." *Wall* (Fall 1952), pp. 23–24.
130. Ingrisano, Michael N., Jr. "A Note on a Critique of F. Scott Fitzgerald." *American Literature* 24 (January 1953):539–40.
131. Steinberg, A. H. "Hardness, Light, and Psychiatry in *Tender Is the Night*." *Literature and Psychology* 3 (February 1953): 3–8. Reprinted in revised form in P138 and B81, pp. 138–43.
132. Bicknell, John W. "The Waste Land of F. Scott Fitzgerald." *Virginia Quarterly Review* 30 (Autumn 1954):556–72 [564–66 et passim].
133. Nishi, Kazuyo. "A Study of F. Scott Fitzgerald – Focusing on *Tender Is the Night*." *Gunma Daigaku Kiyo* 3 (February 1954):103–15.
134. Shockley, Martin Staples. "Harsh Will Be the Morning." *Arizona Quarterly* 10 (Summer 1954):127–35 [129–30 et passim].
135. Frohock, W. M. "Manners, Morals, and Scott Fitzgerald." *Southwest Review* 40 (Summer 1955):220–28. Reprinted in B36.
136. Kennedy, William F. "Are Our Novelists Hostile to the American Economic System?" *Dalhousie Review* 35 (Spring 1955):32–44 [34–35].
137. Lubell, Albert J. "The Fitzgerald Revival." *South Atlantic Quarterly* 54 (January 1955):95–106.
138. Steinberg, A. H. "Fitzgerald's Portrait of a Psychiatrist." *University of Kansas City Review* 21 (March 1955):219–22. Revised version of P131, reprinted in B81, pp. 138–43.
139. Elkin, P. K. "The Popularity of F. Scott Fitzgerald." *Australian Quarterly* 29 (June 1957):93–101 [passim].
140. Giles, Barbara. "The Dream of F. Scott Fitzgerald." *Mainstream* 10 (March 1957):1–12.
141. Schoenwald, Richard L. "F. Scott Fitzgerald as John Keats." *Boston University Studies in English* 3 (Spring 1957):12–21. Reprinted in P147.
142. Wilson, Robert N. "Fitzgerald as Icarus." *Antioch Review* 17 (December 1957):481–92.
143. Hujikawa, Genjin. "*Tender Is the Night*." *Meigjo Daigaku Rikogokubu Kenkyuhokoku*, no. 3 (December 1958), pp. 101–15.
144. Litvin, Martin. "Fitzgerald and the Best in Man," *Lincoln County News*, 10 October 1958, pp. 5, 6.
145. Morris, Wright. "The Ability to Function: A Reappraisal of Fitzgerald and Hemingway." *New World Writing*, no. 13 (June 1958), pp. 34–51 [41–42 et passim]. Reprinted in B30 and B49, pp. 25–31.
146. Pritchett, V. S. "Scott Fitzgerald." *New Statesman* NS 56 (11 October 1958):494–95.
147. Schoenwald, Richard L. "F. Scott Fitzgerald as John Keats." *MIT Publications in the Humanities*, no. 28 (1958), pp. 12–21. Reprint of P141.
148. Stanton, Robert. " 'Daddy's Girl': Symbol and Theme in 'Tender Is the Night.' " *Modern Fiction Studies* 4 (Summer 1958):136–42. Reprinted in B81,

pp. 156–64.
149. "Echoes of the Jazz Age." *Times* (London), 19 November 1959, p. 15.
150. "Our Yesterdays." *Baltimore Evening Sun* (11 May 1959) p. 20.
151. "The Round-Up." *Times Literary Supplement* (London), 27 November 1959, p. 695.
152. Amis Kingsley. "The Crack-Up." *Spectator* (London), 203, no. 6856 (20 November 1959):719.
153. Bruccoli, Matthew J. "An American Classic — F. Scott Fitzgerald Novel 25 Years Old in April." *Richmond News Leader*, 1 April 1959, p. 13.
154. — — —. "Cinema Notes." *Fitzgerald Newsletter*, no. 5 (Spring 1959):2.
155. Decter, Midge. "Fitzgerald at the End." *Partisan Review* 26 (Spring 1959):303–12 [passim]. Reprinted in B107, pp. 135–42.
156. Heppenstall, Rayner. "Jazz Age Echoes." *Observer* (London), 15 November 1959, p. 21.
157. Kuehl, John R. "Scott Fitzgerald: Romantic and Realist." *Texas Studies in Literature and Language* 1 (Autumn 1959):412–26 [418–23]. Reprinted in B81, pp. 1–19.
158. [Manning, Don]. "Dr. Diver and Dr. Zhivago." *Fitzgerald Newsletter*, no. 5 (Spring 1959):4.
159. Powell, Anthony. "More Scott Fitzgerald." *Daily Telegraph and Morning Post* (London), 11 December 1959, p. 18.

The 1960s

160. Allen, Walter. "An Age and an Image." *New Statesman*, N.S. 59 (9 January 1960):48–49.
161. B., M. A. "Golden Boy." *Tablet* (London) 214 (5 March 1960):230.
162. [Bruccoli, Matthew J.]. "New F. Reprints." *Fitzgerald Newsletter*, no. 9 (Spring 1960):2.
163. Friedrich, Otto. "Reappraisals — F. Scott Fitzgerald: Money, Money, Money." *American Scholar* 29 (Summer 1960):392–405 [399–402].
164. Hujikawa, Genjin. "*Tender Is the Night* Again." *American Literature Review* 33 (November 1960):5–7.
165. Irwin, William R. "Dos Passos and Fitzgerald as Reviewers of the American Social Scene." *Die Neueren Sprachen*, 9 (September 1960):417–28.
166. Jacobson, Dan. "F. Scott Fitzgerald." *Encounter* 14 (June 1960):71–77 [passim].
167. Lemaire, Marcel. "Failure and Success of Francis Scott Fitzgerald's Work." *Revue des Langues Vivantes* 26 (January–February 1960):13–45.
168. Quinlan, G. C. "A Note on the *RSV TITN*." *Fitzgerald Newsletter*, no. 9 (Spring 1960):1.
169. Sherwood, John. "A Beautiful Time, Baby." *Baltimore Sun*, 18 September 1960, sec. A, p. 3.
170. Bedingfield, Dolores. "Fitzgerald's Corruptible Dream." *Dalhousie Review* 41 (Winter 1961–62):513–21.
171. Bruccoli, Matthew J. "*Tender Is the Night* and the Reviewers." *Modern Fiction Studies* 7 (Spring 1961):49–54.
172. Hall, William F. "Dialogue and Theme in *Tender Is the Night*." *Modern Language Notes* 76 (November 1961):616–22. Reprinted in B81, pp. 144–50.

173. Hujikawa, Genjin. "A Reappraisal of 'Tender Is the Night.' " *Toyo Daigaku Kyoyobu Kiyo*, no. 2 (February 1961):20–31.

174. Kreuter, Kent and Gretchen. "The Moralism of the Later Fitzgerald." *Modern Fiction Studies* 7 (Spring 1961):71–81 [72, 75–77]. Reprinted in B81, pp. 48–60.

175. Mizener, Arthur. "Scott Fitzgerald and the Top Girl." *Atlantic Monthly* 207 (March 1961):55–60.

176. Phillips, Robert S. "Fitzgerald and *The Day of the Locust*." *Fitzgerald Newsletter*, no. 15 (Fall 1961):2–3.

177. Stevens, A. Wilber. "Fitzgerald's *Tender Is the Night*: The Idea as Morality." *Brigham Young University Studies* 3 (Spring and Summer 1961):95–104.

178. White, Eugene. "The 'Intricate Destiny' of Dick Diver." *Modern Fiction Studies* 7 (Spring 1961):55–62. Reprinted in B81, pp. 117–26.

179. Bryer, Jackson R. "F. Scott Fitzgerald and His Critics: A Bibliographical Record." *Bulletin of Bibliography* 23 (January–April 1962):155–58; 23 (May–August 1962), 180–83; 23 (September–December 1962), 201–08. Earlier version of B70.

180. Cardwell, Guy A. "The Lyric World of F. Scott Fitzgerald." *Virginia Quarterly Review* 38 (Spring 1962):299–323 [316–22].

181. Littlejohn, David. "Fitzgerald's Grand Illusion." *Commonweal* 76 (11 May 1962):168–69. Reprinted in B84.

182. Ridgely, Joseph Vincent. "Mencken, Fitzgerald and *Tender Is the Night*." *Menckeniana*, no 3 (Fall 1962):4–5.

183. Tomkins, Calvin. "Living Well Is the Best Revenge." *New Yorker* 38 (28 July 1962):31–32, 34, 36, 38, 43–44, 46–47, 49–50, 52, 54, 56–69. Reprinted in B96.

184. [Bruccoli, Matthew J.]. "The Chord Sale." *Fitzgerald Newsletter*, no. 21 (Spring 1963):6.

185. — — —. "Correction – RSV TITN." *Fitzgerald Newsletter*, no. 20 (Winter 1963):7.

186. Bryer, Jackson R. "F. Scott Fitzgerald: A Review of Research and Scholarship." *Texas Studies in Literature and Language* 5 (Spring 1963):147–63 [156–57 et passim].

187. Hobsbaum, Philip. "Scott Fitzgerald and His Critics: The Appreciation of Minor Art." *British Association for American Studies Bulletin*, n.s., No. 6 (June 1963), pp. 31–41.

188. Hyman, Stanley Edgar. "The Great Fitzgerald." *New Leader* 46 (9 December 1963):19–20.

189. Light, James F. "Political Conscience in the Novels of F. Scott Fitzgerald." *Ball State Teachers College Forum* 4 (Spring 1963):13–25 [19–22].

190. Lucas, John. "In Praise of Scott Fitzgerald." *Critical Quarterly* 5 (Summer 1963):132–47.

191. Mizener, Arthur. "The Voice of Scott Fitzgerald's Prose." *Essays and Studies* (English Association) 16 (1963):56–67.

192. Quemada, David V. "The Other Side of Paradise: Satire in F. Scott Fitzgerald." *Silliman Journal* 10 (Third Quarter 1963):272–88.

193. Way, Brian. "Scott Fitzgerald." *New Left Review*, no. 21 (October 1963):36–51.

194. Bourjailly, Vance. "Fitzgerald Attends My Fitzgerald Seminar." *Esquire* 62

(September 1964):111, 113, 193–96. Reprinted in B90, pp. 107–22.

195. Bruccoli, Matthew J. "Material for a Centenary Edition of *Tender Is the Night.*" *Studies in Bibliography* 17 (1964):177–93.

196. Cowley, Malcolm. "A Ghost Story of the Jazz Age: Reminiscences of Twenty-Four Hours with F. Scott Fitzgerald." *Saturday Review* 47 (25 January 1964):20–21.

197. Grube, John. "*Tender Is the Night:* Keats and Scott Fitzgerald." *Dalhousie Review* 44 (Winter 1964–65):433–41. Reprinted in B81, pp. 179–89.

198. Long, Robert E. "*Sister Carrie* and the Rhythm of Failure in Fitzgerald." *Fitzgerald Newsletter*, no. 25 (Spring 1964):2–4.

199. Morrill, Thomas. "F. Scott Fitzgerald — Under the Figlinden Tree." *Trace*, no. 53 (Summer 1964):97–104, 185–202.

200. Nagase, Hiroshi. "The Tragedy of Dick — On *Tender Is the Night.*" *Chameleon*, no. 7 (Aug. 1964):48–62.

201. Skipp, Francis E. "The Fitzgerald Reader." *South Atlantic Quarterly* 63 (Summer 1964):443–44.

202. B[ruccoli], M[atthew] J. "Inscribed *Tender Is the Night.*" *Fitzgerald Newsletter*, no. 31 (Fall 1965):4.

203. [Bruccoli, Matthew J.]. "A Source for the Station Shooting in *TITN.*" *Fitzgerald Newsletter*, no. 29 (Spring 1965):6–7.

204. Ellis, James. "Fitzgerald's Fragmented Hero: Dick Diver." *University Review* 32 (October 1965):43–49. Reprinted in B81, pp. 127–37.

205. Le Vot, André E. "Gold Star Mothers: Mencken's Metaphor in *Tender Is the Night?*" *Menckeniana*, no. 14 (Summer 1965):3.

206. Macauley, Robie. " 'Let Me Tell You About the Rich. . . .' " *Kenyon Review* 27 (Autumn 1965):645–71 [667–69].

207. Millard, G. C. "F. Scott Fitzgerald: *The Great Gatsby, Tender Is the Night, The Last Tycoon.*" *English Studies in Africa* 8 (March 1965):5–30 [19–26]. Reprinted in B81, pp. 20–47.

208. Riddel, Joseph N. "F. Scott Fitzgerald, the Jamesian Inheritance, and the Morality of Fiction." *Modern Fiction Studies* 11 (Winter 1965–66):331–50 [348–49].

209. Wasserstrom, William, "The Strange Case of F. Scott Fitzgerald and A. Hyd (Hid)ell — A Note on the Displaced Person in American Life and Literature." *Columbia University Forum* 8 (Fall 1965):5–11.

210. Whitehead, Lee M. " 'Tender Is the Night' and George Herbert Mead: An 'Actor's' Tragedy." *Literature and Psychology* 15 (Summer 1965):180–91. Reprinted in B81, pp. 165–78.

211. Adkinson, R. V. "Novelist as Mythmaker: A View of F. Scott Fitzgerald." *Revue des Langues Vivantes* 32 (July–August 1966):413–19 [passim].

212. Bryer, Jackson R. "A Psychiatrist Reviews *Tender Is the Night.*" *Literature and Psychology* 16 (Summer 1966):198–99.

213. Sisk, John P. "F. Scott Fitzgerald's Discovery of Illusion." *Gordon Review* 10 (1966):12–23.

214. Wycherley, H. Alan. "Fitzgerald Revisited." *Texas Studies in Literature and Language* 8 (Summer 1966):277–83.

215. Foster, Richard. "Fitzgerald's Imagination: A Parable for Criticism." *Minnesota Review* 7, no. 2 (1967):144–56.

216. Gifford, Thomas. "The Fellow Who Went on So About Flappers, Wasn't

He?" *Twin Citian* 10 (October 1967):20–24.

217. Koenigsberg, Richard A. "F. Scott Fitzgerald: Literature and the Work of Mourning." *American Imago* 24 (Fall 1967):248–70 [255, 256 et passim].

218. LaHood, Marvin J. "Sensuality and Asceticism in *Tender Is the Night.*" *English Record*, 17 (February 1967):9–12. Reprinted in B81, pp. 151–55.

219. Long, Robert Emmet. "Dreiser and Frederic: The Upstate New York Exile of Dick Diver." *Fitzgerald Newsletter*, no. 37 (Spring 1967):1–2.

220. Nestrick, William V. "F. Scott Fitzgerald's Types and Narrators." *Revue des Langues Vivantes* 33 (March–April 1967):164–84 [169–84].

221. Spencer, Benjamin T. "Fitzgerald and the American Ambivalence." *South Atlantic Quarterly* 66 (Summer 1967):367–81 [passim].

222. Tamke, Alexander R. "Abe North as Abe Lincoln in *TITN.*" *Fitzgerald Newsletter*, no. 36 (Winter 1967):6–7.

223. Foster, Richard. "Mailer and the Fitzgerald Tradition." *Novel* 1 (Spring 1968):219–30 [passim]. Reprinted in B101.

224. Gross, Theodore L. "F. Scott Fitzgerald: The Hero in Retrospect." *South Atlantic Quarterly* 67 (Winter 1968):64–77 [68–73 et passim]. Reprinted in B92.

225. Gindin, James. "Gods and Fathers in F. Scott Fitzgerald's Novels." *Modern Language Quarterly* 30 (March 1969):64–85 [74–80].

226. Hart, Jeffrey. "Men and Letters — Fitzgerald and Hemingway: The Difficult Friend." *National Review* 21 (14 January 1969): 29–31.

227. Rao, E. Nageswara. "The Structure of *Tender Is the Night.*" *Literary Criterion* 8, no. 4 (1969):54–62.

The 1970s

228. Coleman, Tom C., III. "The Rise of Dr. Diver." *Discourse* 13 (Spring 1970):226–38.

229. Samsell, R. L. "Won't You Come Home, Dick Diver?" *Fitzgerald / Hemingway Annual* 2 (1970):34–42.

230. West, James L. W., III. "James Agee's Early Tribute to *Tender Is the Night.*" *Fitzgerald / Hemingway Annual* 2 (1970):226–27.

231. ———. "The Wrong Duel in *Tender Is the Night.*" *Fitzgerald / Hemingway Annual* 2 (1970):231.

232. Bahnks, Jean. "Letters to the Editor." *Galena Gazette*, 4 March 1971.

233. Burton, Mary E. "The Counter-Transference of Dr. Diver." *ELH* 38 (September 1971):459–71.

234. Coleman, Tom C., III. "Nicole Warren Diver and Scott Fitzgerald: The Girl and the Egotist." *Studies in the Novel* 3 (Spring 1971):34–43.

235. Dahlie, Hallvard. "Alienation and Disintegration in *Tender Is the Night.*" *Humanities Association (of Canada) Bulletin* 22 (Fall 1971):3–8.

236. Gere, Anne R. "Color in Fitzgerald's Novels." *Fitzgerald / Hemingway Annual* 3 (1971):333–39.

237. Gollin, Rita K. "Modes of Travel in *Tender Is the Night.*" *Studies in the Twentieth Century*, no. 8 (Fall 1971):103–14.

238. Hoban, Brendan. " 'Breakdown' in the Novels of Scott Fitzgerald." *Zenith* 1 (1971):51, 53–57.

239. B[ruccoli], M[atthew] J. "Malcolm Lowry's Film Treatment for *Tender Is the*

Night." Fitzgerald / Hemingway Annual 4 (1972):337.
240. Prigozy, Ruth. "Gatsby's Guest List and Fitzgerald's Technique of Naming." *Fitzgerald / Hemingway Annual* 4 (1972):99–112 [109].
241. Robson, Vincent. "The Psychosocial Conflict and the Distortion of Time: A Study of Diver's Disintegration in *Tender Is the Night." Language and Literature* 1, no. 2 (1972):55–64.
242. Stark, John. "The Style of *Tender Is the Night." Fitzgerald / Hemingway Annual* 4 (1972):89–95.
243. Tasaka, Takashi. "The Ethic and Aesthetic Aspects of *Tender Is the Night." Studies in American Literature*, no. 8 (March 1972):15–23.
244. Buntain, Lucy M. "A Note on the Editions of *Tender Is the Night." Studies in American Fiction* 1 (Autumn 1973):208–13.
245. Donaldson, Soctt. " 'No, I Am Not Prince Charming': Fairy Tales in *Tender Is the Night." Fitzgerald / Hemingway Annual* 5 (1973):105–12.
246. Farrell, James T. "F. Scott Fitzgerald and Romanticism." *Thought* 25 (5 May 1973):15–17.
247. Gingrich, Arnold. "Scott, Ernest and Whoever." *Esquire* 80 (October 1973):151–54, 374, 376, 380.
248. Hunt, Jan, and John M. Suarez. "The Evasion of Adult Love in Fitzgerald's Fiction." *Centennial Review* 17 (Spring 1973):152–69 [158–59 et passim].
249. Maimon, Elaine P. "F. Scott Fitzgerald's Book Sales." *Fitzgerald / Hemingway Annual* 5 (1973):165–73 [passim].
250. Monteiro, George. "The Limits of Professionalism: A Sociological Approach to Faulkner, Fitzgerald and Hemingway." *Criticism* 15 (Spring 1973): 145–55 [148–49].
251. Murphy, George D. "The Unconscious Dimension of *Tender Is the Night." Studies in the Novel* 5 (Fall 1973):314–23.
252. Schulte, F. G. F. "Technical Potential and Achievement in *Tender Is the Night." Dutch Quarterly Review of Anglo-American Letters* 3, no. 2 (1973):49–55.
253. Cowley, Malcolm. "The Fitzgerald Revival, 1941–1953." *Fitzgerald / Hemingway Annual* 6 (1974):11–13 [13].
254. Greiff, Louis K. "Perfect Marriage in *Tender Is the Night*: A Study in the Progress of a Symbol." *Fitzgerald / Hemingway Annual* 6 (1974):63–73.
255. Severo, Richard. "For Fitzgerald's Works, It's Roaring 70's." *New York Times*, 20 March 1974, p. 36.
256. Dudley, Juanita Williams. "Dr. Diver, Vivisectionist." *College Literature* 2 (Spring 1975):128–34.
257. Foster, Richard. "Time's Exile: Dick Diver and the Heroic Idea." *Mosaic* 8 (Spring 1975):89–108.
258. Higgins, Brian, and Hershel Parker. "Sober Second Thoughts: Fitzgerald's 'Final Version' of *Tender Is the Night." Proof* 4 (1975):129–52.
259. Littleton, Taylor. "A Letter from Zelda Fitzgerald." *Fitzgerald / Hemingway Annual* 7 (1975):3–6.
260. Qualls, Barry V. "Physician in the Counting House: The Religious Motif in *Tender Is the Night." Essays in Literature* 2 (Fall 1975):192–208.
261. Robillard, Douglas. "The Paradises of Scott Fitzgerald." *Essays in Arts and Sciences* 4 (May 1975):64–73.
262. Robinson, Jeffrey. "Fitzgerald's Riviera —'disappeared with time.' " *Christian*

Science Monitor, 8 April 1975, p. 19.

263. Wheelock, Alan S. "As Ever, 'Daddy's Girl': Incest Motifs in *Day for Night."* *Gypsy Scholar* 2 (Spring 1975):69–75.

264. Whitman, Alden. "Sara Murphy, Patron of Writers and Artists in France, 91, Dead." *New York Times,* 11 October 1975, p. 34.

265. Fujitani, Seiwa. "On the Tragic Sense of Love in the Novels of F. Scott Fitzgerald—Chiefly in the Case of *The Last Tycoon."* *Otemon Gakuin Daigaku Bungakubu Kiyo* 10 (December 1976):65–73.

266. Miller, Linda Patterson. " 'As a Friend You Have Never Failed Me': The Fitzgerald-Murphy Correspondence." *Journal of Modern Literature* 5 (September 1976):357–82 [364–65 et passim].

267. Monteiro, George. "Henry James and Scott Fitzgerald: A Source." *Notes on Contemporary Literature* 6 (March 1976):4–6.

268. Perlmutter, Ruth. "Malcolm Lowry's Unpublished Filmscript of *Tender Is the Night."* *American Quarterly* 28 (Winter 1976):561–74.

269. Prigozy, Ruth. " 'Poor Butterfly': F. Scott Fitzgerald and Popular Music." *Prospects: Annual of American Cultural Studies* 2 (1976):41–67 [passim].

270. Wilt, Judith. "The Spinning Story: Gothic Motifs in *Tender Is the Night."* *Fitzgerald / Hemingway Annual* 8 (1976):79–95.

271. Adams, Michael. "Dick Diver and Constance Talmadge." *Fitzgerald / Hemingway Annual* 9 (1977):61–62.

272. ———. "Fitzgerald Filmography." *Fitzgerald / Hemingway Annual* 9 (1977):101–09 [108].

273. Arnold, Edwin T. "The Motion Picture as Metaphor in the Works of F. Scott Fitzgerald." *Fitzgerald / Hemingway Annual* 9 (1977):43–60 [53–56].

274. DiBattista, Maria. "The Aesthetic of Forbearance: Fitzgerald's *Tender Is the Night."* *Novel* 11 (Fall 1977):26–39.

275. McBride, Margaret. "The Divine Dick Diver." *Notes on Modern American Literature* 1 (Fall 1977), item 28.

276. McNicholas, Mary Verity, O.P. "Fitzgerald's Women in *Tender Is the Night."* *College Literature* 4 (Winter 1977):40–70.

277. Wasserstrom, William. "The Goad of Guilt: Henry Adams, Scott and Zelda." *Journal of Modern Literature* 6 (April 1977):289–310 [305–07].

278. Wilson, Raymond J. "Henry James and F. Scott Fitzgerald: Americans Abroad." *Research Studies* 45 (June 1977):82–91.

279. Grenberg, Bruce L. "Fitzgerald's 'Figured Curtain': Personality and History in *Tender Is the Night."* *Fitzgerald / Hemingway Annual* 10 (1978):105–36.

280. Kolbenschlag, Madonna C. "Madness and Sexual Mythology in Scott Fitzgerald." *International Journal of Women's Studies* 1 (May–June 1978):263–71.

281. Roulston, Robert. "Dick Diver's Plunge into the Romantic Void: The Setting of *Tender Is the Night." South Atlantic Quarterly* 77 (Winter 1978):85–97.

282. ———. "Slumbering with the Just: A Maryland Lens for *Tender Is the Night." Southern Quarterly* 16 (January 1978):125–37.

283. West, Suzanne. "Nicole's Gardens." *Fitzgerald / Hemingway Annual* 10 (1978):85–95.

284. Berman, Jeffrey. *"Tender Is the Night:* Fitzgerald's *A Psychology for Psychiatrists." Literature and Psychology* 29, no. 1 & 2 (1979):34–48.

285. Bruccoli, Matthew J. "Bennett Cerf's Fan Letter on *Tender Is the Night:* A

Source for Abe North's Death." *Fitzgerald / Hemingway Annual* 11 (1979):229–30.

286. Deegan, Thomas. "Dick Diver's Childishness in *Tender Is the Night.*" *Fitzgerald / Hemingway Annual* 11 (1979):129–33.

287. Doughty, Peter. "The Seating Arrangement in *Tender Is the Night.*" *Fitzgerald / Hemingway Annual* 11 (1979):159–61.

288. Fairey, Wendy. "*The Last Tycoon*: the Dilemma of Maturity for F. Scott Fitzgerald." *Fitzgerald / Hemingway Annual* 11 (1979):65–78 [73 et passim].

289. Fenstermaker, J. J. "The Literary Reputation of F. Scott Fitzgerald 1940–1941: Appraisal and Reappraisal." *Fitzgerald / Hemingway Annual* 11 (1979):79–90.

290. Ferguson, Robert A. "The Grotesque in the Novels of F. Scott Fitzgerald." *South Atlantic Quarterly* 78 (Autumn 1979):460–77 [468–74 et passim].

291. Greenwald, Fay T. "Fitzgerald's Female Narrators." *Mid-Hudson Language Studies* 2 (1979):116–33 [119–25 et passim].

292. Kirby, Joan. "Spengler and Apocalyptic Typology in F. Scott Fitzgerald's *Tender Is the Night.*" *Southern Review: Literary and Interdisciplinary Essays* 12, no. 3 (November 1979):246–61.

293. Shepherd, Allen. "Dick Diver in Nashville: a Note on Robert Penn Warren's *A Place to Come to.*" *Fitzgerald / Hemingway Annual* 11 (1979):173–75.

294. Trouard, Dawn. "Fitzgerald's Missed Moments: Surrealistic Style in His Major Novels." *Fitzgerald / Hemingway Annual* 11 (1979):189–205.

The 1980s

295. Bryer, Jackson R. "Four Decades of Fitzgerald Studies: The Best and the Brightest." *Twentieth Century Literature* 26 (Summer 1980):247–67.

296. Donaldson, Scott. "The Crisis of Fitzgerald's 'Crack-Up.'" *Twentieth Century Literature* 26 (Summer 1980):171–88 [passim].

297. Fedo, David. "Women in the Fiction of F. Scott Fitzgerald." *Ball State University Forum* 21, no. 2 (1980):26–33 [31–33 et passim].

298. Horne, Lewis B. "The Gesture of Pity in *Jude the Obscure* and *Tender Is the Night.*" *Ariel: A Review of International English Literature* 11, no. 2 (April 1980):53–62.

299. Lehan, Richard. "F. Scott Fitzgerald and Romantic Destiny." *Twentieth Century Literature* 26 (Summer 1980):137–56 [146–50 et passim].

300. Perosa, Sergio. "Fitzgerald Studies in the 1970s." *Twentieth Century Literature* 26 (Summer 1980):222–46.

301. Prigozy, Ruth. "From Griffith's Girls to *Daddy's Girl*: The Masks of Innocence in *Tender Is the Night.*" *Twentieth Century Literature* 26 (Summer 1980):189–221.

302. Ryan, Lindel. "F. Scott Fitzgerald and the Battle of the Sexes." *LiNQ (Literature in North Queensland* 8, no. 3 (1980):84–94.

303. Donaldson, Scott. "The Political Development of F. Scott Fitzgerald." *Prospects: An Annual Journal of American Cultural Studies* 6 (1981):313–55.

304. Howell, John M. "Dr. Tom Rennie and *Tender Is the Night.*" *ICarbS* 4, no. 2 (Spring–Summer 1981):111–15.

305. Gervais, Ronald J. "The Socialist and the Silk Stockings: Fitzgerald's Double Allegiance." *Mosaic* 15 (June 1982):79–92.

Books

The 1930s and 1940s

1. Hatcher, Harlan. *Creating the Modern American Novel*. New York: Farrar and Rinehart, 1935, pp. 81–82.
2. Muller, Herbert J. *Modern Fiction — A Study of Values*. New York: Funk & Wagnalls, 1937, pp. 384–85.
3. Barnett, James Harwood. *Divorce and the American Novel, 1858–1937*. Philadelphia: University of Pennsylvania Press, 1939, pp. 126–27.
4. Cargill, Oscar. *Intellectual America*. New York: Macmillan, 1941, pp. 342–46 [344].
5. Geismar, Maxwell. "F. Scott Fitzgerald: Orestes at the Ritz," in *The Last of the Provincials*. Boston: Houghton Mifflin Co., 1943, pp. 287–352 [327–33, 336–37 et passim].
6. Adams, J. Donald. *The Shape of Books to Come*. New York: The Viking Press, 1944, pp. 89–90 et passim.
7. Cunliffe, Marcus. *The Literature of the United States*. Harmondsworth, England: Penguin Books, 1945, pp. 275–79; rev. ed. 1961, pp. 276–80.
8. Wescott, Glenway. "The Moral of F. Scott Fitzgerald," in *The Crack-Up*. Ed. Edmund Wilson. New York: New Directions, 1945, pp. 323–37. Reprints P80.
9. Gray, James. "Tenderly Tolls the Bell for Three Soldiers — Scott Fitzgerald," in *On Second Thought*. Minneapolis: University of Minnesota Press, 1946, pp. 61–67 [63–65 et passim]. Reprints P37.
10. Mizener, Arthur. "F. Scott Fitzgerald (1896–1940): The Poet of Borrowed time," in *The Lives of Eighteen from Princeton*. Ed. Willard Thorp. Princeton: Princeton University Press, 1946, pp. 333–53 [347–50]. Slightly revised version of P96; reprinted in B18, pp. 23–45; and B20.
11. Bishop, John Peale. "The Missing All," in *The Collected Essays of John Peale Bishop*. Ed. Edmund Wilson. New York: Charles Scribner's Sons, 1948, pp. 66–77 [69, 73]. Reprints P75.
12. Troy, William. "Scott Fitzgerald: The Authority of Failure," in *Forms of Modern Fiction*. Ed. William Van O'Connor. Minneapolis: University of Minnesota Press, 1948, pp. 80–86. Reprints P90.

The 1950s

13. Trilling, Lionel. "F. Scott Fitzgerald," in *The Liberal Imagination*. New York: The Viking Press, 1950, pp. 243–54 [246]. Reprints P89.
14. Aldridge, John W. "Fitzgerald — The Horror and the Vision of Paradise," in *After the Lost Generation*. New York: McGraw-Hill, 1951, pp. 44–58 [52–55 et passim]. Reprinted in B49, pp. 32–42.
15. Cowley, Malcolm. "Introduction," in *Tender Is the Night*. New York: Charles Scribner's Sons, 1951, pp. ix–xviii. Reprints P110; reprinted in B22.
16. Hoffman, Frederick J. "The American Novel Between Wars — IV," in *The Modern Novel in America, 1900–1950*. Chicago: Henry Regnery, 1951, pp. 120–30 [127–28].
17. Hughes, Riley. "F. Scott Fitzgerald: The Touch of Disaster," in *Fifty Years of*

the American Novel, a Christian Appraisal. Ed. Harold C. Gardiner, S.J. New York: Charles Scribner's Sons, 1951, pp. 135–49 [143–44 et passim]. Reprints P113.

18. Kazin, Alfred, ed. "Introduction," in *F. Scott Fitzgerald: The Man and His Work.* Cleveland and New York: The World Pub. Co., 1951, pp. 11–19 [passim]. Reprints P22, P23, P35, P40, P79, P80, P82, P84, P86, P89, P90, P91, P104, and B10.

19. Mizener, Arthur. *The Far Side of Paradise.* Boston: Houghton Mifflin Co., 1951, pp. 238–51 et passim; rev. ed. Boston: Houghton Mifflin Co., 1965, pp. 174–75, 249–51, 255–56, 263–79, 345–52, et passim. Excerpted in P116.

20. — — —. "F. Scott Fitzgerald: The Poet of Borrowed Time," in *Critiques and Essays on Modern Fiction 1920–1951.* Ed. John W. Aldridge. New York: Ronald Press, 1952, pp. 286–302 [297–300]. Reprints B10; slightly revised version of P96.

21. Brooks, Van Wyck. *The Writer in America.* New York: E. P. Dutton & Co., 1953, pp. 70–71.

22. Cowley, Malcolm. "Introduction" to *Tender Is the Night,* in *Three Novels of F. Scott Fitzgerald.* New York: Charles Scribner's Sons, 1953, pp. iii–xii. Reprints P110 and B15.

23. Fiedler, Leslie A. "Some Notes on F. Scott Fitzgerald," in *An End to Innocence: Essays on Culture and Politics.* Boston: The Beacon Press, 1955, pp. 174–82. Reprints P111.

24. Hoffman, Frederick J. *The Twenties.* New York: The Viking Press, 1955, pp. 374–75.

25. Kazin, Alfred. "Fitzgerald: An American Confession," in *The Inmost Leaf.* New York: Harcourt, Brace, 1955, pp. 116–26. Reprints P86.

26. Cady, Edwin Harrison, Frederick J. Hoffman and Roy Harvey Pearce, eds. "F(rancis) Scott Fitzgerald, 1896–1940," in *The Growth of American Literature: A Critical and Historical Survey.* New York: American Book Co., II, 1956, 530–32 [531].

27. Hoffman, Frederick J. *Freudianism and the Literary Mind.* Baton Rouge: Louisiana State University Press, 1957, pp. 264–71.

28. Miller, James E., Jr. *The Fictional Technique of Scott Fitzgerald.* The Hague: Martinus Nijhoff, 1957, pp. 110–11; for rev. ed. see B59.

29. Trilling, Lionel. "F. Scott Fitzgerald," in *Literature in America.* Ed. Philip Rahv. New York: Meridian Books, 1957, pp. 400–08. Reprints P89.

30. Morris, Wright. "The Function of Nostalgia — F. Scott Fitzgerald," in *The Territory Ahead.* New York: Harcourt, Brace & World, 1958, pp. 157–70. [167–69]. Reprints P145.

31. Wasserstrom, William. *Heiress of All the Ages: Sex and Sentiment in the Genteel Tradition.* Minneapolis: University of Minnesota Press, 1959, pp. 111–14.

The 1960s

32. Bezanson, Walter. "Scott Fitzgerald: Bedeviled Prince Charming," in *The Young Rebel in American Literature.* Ed. Carl Bode. New York: Frederick A. Praeger, 1960, pp. 79–94 [passim].

33. Fiedler, Leslie A. *Love and Death in the American Novel.* New York:

Criterion Books, 1960, pp. 301–03; rev. ed. New York: Stein and Day, 1966, pp. 313–15.

34. Thurber, James. " 'Scott in Thorns,' " in *Our Times — The Best From "The Reporter."* Ed. Max Ascoli. New York: Farrar, Straus, and Cudahy, 1960, pp. 427–35. Reprints P121.

35. Booth, Wayne. *The Rhetoric of Fiction.* Chicago and London: University of Chicago Press, 1961, pp. 190–95.

36. Frohock, W. M. "Scott Fitzgerald: Manners and Morals," in *Strangers to This Ground: Cultural Diversity in Contemporary American Writing.* Dallas: Southern Methodist University Press, 1961, pp. 36–62 [passim]. Reprints P135.

37. Hale, Nancy. *The Realities of Fiction.* Boston: Little, Brown and Co., 1961, pp. 203–209 [207].

38. Shain, Charles E. *F. Scott Fitzgerald.* University of Minnesota Pamphlets on American Writers, no. 15. Minneapolis: University of Minnesota Press, 1961, pp. 35–45 [35–42]. Reprinted in B62.

39. Stallman, R. W. "By the Dawn's Early Light *Tender Is the Night,*" in *The Houses that James Built and Other Literary Studies.* East Lansing: Michigan State University Press, 1961, pp. 158–72.

40. Hoffman, Frederick J., ed. *The Great Gatsby: A Study.* New York: Charles Scribner's Sons, 1962. Reprints P80, P89, P90 and P124 (in revised form).

41. Moore, Harry T. "The Present-Day American Novel," in *Essays by Divers Hands, Being the Transactions of the Royal Society of Literature.* Ed. Peter Green. New Series. Vol. 31. London and New York: Oxford University Press, 1962, pp. 123–42 [123–24 et passim].

42. Schorer, Mark. "Sherwood Anderson — F. Scott Fitzgerald — Ernest Hemingway," in *Major Writers of America.* Gen. Ed. Perry Miller. New York: Harcourt, Brace & World, 1962, pp. 671–84 [682]. Reprinted in expanded form in B77.

43. Thurber, James. " 'Scott in Thorns,' " in *Credos and Curios.* New York: Harper & Row, 1962, pp. 153–63. Reprints P121.

44. Turnbull, Andrew. *Scott Fitzgerald.* New York: Charles Scribner's Sons, 1962, pp. 241–46, 302–04, et passim.

45. Wescott, Glenway. "Glenway Wescott on F. Scott Fitzgerald," in *Novelists on Novelists — An Anthology.* Ed. Louis Kronenberger. Garden City, N.Y.: Doubleday Anchor, 1962, pp. 374–87. Reprints P80.

46. Bruccoli, Matthew J. *The Composition of Tender Is the Night: A Study of the Manuscripts.* Pittsburgh: University of Pittsburgh Press, 1963. Selection reprinted in revised form in B90, pp. 92–106.

47. Eble, Kenneth. *F. Scott Fitzgerald.* New York: Twayne Publishers, 1963, pp. 134–39 et passim; rev. ed. Boston: Twayne, 1977, pp. 123–25, 133–40, et passim.

48. Goldhurst, William. *F. Scott Fitzgerald and His Contemporaries.* Cleveland and New York: The World Pub. Co., 1963, pp. 65, 115–19, 168–69, 200–04, 206–16, et passim.

49. Mizener, Arthur, ed. "Introduction," in *F. Scott Fitzgerald: A Collection of Critical Essays.* Englewood Cliffs, N.J.: Prentice-Hall, 1963, pp. 1–10 [passim]. Reprints P40, P89, P90, P91, P111, P119, P124 (in revised form), P128, P145, and B14.

50. — — —. "Introduction," in *The Fitzgerald Reader*. New York: Charles Scribner's Sons, 1963, pp. xv–xxvii [xxiv–xxv et passim].
51. — — —. *The Sense of Life in the Modern Novel*. Boston: Houghton Mifflin Co., 1963, p. 156 et passim.
52. Shannon, William V. *The American Irish*. New York: Macmillan, 1963, pp. 242–44.
53. Troy, William. "Scott Fitzgerald – the Authority of Failure," in *Modern American Fiction – Essays in Criticism*. Ed. A. Walton Litz. New York: Oxford University Press, 1963, pp. 132–37. Reprints P90.
54. Turnbull, Andrew, ed. *The Letters of F. Scott Fitzgerald*. New York: Charles Scribner's Sons, 1963, pp. 231–34, 236–42, 246–48, 268, 281, 308–10, 346–47, 362–63, 423, 507, 510–13, 532, 536–37, 540–41, 566–67, 570 et passim.
55. West, Paul. *The Modern Novel*. London: Hutchinson & Co., 1963, II, 242 et passim.
56. Allen, Walter. *The Modern Novel in Britain and the United States*. New York: E. P. Dutton & Co., 1964, p. 91.
57. Cross, K. G. W. *F. Scott Fitzgerald*. New York: Grove Press; Edinburgh: Oliver and Boyd, 1964, pp. 78–91 et passim.
58. Graham, Sheilah. *The Rest of the Story*. New York: Coward-McCann, 1964, passim.
59. Miller, James E., Jr. *F. Scott Fitzgerald: His Art and His Technique*. New York: New York University Press, 1964, pp. 131–48 et passim. Rev. ed. of B28; reprinted in B81, pp. 86–101.
60. Millgate, Michael. "F. Scott Fitzgerald," in *American Social Fiction: James to Cozzens*. Edinburgh and London: Oliver & Boyd, 1964, pp. 107–27 [passim].
61. O'Hara, John. "In Memory of Scott Fitzgerald," in *The Faces of Five Decades: Selections from Fifty Years of The New Republic, 1914–1964*. Ed. Robert B. Luce, New York: Simon and Schuster, 1964, pp. 275–76. Reprints P78.
62. Shain, Charles E. "F. Scott Fitzgerald," in *Seven Modern American Novelists*. Ed. William Van O'Connor. Minneapolis: University of Minnesota Press, 1964, pp. 81–117 [111–14 et passim]. Reprints B38.
63. Anderson, Charles R. "Scott Fitzgerald, 1896–1940," in *American Literary Masters*. Gen. Ed. Charles R. Anderson. New York: Holt, Rinehart and Winston, 1965, 951–70 [965–66, 968].
64. Perosa, Sergio. *The Art of F. Scott Fitzgerald*. Trans. Charles Matz and Sergio Perosa. Ann Arbor: University of Michigan Press, 1965, pp. 102–30.
65. Piper, Henry Dan. *F. Scott Fitzgerald: A Critical Portrait*. New York: Holt, Rinehart and Winston, 1965, pp. 205–28 et passim.
66. Doherty, William E. "*Tender Is the Night* and the 'Ode to a Nightingale,' " in *Explorations of Literature*. Ed. Rima Drell Reck. Baton Rouge: Louisiana State University Press, 1966, pp. 100–14. Reprinted in B81, pp. 190–206 and B107, pp. 112-26.
67. Hoffman, Frederick J. "The 'Irresistible Lothario': F. Scott Fitzgerald's Romantic Hero," *The Twenties: Poetry and Prose*. Eds. Richard E. Langford and William E. Taylor. Deland, Fla.: Everett / Edwards, 1966, pp. 59–61.
68. Lehan, Richard D. *F. Scott Fitzgerald and the Craft of Fiction*. Carbondale and Edwardsville: Southern Illinois University Press, 1966, pp. 33–35,

123-48, 176-78 et passim. Preface by Harry Moore, pp. v-x [vii-ix et passim]. Selection from Lehan reprinted in B81, pp. 61-85.

69. Weimer, David. "Lost City: F. Scott Fitzgerald," in *The City as Metaphor.* New York: Random House, 1966, pp. 88-103. [95-96 et passim].

70. Bryer, Jackson R. *The Critical Reputation of F. Scott Fitzgerald: A Bibliographical Study.* Hamden, Ct.: Archon Books, 1967, pp. 77-90 et passim; *Supplement,* 1984, passim.

71. Cowley, Malcolm. "Fitzgerald's Goodbye to His Generation," in *Think Back on Us . . . A Contemporary Chronicle of the 1930's.* Ed. Henry Dan Piper. Carbondale and Edwardsville: Southern Illinois University Press, 1967, pp. 225-28. Reprints P28.

72. Mizener, Arthur. *Twelve Great American Novels.* New York: New American Library, 1967, pp. 104-19 et passim. Reprinted in B81, pp. 102-16.

73. Moseley, Edwin M. "Tender Is the Night: Healer and Scapegoat," in *F. Scott Fitzgerald: A Critical Essay.* Grand Rapids, Mich.: William B. Eerdmans Pub. Co., 1967, pp. 36-41.

74. Sklar, Robert. *F. Scott Fitzgerald: The Last Laöcoon.* New York: Oxford University Press, 1967, pp. 249-92 et passim.

75. Hindus, Milton. *F. Scott Fitzgerald: An Introduction and Interpretation.* New York: Holt, Rinehart and Winston, 1968, pp. 50-69.

76. Mizener, Arthur. "On F. Scott Fitzgerald," in *Talks with Authors.* Ed. Charles F. Madden. Carbondale and Edwardsville: Southern Illinois University Press, 1968, pp. 23-37.

77. Schorer, Mark. "Some Relationships: Gertrude Stein, Sherwood Anderson, F. Scott Fitzgerald, and Ernest Hemingway," in *The World We Imagine.* New York: Farrar, Straus and Giroux, 1968, pp. 299-382 [359-63 et passim]. Reprints in expanded form B42.

78. Trachtenberg, Alan. "The Journey Back: Myth and History in *Tender Is the Night*," in *Experience in the Novel: Selected Papers from the English Institute.* Ed. Roy Harvey Pearce. New York: Columbia University Press, 1968, pp. 133-62.

79. Blake, Nelson Manfred. "The Pleasure Domes of West Egg and Tarmes," in *Novelists' America: Fiction as History, 1910-1940.* Syracuse, N.Y.: Syracuse University Press, 1969, pp. 45-74 [71-73 et passim].

80. Bryer, Jackson. R., ed. "F. Scott Fitzgerald," in *Fifteen Modern American Authors: A Survey of Research and Criticism.* Durham, N.C.: Duke University Press, 1969, pp. 211-38 [passim]; revised and expanded edition, *Sixteen Modern American Authors: A Survey of Research and Criticism.* New York: W. W. Norton & Co., 1973, pp. 277-321 [passim].

81. LaHood, Marvin J., ed. "Introduction," in *Tender Is the Night: Essays in Criticism.* Bloomington & London: Indiana University Press, 1969, pp. ix-xi. Reprints P138, P148, P157, P172, P174, P178, P197, P204, P207, P210, P218, B59, B66, B68, and B72.

82. Spatz, Jonas. *Hollywood in Fiction: Some Versions of the American Myth.* The Hague and Paris: Mouton & Co., 1969, pp. 87-88, 115-16 et passim.

The 1970s

83. Kinahan, Frank. "Focus on F. Scott Fitzgerald's *Tender Is the Night*," in *American Dreams, American Nightmares.* Ed. David Madden. Carbondale

and Edwardsville: Southern Illinois University Press, 1970, pp. 115–28.
84. Littlejohn, David. "Three Glimpses of Scott Fitzgerald," in *Interruptions.* New York: Grossman Publishers, 1970, pp. 91–105 [94 et passim]. Reprints P181.
85. Milford, Nancy. *Zelda, A Biography.* New York: Harper & Row, 1970, pp. 286–87 et passim.
86. Stern, Milton R. *The Golden Moment: The Novels of F. Scott Fitzgerald.* Urbana: University of Illinois Press, 1970, pp. 289–462 et passim.
87. Bigsby, C. W. E. "The Two Identities of F. Scott Fitzgerald," in *The American Novel and the Nineteen Twenties.* Stratford-Upon-Avon Studies 13. Eds. Malcolm Bradbury and David Palmer. London: Edward Arnold, 1971, pp. 128–49.
88. Bradbury, Malcolm. "Style of Life, Style of Art and the American Novelist in the Nineteen Twenties," in *The American Novel and the Nineteen Twenties.* Stratford-Upon-Avon Studies 13. Eds. Malcolm Bradbury and David Palmer. London: Edward Arnold, 1971, pp. 11–35 [29–34 et passim].
89. Bruccoli, Matthew J. and Jackson R. Bryer, eds. *F. Scott Fitzgerald in His Own Time: A Miscellany.* Kent, Oh.: Kent State University Press, 1971. Reprints P5, P14, P21, P22, P23, P28, P31, P57, P58, P65, P72, P76, and P77.
90. Bruccoli, Matthew J., ed. *Profile of F. Scott Fitzgerald.* Columbus, Oh.: Charles E. Merrill Pub. Co., 1971. Reprints P194 and a revised section of B46.
91. Glicksberg, Charles I. "Fitzgerald and the Jazz Age," in *The Sexual Revolution in Modern American Literature.* The Hague: Martinus Nijhoff, 1971, pp. 58–67 [64–65].
92. Gross, Theodore L. "F. Scott Fitzgerald: The Hero in Retrospect," in *The Heroic Ideal in American Literature.* New York: The Free Press, 1971, pp. 221–39 [229–34 et passim]. Reprints P224.
93. Kuehl, John, and Jackson R. Bryer, eds. *Dear Scott / Dear Max: The Fitzgerald-Perkins Correspondence.* New York: Charles Scribner's Sons, 1971, pp. 181–95, 250–51 et passim.
94. Latham, Aaron. *Crazy Sundays: F. Scott Fitzgerald in Hollywood.* New York: Viking Press, 1971, pp. 75–95 et passim.
95. Mayfield, Sara. *Exiles from Paradise.* New York: Delacorte Press, 1971, pp. 202–21.
96. Tomkins, Calvin. *Living Well Is the Best Revenge.* New York: The Viking Press, 1971, pp. 3–6, 124–25, 128, et passim. Reprints P183.
97. Bruccoli, Matthew J., ed. *As Ever, Scott Fitz—: Letters Between F. Scott Fitzgerald and His Literary Agent, Harold Ober: 1919–1940.* Philadelphia and New York: J. B. Lippincott Co., 1972, pp. 89–90, 153–54, 167–70, 199–204, 211–12, 215–19, 340–41, 347–48, 353–54 et passim.
98. — — —. *F. Scott Fitzgerald: A Descriptive Bibliography.* Pittsburgh: University of Pittsburgh Press, 1972, see esp. pp. 78–92; *Supplement,* 1980, see esp. pp. 13–14.
99. — — —." 'A Might Collation': Animadversions on the Text of F. Scott Fitzgerald," in *Editing Twentieth Century Texts.* Ed. Francess G. Halpenny. Toronto: University of Toronto Press, 1972, pp. 28–50.
100. Callahan, John F. *The Illusions of a Nation: Myth and History in the Novels*

of F. Scott Fitzgerald. Urbana: University of Illinois Press, 1972, pp. 62–199 et passim.

101. Foster, Richard. "Mailer and the Fitzgerald Tradition" in *Norman Mailer: A Collection of Critical Essays.* Ed. Leo Braudy. Englewood Cliffs, N.J.: Prentice-Hall, 1972, pp. 127–42. Reprints P223.

102. Harrison, Gilbert A. *The Critic as Artist: Essays on Books 1920–1970.* New York: Liveright, 1972, pp. 86–90. Reprints P28.

103. Mizener, Arthur. *F. Scott Fitzgerald and His World.* London: Thames and Hudson, 1972, pp. 83–84, 92–95 et passim.

104. Nelson, Gerald B. *Ten Versions of America.* New York: Alfred A. Knopf, 1972, pp. 43–60 et passim.

105. Selznick, David O. *Memo from David O. Selznick.* Ed. Rudy Behlmer. New York: The Viking Press, 1972, pp. 443–68 et passim. "Editor's Foreword," pp. xiv–xix [xviii–xix].

106. Cowley, Malcolm. *A Second Flowering: Works and Days of the Lost Generation.* New York: The Viking Press, 1973, passim.

107. Eble, Kenneth E., ed. *F. Scott Fitzgerald: A Collection of Criticism.* New York: McGraw-Hill, 1973. Reprints P155 and B66.

108. Fahey, William A. *F. Scott Fitzgerald and the American Dream.* New York: Crowell, 1973, pp. 94–114 et passim.

109. Bruccoli, Matthew, Scottie Fitzgerald Smith and Joan P. Kerr, eds. *The Romantic Egoists.* New York: Charles Scribner's Sons, 1974, pp. 193–94, 196–203, et passim.

110. Buttita, Tony. *After the Good Gay Times: Asheville – Summer of '35, a Season with F. Scott Fitzgerald.* New York: The Viking Press, 1974, passim.

111. Greenfield, Howard. *F. Scott Fitzgerald.* New York: Crown Publishers, 1974, pp. 104–07 et passim.

112. Huonder, Eugen. *The Functional Significance of Setting in the Novels of Francis Scott Fitzgerald.* European University Papers. Series XIV, Anglo-Saxon Language and Literature, Bd. 20. Bern: Herbert Lang; Frankfurt/M.: Peter Lang, 1974, 77–101 et passim.

113. Welland, Dennis. "The Language of American Fiction Between the Wars," in *History of Literature in the English Language, Volume 9: American Literature since 1900.* Ed. Marcus Cunliffe. London: Barrie & Jenkins, 1975, pp. 48–72 [68–69].

114. Dardis, Tom. *Some Time in the Sun: The Hollywood Years of Fitzgerald, Faulkner, Nathanael West, Aldous Huxley, and James Agee.* New York: Charles Scribner's Sons, 1976, pp. 22–23 et passim.

115. Francis, John. "F. Scott Fitzgerald's Women," in *American Literature: A Study and Research Guide.* Eds. Lewis Leary and John Auchard. New York: St. Martin's Press, 1976, pp. 157–73. Sample research paper.

116. Graham, Sheilah. *The Real F. Scott Fitzgerald: Thirty-Five Years Later.* New York: Grosset & Dunlap, 1976, pp. 176–77 et passim.

117. Lowry, Malcolm, and Margerie Lowry. *Notes on a Screenplay for F. Scott Fitzgerald's Tender Is the Night.* Bloomfield Hills, Mich. and Columbia S.C.: Bruccoli Clark, 1976.

118. Martin, Marjorie. *Fitzgerald's Image of Women: Anima Projections in Tender Is the Night.* English Studies Collections, no. 6. East Meadow, N.Y.: English Studies Collections, Inc., 1976. 17 pp.

119. Moorty, S. S. "Norris and Fitzgerald as Moralists," in *Studies in American Literature: Essays in Honour of William Mulder*. Eds. Jagdish Chander and Narindar S. Pradhan. Delhi: Oxford University Press, 1976, pp. 119–26 [passim].

120. Meyers, Jeffrey. "Scott and Zelda Fitzgerald: The Artist and the Model," in *Married to Genius*. New York: Barnes & Noble, 1977, pp. 190–210.

121. Milne, Gordon. *The Sense of Society: A History of the American Novel of Manners*. Rutherford, N.J.: Fairleigh Dickinson University Press, 1977, pp. 218–21.

122. Allen, Joan M. *Candles and Carnival Lights: The Catholic Sensibility of F. Scott Fitzgerald*. New York: New University Press, 1978, pp. 124–31 et passim.

123. Berg, A. Scott. *Max Perkins: Editor of Genius*. New York: E. P. Dutton, 1978, pp. 228–34.

124. Bruccoli, Matthew J. *Scott and Ernest: The Authority of Failure and the Authority of Success*. New York: Random House, 1978, pp. 40–41, 112–23, 152 et passim.

125. Bryer, Jackson R., ed. "Introduction," in *F. Scott Fitzgerald: The Critical Reception*. [New York]: Burt Franklin & Co., 1978, xi–xxvi [xx–xxii]. Reprints many reviews of *Tender Is the Night*.

126. Gallo, Rose Adrienne. *F. Scott Fitzgerald*. New York: Ungar, 1978, pp. 57–81.

127. Horodowich, Peggi Maki. "Linguistics and Literary Style: Deriving F. Scott Fitzgerald's Linguistic Contours," in *Papers From the 1977 Mid-America Linguistics Conference*. Eds. Donald M. Lance and Daniel E. Gulstad. Columbia: Linguistics Area Program, University of Missouri, 1978, pp. 461–72.

128. Sivaramkrishna, M. *Icarus of the Jazz Age: A Study of the Novels of F. Scott Fitzgerald*. Hyderabad: Department of Publications and Press, Osmania University, 1978, pp. 119–42 et passim.

129. Bruccoli, Matthew J., ed. *The Notebooks of F. Scott Fitzgerald*. New York and London: Harcourt Brace Jovanovich, 1979, passim.

130. Girgus, Sam B. "Beyond the Diver Complex: The Dynamics of Modern Individualism in F. Scott Fitzgerald," in *The Law of the Heart: Individualism and the Modern Self in American Literature*. Austin: University of Texas Press, 1979, pp. 108–28.

131. Ousby, Ian. "The Lost Generation," in *A Reader's Guide to Fifty American Novels*. London: Heinemann; New York: Barnes & Noble, 1979, pp. 205–76 [221–26 et passim].

132. Rao, B. Ramachandra. *The American Fictional Hero: An Analysis of the Works of Fitzgerald, Wolfe, Farrell, Dos Passos and Steinbeck*. English Language and Literature, no. 4. Chandigarh: Bahri, 1979, pp. 13–27 [23–25].

133. Rhodes, Robert E. "F. Scott Fitzgerald: All My Fathers," in *Irish-American Fiction*. Eds. Robert E. Rhodes and Daniel J. Casey. New York: AMS Press, 1979, pp. 29–51 [43–45 et passim].

134. Stavola, Thomas J. *Scott Fitzgerald: Crisis in an American Identity*. New York: Barnes & Noble Books, 1979, pp. 145–65 et passim.

The 1980s

135. Bruccoli, Matthew J., and Margaret M. Duggan, eds. *Correspondence of F. Scott Fitzgerald*. New York: Random House, 1980, pp. 221–22, 15–33, 358–59, 366–67, 490–91, et passim.
136. Way, Brian. *F. Scott Fitzgerald and the Art of Social Fiction*. New York: St. Martin's Press, 1980, pp. 119–48 et passim.
137. Bruccoli, Matthew J. *Some Sort of Epic Grandeur: The Life of F. Scott Fitzgerald*. New York and London: Harcourt Brace Jovanovich, 1981, pp. 335–43, 362–81, 511–23, et passim.
138. Messinger, Christopher. *Sport and the Spirit of Play in American Fiction: Hawthorne to Faulkner*. New York: Columbia University Press, 1981, pp. 202–03 et passim.
139. McCay, Mary A. "Fitzgerald's Women: Beyond Winter Dreams," in *American Novelists Revisited: Essays in Feminist Criticism*. Ed. Fritz Fleischmann. Boston: G. K. Hall & Co., 1982, pp. 311–24.
140. Donaldson, Scott. *Fool for Love*. New York: Congdon & Weed, 1983, pp. 119–24, 193–97 et passim.
141. Le Vot, André. *F. Scott Fitzgerald: A Biography*. Trans. William Byron. Garden City, N.Y.: Doubleday & Co., 1983, passim.

INDEX